ERASING BARRICADES
Woman in Indian Literature

ERASING BARRICADES
Woman in Indian Literature

Edited by

Nibir K. Ghosh
Sujata
Sunita Rani Ghosh

AUTHORSPRESS
Publishers of Scholarly Books

Worldwide Circulation through Authorspress Global Network
First Published 2010
by
Authorspress
E-35/103, Jawahar Park
Laxmi Nagar, Delhi-110 092
e-mail: authorspress@yahoo.com

Erasing Barricades: Woman in Indian Literature
ISBN 978-81-7273-533-3

Printed in India at Tarun Offset, Delhi.

Foreword

Writing has not always been considered a suitable career for a woman. Indeed, literature has traditionally been such a male-orientated field in the past that it was common for women authors to adopt a masculine pseudonym in order to be taken seriously, as we are aware with such British novelists as Currer Bell (Charlotte Bronte) and George Eliot (Mary Anne Evans). If women wanted their writing to be more than an occasional pastime, they were often forced to forego a conventional family life. Even today, women writers may argue that they are not offered the respect given to male authors and many woman writers still struggle to win recognition as professional authors.

The essential subversiveness of women's writing may be part of the reason why, throughout history, so many works by women have been undervalued and under-recognised. What better way to disarm something that threatens the male-dominated literary culture, than to claim that it is inferior, frivolous, and less important than a corresponding work by a man?

We may inquire whether there are indisputable differences, imaginable and cognitive, between the literary works of women and those of men. If these differences are so substantial as to make an authentic difference, does this in turn make necessary different aesthetic standards for judging the achievements of men and of women writers? Are women novelists such as Kamala Das and Anita Desai to be read as though they have more in common with Charlotte Bronte or George Eliot than with modern British male novelists, such as Martin Amis or Ian McEwan?

In the last two decades, a radical shift has taken place in the study of Indian women writers and they have begun to take their rightful place beside male novelists and poets. First and foremost, their work is now being taken seriously, and, as a result, a full array of theoretical approaches – postmodern, feminist, psychoanalytic, culturalist, multiculturalist – are employed to analyse a group of writers often neglected in the past. Despite the theoretical sophistication brought to bear in analysing the most popular Indian women poets and novelists, the one topic that is still virtually ignored is the issue of aesthetic seriousness. The essays in this collection strive to address the cultural and ideological significance of women's literary achievements.

Changes occurred in India after Partition and Independence, in the arenas of politics, culture and domesticity. As the country departed from the colonial attitudes of the past, there was a considerable growth culturally, with many women writers expressing their new found freedom and independence. Although there has always been a focus in India on the arts, they have been strongly influenced by overseas cultures, mainly American and British. This is especially so since media, such as television and computers, appeared in the home. During this time the Indian literary scene has also undergone a period of development. Many women authors have brought a radical new approach to writing that has not been seen before in the country. This new culture offers an alternative to the mainstream ideals that were dominant in India during the past decades.

This increasing international awareness via the media saw Indian society moving away from the restrictions of the 1940s, towards a more pluralistic society. Increasing numbers of artists became dissatisfied with the way society operated and began to revolt from established traditions. This saw an increase in dissident voices from such groups as students and women. As these overseas influences began to emerge in society, so too could they be seen in literature, especially within the novels and poetry being written by women.

There are many women writing poetry, prose and criticism in India today, producing a heterogeneous, prodigious, and challenging body of writings. This collection will be of value both to readers of poetry and novels and to those who seek to consider some of the critical debates that negotiate such challenging writings. Through the dialogue between theory and text, discussion and even controversy about these authors can be raised. The issues surrounding poetry, prose, gender and place are brought to the forefront and, like all pieces of critical writing, the essays themselves reflect the intersections of text and reader.

Because the writers themselves, and the work discussed here, indicate great variety in temperament, style and intent, it also becomes crucial to consider what actually serves to constitute these disparate writers as a 'group'. By implication the gender-specific focus of these essays suggest that not only are these writers defined by their experience as writers working in an Indian environment and an Indian literary scene, diverse and regionalised as these scenes may be, but also that their work is further influenced by their experience as women living in a patriarchal society. In turn, however, these categories raise some crucial difficulties of definition. That is, how do we define India, 'Indianness', and the experience of writing in this complex cultural context? What is the influence of the Indian environment and landscape on the production of novels and poetry? And what is the relation between the forms of culture, language and historical experiences in India? As we see in the essays, these women writers bonded in some of their philosophies and in the tools of their trade are sharply differentiated by the facts of their history and its consequences for their social experiences.

This collection of essays on Indian women writers goes a long way towards addressing some of these issues. If there is anything that the wide range of women's writing mentioned in this volume have in common – besides their literary talent, and secondly their gender – it's a certain bravery that impelled them to write in the first place. The mention of these writers and the accounts of their work remind us of how many women, in every age and culture, transcended the traditional barriers that have kept their work from being written, published and read.

Patricia Prime

Preface

Erasing barricades can be a complex task, especially when it concerns the fate and predicament of half of the human world that has hitherto been confined to the obscurity of a life akin to that of "flies to wanton boys." The complexity of transforming the agony of silence into language and action is heightened when one begins to question every generalisation rather than accept any that is not confirmed by our own experiences. In the context of the changing times, when considerations of empowerment in human relationships are no longer the sole prerogative of the male, it is worthwhile to explore the paradigm shifts that have led women to challenge the voices of tradition and Freudian sophistication imposed by the patriarchal order to keep women in perpetual subjection. As a case in point, one may look at a few lines from Imtiaz Dharker:

> Look hard at my face.
> This is how faces look
> after they have broken through
> brick walls, glass ceilings,
> seductive cloth, cages
> of gold, curtains of fire.

Increasingly conscious of the barriers, the obstacles, the impediments, and the stumbling blocks that hindered woman from putting herself into the text of her own life, women writers and activists have taken upon themselves, often with pleasure, the onerous task of affirming that a woman is not a mere vehicle, a vessel, with no needs or desires of her own, and that she is well on her way to go out and snatch life with both hands without the feeling of guilt or remorse.

The essays in this volume, contributed by distinguished academics, scholars, creative writers from different parts of India and two other major continents of the globe, showcase, through insightful critical evaluation of creative renderings, the exciting voyage of woman through extensive barricades of existence to the lyrical articulation of her agony and ecstasy. The kaleidoscopic range and variety of perceptions — that cut across frontiers of language, genre, region, class, culture, community and religion — provide the intrinsic link between truth and perspective, between what we see and the angle from which we see it. A unique feature of this memorable anthology is the harmonious blend of English and Hindi in the expression of viewpoints seminal to human concern.

Before closing the prefatory note, we are immensely happy to put on record our sincere gratitude to all those who made this adventurous enterprise a great success. We are grateful to all the contributors for making the daunting task of erasing barricades extremely gratifying. Our special thanks go to Patricia Prime and Kathleen Alcala for enriching the volume with the infinite richness of their individual perceptions. We are no less indebted to Dr. Eunice de Souza for enhancing the beauty of the anthology with her poetic touch. We gratefully acknowledge the invaluable cooperation we have received from Mr. K.K. Srivastava and Mr. K.C. Jain in the completion of this project. Words of thanks will be poor recompense for Mr. Sudarshan Kcherry of Authorspress whose daring maiden venture in the arena of bilingual production, brought out so aesthetically, deserves our special appreciation.

Editors

Nibir K. Ghosh

Sujata

Sunita Rani Ghosh

Contents

Miss Louise

from *Fix,* published by Newground Bombay, 1979

She dreamt of descending
curving staircases
ivory fan aflutter
of children in sailor suits
and organza dresses
till her dream rotted her innards
but no one knew:
innards weren't permitted
in her time.

Shaking her graying ringlets:
"My girl, I can't even
go to Church you know
I unsettle the priests
so completely. Only yesterday
that handsome Fr Hans was saying,
'Miss Louise, I feel an arrow
through my heart.'
But no one will believe me
if I tell them. It's always
been the same. They'll say.
'Yes Louisa, we know, professors
loved you in your youth,
judges in your prime."

Eunice de Souza

1 Introduction: Women and Contemporary Literature

— Nibir K. Ghosh

> I was elected by the women of Ireland, who instead of rocking the cradle, rocked the system.
>
> —*Mary Robinson*

> Being a woman is like being Irish. Everyone says you're important and nice but you take second place all the same.
>
> —*Iris Murdoch*

> Women are a huge powerhouse in today's India. Look around you. There are women racing in all kinds of fields... finance, literature, broadcasting, art, IT, design, law, science, medicine, education – and are a huge powerhouse in today's India. A powerhouse, true And yet this is a powerhouse with over 90% of the power switched off. These are women who don't even know they have choices.
>
> —*Imtiaz Dharker*

The Backdrop

The *Bible* says the Lord God created Eve out of the rib cage of Adam, giving thereby a derivative nature to her existence. There is an equally charming myth associated with the creation of woman by the Supreme Creator, "Bramha". Bramha first created man and, in his generosity, wished to give man a companion. He borrowed several components from the beautiful creation of nature and made woman out of them. Hence the reference of woman as Prakriti. Bramha presented woman to his earlier creation man saying, "She will serve you lifelong and if you cannot live with her, neither can you live without her."

Both myths indicate that woman is either an "after thought" of a male God or a play-mate created for man as a psychic compensation for his innate loneliness. If the primordial myth gave woman her ritually prescribed status, all literatures since time immemorial expose the desperate marginality of female existence whether these women have lived in solitude, in extended families or in nuclear families, be it in ancient Athens or the world of Manu. Though Manu, the lawgiver, accepts that "A woman's body must not be struck hard, even with a flower, because it is sacred," he is well known for stating: "A woman is never fit for independence. Her father protects (her) in childhood, her husband protects (her) in youth and her sons protect (her) in old age.... Day and night woman must be kept in dependence by the males."

It ought not to be surprising, therefore, that in the world's most powerful democracy, when the Statue of Liberty, which portrays a woman holding the torch of freedom, was opened to the public on October 28, 1886, no woman was invited to the ceremonies on this important occasion. Even to the nineteenth century conservative in America, the idea of equal rights for women had appeared ridiculous and unwarranted as can be evidenced from the following statement:

> The power of woman is in her dependence....But, when she assumes the place and tone of man as a public reformer, our care and protection of her seem unnecessary; she yields the power which God has given her for protection, and her character becomes unnatural. If the vine, whose strength and beauty is to lean upon the trellis-work and half conceal its clusters, thinks to assume the independence and overshading nature of the elm, it will not only cease to bear fruit, but will fall in shame and dishonour into the dust.

These social stereotypes have been reinforced by archetypes for ages, amply supported by Freud's classic finding ascertaining that "Anatomy is Destiny."

Articulating Silence : Virginia Woolf's *A Room of One's Own*

Important questions — like, Who is the real woman? Where is the real woman? What is her real entity? Has she an identity of her own? — lay submerged in the conspiracy of silence. Mention must here be made of Virginia Woolf's *A Room of One's Own* (1929), a document that veritably challenged the paradigms of such a silence. In passionately reclaiming the woman's voice muted by patriarchal society – where men have all the power and money, hold all the important positions, make all the important decisions – Virginia Woolf's narrator in the essay explores the British Museum in London and is dismayed to find that though there are too many books written about women (almost all by men) there are hardly any books by women on men or by women on women.

Reflecting on such a great disparity, the narrator gives convincing evidence why genius has so infrequently flowered among women. In *A Room of One's Own,* Woolf ponders the significant question of whether or not a woman could produce art of the high quality of Shakespeare. In doing so, she examines women's historical experience as well as the distinctive struggle of the woman artist. She says "genius like Shakespeare's is not born among labouring, uneducated, servile people." In her view, some kind of genius must have existed among women then, as it exists among the working class, although it never translated to paper. The narrator argues that the difficulties of writing - especially the indifference of the world to one's art - are compounded for women, who are actively disdained by the male establishment. By boldly advocating the fact that both the freedom from economic dependence and the freedom from fetters to the mind and body are conditions of the possibility of genius and its full expression, Woolf laid the foundation of the feminist movement. She asserts how Judith Shakespeare still lives within all women, and that if women are given 500 pounds a year and a room of one's own, that is money and privacy, she will be reborn. Woolf's essay raises three inextricable issues: women and what they are like; women and the fiction they write; and women and what is written about them.

In breaking the conspiracy of silence and in giving expression to the untold stories of women, the revolutionary roles played by the Feminist Press in New York and Kali for Women in New Delhi need not be overemphasized. The Mission of the Feminist Press is to publish and promote the most potent voices of women from all eras and all regions of the globe. The Press has brought more than 500 critically acclaimed works by and about women into print, enriching the literary canon, expanding the historical record, and influencing public discourse about issues fundamental to women. The Feminist Press continues to bring vital new voices to public attention.

Started in 1984, in a Delhi garage by Ritu Menon and Urvashi Butalia, Kali for Women has been providing a viable publishing mouthpiece to Indian feminism. Kali's objective is to increase the body of knowledge on women in the Third World, to give voice to such knowledge as already exists and to provide a forum for women writers. Apart from publishing English translations of significant fictional writings by women from various Indian languages, Kali also seeks to redefine issues of women's lives in a positive way. Kali for Women has now split into two independent imprints. The co-founders of Kali, Urvashi Butalia and Ritu Menon, have established their independent publishing imprints - Zubaan and Women Unlimited respectively.

Henrik Ibsen's *A Doll's House*

When Nora in Ibsen's *A Doll's House* (1879) tells her husband Torvald Helmer before leaving him for good, "Our house has never been anything but a play-room. I have been your doll wife, just as at home I was daddy's doll child. And the children in turn have been my dolls. I thought it was fun when you came and played with me, just as they thought it was fun when I went and played with them. That's been our marriage," she comes to the point where she takes a drastic step ahead of her time. The play created a sensation when it was first produced and many women refused to play the part of a woman who deserts her husband and children.

Erica Jong's *Fear of Flying*

Erica Jong advocates both emotional and economic autonomy as imperatives in the woman's struggle for liberation. What is significant in Erica's stance is that she is not unaware of the ground realities and the attendant hazards of Nora's decision in Ibsen's play. She takes into account all the dialectics involved in theories of Western Feminism propounded by Germaine Greer, Kate Millet, Ellaine Showalter, Simone de Beavoir and the rest and yet she is highly critical of the "whole package of lies that passes for feminism." She states that fulfilment cannot be attained through idle flights of fancy, martyrdom or suicide. Fulfilment lies in exploring the "inner space" of the self to conquer one's own "sense of vulnerability".

In Erica Jong's view the awakened Eve, especially in the American context, has gathered the confidence to voice her protest against the tyranny of man not by virtue of her legal battles or the attainment of political rights of equality but through her rejection of roles imposed upon her by a male-dominated society and through her discovery and acceptance of the true essence of her own selfhood. At the end of the novel, Isadora Duncan, the protagonist, is seen musing over the ambivalence of the choice she had made. Commenting on the powerful status of the institution of marriage, she states in the novel: "In 19th century novels, they get married. In 20th century novels they get divorced. Can you have an ending in which they do neither? But whatever happened, I knew I would survive it....Surviving meant being born over and over. It wasn't easy, and it was always painful. But there wasn't any other choice except death."

Erica Jong's *Fear of Flying* also brings to the fore the misconception that we in India normally have about the Western idea of marriage and family life. One tends to believe as a result of such misconception that the woman in Western society is endowed with all kinds of freedom that are denied to womenfolk in India, especially the right to live as one desires. Tired of playing the game of musical beds, the protagonist becomes aware of ground realities even in the most powerful democracy in the world: "It is heresy in America to embrace any way of life, except as half of a couple. Solitude is un-American. It may be condoned in a man....But a woman is always presumed to be alone as a result of abandonment, not choice....There is no dignified way for a woman to live alone. Oh! She can get along financially perhaps (though not nearly as well as a man), but emotionally she is never left in peace. Her friends, her family, her fellow workers never let her forget that her husbandlessness, her childlessness — her selfishness, in short — is a reproach to the American way of life.

Doris Lessing

While talking of the fate and predicament of women in

contemporary literature, one cannot ignore the dominant presence of Doris Lessing in any discourse both as a creator and a protagonist. In awarding the 2007 Nobel Prize for Literature to Doris Lessing, the Swedish Academy cited her as "that epicist of the female experience, who with scepticism, fire and visionary power has subjected a divided civilisation to scrutiny." The award, that came a few days before her 88th birthday makes her the oldest recipient of the coveted honour. Author of dozens of books of fiction, as well as plays, non fiction and two volumes of autobiography, she is the 11th woman to win the Nobel Prize in Literature.

Lessing wrote persuasively about politics, feminism, Communism and black-white relations in Africa before moving on to explore the emotional dimensions of the human psyche in her groundbreaking 1962 novel entitled *The Golden Notebook* which took the world by storm. Her focus has always been her concern about the inner lives of women and she is extremely articulate in rejecting the notion that they should abandon their lives to marriage and children. Having known what it means to be intelligent and frustrated and female in an essentially male-dominated world, she states: "Any human anywhere will blossom in a hundred unexpected talents and capacities simply by being given the opportunity to do so." She critically and realistically explores the controversial questions being debated the world over – the stereotypes, marriage, motherhood, the predicament of emancipated women, sisterhood and finally arrives at the conclusion that to be free one must be self contained.

Lessing motivates us all to demonstrate an optimistic approach to life and its complexities and suggests that we ought not to wallow in self-pity, regret, sentimentality or seek to evade responsibilities. Instead we are to face each problem as it comes. She emphasizes the need for positive engagement with the world and prefers a delicate balancing of social responsibility and self-interest. In spite of the cosmic misalignments, humanity has the ultimate choice for good or evil, she says. According to her, "The New Jerusalem does not come down from heaven—it is constructed by humanity in whatever geometric shape they want....What is a hero without love for mankind."

Indian Literature

Images of woman in Indian literature is characterised by contradiction – there is a conventional image and there is a protesting voice. Postindependence literature reveals the woman's quest for her identity giving rise to a number of issues. The new woman is emerging and there are a number of new themes and issues to be taken by the future. However, two overall views of woman have been dominating Indian literature from ages: The Sita and the Draupadi archetypes. There is silent suffering with utmost loyalty to man in the Sita type and woman as an individual demanding social justice in the Draupadi types. Sita absorbs all inflicted misery and humiliation of the male ego whereas Draupadi challenges the male ego to the epitonic limits of human excellence. Sita accepts, accommodates and withdraws. Draupadi resents, rejects and involves herself in the process of life as a protagonist. These two feminine archetypes define the limits of feminine experience in reality, especially the Indian Reality. The gender divide in modern Indian literature moves between new iconisations of these two bold and primordial figures.

Pratibha Ray's *Yajnaseni*

As an appropriate illustration of the two primordial figures mentioned above, Pratibha Ray's novel foregrounds the anguish and anger of Yagnaseni who rightly questions whether man has the right to consider woman merely as his movable or immovable property. Placed on the brink of utter humiliation when brought dragging to the court by Dushshasana, Yagnaseni doesn't plead for mercy but demands justice. Pratibha Ray's protagonist Yagnaseni boldly affirms the stand she had taken in that critical moment, a stand no less significant in today's India than it was in that mythological space: "When that wicked man was stripping me, helpless like chaste Sita I could have disappeared into the depths of the earth to hide my shame. If I had prayed, would not the earth have opened? But I did not do so. If I had done so my modesty would have been protected but the wicked would not have been punished. In the future this problem would remain unresolved for women....The remaining days of my life I will fight against injustice, adharma, sin. Though the world may call me an ogress because of this, the world must know that woman who creates, is auspicious, is also the destroyer of the sinful and the wicked....Let the world know that while a woman's heart is delicate, it is not weak."

According to Ray, Draupadi is a challenge of womanhood, the embodied form of action, knowledge, devotion and power. Such a woman who has faced torment, insult, mental and emotional dilemma like Yajnaseni Draupadi — has not yet been born on this earth. Yet, the pain and the agony of mythical Draupadi is not an anachronism in contemporary Indian society, a fact that is highlighted by Ray through the narrative she recounts in the "Afterword" to *Yagnaseni — The Story of Draupadi*:

> All of us know something of Krishnaa's sacrifice, dedication, strength of character. The name of the younger sister of a lady known to me is Krishnaa. Leaving her debauched drunkard of husband she is living in her father's house. Everyone said Krishnaa should remarry. But in our society today the remarriage of one discarded by her husband is not that simple and easy. For diverting her mind, Krishnaa went away to her brother in West Germany. Sometime later, she married a young man there. She has two children now, a son and a daughter. Her conjugal life is comfortable. But the peculiar thing is that those who were at one time sympathetic towards Krishnaa, said after the second marriage, "Well, when her very name is Krishnaa, she could be happy only after taking a second husband. Arre! The Krishnaa of *Mahabharata* took five husbands, and still not being satisfied, was attracted to Karna and Krishna."

After such knowledge, what forgiveness! It is interesting to note, sad though it is, how societal attitudes refuse to acknowledge the need for change in spite of epoch making advancements and technological future shocks. In Arundhati Roy's *The God of Small Things,* the novel that won her the Man Booker Prize, we are brought in touch with the harsh realities that reflect the social and cultural stigma of divorce in India and the fate of the "wretched Man-less woman": "a married daughter had no position in her parents' home. As for a divorced daughter according to Baby Kochamma, she had no position anywhere at all." Let us not forget that the novel's location is Kerala, the province which has the highest literacy rate in India.

Mahashweta Devi's "Draupadi"

On the other extreme, and contrary to the stereotypical patterns of the female image, the hope, perhaps, sadly lies in the emergence of the exceptional woman like Dopdi in Mahashweta's story "Draupadi" who can live on her own terms by rejecting the stereotyped image of the 'truly virtuous woman' who is ever willing to conform to the standards set by a male-dominated society. Unlike the legendary Draupadi in *Mahabharata* who in her helplessness pleads to Lord Krishna to protect her from being ignominiously disrobed in public, Mahashweta's protagonist subverts the stereotypes of "female virtue and modesty" by boldly daring the exploiters of her modesty to touch her again: "What's the use of clothes? You can strip me, but how can you clothe me again? Are you a man?...There isn't a man here that I should be ashamed. I will not let you put my cloth on me. What more can you do?"

The Contemporary Scene

The image of woman in literature emerges out of the existing world. In India, which has been regarded by sociologists as a traditionally maledominated society, both men and women writers have seen woman in this relationship with man, primarily as mother, wife, mistress and sex objects. Woman as an achiever is either non-existent or considered an exception. A woman's individual self has very little recognition. But we have to remember that family plays a pivotal role in the Indian scheme of life. The new woman in Indian literature does not break the family but dreams to make the family "Home Sweet Home". Be it small or big, be it in the courtyard or in the courtroom woman is the cause of all action. But they are still walking on a tight rope to achieve their human rights and social justice. Indian women at the turn of the century are in a transitional phase *via-a-vis* the interface of tradition and modernity. Though women writers are tolerant and respectful towards the traditional obligations, they are still confident of their own new self and sensitive to the dogmatisation of traditional values.

At the turn of the new millennium Indian literature as far as the feminist thrust is concerned, is not free from family, history and social modernism. The women are more educated, sophisticated and even rebeliious but the woman herself is wary of shedding off the traditional values which forms part of her inherited consciousness. Once upon a time, not very long ago, the story of Savitri was held up as a prime example of the lengths to which a wife could go in aiding her husband. The myth relates how the good wife saves her husband from death, follows him anywhere, proves her virtue, remains under his control and gives him her power. We must however admit that the times are changing even if the pace of change is marginal. As an evidence of the changing scenario we may look at a statement by Anees Jung in her pioneering book titled *Unveiling India: A Woman's Journey* (1988):

> Not long ago a woman who spoke about herself was considered a loose woman. To voice a pain, to divulge a secret, was considered sacrilege, a breach of family trust. Today, voices are raised without fear, and are heard outside the walls of homes that once kept a woman protected, also isolated. Some of the women who speak here have stepped out. Others who have not, are beginning to be aware, eager to find expression. But let them speak for themselves....Their looks have not changed, their manner has. Individually they have gained a name, collectively an identity. Their new power was not imposed upon them but already existed, enclosed within walls. Now that power has stirred out into the open. Their new strength stems from personalities defining their own terms, lending grace to living.

Anees Jung exemplifies another writer in search of new images of women. She explains the change that has taken place in Indian society so that now women will tell their own stories. Jung herself, who grew up completely secluded in purdah, has remained unmarried and become a successful writer. She says about herself: "My reality no longer has one face. I have stepped out of an enclosed reality into one that is larger, more diverse, and mobile....I continue to live out an experience for which I have yet to find a name."

Conclusion

To return to the epigraphs with which I opened the deliberations, it becomes imperative to realise that women empowerment is a very complex issue endowed with subtle shades of variant approaches that require the perfect poise to navigate between rocking the cradle and the system in order to restore a major share of the power that currently stands switched off. Perhaps, what is needed is that every feminist worth the name must learn to acknowledge what she has in common with others of her sex who are all similarly shackled by conventional notions of her predicament. Neither the path of open confrontation nor an uneasy truce but the confidence to move in harmonious unison as co-partner in the power game, without compromising honour and dignity as an individual, ought to be the real goal of woman's emancipation.

It must be borne in mind that specific reforms related to the emancipation and empowerment of women must supplement the basic need for a change in attitude towards women, since women need self-trust, self-reliance, and self-respect in order to assert their individual identity and existence. The fact cannot be ignored that sex is the only instance in which representatives of the unequal groups live in more intimate association with each other than with members of their own group to a greater extent than any other underprivileged group. Femininity must, therefore, exist as the complement to masculine power, not as its subversive supplement, an excess that would undermine the boundaries of gender. As such, it would be appropriate to bear in mind the words of Betty Friedan that come at the end of her *The Feminine Mystique*:

> Who knows what women can be when they are finally free to become themselves? Who knows what women's intelligence will contribute when it can be nourished without denying love? Who knows of the possibilities of love when men and women share not only children, home, and garden, not only the fulfillment of their biological roles, but the responsibilities and passions of the work that creates the human future. It has barely begun, the search of women for themselves. But the time is at hand when the voices of the feminine mystique can no longer drown out the inner voice that is driving women on to become complete.

I am optimistic that this grand collection of essays will bring to the fore multipie facets of women's experiences: the power, the passion, the pain, the hopelessness, the fury, the joy. It will be a rewarding experience to see distinguished scholars from different parts of the nation shed light on the diversity of women and the diversity within each woman as portrayed in literature. It is intrinsically significant to ask how these experiences touch women writing on the whole. Do these writings address seminal questions and issues? How do women themselves view such writings? Is it marginal or central to their lives? What is the relationship between such writing and the political involvement of the writers? What are their concerns, and what is the creative energy at work?

Much heat and light is bound to be generated in the ensuing discussions as scholars proclaim in unison: "Why should boys have all the fun?"

2 Testimonios

— Kathleen Alcalá

There is a term in Spanish, *testimonios*, which means 'to bear witness'. It is an art form, usually oral, in which tribute is paid to a specific person, living or dead. It is the sort of speech that might be given at a dinner party for a retiree, or at the other end of the scale, on behalf of a whole group of people who will never have a voice, because they do not read or write or are denied access to their basic human rights. I have been exploring this as a written form, and I would like to discuss the work of several contemporary writers who have chosen to bear witness on behalf of people far different from themselves.

Elena Poniatowska is a Mexican journalist who has written about several major events in Mexican history, both before and during her lifetime. She is best known for her 1971 work *La noche de Tlatelolco* (published in English as *Massacre in Mexico*), in which she relates her interviews with the survivors and families of those who died in the 1968 Tlatelolco Massacre in Mexico City.

Some years ago, Elena learned about a woman living in Mexico City who had fought during the Mexican Revolution. Known as Adelitas, these women bore arms alongside their male counterparts to overthrow the royalist-leaning upper classes of Mexico during its long and turbulent transition from a Spanish territory. Elena sought her out, but the woman, Jesusa Palancares, refused to speak with her. In 1964, Jesusa was already eighty-seven years old. She had long before lost faith in her fellow humans, and now took comfort from her religious practice of spiritualism and her sympathy with animals. Elena pursued her for months, bringing her groceries, sweeping out her modest room for her, begging the woman to share her story.

Finally, Jesusa relented, and every Wednesday afternoon, began to spin out her incredible tale. This took over two years, and Elena lost and found her several times over the course of the interviews as the woman's circumstances and addresses changed. Always poor, never able to have children herself, Jesusa had ridden into battle with her husband and her father as a 15-year-old, part of a war that would forever change the world. But the world was never that different for her. She lived in poverty all her life, raised several foster children and sheltered many animals, and remained self-sufficient until the end.

Elena, from the upper-classes herself, did not hesitate to pursue this story, perhaps the greatest of her journalistic career, because it was the most difficult to obtain.

Margaret Atwood is a Canadian writer of short stories, poetry, and novels. Among them are *The Handmaid's Tale,* a cautionary story set in the future about a society dominated by religious zealots, and *Alias Grace,* a historical novel based on a true case in the 1800s of a young housemaid accused of murder. Although written twenty years ago, *The Handmaid's Tale* rings closer to the truth today than when it was written. The book is not just about distopia, but about what it means to let go of power, to let others control your life because it is pleasant and convenient, at least for awhile. The disturbing narrator of this book, Offred, upsets us because she is so close to what we might be.

Alias Grace takes a case from the Canadian judicial system and re-examines it in such a way that we can also see how a woman can be both the victim and manipulator in such a way that we do not know whether to sympathise with the young and beautiful protagonist or dismiss her. Atwood loves this two-edged sword, and wields it beautifully in her books.

A.S. Byatt is the British author of a number of novels, story collections and non fiction books. Probably the best-known of these writers, she creates hothouse environments in which her characters eventually explode into emotional chaos. As part of a lecture series at Harvard University, Byatt researched the many stories about Sheherezade and the power of storytelling. In one, she discovered, the young storyteller gives birth to three children while spinning out her linked tales in order to save her life for 1001 nights. Byatt tells us that "Narration is as much part of human nature as breath and the circulation of the blood" (Atwood, 166). By reminding us that Sheherezade may well have once been a living, breathing human being, she helps us remember, as Toni Morrison might say, that we tell stories in order to save our lives.

Finally, I would like to mention a writer who lives near me, Mary Woodward. Woodward recently wrote and published a book about her parents Milly and Walt Woodward, who defied the local authorities, death threats, and were ostrasized by their community for honouring the free speech rights of some of their neighbours. The publishers of *The Bainbridge Review* during World War II, the Woodwards asked members of the high school class of 1942 to continue to act as correspondents for the paper while incarcerated with their families in concentration camps. Bainbridge Island was the first place from which Japanese Americans were removed as possible threats to the community. These families, for the most part, lost everything, unless they were able to find sympathizers to "hold" property for them while they were gone. A few families managed to return and build their businesses back up, and a national memorial to the Japanese American families on Bainbridge is under construction. The Woodwards honoured these people by bearing testimony, and Mary has honoured her parents by writing this book in cooperation with the Bainbridge Island Japanese American community.

These writers cover a range of experiences, success, and subject matter, but all have chosen to write about people and places outside of the current situation, and outside of their own personal experiences in society. None of them needed to do it, but have so chosen to use their gifts. I have maintained elsewhere that writing is a political act, and by highlighting these lives, fictional, mythical or historical, these four women writers have beautifully fulfilled that mission.

Work Cited

Atwood, Margaret. *The Handmaid's Tale*, Everyman's Library: New York, 200).

— *Alias Grace,* Nan A. Talese: New York, 1996.

Byatt, A.S. *On Histories and Stories – Selected Essays,* Harvard University Press: Cambridge, Massachusetts, 2001.

Poniatowska, Elena. *Here's to You, Jesusa!* Farrar Strauss Giroux: New York, 2001 (in English).

Woodward, Mary. *In Defense of Our Neighbors,* Fenwick Publishing: Bainbridge, 2008.

3 Recasting Representations

— **Shanker A. Dutt**

The beautiful city of Agra is renowned for its people, its culture, its history and the magnificence of its architecture. Among its many wonders, to most people around the world, the Taj remains the most magical, casting a rare spell on the beholder. But let us pause here a moment. How is the Taj represented to the world in books of history, in tourism brochures and in websites? Is the dominant information about an Emperor who ordered the building of one of the wonders of the modern world or the Empress it commemorates? Diagonally across the river is another magnificent mausoleum. However, in this case the dominant information is not about the builder but the one to whom the sepulchral architecture is commemorated. In the case of the Taj, it is Emperor Shah Jahan whose identity is privileged as the subject of creation. In the second instance, the monument is known as Itmad-ud-Doula's tomb. Noor Jahan remains an afterthought.

Forms of representation in most formal human expressions have denied subjecthood to women, relegating their roles to the shadows of passivity, acted upon, rather than acting, spatially at the margins of subordination. However, history and architecture have fortuitously amalgamated to put Mumtaz at the centre of the Taj's symmetrical design. In doing so, in one of the most fascinating ironies of history, the patriarchal paradigm that constructs epistemes stands deconstructed. The story of the Taj in many ways replicates the history of the manner in which women have been represented in literature, negotiating and contesting patriarchal space in a dynamic continuum.

Women's writing and the construct of women by men is of immense value for it maps civilisational priorities at a given moment in time. Not only does it represent the being and consciousness of half of global humanity, it endorses a cultural construct framed by engagement and negotiation with or resistance to social structures. Woman's mediations with traditional cultural signifiers such as kinship, marriage and procreation and its interrogation of values and structures amplified and created by dominant discourses inscribe the female subjectivity in literary texts. However, to speak of an overarching theory of a woman's right to self-determination, as a starting definition to feminism, is perilous. Social, cultural, economic structural differences across global locations differentiate women's writings and feminist subjectivities. The absence of overt statement of affiliations may also be seen in different ways: from the Althusserian interpellation, Zizek's consensual interpellation to plain fear of marginalisation and victimhood. These silences are often significations of nascent resistance for they seek to express much that is subliminal or suppressed. Much of women's writings that are labelled feminist deconstruct literary forms and socio-political constructs. They struggle against patriarchal inheritance and speak their mothers.

In the September 2007 edition of *Re-Markings*, edited by Dr. Nibir Ghosh, to which I had made a humble contribution, the back cover carried an Iris Murdoch quote which I reckon is significant for this insightful seminar entitled *Women's Representation in Contemporary Literature*: "Being a woman is like being Irish. Everyone says you are important and nice but you take second place all the same."

Faith Wilding's play *Waiting*, succinctly expresses the denial of agency and the contours of coded subordination mapped on an emotional landscape:

> Waiting for someone to pick me up
> Waiting for someone to hold me...
> Waiting for somebody...
> Waiting to wear make-up
> Waiting for my pimples to go away...
> Waiting for my children to come home from school
> *Waiting for them to grow up, to leave home*
> Waiting to be myself
> Waiting for excitement

Waiting for my flesh to sag
Waiting for the pain to go away
Waiting for the struggle to end
Waiting for release.

I anticipate that the academic deliberations at this conference will debate and explore representations that are equitable and fair to both women and men instead of attempting to replace one centre with another as a substitution of hierarchies.

The famous Ghosh apart from the eminently academic one of this city, lives in Brooklyn, not far from Suketu Mehta of Maximum City fame and until his tragic death, Agha Shahid Ali. This is Amitav Ghosh. I wish to share some of my views on Ghosh's women and the fundamental impulse behind writing women back to the centre in *The Shadow Lines* and how he followed the model in *The Glass Palace, The Hungry Tide* and *Sea of Poppies.* In his collection of prose writings *Imam and the Indian*, a piece called *Ghosts of Mrs. Gandhi* describes the difference between disinterestedness in aesthetics and a writer's responsibility toward the affirmation of humanity.The year 1984 fulfilled its apocalyptic portents most devastatingly in India. The list includes separatist violence in Punjab and Operation Blue Star, the Bhopal Gas tragedy, the assassination of Indira Gandhi followed by brutal pogroms against a hapless community. The 31st of October for Ghosh began like any other day. Back from Oxford after obtaining a doctoral degree, he was teaching in Delhi University. On that morning, arriving at the University, he noted a perceptible change in the conduct of the students as they huddled around transistors and in the lecture-room, were fidgeting with distraction. Gradually the news filtered that Mrs. Gandhi had been shot by her bodyguards and was battling for her life. At about 1:30 p.m. the first reliable report of her death was broadcast from Pakistan. The writer left the university with a friend Hari Sen as he needed to make a long distance phone call and was invited to use Hari's family phone.

A middle-aged Sikh had hurriedly entered the bus at a stop in Connaught Place and it was unfortunate that the bus would take the route past the hospital where Indira Gandhi's body then lay. By then, certain loyalists in her party had begun to incite the crowds to seek revenge. Lumpens armed with instruments of hate and vengeance were on the predatory hunt for Sikhs. It was then that a short stout woman, who understood the situation, gestured urgently and hissed at him to get down between the seats and keep out of sight. He hurriedly eased himself in the footspace between the seats. That woman's timely intervention along with the driver's denial of Sikh presence among passengers saved him from the wrath of insane violence.

As the violence spiralled in all its brutal inhumanity, sanity was articulated through hoary Gandhian staples for peace by ordinary members of civil society many of whom were women. On one such occasion, members of the Nagrik Ekta Manch were confronted by a determined mob, its members advancing towards the peaceniks brandishing instruments of hurt. As they braced for the attack, something extraordinary happened. The women who comprised more than half the group stepped out and formed a protective cordon around the group. The salwar kameezes and sarees became a fluttering barrier against the approaching menace. The thugs faltered and moments later they had vanished (Ghosh: 2002: 46-58). I believe Ghosh's women characters in his novels from *The Shadow Lines* to *Sea of Poppies* were born out of these two experiences.

In *The Shadow Lines,* Thamma, Ila and May are agents of action and central devises in the interrogation of essentialist notions of belonging and identity. While Thamma represents a metaphor for the anti-colonial phase in history, Ila represents the postnational transit lounge of cultures with a few qualifications. Thamma's agency is doubly emphasised through the spatial dimensions of the flat in Gole Park where the homogenising codes prefigures the narrated nation. Ila's quest of freedom "from your bloody culture" is an act of seeking alternatives to oppressive structures but she exercises her will and choice to commit herself to Nick though he may move an entire massage parlour to her home. In many ways Moyna in *The Hungry Tide* is a subaltern recast of the metropolitan Ila in their moral choice of commitments. The strength, resilience and vulnerability of Thamma may be followed in Nilima in *The Hungry Tide*. In Ghosh's masterly narrative Kanai Dutt is cast together by chance circumstance with a cetologist from the U.S., Piyali Roy, who has come to study freshwater dolphins, the

Oracella brevirostris in the tide country. The multiple histories of the Sundarbans come alive through the diary of the Marxist schoolteacher Nirmal who settles with his wife Nilima in Lucibari. Nilima's worldly pragmatism is exemplified in "...you live in a dream world of poetry and fuzzy ideas about revolution. To build something is not the same as dreaming of it: building is always a matter of well-chosen compromises." Sharing narrative space with Nilima and Piya are the products of postcolonial subalternisation, Kusum and Moyna. In the courage that Kusum displays under compelling adversity, she attains a stature far beyond her classified socio-economic identity. In Ghosh's narrative, the State's assault on unarmed settlers of Morichjhapi to evict them is carried out with ruthless repression. The Hamilton experiment of setting up a community "that could not bring all their petty little divisions and differences...there would be no Brahmins or Untouchables, no Bengalis, no Oriyas. Everyone would have to live and work together" (HT: 51-52). This would be a "model for all of India; it would be a new kind of country." Nirmal sees the Morichjhapi experiment as history from below: "an experiment imagined not by those with learning and power but by those without" (HT: 171). The right to dream and the right to fulfil those dreams are not restricted to the privileged but the powerless, the illiterates and the poor. This idea is exemplified in Kusum who becomes Nirmal's ideal of subaltern resistance and rekindles his ardour for revolution and for life.

Against the rigidities of social codes, Deeti and Paulette in *Sea of Poppies* reach across to a hybrid world that accommodated plural community bonds. Paulett's concealed resistance to Western dresses, her preference for the saree, her sisterly loyalty to Jodu and gumption to board the *Ibis* in disguise combines with Deeti's subaltern rebellion, her dalitisation and moral choices to create a new solidarity within the fragile community in the *Ibis*: "In the escalating din, Deeti's song was almost inaudible at first, but when the other women grew aware of it they joined their voices to hers, one by one....The women's voices grew in strength and confidence" (SP: 2008: 398).

Bondings based on ideology or common necessities may be traced from the Eurocentric but progressive Alan's group to the multicultural Ila's in *The Shadow Lines*, inclusiveness of the subaltern female affinities as with Piya, Moyna and Nilima in *The Hungry Tide* and a strong resilient solidarity aboard the *Ibis* in *Sea of Poppies*. By affirming agency, Ghosh has indeed written women and marginalised social formations back to the centre.

Works Cited

Ghosh, Amitav. *The Imam and the Indian*, Delhi: Ravi Dayal & Permanent Black, 2002.

— *The Shadow Lines*, New Delhi: OUP, 1988.

— *The Glass Palace*, Delhi: Ravi Dayal & Permanent Black, 2000.

— *The Hungry Tide*, New York: Mariner Books, 2006.

— *Sea of Poppies*, New Delhi: Viking Penguin, 2008.

Ghosh, Nibir K. *Re-Markings*, Vol. 6 No. 2, Sept. 2007.

Wilding, Faith. *Waiting* was performed at Womanhouse in Los Angeles sponsored by the Feminist Art Program, California Institute of the Arts.

4 Women in Contemporary Indian English Literature

— T. S. Anand

Indian English novelists, apart from dealing with various social and psychological issues, have been focusing on the changing place, position, roles and problems of women. Women in Indian society, though they constitute almost half of the world's population, have not been treated on par with men in various spheres of human activity. They have been pilloried, oppressed, suppressed, repressed, victimised and marginalised. Under the impact of patriarchal values, the values of sacrifice, submissiveness, excessive endurance, series of adjustments and self-effacement have been demanded and desired from them alone. Any deviation from the norm incurred a woman epithets like a shrew, a witch, a monster or in other such derogatory terms. The writers, both male and female of almost all the countries and cultures, have been grappling with the culture and context specific problems and issues related with women. This paper focuses on some of the Indian literary texts in English (Fiction and Poetry) to examine the portrayal of the changing images of woman since late nineteenth century to the present one.

In all human societies, socio-politico-historical factors play a significant role in constructing the traditional images, roles and value patterns for women which are transmitted from one generation to another through myths, legends and folklores. The *Manusmiriti*, also known as "Manava Dharmashastra", hailed as the earliest and the most authoritative book representing Hindu life and culture spoke not only for the dependence of woman in all the stages of her life on her father, husband and son but also denied her equal status with man and independence in any action. Manu regarded woman by nature to be more emotional and less rational than man and also declared that while creating her, God allotted to woman a love of her bed, of her seat and of ornaments, impure desires, wrath, dishonesty, malice and base conduct. She was declared by Manu not only to be kept under the control of man and was denied "sensual enjoyment," he also laid a mandate for her: "Even though destitute of virtue or seeking pleasure elsewhere or devoid of good qualities yet a husband must be constantly worshipped as a god by a faithful wife." Ever since, these dual standards advocated by Manu have had a lasting impact on man-woman relationship in Indian culture, which has resulted in woman's exploitation and subjugation in marital relationship. He also gave his verdict against widow remarriage and put several restrictions on the economic and political roles of women in society and by dividing society into four *Varnas,* he equated women with the lowest class, i.e., Shudras.

The freedom of India in 1947 bestowed upon Indian women equal status, opportunities and rights in all fields. Many laws were enacted to give them the rights of equal share in the parents' property and protection in case of any kind of violence to their person. During this period of sixtytwo years, with the dissemination of awareness through education and transformation of the earlier mindsets, and the impact of Women's Liberation Movement and women's economic upliftment, a new Indian woman has emerged with her own desires, ambitions and quests to smash the shackles of ages-old biases, beliefs and customs which had devalued her person and undermined her potential. In the process of their fight against the repressive forces of tradition and prescriptive roles based on idealised models of a bygone era, and their desire for free and new horizons created ambiguities, confusions and reactions as they resolutely defied the restrictive social practices and carved a niche for themselves. The female protagonists in R.K. Narayan's *The Guide* and *The Painter of Signs,* Mulk Raj Anand's *Gauri,* Nayantara Sahgal's *Storm in Chandigarh* and *The Day in Shadow,* Kamala Das's autobiography *My Story,* her novel *Alphabet of Lust,* Amrita Pritam's *The Revenue Stamp,* Manju Kapur's *Difficult Daughters* illustrate this viewpoint.

Rama Mehta in her *Inside the Haveli* and Shashi Deshpande in almost all her novels, though show their educated female protagonists feeling oppressed and undergoing inner conflict in given circumstances after their marriage yet while portraying and speaking for the self-assertion of these female protagonists, these writers advocate a healthy blend of tradition and modernity.

Whereas Kamala Markandaya delineates the sufferings and miseries of rural women in her early novels who resign themselves to their fate and adhere to their traditionally assigned roles, Nayantara Sahgal advocates new morality and new understanding in man-woman relationship, especially in the upper class. Anita Desai's female protagonists in most of her novels are shown passing through various psychological conflicts. Arundhati Roy, in her novel, *The God of Small Things,* through the three generations of women, has projected the phases of silent suffering, revolt and making a way for oneself. Kiran Desai too in her *Inheritance of Loss* through various women characters has thrown light on the oppression and repression of woman like Nimi by her highly educated husband, and has also shown liberated woman like Noni, living the life in her own way.

In India, since a woman is considered to be an embodiment of sacrifice, silent suffering, humility, faith and knowledge, she should be virtuous, chaste, submissive, homely, graceful, and devoted to her husband and his family. She must seek pleasure in these relationships. These attitudes exemplify the belief that woman should not have any right on her own; that she has only duties in relation to man. Kamala Das also articulates the plight and predicament of women whom she considers doomed to live in an intensely man-made world:

> Dress in sarees, be girl
> Be wife, they said — Be embroidered, be cook,
> Be a quarreler with servants, fit in, Oh,
> Belong cried the categorizers ("An Introduction").

In a patriarchal society, the birth of a female child is traditionally less welcome than that of the male. Being born a boy is itself a privilege. Girls arrive in the world as undesirable creatures and the lifelong battle against their formidable foe, i.e., their sex begins as Eunice de Souza expresses:

> I heard it said
> My parents wanted a boy

I've done my best to qualify
I hid the bloodstains
on my clothes
I let my breast-sag ("deSouza Prabhu").

The same crisis has been faced by many women poets. Even a poet like Monika Varma has felt this pressure:

I climbed tree....
Get down at once
It is most unsuitable for young ladies,
the governess, Louisa. M. Bayley said
("Disremember Me Doves").

The secondary status becomes more obvious as a girl grows up. She is prevented from developing her own individuality, constantly reminded that she is destined for man, and the one who gets the most masculine attention is the luckiest one. Entire rearing and gearing up of a girl is male-oriented and her salvation lies in marriage. Parents, grandparents, uncles, aunts—all condition her for this destiny right since her childhood. Sujata Bhatt in "Light" expresses this tragic fate of being a daughter:

When I was seventeen
My grandmother said
"Get her married
before the light
goes out of her face."

Sunita Jain's mother also forced her into marriage: "I felt pain when I came to my 'sasural' as I became someone's bhabi', 'chachi', and 'mami' at the tender age of 18."

Ironically, these girls believe that marriage is an escape from the control of parents and society. In reality, it turns out to be only an exchange of masters as Imtiaz Dharker's Fatimah, a Muslim girl, elopes with an English boy to free herself from the closed Muslim world:

And there you are with your English boy
Who was going to set you free,
Trying to smile and be accepted,
Always on your knees (*Purdha and Other Poems*).

Marriage turns out to be a trap which negates her rights to individuality, independence and self-realisation. It thwarts the growth of individuality as Lalitha Venkateswaran discovers:

> All learning would be stormed by me.
> I would sing, make speeches, read the news;
> Write, act, run offices and marathons
> I would concentrate upon myself.

But even in marriage the "power politics" to use a phrase from Kate Millett, operates in such a subtle manner as reduces the status of a woman to a mere utility item, an object for decoration, for possession and for man's sexual gratification. Mamta Kalia complains on being drowned in the domestic world:

> I, no longer feel I'm Mamta Kalia
> I am Kamla
> Or Vimla
> Or Kanta or Shanta ("Anonymous").

Likewise, the traditional drudgery of household chores threatens a woman's freedom as an individual:

> Unmade beds, dirty linen
> Papers wrongfolded, slippers thrown,
> ....
> A sinkful of plates
> And a head full of ache
> ("Love Made a Housewife Out of Me").

Sunita Jain too displays symptoms of discontentment with the domestic duties as "years of washing dishes" give her a "creasing forehead". Her poem "Knife" aptly sums up the depressing influence of household drudgery:

> My chapped feet,
> my hands grown rough with domestic duties,
> where shall I hide these.

Marriage involves not only the commitment to one's husband but also to those in the inner circle of the husband. Behroze Shroff has exposed this reality of Indian marriage, wifehood and motherhood in her poem "Mother" wherein the girl's cherished dreams are destroyed at a tender age of nineteen: "Your youth and energy were harnessed/ To serve a mother-in-law's sick bed" as the young married woman takes his name, his religion, family and class.

Gauri Deshpande expresses candidly about the position of a woman in marriage:

she could with such ease
be enslaved by your skillful hands,
condescend to warm your bed
stiffen your manhood/and bear your spawn.

Mamta Kalia's "I am a Great Fool" also presents the poet's sense of ennui in her matrimonial relationship, where she finds marriage as hazardous to keeping love alive. She cries in disillusionment:

am a great fool
To think that marriage is bliss,
Was it last month or last year
That we exchanged a kiss.

Extramarital relations are no solutions to the marital problems. The commission of adultery in case of Kamala Daș could not fulfil her quest for an ideal lover.

After that love became a swivel-door
When one went out, another came in,
Then I lost count for always in my arms
Was a substitute for a substitute ("Substitute").

It is only love, candour, consent, companionship and tenderness within marriage that a woman longs for. Instead of this, marriage turns out to be an unpleasant experience. Contemporary Indian women poets realised that real self or natural self is totally denied to a married woman and who knows it better than Kamala Das. A woman in marriage has to play imposed roles:

I must pose
I must pretend,

I must act the role
of a happy woman,
Happy wife ("The Suicide").

Love for a man is a temporary refuge from boredom and loneliness. For a woman love means complete emotional involvement. She wants a lasting and stable relationship with man. Man looks upon sex as a means of self-gratification and sensual pleasure whereas woman relates it to the emotional fulfillment and meaning in life. Sex seems to a woman a mere dry activity that leaves her unsatisfied as men do not penetrate into the "plunging depths" of their "souls/and bodies."

The lack of emotional content in man-woman relationship has been the cause of frustration in Kamala Das also. She describes her experiences in "Convicts":

That was the only kind of love
This hacking at each other's parts
Like convicts hacking, breaking clods
At noon.

Suniti Namjoshi's poetry shows her disillusionment in love in "Beauty and the Beast":

Beauty loved the ugly beast
And thinking 'twas a prince she'd wed
Waited for his shape to change,
And found there were two beasts in bed.

A woman is considered to be an instrument for continuing her husband's family. The pressures of maternity for a son's birth is usually faced by a woman. Behroze Shroff expresses that even at the risk of a woman's life her "production unit" is made to function again and a son is made to born:

Like a bucket of water
Scraped out of low-lying well,
a son was obtained from you ("In Their Own Voice").

Even the economically independent woman's lot is no better. She has to manage her wifely and professional obligations, hence bear the double burden. Mamta Kalia portrays a working woman who has to bear the drudgery of her workplace, and also manage "sinkful of plates." A working woman finds no enjoyment in sex even.

They made love
And ate sandwiches
And looked at each other's face –
Two empty cans ("They Made Love").

The contemporary Indian women's poetry has broken the boundaries of tradition while describing the conflict between the old and the new, and it expresses the desire of woman to break free of the bonds that have restricted her since times immemorial. It expresses a woman's longing for independence and freedom, quest for an individual identity, hunger for establishing a meaningful relationship with a man, with the outside world.

Kamala Das protests against this "soul-killing" subjugation and asks: "Woman, is this happiness, this lying buried/ Beneath a man?" Her poems are powerful expression of her feminine sensibility which seek self-realisation through man's love. She revolts against conventions, and struggles to realise her desire for ideal love through extramarital sexual relationships. The urge for freedom from living with the husband makes her rebellious: "I shall some day leave, leave the cocoon/ You built around me with morning tea."

Mamta Kalia also rebels against patriarchy. Her poems are haunted by the memories of her father:

You suspect I am having a love-affair these days,
But you are too shy to have it confirmed
What if my tummy starts showing gradually
And I refuse to have it curetted? ("Tribute to Papa").

Monika Varma's anguished cry in "Give me Space," sums up her feelings of repression perhaps under the pressure of patriarchy. She urges for a space "for one little day" before she dies: "Give me space...space not just to exist/ but to live..."

The freedom-loving feminine selves of the women poets often lead to an ego clash with their husbands. And it becomes difficult for both of them to arrive at a consensus as it is in the case of Mamta Kalia:

Every time I open my mouth
You feel let down,
And every time you discuss your pay scale,
I try hard not to frown.
If this goes on where will we end?
Or have we ended before we have begun?

Contemporary Indo-Anglian women poetry appears to be seriously involved in the power struggle to dislodge patriarchy. These poets question the very foundations of patriarchal assumptions. There has been an increasing tendency among them to redefine their own selves. Vijaya Goel tries to jolt women out of their complacency:

You are the power of this earth
The creator of man,
Yet you lie at his feet,
Begging to survive! ("She").

In forging new identities, new metaphors and symbols, new bonds and new meanings, these poets experience conflict between their personal values and larger social practices. The weight of an entire cultural tradition that has relegated and marginalised them is too great to be either borne or cast off. Their attitude becomes double edged: rebellious and tender. Their struggle with themselves and the world outside takes the form of a conflict between passivity and rebellion against the male-oriented universe. Torn between their feminist desires on one side and their stereotyped social roles on the other, the poems of these poets are constructed differently as compared to the poems of the male writers.

In their search for trust, companionship, security, love and dignity, the hungry self of post-independence Indian women poets confront a variety of anomalies, contradictions and paradoxes. They find themselves caught between the conflict of tradition-bound self and the self looking for liberation from all kinds of restraints. The dualities within them leave them sad, lonely and empty. Vacillating between passivity and rebellion they get frustrated and disappointed. But this tendency of charting out a 'new woman' who questions and protests rather than live in ignominy, leads her to tread on problematic grounds, resulting in her divided existence.

Works Cited

Bajaj, Rashmi. *Women Indo-Anglian Poets: A Critique,* New Delhi: Asian Publication Services, 1996.

Bhongle, Rangrao. "Eunice De Souza: A Poet of Our Times," Surya Nath Pandey ed. *Contemporary Indian Women Writers in English: A Feminist Perspective,* New Delhi: Atlantic Publishers and Distributors, 1999: 40-46.

De Souza, Eunice. *Nine Indian Women Poets: An Anthology,* New Delhi: Oxford University Press, 1997.

—*Talking Poems: Conversations with Poets,* New Delhi: Oxford University Press, 1999.

Dwivedi, A.N. "Suniti Namjoshi: Art and Artifice in Her Work." *Papers on Indian Writing in English,* Delhi: Amar Prakashan, 1991.

Iyengar, K.R. Srinivasa. *Indian Writing in English,* Jalandhar: Sterling Publishers Pvt. Ltd., 1985.

Kaur, Tejinder. "Changing Facets of Indian Women and Women's Issues in Selected Indian English Fiction: A Study", in *Trends in Indian English Literature,* eds. T.S. Anand-Shalini Gupta, New Delhi: Creative Books, 2008.

King, Bruce. *Modern Indian Poetry in English,* Delhi: Oxford University Press, 1987.

Naik, M.K. "Echo and Voice in Indian Poetry in English". Chirantan Kulshrestha ed. *Contemporary Indian English Verse: An Evaluation,* New Delhi: Arnold-Heinmann Publishers, 1980: 26-40.

5 Feminism Incorporated: The Construction of Resistant Female Subjects in Two Literary Texts

— Rajesh Kumar Sharma

The common opinion in India is that feminism as a modern sensibility arrived here from the West in the 1970s and 1980s.[1] The opinion might be correct with regard to the critical practice but it is evidently not so with regard to the literary practice. The feminist sensibility has long and deeply informed the literary practice in India, a fact that is also borne out by the two texts considered in this essay: Dharmavir Bharati's *Kanupriya* and Shiv Kumar Batalavi's *Loona*. *Kanupriya* is a long dramatic monologue in four parts written in Hindi in 1959, while *Loona* is a poetic drama written in Punjabi in 1965.

This essay examines the construction of resistant female subjects and the forms and limits of the resistance *vis-à-vis* the patriarchal-phallogocentric order in these two texts.

Both Loona and Puran, the protagonists of Shiv Kumar Batalavi's poetic drama, belong among the ironic martyrs in literature. The prince among these martyrs is Kafka's K. who, in a moment of ironic illumination on the threshold of death, would have "the shame of it to outlive him" (*The Trial*, 251). He has turned persecution and murder into the fine art of courting suicide and would, finally, transmute it into salvation and martyrdom. Unlike K.'s ironic martyrdom, that of Loona and Puran is, however, both mixed and ironic.

Loona concedes victory to patriarchy when the flames of her *ressentiment*[2] consume the man whose body she craves, though she asserts at the same time that her act would confer immortality on him. Post-execution, he would blossom, she says, like the Ashoka tree under the touch of a virgin's foot. Moreover, his sacrifice would save from the pain of guilt those young men who may find themselves in his situation in future. Loona's rationalisation is stretched between the contradictory edges of an injured woman's personal and historical vengeance on the one hand and a lover's humane and redeeming benevolence on the other (201-04).

She is aware that in a world that might never know of her benevolence, she would earn infamy. But she would happily be an unrecognised martyr. The infamy would be the price she would pay to protect other poor girls from the Salwans of the future. Her motivating hope is that after her intervention such aberration from social norms would not recur.

Loona breaks, thus, in order to save. From a protagonist of transgression and defiance, she becomes a champion of justice and the law. To the extent that the quiet shift in her self-imagined role is scripted within the regime of patriarchal norms that control a young woman's sexuality, her martyrdom comes to eventually reinforce the order against which she had risen in revolt. Her potentially revolutionary martyrdom, consequently, mutates into a propitiatory sacrifice and her resistant discourse ends up being no more than inoculation.[3] It would thwart systemically disruptive resistance that might subvert the dominant order.

Puran, too, aspires for martyrdom. He would die in order to save others from reliving the fate that has doomed him and his people, including Salwan, Ichharan and Loona. But the efficient cause of his execution is his silence: he cannot bring himself to tell his father that the real problem is the old man's aberrant lust. Whether Puran dies to cover up his father's sin or is simply speechless (given the phallogocentric character of the Symbolic Order that confers speech) against his father's transgression, his in/action only affirms his status as a true Oedipal son by perpetuating the order of the fathers. Indeed, his Oedipal credentials entail that his crime should be *sculpted,* not just *inscribed* as in Kafka's penal colony,[4] on his desired and despised body, desired by Loona but despised by himself. The despiser of the body would experience the body in excruciating ecstasy as the axe falls on his limb after limb. On the other hand, the sentence passed on him is also the "untouchable" Loona's vengeance against his inaccessible body and the site of Salwan's displaced fear of carnality as well as of his repressed desire for his own object of desire, Loona.

The ideological opposition that Puran raises between the body and the soul articulates his scorn for the body: he regards love as a duel of two bodies that dishonours the soul (169). He tells Loona he might have given her his love had she wanted disembodied love, but she desired sensual gratification (176). Loona's clinching evidence against Puran – persuading Salwan that Puran attempted to seduce her – is, quite aptly, a physical inscription: the trace of an injury obviously self-inflicted but attributed to Puran (197).

That Puran incarnates the phallogocentric fantasy is suggested also in his judgement of Loona as a diversion and hindrance in the linear course of life that should, ideally, move towards a masculine orgasmic dissolution (231). The phallogocentric ideal of dissolution, in which differences cease to be, is spelt out in Puran's letter to her (188-89). The linear conception of human life, however, is set against another conception that the text makes available: that of human life as change, eternal wandering and Dionysiac intoxication (26). The alternative conception is, however, not worked out but relegated to the position of the textual noise.[5]

Broadly, the discursive structure of *Loona* is binary-dialogic, almost polemical. Two discourses, the patriarchal and the anti-patriarchal, collide. The former is articulated through Puran, Salwan, Kunta and Mathari; the latter through Loona, Ira, Ichharan and Goli. The collision makes the text manifestly anti-patriarchal at the level of polemics. But at the level of the Symbolic it accomplishes little more than problematising the patriarchal-phallogocentric order. Indeed, it even appears to slide into complicity with that order. And this is notwithstanding the presence of inter-crossing discursive threads and extra-discursive excesses and eruptions, such as Puran's femininity, Salwan's transgression of the norms, Ichhran's complicitous critique of patriarchy and Loona's self-perception as fire against Salwan's view of her as an erotic feminine stereotype.

This is not, however, to belittle the usefulness of rational discourse, deployed in the text, in women's struggle for an equal world. In fact, by rewriting as Loona's what had come down in folklore as Puran's story, Batalavi makes his preliminary intervention in the order of signification. Subsequently, in the overall scheme, the patriarchal voices are made to sound feeble and unconvincing in contrast to the high and impassioned voices of resistance. Such moves are undoubtedly significant. Salwan virtually discards his "unbeautiful" wife of many years, Ichharan, to buy and wed Loona, a poor "untouchable" girl who is young enough to be his son's bride but whose feminine beauty has aroused his lust (58). Loona, on the contrary, neatly steps out of and shatters the stereotype that had lured the old man and, in so doing, exposes his calamitous folly. Kunta, the wife of Salwan's friend King Varman, may consider woman to be no more than man's adjunct (68) and Mathari may glorify woman as the immortal creatrix (86-7), yet their ghostly voices are mere whispers before Loona's loud wail that rises from a lucid apprehension of her situation. Indeed, her wail is attended by an entire symphony of anger, protest and despair represented by Ira, Ichharan and Goli. Goli voices sheer hatred of the patriarchal male seen as fickle, secretive, wily and unfaithful (99-102). Maternity, she says, is an imaginary luxury that men fabricate to trap women in a web of false consciousness (112). Ichharan laments her reduction to an object of exchange in Salwan's world in which women are mere bodies to be transacted (97).

In the fitness of things, it falls to Loona and Ira to offer the most powerful articulation of resistance. Between them, they launch the most comprehensive and aggressive assault on the patriarchal order. Loona's self-perception as fire is a fruit of her long sortie into the territory of "timeless" phallogocentric signs during which she grabs also the Apolline right to speak and prophesy. The fire will speak and one day from the eyes of every fire will flow the offspring not of tears but of mutinous conflagration (78). She rejects silence and the authority of religions and also denounces the notion of destiny (79-80). At the same time, she understands that a woman is not quite free to author her destiny in the prevailing social order that despises daughters and regards them as a burden (85). She comprehends too the ubiquity of women's oppression, including their self-alienation and poverty of rights.

Although Loona can perceive her self-alienation with something like a tragic protagonist's lucidity (131-38), yet it is left to Ira to universalise Loona's little world in which something has gone fundamentally and disastrously wrong. To Ira, every woman is a Loona, every man a Salwan and every woman's life a prolonged act of suicide. In an intuitive insight that slices through the phallogocentric Symbolic, the world lies before Ira "exposed in its impotence" (139-40). It is a world of the dead (141). Her sincere but ironic advice to Loona is, therefore, to kill the inner Loona by smothering the fire and joining the community of the dead. The winds of time will scatter away the pain.

But Loona ignores Ira's advice. Instead, she approaches Puran in the misery and self-abasement (145-48; 154-55) of frustrated desire. However, the Oedipal son who reproached his mother (Ichharan) for abandoning him after her husband's second marriage reproaches her too for lacking in proper maternity that, for him, constitutes the essence of femininity (159-60). He is not prepared to look under the Symbolic and glimpse the subterranean lava of Loona's unmet desire. The surplus of her desire eventually consumes him, though it does not spare Loona either.

It is a double sacrifice, indeed the double martyrdom reappropriated as sacrifice by the patriarchal-phallogocentric order at whose altar it is made. The Sutradhar had anticipated a wasted sacrifice (37). In the end, is it a wasted sacrifice or a wasted martyrdom? Would it, or would it not, revitalise the order which it was supposed to propitiate? Or would it unleash transformations in the order, however molecular? Do any lines lead from resistance to revolution? Or, is Loona's resistance a self-enclosed event destined to self-destruct? The many-tongued answers lurk in the liminalities of the text where it merges into the Symbolic Order.

****

Of the two texts considered here, Dharmavir Bharati's *Kanupriya* is the more radical in terms of the intervention in the patriarchal-phallogocentric order. Kanupriya means the beloved of Kanu, which is one of the names of Krishna. Unlike Loona, this subject-protagonist is initially inscribed in the sexual economy of the text by virtue of her objectification in a heterosexual relationship. She is the other who derives her being from the self that is Krishna, so that she is seen not *in* herself but *as* Krishna's beloved. But this titular inscription has been entirely overwritten by the time the text ends, with Krishna becoming an object in Kanupriya's apocalyptic oneiric vision. The overwriting happens gradually but comprehensively as the text engages and problematises an entire masculinist appropriation of the predominant philosophical discourse of the Indian civilization articulated in the *Bhagavad Gita*. What is perhaps even more significant is that the engagement and problematisation are performed simultaneously within the order of the phallomorphic discursive rationality that is under challenge and in the darkness beyond its margins. This double performance is achieved by means of dissolving Kanupriya's interpellated phallomorphic subjectivity into fluidity, a process, a becoming-cosmic[6] on the one hand and by means of relativising the infinite and eternal wisdom propounded by Krishna on the other. Since subjectivity is the keystone of the structure of the phallogocentric Symbolic Order, the most efficacious strike on that order would be its dissolution into a subjectivity. The subjectivity that arises in the wake of the dissolution and cosmicisation is no longer alienated in phallogocentrism; rather it is capable of othering and reflection. For Kanupriya's oneiric vision of the cosmic sea is not only the other of Krishna's *virat rupa*, the cosmic form that he reveals to Arjuna, but it is also the de-absolutisng ground of that cosmic form. Kanupriya is, therefore, not just a resistant female subject but also a revolutionary one who, from her self-created revolutionary subjective space, displaces the self-evident truth(s) of the patriarchal-phallogocentric rationality.

In the First Song of *Poorvaraga*, Kanupriya speaks to the Ashoka tree that has blossomed to the touch of her feet. She has been always sleeping in the tree, she says, and her touch is only a reminder to the tree of her unseen presence in its every fibre (11-2). The becoming-cosmic is really being-cosmic. The subject is tantra as well as a *tantu* (fibre) in the tantra. The organism awakens into anorganism, the subject into a subject, and the organized Oedipal body into the body without organs.[7] Krishna has always been there in Kanupriya: she has only to listen as he plays as music in the strings of her body (Second Song, 13). The subject is endless lines of flow from and into other subjects and objects. In the Fourth Song, the dark Yamuna is Krishna and Kanupriya is bathing in its waters (16). In Kanupriya's encounter with the tree and the river thus, the cosmic, unorganized, unsignified, unsubjectified ground shines and floods the pure perception.

In the First Song of *Manjari Parinaya,* Kanupriya speaks to her mind. The mind would not plunge into affective intensities; it balks at the verge. The Song ends with her resolve to take the plunge some day (25). In the Second Song, the body emerges as the bridge to the being: it leads to the being through self-emptying. Kanupriya experiences herself as molecular, as "pure fragrance" (27). In her lover's hands, she is a recreated artifice everyday. In his spontaneous, effortless game, Krishna evacuates to fulfill and fulfills to evacuate her (28). Kanupriya responds with childlike effortlessness (29). She forgets the common language (31). Momentarily, the in-forming order of language is innocently cast away.

From a reflexive distance, Kanupriya would later use language to capture the relationship with her lover. But the relationship eludes language, and she gives up. Her Krishna is the dark sea (38). Language cannot signify the mystery of their primordial, divine relationship. She is Shakti, Vishnu's Yogamaya, who pervades all. She is Krishna's embodied beloved, but self-aware as his bride in all space and time (36-7). Yet she cannot take a measure of the relationship.

In *Srishti Sankalpa,* the teleology of the Creation is recoded as Kanupriya reveals herself as the meaning of the divine will to create. She is the Creator's Divine Companion. The cycles of creation are endless repetitions of the divine lovemaking, erotic eternal returns (41-4), not stages along the straight line of some phallomorphic teleology. The positioning of the female principle in the centre of cyclical circularity instead of in the teleological margin (as in the modern Western cultural narrative)[8] inscribes difference into the dominant contemporary cartography of time and space, recoding it non-phallomorphically.

The becoming-cosmic sends fear into Kanupriya's human heart (*Adim Bhaya,* 45-9). If the cosmos, being the object of Krishna's primal love-making, is her ludic body (*leelatana*), her human body is a simulated body (*chhayatana*) that must suffer loss and separation. In the interspace of this cosmic-corporeal duality, Kanupriya seeks the existential justification of human embodiment.

The human fear arising from her becoming-cosmic prepares her for self-emptying. She decorporealises and becomes cosmic (*Kelisakhi,* 50-4).

But now history erupts into the eternal present of affective intensities. Krishna has been long gone to make history. Kanupriya falls back into the contingent body amid ruins of the memories of love. She can recognise neither Krishna nor herself. History casts doubts over the truth of intensities in which she had once become cosmic (*Vipralabdha*, 57-9). Krishna has passed over her into history: her body that had once been a bridge to the being has been used by history as its own bridge (60). Kanupriya is divided. On the one hand is the greatness Krishna has gained in history, on the other is the loss she has suffered, the loss of the eternal present of love. She must search for the truth between timeless intensities on the one hand and history on the other (63).

At this point, she contemplates Krishna's historic project. The contemplation is both a historicizing critique of Krishna's project and an overcoming of history, for the latter has abandoned woman to dereliction by treating her as the eternal outsider. Kanupriya surveys the landscape of her memories of love that the armies of her lover are now laying waste. Nobody and nothing is safe in the way of war-drunk armies. She too must seek cover. The Ashoka tree that once shaded their love would be cut down for it stands in the way of the armies. She and her love stand forgotten in the incredible inhumanity of the war. Yet, with irony though, she must take pride in her lover who commands such wonderful armies (64-6).

She turns to Krishna himself (in his absence) for an answer to her question. Where is the truth? In the intensities that pulsate in the cosmos and lift her into being-cosmic or in the war that would write history and that has drawn Krishna into history? His history eludes her: she confesses her ignorance. Let him explain to her, as he did to Arjuna, what is truth and what is meaningfulness (67-9).

But she is afraid he can explain nothing to her, for she would not find anything in mere words. Words are absences. Unlike Arjuna, whom Krishna's words have reportedly brought enlightenment, she must receive Krishna himself as an embodied intensity who would set on fire her numbed senses. Should he speak, his glowing words would fall throbbing on her, but miss to communicate any history (70-2). She is thus poised to leap, beyond *signifiance*,[9] beyond history and words, into the sea of sheer intensities.

And so she has the dream vision of the cosmic sea pulsating with tides of war-like restiveness. She sees that war and death have engulfed all Creation and Krishna is quickly shifting his acts: sometimes he is arbitrating, sometimes aloof, sometimes engrossed in war. At last, disappointed and hurt, he retires beside her. The poison of war, with its futile and rampant death, has spread uncontrollably. He has flailed his arms and screamed from the shore, but none has heeded his words. Helpless and exhausted, he goes to sleep like an infant on Kanupriya's breast. He dreams and murmurs that there is no test to know the true from the false and justice from injustice. Perhaps chance is all. He, the fountain of eternal wisdom to Arjuna, is probably as ignorant as anyone else beside the infinite sea of existence. Kanupriya sees him innocently confessing his utter ignorance to Arjuna. He has given up history and become the sea. And he remembers Kanupriya and calls out to her (73-7).

Kanupriya arrives to his dream-call. She reminds him how she had kept herself apart and not dissolved into him, how she had withheld herself in time and space, how she had abided in history and avoided the temptation of eternity (17-8). She wanted to ensure that the next time history was made she would be by his side, for without her his words have no meaning and cry for blood. The poem ends with Kanupriya waiting for Krishna. His fingers have yet not begun to weave meaning into history (78-9).

The oneiric and the real dissolve in the cusp of Krishna's dream-call, Kanupriya's arrival and her ascetic wait in the hope that history would be written afresh as a shared and humane (non-masculinist) project. History would no longer be indifferent. Certainly not to the intensities.

Works Cited

Batalavi, Shiv Kumar. *Loona,* Amritsar: Lok Sahit Prakashan, n.d.

Bharati, Dharmavir. *Kanupriya,* New Delhi: Bharatiya Jnanapith, 1959.

Kafka, Franz. *The Trial,* Trans. Willa and Edwin Muir. Middlesex: Penguin, 1984.

Notes & References

1. Feminism denotes, among other things, a certain kind of critical gender sensibility to the patriarchal and phallogocentric order.

2. The concept of *ressentiment* is considered to be among Nietzsche's major contributions to psychology. He writes: "While the noble man lives in trust and openness with himself ... the man of *ressentiment* is neither upright nor naïve nor honest and straightforward with himself. His soul *squints;* his spirit loves hiding places, secret paths and back doors, everything covert entices him as *his* world, *his* security, *his* refreshment; he understands how to keep silent, how not to forget, how to wait, how to be provisionally self-deprecating and humble." Friedrich Nietzsche, *On the Genealogy of Morals,* trans. & ed. Walter Kaufmann (New York: Vintage, 1989) 38.
3. Roland Barthes enumerates inoculation among the ways the myth functions to suppress history and difference. See his *Mythologies,* trans. Annete Lavers (London: Paladin-HarperCollins, 1973).
4. See Kafka's short story "In the Penal Colony". *Selected Short Stories,* trans. Willa and Edwin Muir (New Delhi: Srishti, 1998) 191-227.
5. The concept of noise as the necessary condition of communication has been quite innovatively elaborated by Michel Serres. See John Lechte *Fifty Key Contemporary Thinkers* (London: Routledge, 1994).
6. Gilles Deleuze and Felix Guattari, *A Thousand Plateaus: Capitalism and Schizophrenia,* trans. Brian Massumi (London: Athlone, 1999). See chapter "1730: Becoming-Intense, Becoming-Animal, Becoming-Imperceptible . . ."
7. Gilles Deleuze and Felix Guattari, *A Thousand Plateaus: Capitalism and Schizophrenia.* See particularly the chapter "November 28, 1947: How Do You Make Yourself A Body Without Organs?"
8. Irigaray laments the complete rupture that has come to separate the modern Western culture from its pagan past as a result of which the modern Western subject has no access to authentic difference in the order of the Imaginary. The only Imaginary available to him/her is phallomorphic.
9. This is a French term imported into English by Brian Massumi, the translator of Deleuze and Guattari's *A Thousand Plateaus: Capitalism and Schizophrenia.* Borrowed, according to Massumi, from Benveniste, it means "signifying regime of signs". In Gilles Deleuze and Felix Guattari, *A Thousand Plateaus: Capitalism and Schizophrenia,* xviii.

6
Women Occupants of Gandhian Literary Space

— **Muniba Sami**

Some of the novels written by Indian writers in English before and after independence make use of the issue of women's participation in India's struggle for independence. Gandhi's involvement of women in the freedom movement invites comparisons and contrasts with the participation of the fictional female characters/heroines who joined the Satyagraha in response to his call. One sees in these novels a reworking of his esteem of women in combination with their role in the nationalist struggle. The textual representations allow the reader to see the manner and extent to which they are marginalised in the essentialist representations of nationalist discourse, revealing at the same time the author's own perspectives *vis-à-vis* the women's position in the patriarchal set-up.

In Raja Rao's *Kanthapura* the involvement of the village women in political activity cannot simply be seen at the level of local participation depicted in the novel. Rumina Sethi sees Rao's intrusion of his own political interests as well as his position within the brahminic intelligentsia. The two prominent Gandhian heroines, Rangamma and Ratna, who are natural leaders of the village women in the novel, happen to be Brahmin widows. The predominantly patriarchal order and specially the stronghold of chauvinistic brahminic culture was contemptuous of Gandhi's encouragement to women to step out of their domestic space and enter the public domain. By making grandmother Achakka, the narrator also a Brahmin widow, Rao is able to invite sympathetic comment on the Gandhian women activists' political involvement which permits (despite the pervasiveness of the dominant

Brahmin patriarchy in the novel) both Brahmin and non-Brahmin women equal participation with men in Gandhi's programme. Having been married they can qualify as the spiritual "nation mothers." A single woman, unmarried and young cannot, as she would be a potential symbol of desire (a temptress) of the material/physical world and as such a threat to the sexless Mother India image that the nationalists were trying to create. In order to remain within the great cultural tradition defining the nation, the woman who is traditionally seen as evil, a temptress needs to become 'pure' by the denial of feminine eroticism before she can acquire the Mother India status. This link, for the nationalist, also served to stake claim to the land of one's birth which had been forcibly controlled by foreigners.

In the novel, Rao uses both female activists, Rangamma and fifteen-year-old Ratna as mother figure. Although Ratna's feminine sexuality does initially come in the way of the Gandhian Moorthy's journey towards achieving the status of *brahmachari*, Rao overcomes this 'aberration' by making not only Moorthy fast to purify himself to achieve full sublimation but Ratna too is made to evolve spiritually through her full support to Moorthy during a fainting trance at the end of his three-day fast by falling prostate after offering the following prayer as a form of 'cleansing' process: "'God, God," she said, "keep him strong and virtuous, and may he rise out of this holier and greater; God I shall offer ten coconuts and a kum kum worship. God, keep him alive for me." Then she rose and fell prostrate before the god in the sanctum'" (Rao: 2001:72).

Rangamma is a surrogate mother to Moorthy especially after the death of his mother while Ratna displays a maternal care for the fasting hero. By following Gandhi, Rao 'liberates' the women including Brahmin widows from a restrictive life by allowing the home to be infiltrated by politics enabling the women to participate in the nationalist struggle without transgressing the patriarchal boundaries, both literally and figuratively. Even though Gandhi advocated equal rights for women in all spheres and sought social reforms, his image of the Indian woman remained fixed on the symbology of the mother and as such they entered public life to play maternal roles. His role for women within the national struggle appears largely limited to the domestic sphere. He believed men and women to be playing complementary but different roles and insisted that service to the husband, his family and country, in that order of preference, should be accepted as the 'primary duties' of women. But he also argued against the traditional stereotype of the weak and inferior women, asserting that women were not weak (as rendered by custom) because they possessed moral strength if not physical strength of men.

By imputing moral strength to women as almost being inherent or genetic to their mental make-up, Gandhi created yet another myth. He did not visualise a complete revolution or transformation of women's roles. His roles for women are dictated by different circumstances and levels of participation which appear to be contradictory. He advocated the fulfilment of only their primary duties for women who bore family responsibilities of looking after children and the aged, which were not to be given up for the sake of the national movement and yet he hoped women would sacrifice the pleasure of housekeeping and childbearing. If already married, he expected them to remain celibate for the sake of the national movement. He also expected his workers who had dedicated themselves entirely to the national struggle to stay single in clear pursuit of their goal.

Gandhi's image of the Indian woman undoubtedly possessed freedom but the woman's role was limited within the boundaries delineated by the patriarchal system. Any form of family resistance to the women's participation was broken down with the assurance that they would not overstep the boundaries of their traditional roles. Thus his involvement of women in the freedom struggle was a strategic tactic and attempted to both harness and limit their agency.

In *Kanthapura,* Rao's nationalistic belief in the 'protection' of women's domestic sphere is made evident in Rangamma's advice to women in their national activity as members of Sevika Sangh.

She exhorts them to first do their housework and not forget their husbands and children before helping others through the Sevika Sangh. While allowing flexibility, like Gandhi, Rao through Rangamma's attitude insists on preserving what Partha Chatterjee points to as the "differences between socially approved male and female conduct" (Chatterjee:1993:130). Again, like Gandhi, Rao creates categories of women: those who owe their services first to the home, and those who have no familial responsibilities and can therefore serve the nation. Since neither Rangamma nor Ratna has a husband and children they can be accommodated within the Gandhian parameters of chastity and abstinence.

What is striking about the novel is the role of Achakka in the framework of nationalist ideology. Her voice-over anonymity does not quite prepare the reader with her exaltation into the image of Rani Lakshmi Bai. The grandmother emerges from the margins from being merely an oral storyteller into assuming dimensions of a character who is no longer prepared to do what Rangamma advocates. She is not content to make a contribution to the freedom struggle only in terms of spinning but as Sethi points out, "is impatient to move beyond an auxiliary role in the freedom struggle in the same way as the women who had urged Gandhi to let them join the famous Dandi march. Gandhi had read their eagerness as a 'healthy' sign, yet refused them participation with ambiguous reasoning that they were 'destined' to make a far greater contribution to India's programme for independence in ways other than merely breaking salt laws"' (Sethi: 2006:143). Chaman Nahal's fictional account of Gandhi's gentle persuasion of Kusum – another Gandhian heroine in *The Salt of Life* – to join the Dandi march appears to contradict this historical fact. Not only does Sethi cite Gandhi's "To the women of India" (121), to support her statement but political theorists like Bhikhu Parekh and historical accounts confirm that the seventy-eight carefully chosen associates representing various regions and religions who accompanied Gandhi on his twenty-four-day march to Dandi were all males. He was joined subsequently by hundreds of people, men and women, mainly peasants from the surrounding villages.

Achakka feels magnified into Lakshmibai and is possessed by *Shakti* or the primal power which renders the male principle in the godhead, *purusha,* passive and weak. But as Sethi points out, "At the level of *Shakti,* the female point of view assumes more significance than Rao is prepared to allow" (Sethi: 2006:141). The women-power grows as the women believe the power of Kenchamma, the village goddess, to be present in each one of them. In fact, they are unnerved by the fear of their own unnatural courage and engage in a battle against the colonial might of the Red men even as Kenchamma did to kill the demon. Kenchamma's abiding presence in their lives helps them albeit with initial misgivings, to take to Gandhi easily as they correlate the feminine principle in Gandhi sainthood with their mountain goddess.

While Rangamma does not envisage any fundamental change in the traditional role of women, Achakka as the voice of dominant matriarchy unconsciously assumes authority and challenges the idea of a rigid division of labour between the sexes thus posing a threat not only to the brahminic partriarchal system, but the ideological level of the novel as well. Within the nationalist ideology women-power must not be allowed to go unchecked. So in the novel too, the awakening *Shakti* is restrained as the power of Kenchamma the mother-goddess takes over from Kenchamma the woman. Just as Gandhi did not intend to wage a feminist struggle as his programme for women complemented their household roles, so also "Rao secures their participation within limits so as not to upset the traditional Hindu image of the Indian woman, thereby freezing third-world women in time, space, and history" (Ibid: 144). Within both domestic and public living, the Kanthapura women, apart from spiritual upliftment, achieve little in altering the private domain.

Bharati in R.K. Narayan's *Waiting for the Mahatma* is yet another Gandhian heroine who is given a more prominent role than Rangamma or Ratna. But she is conceived in a detached, down-to-earth, uninvolved sort of way. While she both represents and carries the spirit of India in her name, unlike Rao, Narayan does not transpose the mother-image onto her, to become 'Bharat Mata' as her name appears to suggest. Ratna and Bharati share a number of personality traits. Both radiate freshness of youth, self-confidence and energy. Fired by missionary zeal, they exhibit their sense of duty, commitment and devotion to their ideology. Although Ratna is a widow, both are young, single and attractive. But the conception of their character could not provide a sharper contrast as the sensibility, perspective and the chosen techniques of the two authors have nothing in common. While Rao's tone is serious, idealistic and committed, Narayan's is comic, gently ironic and non-committed. Narayan's amused and tolerant humour not only lends him a seemingly objective stance by creating a distance between him and his characters but also determines the nature of his characterisation.

Waiting for the Mahatma can be read as an allegory of Indian nationalism with Sriram representing the adolescent nation which sleeps, eats, sits and walks pointlessly (as Sriram does), discontented within its circumscribed universe, cosseted by layers of customs till it is awakened out of its age-long somnolence by the beauty of Gandhian ideology (in the form of Bharati) bringing about a total disenchantment with the colonial rule (of the apple-cheeked queen of the portrait). Sriram's mother's dim portrait "which for years hung too high on the wall for him to see" (Narayan: 1999:5) and which he was not too pleased with when he grew tall enough to study the picture can be seen as a metonymic use of the erosion of India's ancient traditions.

Like Sriram, the nascent nation came under the spell of Gandhian ideology without understanding it fully or realising its full implication. The novel is really about the limitation of perceptions during the growth and the maturity of national consciousness. The root of nationalistic zeal lay in the lack of genuine ideological conviction. The stages in the transformation of Sriram represent the stages in the evolution of India's national consciousness but without ever really acquiring a full grasp of Gandhian doctrines. The nation's lapsing into violence with a sort of misty responsibility during the Quit India Movement of fortytwo, is represented by Sriram's acts of destruction with indiscriminate enthusiasm in the mistaken belief of having followed Gandhi's way of 'do or die' principle.

Seen in the light of this allegorical reading, Bharati represents the idea of "Gandhi's India" rather than the mythical image of Mother India of the nationalist discourse. Had the latter been the author's intention, he would have positioned Bharati (the way Rangamma and Ratna in *Kanthapura* have been positioned) within the narrow parameters and well-defined boundaries delineated by the tradition of the patriarchal system. Instead, Narayan contextualises her origin within the framework of the national movement by making her father die in the non-cooperation movement. A feminist, however, may charge Narayan with adopting a gendered perspective in making Bharati an orphan, thereby qualifying her as an ideal candidate for the role of Mother India. The allegorical reading here may bail the author out by looking at Bharati as am emblematic daughter of India even as Sriram may also be seen as the emblematic son, both representing in spirit and body, the vision of Gandhi's India of the future. The answer to yet another feminine questioning of Narayan's preference for the use of a female character rather than a male one (like Moorthy in *Kanthapura*) to represent Gandhian ideology, would be to see Bharati as an appropriate trope to represent the 'woman' in Gandhi rather than the ideal of Indian womanhood. Of course, one cannot deny the fact that Narayan does present Bharati as an 'ideal' woman but she is Gandhi's ideal, not the author's. Narayan's non-commitment to any ideology coupled with his mildly ironic detachment from his characters is a testimony to the neutral position he takes also in terms of the gender perspectives.

In *Salt of Life,* Nahal makes the fictitious character of Kusum the torch-bearer of Gandhian ideology and philosophy. She is one of the most trusted followers of Gandhi and is made to function like the sounding board for his inspirational idea of the Salt Satyagraha. While trying to board a train to Bombay to see her thirteenyear-old son who was injured in the violent aftermath of the Dandi March, she becomes the victim of a racial conflict at Wazirabad station. It is almost a repeat of Gandhi's famous

Martizburg experience of racism in South Africa. Her Gandhian revolt against this injustice sparks off a spontaneous agitation amongst the station-crowd which she is quick to control in order to prevent it from becoming violent. The news spreads like wild fire and the administration are in a state of confusion. Nahal lends this scene a metonymic significance in transforming Kusum into becoming the incarnation of Shakti in fierce opposition to British injustice represented by the racial attitude of Mr. Percy Wand, an officer of the Indian Political Service. After demanding a bucket of water from the engine driver, she proceeds to prepare salt in the middle of the railway platform to fight the British demon, the British *Mahishasur*, Percy, a devil incarnate: "Kusum the Shakti would lead these multitudes today against the might of the Empire, and she loosened her hair and spread it on her shoulders like a goddess. Yes, Kusum the Shakti would stand on that track alone, unaided by anything but her own innate fire, let them all disperse or fall back she would single-handed see how the train was able to budge forward an inch" (Nahal: *The Salt of Life*: 1993: 278).

Kusum almost becomes the incarnation of *Kali* or *Durga*, the manifestations of Shakti. But in spite of being the role model of a Gandhian woman, living and working in strict adherence to the rules of Sabarmati Ashram, Kusum, unlike Bharati, makes a conscious choice of leaving the ashram to lead a different life by marrying Raja Vishal Chand even at the cost of Gandhi's disapproval. Hence, in the light of this background Nahal's use of *Shakti* image (a typical patriarchic mythical figure of female power representing the role of the protectress in nationalist discourse, repeatedly invoked to stand for the motherland) to exalt Kusum into the image of Shakti, appears to run counter to his image of a woman on her way to emancipation. But the narrative perspective of the text elsewhere, unlike Rao's, does not support the imposition of the patriarchal construct of ideal womanhood on his women characters. On the contrary, there is an attempt by his Gandhian women, namely, Kusum and Rehana, to break free, although unsuccessfully, from the limiting confines of Gandhian feminism itself. Yet, another way to read Nahal's use of the Shakti trope is to see its use as a subversion of the myth in empowering Indian women in demolishing the barriers between the home and the world. This view finds support in the text itself without taking away from the dignity and the nobility of a great soul – the Mahatma. Nahal writes:

> She (Kusum) was wrong when she thought she had broken with Gandhi. Who could sever a bond so elaborate and convincing? Yet it went deeper than Gandhi; it was the spirit in her that could not be broken, or beaten, or bent – under any circumstance. Yet slowly she was getting to know the epitome of womanhood. Once she thought the beloved to be that personification. Or she thought it to be her duty. Recently, she even thought sensuality to be that personification, the source, the womb, from which life begins and where all life's searches end….Yet the woman in her had remained ungratified…..She had partitioned off the woman into little chambers and mistaken the crumbs for the wholes….She wondered why piety alone was the code recommended for the woman. Why were all the mythical Indian heroines clad in the sickly garb of virtue (read 'sexual purity' in the context)? (Nahal: *The Salt of Life*: 1993: 275 – 276).

Kusum and the other fictitious torch-bearers of Gandhian movement like Bharati and Ratna, the young heroines of *Waiting for the Mahatma* and *Kanthapura* respectively represent thousands of women who actively fought in anti-colonial struggles not only as followers but also as leaders in their own right. Women had not only become the metaphor for indigenous culture but they too often, like their male counterpart, appropriated the iconography of motherhood. Although Narayan in *Waiting for the Mahatma* does not impose such an iconography onto Bharati whose name is meant merely to carry the significance of India, the 'naturalised' association of the mother icon with the woman, through constant use, tempts the reader to impose this iconography onto Bharati. Both she and Ratna represent middle class young educated women who were mobilised and allowed participation in the nationalist movement from 1920s onward when Gandhi became the prime mover of the nationalist movement.

But even though the role of women in anti-colonial struggle may be seen to be merely contributory, the very exposure to political engagement in public sphere opened up new spaces for them enabling them to challenge certain notions of motherhood as well as female roles.

Works Cited

Chatterji, Partha. *The Nation and its Fragments,* Delhi:OUP, 1993.

Nahal, Chaman. *The Salt of Life,* New Delhi: Allied Publishers, 1993.

Narayan, R.K. *Waiting for the Mahatma,* Mysore: Indian Thought Pub., 1999.

Rao, Raja. *Kanthapura,* New Delhi: Orient Paperbacks, 2001.

Sethi, Rumina. *The Myths of Nation,* New Delhi: OUP, 2006.

7 Quest for Self in Shashi Deshpande's *That Long Silence*

— **Sujata**

Shashi Deshpande portrays the subjugation of women to prove her identity, wanting to think beyond the limitations imposed by her relationships. Her women characters feel the need of playing an assertive role in their lives, but they still are bound by their responsibility of nurturing various relationships which the society and their biological nature have imposed upon them. A woman should not be confined to the relations she bears to a man, but at the same time these relations should not be denied to her. A woman enjoys various relationships of wife, mother, friend and so on and still yearns to be herself without requiring a sheltering gap of male presence behind her. She desires to exhibit an energy that can erase her conditioning and free her from her psychic fears and the bondage of centuries.

Jaya, the protagonist of *That Long Silence*, truly represents these shades of the contemporary woman. She wants to know and understand her own bare self leaving all other extra details, as that alone can prove to be a source of strength in her tedious, lonely journey towards true selfhood. The novel centres on the process of Jaya's realising herself. Shashi Deshpande says about the novel: "And I wrote *That Long Silence*, almost entirely a woman's novel, nevertheless, a book about silencing of one half of humanity. A lifetime of introspection went into this novel, the one closest to me personally - the thinking and the ideas of this are closest to my own" (quoted in Jain 2000:210).

The novel *That Long Silence* begins with Jaya and her husband Mohan shifting from their cozy and palatial house to their old house in Dadar, Bombay, where they had stayed immediately after getting married when their financial condition was not good. Her husband is accused of financial bungling and an enquiry against him is in process. Mohan is however optimistic and he decides to stay in the Dadar flat to make himself unavailable for the time being and is consoled to know that the children, Rahul and Rati, are away on a long tour with their family friends and it is taken for granted that Jaya will follow him. Jaya recalls: "I remember now that he had assumed I would accompany him, had taken for granted my acquiescence in his place. So had I. Sita followed her husband into exile, Savitri dogging Death to reclaim her husband, Draupadi stoically sharing her husband's travails" (Deshpande 10). That the role of mythical woman would only render her a fool is known to Jaya who uses the metaphor of the bullocks yoked together to describe their position: "Two bullocks yoked together…it is more comfortable for them to move in the same direction. To go in different directions would be painful; and what animal would voluntarily choose pain?" (12). Later she is rudely shocked by Mohan's accusation that she too is indirectly involved in the scam. Mohan bursts out to convince her that all he did was for her and the children.

The memories crowd in her mind. For Jaya, the only way out is an encounter with reality and to express that reality through her writings. Whatever she wrote so far was not the expression of her real self, she has to face her real part, which she calls ghost. As she enters the Dadar house, the ghosts of the past spring out at her. But left alone later, she gets the idea that the ghost most fearful to confront is the ghost of one's own old self. And her past is visualised in a detached way. She sees her past activities as if she were some other person. This woman is a ghost of Jaya, for Jaya has by now deviated from her earlier self. This meeting with her earlier self is like having a stranger thrusting upon oneself, claiming a relationship that is denied.

Jaya begins to understand how women are trapped through the glorification of the role of housewife and the mother. The children are always presented to her as a final argument. It is used as a justification for everything and Jaya is defeated. But she argues that Kusum should be kept in the Dadar flat, away from the children, and Kusum begins to stay there despite Mohan's contempt. Not only Mohan but also Jaya's two brothers and her mother oppose the idea of taking Kusum's responsibility. Yet Jaya sticks to her decision through her sincerity though her sincerity cannot save the poor woman who commits suicide. Jaya's struggles silently against the limitations imposed on her by her husband and also by other members of her family. She is aware that such scattered cases of silent revolt are not enough for asserting her individuality. She begins to prepare herself internally for breaking fresh ground as a writer.

For seventeen long years of her marriage she has successfully controlled her feelings as she has thought it more important to be a loyal, good wife and a caring mother rather then being a good writer. She has suppressed her desires that lead to self-actualisation and fulfilment, in her zeal to play the role of a loyal wife and a caring mother. In order to have a happy martial life, she not only suppresses her writing career but also her association with her one time neighbour, Kamal. Consequently, she fails to project her inner feelings in her stories. Thus, her career as a writer is finished in the early years of her marriage. A short story of hers bags the first prize and also gets published in a magazine. She is on the verge of getting recognition as a writer when Mohan expresses his displeasure at a particular story written by her. The story talks about a man who cannot reach out to his wife except through her body. Mohan suspects that the man portrayed in the story is he himself, and is doubtful that people would take him for the man in the story. Due to his disapproval she stops writing. But she begins to write under a pseudonym. This does not help and her stories are rejected one after another. Kamat, her neighbour, analyses the reason behind the successive rejections and tells her that her stories lack strong emotions, as she has suppressed her anger and frustration. But she cannot express her anger or feelings for fear of damaging her relation with Mohan. She has learnt to control her anger as Mohan considers this trait in a woman as unwomanly. She tells Kamat: "No woman can be angry. Have you ever heard of an angry young woman?" (147). At this Kamat warns her against indulging in selfpity as it would only prove destructive to her. He admonishes her and warns her against 'women are the victim' theory.

Later she begins to write light humorous pieces on the travails of a middle class housewife in a column entitled 'Seeta'. She not only gets encouraging responses from the readers but also a nod of approval from Mohan, which is essential for her to have a happy married life. She stifles her need for being in touch with her inner self and of expressing it creatively in her writing to survive happily in a male-dominated society.

In her zeal to play the role of a loyal wife and a caring mother, she smothers her real self. Like other women, she has been indoctrinated right from her childhood. She does not protest for anything. Her dress and her appearance are proof of her submission to Mohan's liking, replicating an observed family woman. She systematically suppresses her free will as she has been taught the importance and stability of marriage and family to survive in this patriarchal world wherein a woman has to suppress her feelings and has to follow instructions given by her husband without a question. She tolerates everything and never expresses her pain. She thinks, "the emotion that governed my behaviour to him...was the habit of being a wife, of sustaining and supporting him" (98).

Kamat, a widower living above her flat lends depth to Jaya's personality. She is drawn towards him as he treats her as his equal and offers constructive criticism. He even receives her mail at his address to help her to avoid any confrontation with her husband as he disapproves of her writings. He showers his attention on her as he is lonely. Unlike other men he does not have aversion to cooking and such other domestic chores meant to be performed by women exclusively. She feels so much ease in his company that her womanly inhibition withers and she opens up her problems to him. He warns her against wallowing in selfpity and asks her to pursue her literary career by giving expression to her real inner self.

Jaya is challenged by the stoicism of Jeeja, an elderly maidservant. With her ability of self-analysis, she has the courage to acknowledge her emotions. She realises that her fear of losing the comfort of a happy family is at the root of taking the role of 'Seeta'. She decides to erase silence from her life and exhibit the genuine significance of her free, innate and uninhibited personality in totality. She resolves to continue her writings and does not wait for Mohan's consent or approval.

Works Cited

Jain, Jasbir. Ed. *Creative Theory: Writers on Writing,* Delhi: Pen Craft International, 2000.

Deshpande, Shashi. *That Long Silence,* New Delhi: Penguin, 1989. References to the text are from this edition and have been indicated by page numbers in parentheses.

8 Patriarchal Mechanism of Oppression: Images of Women in Contemporary Indian English Drama

— Anju Bala Agrawal

Patriarchy is described as a political-social system that insists that males are inherently dominating, superior to females, and endowed with a right to dominate and subjugate them. It operates in direct and subtle ways to achieve and maintain gender inequalities essential for subjugation and subordination of women. As a result women are forced to undergo different kinds of oppressions in every walk of life. Adrienne Rich defines patriarchy as the "power of the fathers: a familial, social, ideological, political system in which men—by force, direct pressure, or through ritual, tradition, law, and language, customs, etiquette, education and the division of labour—determine what part women shall or shall not play and in which female is everywhere subsumed under the male."[1] In fact patriarchy perpetuates inequality between men and women. This paper focuses on the oppressions of women in patriarchy as presented in contemporary Indian English drama and drama in translation with special reference to dramatists like Vijay Tendulakar, Girish Karnad, Mahesh Dattani and Mahashweta Devi.

In most of his major plays, Tendulkar projects women as victims under patriarchal mechanism of oppression. Gender stereotyping is forced upon them. In the patriarchal set-up, her life is limited to purely domestic roles—daughter, mother and wife. A gendered difference is forced upon her from childhood. She has to take care of 'family' values—values which are presumed to be her responsibility and not the male's. Females are expected to be meek, submissive and patient. They should subordinate their desires to those of male selflessly. Such sustained sociological conditioning inhibits and restricts the full development of a women's personality. Even education has been unable to save women from oppression. Let us analyse the major plays of Tendulkar to show different types of oppression faced by women.

In *Kamala,* Jaisingh's feelings towards Kamala and Sarita are not much different. If he expects Kamala to appear at the press conference in her soiled and torn clothes to suit his sense of the dramatic, he expects Sarita to submit to his desire for sex whether she wants it or not. He abuses Sarita by calling her "bitch." Sarita meekly accepts her subordinate position in the house and willingly follows every instruction of Jaisingh. When she sees commodification of Kamala, she realises that there is no essential difference between Kamala and herself. Even Kakasaheb who first sympathises with Sarita and is critical of Jaisingh ends up telling her that men are like that and that her place is beside her. This is an example of oppression in a standard way.

In *Sakharam Binder,* Laxmi and Champa represent two polarities of feminine response to patriarchy. Laxmi is thrown out of her house by her husband but she still considers him God. When she comes to live with Sakharam, she respects him as he is providing her food and shelter. She is the blind follower of patriarchal system. Champa is a figure of revolt. She hates her husband for the physical and sexual torture he inflicted on her. She comes to live with Sakharam and adopts a violent and abusive attitude towards males. Laxmi hates Champa for ill-treating her husband. She upholds the patriarchal value system so much that she sees Champa's death as a kind of divine retribution.

Tendulkar's Sakharam represents the double standard that patriarchy sanctions. He picks up helpless abandoned women and gives them shelter in his house so that they will take care of his physical and domestic needs. He is not bound by the norms of marriage, yet he expects 'his' women to live with decorum as a wife. In the play *Vultures,* Tendulkar demonstrates the bestiality and monstrosity of people under patriarchal system.

Ghasiram Kotwal[2] literally and figuratively occupies a marginal place. The writer has depicted the patriarchal world of Poona

Brahmins where women are treated as commodities and possessions. The patriarchy denies women freedom and an independent identity. They are dominated and controlled by any means. The three women who have a visible presence in this play are Gulabi, the prostitute; Lalita Gauri, Ghasiram's young virgin daughter and later Nana's mistress; and the young Brahmin wife of Nana. They represent different roles allocated to the weaker gender by patriarchy. They are valued in sexual terms only. Ghasiram uses Gauri as the sexual bait. He sends Gauri to Nana to become Kotwal of Poona. Gauri does not express her feelings against this commodification; rather she slips into the role of being Nana's mistress. After some time Nana is bored of Gauri and buys a new Brahmin girl as his wife. Thus, women are so much suppressed by patriarchy that, throughout the play, they neither express their feelings and views nor can they make their own decisions.

In Tendulkar's drama, the organisation of 'family' is patriarchal, in that all men are considered superior to all women though this does not mean that women have no place within it. They are often awarded positions of spiritual reverence and authority. *Silence! The Court is in Session* lays bare sexual politics in patriarchal norms of family and gender relations. Miss Benare, the school teacher in the play, fiercely claims her independence as a person: "My life is my own. I haven't sold it off to any one for a job. My mind is my own. No one can suppress it. No one. I shall do whatever I choose with my life. I'll decide what to do with it."[3]

With this spirit of individualism Benare takes the bold step of getting pregnant with the man she loves, Prof Damle. The game played by the participants in the form of mock court trial represents the violent and merciless way in which a woman trying to have her own way is flouted and insulted in a male-dominated society. Benare with all her flouting of conventions desperately tries to find a husband so that her 'son' will have a father. Why 'son'? Why not 'child'? Whatever patriarchy may do, Benare shows a rare degree of awareness of her marginalisation.

Both Tendulkar and Dattani see women primarily as exploited and marginalized subjects but where Tendulkar's women are victims, Dattani's views cover a wide range. In *Dance Like a Man* and *Where There's a Will,* Dattani draws attention to two inevitable after effects of the patriarchal mindset. In both plays, he presents powerful pictures of dominating fathers destroying their sons for not rising up to their expectation. In *Dance Like a Man,* the father-in-law joins hand with his daughter-in-law to destroy his son's career as a dancer. In *Where There's a Will,* Hasmukh Mehta tries to get even with his son by making his mistress the executor of his will. In these plays, women, who are oriented towards accepting male supremacy from birth, flout patriarchy to gain their goals.

The helplessness of women in Indian society has been depicted in the play *Tara.* How preference is given to a male child over a female child has been highlighted by Dattani in this play. Whenever the question of choice comes between male and female, it is the male who is chosen. *Tara* also brings the bizarre reality of the woman playing second fiddle to man. The most frightening example of women blindly adhering to patriarchal values is found in *Tara.* Tara and Chandan are conjoined twins and they are to be separated through surgical operation. The mother and the maternal grandfather decide to give the boy, the leg that receives most of its blood supply from the girl and hence has a better chance of survival in her. The preference for the beneficence of the male child while staking the life of the female child is pathetic and takes to culmination the feeling of rejection felt by women in our society.

Bravely Fought the Queen presents the exploitation as tolerated by women prevalent in educated urban families. It also shows that women will fight back if they are not heard or suppressed for a very long time. Alka is all armed to fight back and to question the norms set by men for women. We are instantly reminded of the lines spoken by Dolly: "And we can all go—bravely fought the queen! Bravely fought the queen! Full of manly valour."[4] In the patriarchal set up, marriage is not only a means of regulating sexual and reproductive behaviour but also a means of upholding male dominance. A woman who is unable to conceive becomes an aberration; even when the fault is not hers. Uma in *Seven Steps Around the Fire* is repeatedly taken to the doctor by her mother-in-law. The gynaecologist suggests that he wants to see the husband. When Uma tells this to Suresh, he ignores it. To see the doctor, to admit that here might be something wrong with him, that he might be impotent, is something the educated manly police officer could never admit even to himself.

Like his contemporaries, Girish Karnad has also depicted the marginalisation and inferiorisation of women in a male-dominated society. The male has voice, presence and power, whereas the female is silent, absent and powerless. In some plays of Karnad, women are docile and shouted at. The representation of high-caste women in Girish Karnad's play *Tale Danda* is expectedly stereotypical. In the royal household, the position of Queen Rambhavati, King Bijjala's wife is no better than any other servant of the palace. She tells her son: "Do as you wish. Just don't upset your father, that's all. He turns his bad temper on me and I can't take it any longer".[5] Rambhavati does not have a "will of her own." She is devoid of her 'self'. Her not minding the inferiorised position is the outcome of the centuries of internalisation of the patriarchal postulates by women in society. She has an unflinching allegiance to her husband. Elaine Showalter's words appropriately fit Rambhavati's position: "We have seen our foremothers as mindless, downtrodden souls accepting century after century the fetters of their lot with passivity, unheeding or incapable of perceiving their exclusion from society."[6]

The other woman in the palace is Sovideva's wife. She has been discarded and sent to her parents by Sovideva. Sovideva wantonly revels in the arms of a prostitute, Indrani. When Sovideva is in need of help in the aftermath of the beheading of Madhuvarasa and Haralayya, he is advised to visit his father-in-law and bring the queen back. At this juncture, Sovideva's statement is: "Yes, And see our queen again! She is our Queen after all, frigid bitch though she is."[7] This shows that woman is valued for her functional utility only rather than for her intrinsic worth as a human being.

In patriarchy, men command and it is women's lot to obey silently without so much as a protesting sound. Women's slavery leaves men free to pursue their wishes. The most relevant example of the shabby treatment meted out to women is provided by the *sharana* Jagadeva. Jagadeva does not care for his responsibility towards his mother. It is she who will care and attend to her mother-in-law. This shows the condition of women in the traditional Indian society. Women remain a marginalised and suppressed group, without power, without voice and may be even without consciousness of their peripheral position in society.

The play *Nagamandala* mocks at the double standards adopted by the patriarchal society. It is about Rani who represents a typical woman in a male dominated society. Appanna, a wealthy village youth marriages her and brings her to his house when she attains womanhood. Her attitude towards her husband after marriage is that of a traditional wife in a patriarchal society where every husband is worshipped as a god. Appanna has a concubine outside. For her, he leaves behind his own newly wedded young wife waiting for him day and night. He visits her only once in twenty four hours and that too not for her sake but for his meals. He commands his newly wedded wife and treats her with contempt reserved for women in a patriarchal society: "Have you brought in all the bundles... Well then I'll be back tomorrow at noon, Keep my lunch ready. I shall go and eat."[8]

Rani does not dare to question his arrogance. In order to counter this male-chauvinistic vision, Karnad adopts a strange device in which the king Cobra gets sexually involved with Rani. Spending nights with Naga, she becomes pregnant. When Appanna comes to know about Rani's pregnancy, he infuriates and charges Rani with having extramarital relations without bothering what he himself is doing. Here, it is noteworthy that Rani's act is not intentional as she is not aware of Naga. She has to face the chastity ordeal. The situation in which Rani is required to show her chastity is reminiscent of the fire-ordeal through which Sita had to prove her virtue as a devoted wife.

In the patriarchal society, no such ordeal is reserved for man however immoral he may be as a father, husband and brother. When Rani, with the help of Naga proves her chastity, she is considered a goddess. Even Appanna who suppressed her reason by continuous torture, falls at her feet and asks forgiveness. Later, he becomes a devoted husband. This change in Appanna shows a trace of matriarchy at the end. Karnad seems to anticipate that matriarchy is to follow patriarchy if our society is to change for better. Her other female protagonists, like Vishakha in *The Fire and the Rain,* Padmini in *Hayavadana,* are seen breaking the shackles of patriarchal oppressions and trying to get a new meaning to be added to their individuality.

Mahashweta Devi is different from the male dramatists. She focuses on the link between feudalistic set up and patriarchy. She projects women as symbols of resilience and love. It may be due to her being a woman that enables her to recognise this power that emerges when a woman is isolated, victimised or oppressed.

Sujata Chatterjee, the protagonist in *Mother of 1084* is a victim of patriarchal authority of her husband. Despite her affluent background, she takes up a job in the bank as an act of self-assertion against oppression. However, she suffers patiently all the humiliation by her overbearing husband and corrupt children and their spouses. She fails to disconnect herself with them and leads a compromising life till one morning when she is summoned to identify her favourite son Brati's dead body in the police morgue. In a series of encounters with people, she knows about Brati's mission and for whose sake he died. Now she discovers for herself the enormous spread of the power that she had so long identified with her dehumanised household alone. She finds in his sacrifice an articulation of her silent resentment against the patriarchal system she bears all along against the insensitive establishment and revolts.

Bayen is a moving story of a sensitive mother, who, like Sujata, is placed against the powerful patriarchal institution. Chandi, the central character in the play, is a gravedigger. Her job is to bury the dead children and protect them from jackals at night. As long as she remains unmarried and is not blessed with a child, she goes on with her work without any complaint. She is fed up with her work. Having found an image of her baby son in the dead children she buries, she pleads with her husband Malinder, to release her from the constraint thrust on her by the feudal society, by taking her to a town where nobody knows about them. He pays no heed to her complaints. About this time, the gullible people led by

Gourdas, a hypocrite and exploiter, brand her as a witch and condemn her to live away from her son and family. Though she is reduced to the animal status by the society, she is not devoid of human passion. In fact, the separation from her son and society has led to the realisation of her being as a mother and a human being. When Gourdas plans to stop and loot the train by spreading bamboo sticks on the railways, Chandi runs to the spot and dies in an attempt to avert the accident. The defiance of age-old values takes concrete shape as her son, Bhagirath comes forward to acknowledge the dead as his mother.

Through the portrayal of Chandidasi and Sujata, Mahashweta Devi projects the image of women as Shakti—the embodiment of strength, and also one who is capable of boundless love. Sujata and Chandidasi project the dignity of Sita and Sati—the two archetypal quintessential figures of Indian womanhood. Women have this power in spite of patriarchy; it may even be a byproduct of patriarchy. Whatever be the case, it is this kind of positive reinforcement that women require to throw off the restraining shackles of the patriarchal system.

To conclude, contemporary Indian drama reveals the androcentric bias of the prevailing patriarchal order. Various strategies are adopted to highlight its hegemony. The social institutions which influenced this mindset not only become utterly insensitive to the inner needs, longings and aspirations of women but also perpetrate inequality and injustice against women. Women, in spite of the sufferings they undergo, question and at times challenge the basic assumptions of the patriarchal order. Feminism has now emerged as a new way of life, free of "dependence syndrome." A new perspective has dawned on the Indian horizon with the feminine psyche trying to redefine a woman's role in society and reassert her self-identity hitherto denied to her under tne patriarchal order.

References

1. Adrienne Rich, *Of Women Born: Motherhood as Experience and Institution,* London: Virago, 1977, pp. 57-58.
2. Vijay Tendulkar, *Ghasiram Kotwal,* tr. Jayant Karve and Eleanor Zelliot, Calcutta, Seagull Books, 1999, pp. 51-52.

3. Vijay Tendulkar, *Five Plays,* tr, Priya Adarkar, Mumbai, Chennai, OUP, 1995, p.58.
4. Mahesh Dattani, *Collected Plays* New Delhi: Penguin Books, 2000, p.296.
5. Girish Karnad, *Collected Plays: Vol. II,* (New Delhi: Oxford University Pres., 2005), p.15.
6. Elaine Showalter, qtd. Dona Bennet, *Naming the Way Home, Amazing Space: Writing Canadian Women* Longspoon/Newest, p.229.
7. Girish Karnad, *Collected Plays: Vol. II,* p.88.
8. Ibid., *Vol. I,* p.254.

9 Exploring Territories of Indian Feminism

— Arpita Ghosh

Till date no such theory has been evolved which can categorically be referred to as Indian feminism. In the past two decades attempts have been made to lay down an ideology for feminism in India, yet no such solid niche has been carved out as is found in mainstream Western feminism. In this paper, my concern is with the Indian scenario. Some references are made to the evolution of women abroad in order to place the Indian situation in a larger, global context. This would only highlight both the differences and the similarities from the theoretical premises of Western feminism which cut across cultural and societal boundaries.

Feminism possesses no primary text, no definitive theoretical source from which it arose. Its political roots lie in the struggle for equal civil and political rights for women. The concept of self-realisation, freedom and autonomy is drawn from the Enlightenment philosophers who stressed on the equal rights of man. It was during this revolution in United States and France, Mary Wollstonecraft wrote her treatise *A Vindication of the Rights of Woman* (1792), claiming equal rights for women. She attacked the prevailing notion of docile femininity and laid out the principles of emancipation: equal education for boys and girls, an end to prejudice and plea for women to become defined by their profession, not their partner. She declared: "I do not wish them [women] to have power over men; but over themselves."

The development of feminism as theoretical discourse and the growth of women's studies as an academic discipline in the 1970s and 1980s encouraged women to explore a range of different intellectual traditions and theoretical paradigms, drawing upon such diverse sources as Marxism, psychoanalysis and semiotics. According to Alison Jaggar's formulation, feminism defines all those forms of theory and practice that seek, no matter on what grounds and by what means, to end the subordination of women.

Feminist criticism originated primarily as a content-based approach to literature which catalogued the response of the female reader to the sexual stereotyping codified in the literary texts. One of the most influential of these early texts was of course Kate Millett's *Sexual Politics* (1969). This was rapidly followed by numerous other critical studies of 'images of women' in the mainstream literature and culture. The sole concern of feminist criticism was to rediscover a lost tradition of women's literature. Elaine Showalter's ground-breaking text *A Literature of Their Own: British Women Novelists from Brontë to Lessing* (1977) was able to delineate a female counter-tradition within literature, an enormous body of writing which had been forgotten or repressed and which revealed significant patterns of continuity in its themes and pre-occupations.

Summarising the achievements of critical research in this realm, Showalter wrote in an essay "Introduction: The Feminist Critical Revolution": "We now have a coherent, if still incomplete, narrative of female literary history, which describes the evolutionary stages of women's writing during the last 250 years from imitation through protest to self-realization, and defines and traces the connections throughout history and across national boundaries of the recurring images, themes, and plots that emerge from women's social, psychological, and aesthetic experiences in male-dominated cultures."

The criteria for a feminist reading of women's literature within American criticism is largely anchored in a reflectionist model which measures the work and its ability to reproduce realistically female experiences in the same way as texts by male authors reflect a patriarchal perspective. In short, the work of a woman is read as containing an implicit critique or subversion of patriarchal values. As a result, the achievements of feminist criticism include reintroduction of political interests into the interpretation of literary texts instead of expounding the workings of metaphor or metonymy. They are keen to reveal the workings of patriarchal ideology through its representation of gender and inter-personal relations which are deeply embedded within existing social relations.

Following the path tread by Showalter, Susie Tharu and K.Lalita compiled an anthology of two volumes of women writing from thirteen languages which, for the first time, published in English translation, illuminate the lives of women over two millennia of Indian history and extend our understanding of literature, feminism and the making of modern India. In the 'Preface' to the said book, *Women Writing in India 600 B.C. to the Present, Volume I : 600 B.C. to the Early 20th Century* (1991), they have claimed that "we have attempted to make available for English-language readers in India and around the world a group of works that together will illuminate the conditions in which women wrote; bringing more significant women's writing to light; help us reevaluate writers who were reasonably well known but had been misunderstood or dismissed; give us a sense of the themes and literary modes women drew on and made use of; and help us capture what is at stake in the practices of self or agency and of narrative that emerge at the contested margins of patriarchy, empire, and nation." They have meticulously taken special note of women writers who were criticised or spoken about dismissively, and of controversies that involved these women. In the process they have come across debates in which women had intervened; about their roles as wives, companions, and mothers who "also" wrote. The early 20th century, commonly considered a period when the women's movement was at a low ebb, had been a high point of women's creative impetus.

Chandra Talpade Mohanty's edited volume, *Third World Women and the Politics of Feminism* (1991), is a compilation of essays and debates which focuses on the development of feminist theory and politics by third world women. She clubs Indian women with the "third world women" and accounts for their politics of feminism. Here, the term "third world" has been deliberately used preferring it to "postcolonial" or "developing countries." "Third world" refers to the colonised, neocolonised or decolonised countries of Asia, Africa and Latin America. However, scholars often locate "third world women" in terms of underdevelopment, oppressive traditions, high illiteracy, rural and urban poverty, religious fanaticism, and overpopulation of particular Asian, African, Middle Eastern and Latin American countries.

Audre Lorde's poetic cartography in the beginning of the Introduction "Cartographies of Struggle - Third World Women and the Politics of Feminism" gives a different definition.

According to her, the third world is "a world which is definable only in relational terms, a world traversed with intersecting lives of power and resistance, a world which can be understood only in terms of its destructive divisions of gender, colour, class, sexuality, and nation, a world which must be transformed through a necessary process of pivoting the centre (in Bettina Aptheker's terms), for the assumed center (Europe and the United States) will no longer hold."

The early history of the emergence of women's struggles in India encapsulates tensions between progressive and conservative ideas and actions. After all, histories of feminism also document histories of domination and oppression. No non-contradictory or "pure" feminism is possible. In India, the middle-class women's movement essentially attempted to modernize earlier patriarchal regulation of women and pave the way for middle-class women to enter the professions and participate in political movements. However, one cannot deny the fact that it is Indian middle-class men who are the key players in the emergence of the "women question" within Indian nationalist struggles. Male-led social reform movements were thus pre-occupied with legislating and regulating the sexuality of middle-class women, and selectively encouraging women's entry into the public sphere. This observation of Mohanty echoes what Adrienne Rich has said in *Of Woman Born* (1986): "whatever my status or situation, my derived economic class, or my sexual preference, I live under the power of the fathers, and I have access only to so much of privilege or influence as the patriarchy is willing to accede to me, and only for so long as I will pay the price for male approval."

Vrinda Nabar's seminal research work *Caste as Woman* (1995) is an illuminating text which surfaces a totally different perspective to analyse the situation of Indian women. In this book, Nabar draws parallel references with Bell Hooks' *Ain't I A Woman? Black Women and Feminism* (1981), where Hooks has charged that for the West, the term "woman" is synonymous with "white woman." Hooks argued that feminism had its roots in a world-outlook coloured by racial imperialism. In *Feminist Theory: From Margin to Center* (1984), Hooks argued once again for the essential difference between the black and white female experience, seeing it as a difference in perception of what the term 'oppressed' could mean to different social/ethnic/racial groups. In a similar fashion the experiences of the Western women do not fit into the Indian context and hence the need for an indigenous feminist ideology.

In spite of the ongoing efforts of groups of women in India to Indianise the movement, the popular conception of the term "feminism" remains both ignorant and imitative. The Indian Women's Movement has never threatened the *status quo* in any significant way. According to Nabar, one of the reasons for the sustained misapprehension about feminism among the Indian intelligentsia may be the failure of committed feminists in this country to provide a text that would both arouse public attention and be taken seriously, a text that would interest a significant cross-section of readers, young and old, male and female. The boundaries of caste, class and economic disparity may seem to call for a book in itself. But it is hoped that the categories which apply to the Indian woman and the framework within which she is placed are, at one level, all-encompassing.

A primary focus in Nabar's study is the role of tradition in our social existence and the need for feminism to first discredit some of the legacies of this tradition. The tradition born of myth have always oppressed women and done them enormous harm. Most Indian women would relate to the Hindu tradition. The strictures regarding codes of behaviour and forms of social purdah are found in both Hinduism and Islam, and similar patterns may be observed in the other religious groups: Sikhs, Parsis, Christians, Jews, Buddhists and Jains. There is a certain image conjured up by the nomenclature Bharatiyanari, which cuts across religious boundaries, and which women by and large conform to. It is this image which the feminists question in varying degrees of defiance and revolt.

The importance of the hold of tradition and mythology on the Indian subconscious should not be undermined. Very few men or women in the West, even among the more conservative believers, would consciously use the Virgin Mary to uphold present day ideals of female perfection or purity. But the readiness with which most Indian grasp at mythological stereotypes like Sita or Savitri, or their reservation about Draupadi, are an obvious indication that, for us, time future is indeed contained in time past. This may have something to do with a world-outlook which is sentimental, even emotionalistic and melodramatic, rather than pragmatic and utilitarian. However, the myths denuded would reveal a pattern of unequal prescription. Sita does not merely follow Rama into the forest, but has to prove her chastity after being rescued from Ravana who had abducted her. Draupadi is pawned in a game of dice, a clear indication of her status as a dispensable commodity owned by the five Pandava brothers to whom she is married. Both Sita and Draupadi are placed in a higher pedestal as women devoted and committed towards the well-being of their husbands. Such glorification of their virtues are nothing but another ploy of patriarchy to herald female martyrdom as preferable, desirable, and even imperative under the facade of pativrata.

The feminist wave in the West received immediate and widespread exposure in India due to the media-boom in the 70s and 80s. Its persuasive rhetoric wooed a large number of articulate women engaged in trying to break through the conventions of a hidebound, traditionally patriarchal society. However, the stridency of many of the Western feminists lost them their audience in India. Feminism in the West was born of a way of life essentially defined by the philosophy of individualism. In Western society the individual good is more important than the collective good. They, by and large, thrive on the principles of rationality and reasoned argument. In the context of Indian society, whose collective unconscious still operates at a very fundamental level of faith and dogma, such individualism is impractical. If the lot of Indian women has to change then it would have to be done from within. Mere aggression and militancy would be disastrous because Indian conditions are unfavourable for the success of any revolution that has its roots in individualistic values. For something as fundamentally iconoclastic as a female revolt, they would prove fatal.

If the Indian response to feminism was a combination of skepticism and opposition, it was because the language of Western feminism was alien, its priorities remote to the workings of the Indian mind. Most Indian women at all class-levels are in fact ignorant about the real focus of protest. Moreover, the concept that the present condition of woman is man-made and therefore not incontrovertible, cannot be fitted properly into the minds of Indian women. Phrases like *purush-jati* and *stri-jati,* to name only two, assert the belief in the naturalness of differences — differences that are not so much biological as artificial constructs perpetuated through doctrine and dogma. These are passed on from one generation of women to another, mother to daughter, mother-in-law to daughter-in-law. Most Indian women are taught by other women that they have no choices, that this oppressive condition incorporates both *stri-jati* and *stri-dharma*.

The total emotive and spiritual immersion in the husband's being, may not operate in marriages today. Yet there is something in it which is very endemic to our world-view which is interwoven with the symbols of womanhood: *purdah, haveli, chudiyaan, mangal-sutra, kum-kum, sindoor*, or even the colour red itself; of the self-effacing role of the *ardhangini*, of the *saubhagyavati*, of a mother, and finally a widow. Each of these is replete with a mixture of deep unhappiness, feelings that are rarely expressed with total spontaneity, suppressed hopes and dreams, untold tragedies. The orthodox view of the *Bharatiyanari*, an impossibly ideal, lifeless, colourless, oppressed prototype, is still the popularly accepted one. She is an antidote to the corrupting effect of the so-called 'modern', 'liberated' woman who allegedly models herself on the women abroad. The divorced woman, without exception, is viewed as 'Westernised' (i.e. amoral) and unmindful of her duty as a good Indian wife. The embodiments of the 'modern' woman —the working woman, the single/divorced woman, the successful/professional woman—are all up against the most fearsome odds.

In this paper I have discussed why the insights provided by Western feminism are not enough to improve the lot of Indian women. I have also analysed how our embedded cultural heritage and tradition and the stereotypes of Indian womanhood affect our creative impetus. None the less, one cannot deny the fact that those same stereo types could have been our greatest inspiration if we had seen them from a different perspective. All these years we have seen and followed Sita's devotion towards Rama, but we have never tried to look beyond. We have overlooked the self-respect and dignity she had for herself. Had it been so, we would not have been waiting for Western feminism to fit into our Indian context. The fact remains that we have all the ingredients for the formation of an indigenous feminist ideology embedded in our own culture and tradition only. The need of the hour is to analyse those age old stereotypes from a positive perspective, and there lies the compendium of Indian feminism.

Works Cited

Mohanty, Chandra Talpade, Ann Russo, and Lourdes Torres, ed. *Third World Women and the Politics of Feminism*, Bloomington, Indianapolis: Indiana University Press, 1991.

Nabar, Vrinda. *Caste As Woman*, New Delhi: Penguin Books India, 1995.

Rich, Adrienne. *Of Woman Born: Motherhood As Experience and Institution*, New York, London: W. W. Norton & Company, 1995.

Showalter, Elaine, ed. *The New Feminist Criticism: Essays on Women, Literature and Theory*, New York: Pantheon, 1985.

Tharu, Susie and K. Lalita, ed. *Women Writing in India 600 B.C. to the Present, Volume I: 600 B.C. to the Early Twentieth Century*, New Delhi: OUP, India, 1991.

Wollstonecraft, Mary. *A Vindication of the Rights of Woman*, 1792. London: Penguin Books, 1992.

10 "Till Death do Us Part": A Feminist Interpretation of Nayantara Sahgal's *The Day in Shadow*

—Neena Arora

For centuries marriage was considered to be the destiny for woman irrespective of the fact whether she was happily married or was miserable due to constant oppression by man in the patriarchal set up. However, a possibility of freedom from endless suffering in unhappy marriage appeared with divorce, separation or annulments of marriage under law. Divorce is a process of giving legal recognition to the breaking up of a relationship already shattered by irreconcilable disparity in the character of two persons or by broken faith and bitter tensions. For ensuring harmony in the marital relations, an acceptance and adjustment of the wishes, attitudes and sentiments of both the partners is necessary. But when the needs, wishes or individuality of one of the partners is ignored then this results in discord. "Divorce," as Marilyn French says, "like marriage, is morally neutral, it is good; insofar as it ends a long-term intimacy, it is to be lamented."[1] But certainly divorce gives freedom to women to get rid of an existence of suffering due to male-aggression or gender oppression.

In India, traditionally, the matrimonial ties are considered irrevocable. The "Hindu Dharma" expects from a wife complete obedience and devotion to her husband. She is expected to completely merge her ego with her husband's, and to strictly follow the ideal of *Pativrata*: "As a river merging itself in the ocean loses its identity, so a wife was supposed to merge her individuality with that of her husband. Her only concern in life was to see that all services needed by her husband were properly performed by her, the satisfaction of her husband being her sole joy in life...there was no question of raising a word against him even when he was found to be ill-tempered, vicious, diseased or a drunkard."[2]

In India, the blessing for the married woman is always "Sada Suhagan Raho" (i.e. May you never lose your husband). To have a husband was the greatest blessing for a woman even if he was evil because society recognised woman only through the husband. A single woman had no status in society. Hence, there were practices like "Sati" (self-immolation of widows on the pyre of the deceased husband) because a woman's existence without a husband was thought to be meaningless. While some performed Sati willingly, knowing the plight of widows in Hindu society, others were forced to die on the husband's pyre. In this kind of setup, the question of divorce or separation for a married Indian woman did not arise. Hence, for centuries there was no provision for a legal divorce. A woman could not remarry even after the death of her husband, though a man could abandon his wife and remarry anytime.

The concept of marriage as a sacrament and an indissoluble union was pervasive in the West also for centuries, and divorce was only a male's privilege. Woman was seen only in relation to man. She had no life of her own. As Gilbert and Gubar comment in *The Madwoman in the Attic*, to be selfless is not only to be noble, it is to be dead. But the woman who refuses to be selfless and acts on her own initiatives irritates the society and is unwelcome. In the Western societies, there were no grounds for which a woman could divorce her husband until Roman woman gained the right to divorce in the days of the Empire. However, Protestants took a somewhat more liberal stand on the question of divorce. "Luther seems to have believed that only adultery and desertion were adequate grounds for divorce.... However, in addition to adultery and desertion, cruelty and 'refusal to conjugal duty' (which meant refusal of sexual intercourse) were also considered grounds for divorce by most Protestant churches."[3] John Milton wrote a series of pamphlets in favour of divorce in the years between 1643 and 1645 but it was only in 1857 that judicial divorce (divorce granted by a court of law) became available in England. And it was only in 1968 that the divorce laws were made more liberal.

The liberalisation of divorce has come as a great help to save women from endless oppression, or torture in marriage and now apart from the usual grounds of adultery, cruelty, greed etc., divorce can be granted on the mutual-consent basis, if both the partners agree and are bent upon final separation; in America this is known as "no-fault" divorce.

In her novels, Nayantara Sahgal shows her women suffering in marriage and then deciding to come out of the stifling bondage by opting for divorce. Her characters like Simran, Saroj, Rashmi leave their husbands or break the marriage which does not allow them to be free and to live life in their own way. She shows that though divorce frees them from the agony and suffering of a unhappy or unjust relationship still it does not solve the problems and women have to continue to struggle and suffer on various levels—economic, emotional and psychological As such the questions arise: does a sexist society easily accept a woman's freedom? Does a woman find real happiness in her new role as a divorcee? Does she really become free after divorce? These and some other related issues have been explored in Sahgal's many novels but more deeply in *The Day in Shadow* (1971).

Divorce which is admittedly a relief from the painful life of a wrong marriage, is hardly enough to re-establish the woman socially, psychologically or financially. Even after divorce, the aggrieved or relieved woman does not find herself in the same situation as before marriage. Despite the wounds inflicted in the unsuccessful marriage which have to be borne for a long time, a woman has to further bear the onslaughts of a harsh society which does not allow her to be free and happy. Divorce is the beginning of another phase of troubles as it comes out clear after a study of *The Day in Shadow*.

In the past the role of the divorced woman was to withdraw from the society and hide her shame. The divorcee was shunned by friends, and spoken of in hushed whispers by her relatives. The divorcee was not sure whether she was expected to grieve or to celebrate, to feel ashamed or relieved. The Indian society still does not consider divorce to be something good or healthy despite the liberal divorce laws. As Rama Mehta puts it, "the position of the divorced or separated woman... (has) only marginally improved for the upper middle class."[4] Divorce in Indian society in general is considered a social stigma and a big scandal for a woman who is treated as if she is accursed with some disease. Probably, this makes most of the oppressed women dare not break their unhappy marriage and silently accept physical and mental torture instead. However, the trends have changed in recent times. Instead of clinging to a to a sterile and oppressive relationship, more and more women are asserting themselves and are seeking freedom by way of divorce, even if they have to incur wrath of society or their family. Not surprisingly in India both in urban and semi-urban areas divorce rate is in spate and is not limited to affluent upper class alone.

The Day in Shadow is an autobiographical novel of Nayantara Sahgal. Here she narrates the traumatic experiences of Simrit who can be compared with the writer. Incidentally, Sahgal took divorce from her husband Gautam Sahgal in 1970, which was unheard of in those days. In the novel, after long years of her married life Simrit decided to put an end to her unhappy marriage. Through Simrit, Sahgal expounds various aspects of divorce and its implications for a lonely woman.

Simrit's decision of divorce lands her into multifarious problems. In the traditional society, where a married woman is respected more than a single woman, a divorcee is more or less ostracised or shunned as if she were a pollution. The husband's social status or official position becomes a touchstone through which the worth of a woman is measured. After her divorce, Simrit soon realises that it is basically a "husband-centred world"[5] where a free woman has no place; her individual contribution and social standing are meaningless in this male-oriented society. Like Sahgal, Simrit is a journalist and a more well-known writer but finds that people are more interested in her husband and often ask her "what does your husband do?"(6). Instead of showing concern for the agonized lonely woman, they add fuel to the fire by insisting on the "husband" and his status, etc. Simrit reflects on the whole graceless affair: "Wasn't it odd, when you were standing there yourself fully a person, not to be asked what you did?"(6). Shortly after her divorce, in a posh party being attended by top bureaucrats of the Ministry of Petroleum and aristocrats and debonairs of Delhi's upper strata, people are surprised to find her alone. One of the organisers of the party "was studying her solicitously, as if divorce were a disease that left pock marks"(4).

Simrit is a woman with a strong sense of individuality and had "never accepted a world where men did things and women waited for them"(6). Her independent, bold, self-reliant attitude separates her from the traditional women who religiously follow the footsteps of their husband and worship him like god. She is surprised to find that people around her mourn divorce and hesitate to accept it as soothing and life-giving at least to the person who had suffered prolonged suppression and domination. When Som's company lawyer Moolchand visits her, he begins his conversation condoling, "as if someone had died": "I want to tell you how sad I consider all this...so unbelievable...all my sympathies...the children...anything I can do" (54). The Managing Director of Oil Products Ltd., Mr. Shah, whom Simrit meets to ask his advice on the consent terms, also does not consider divorce to be something positive as he believes that "divorce is not part of our tradition" (146). Sadly, no one tries to look into the reason of divorce. Divorce, when it comes to Simrit, is not easy either: "It was painful how the connection continued, like a detached heartbeat. The tissue of a marriage could be dissolved by human acts, but its anatomy went on and on. And skeletons could endure for a million years. Just living together, daily routine produced that uncanny durability. It made the question of whether one had loved or not, been loved or not, been the transgressor or transgressed against, trivial by comparison" (64).

Even after divorce the woman often experiences a sense of inability to control or mould her life. In *The Day in Shadow*, Sahgal reveals the psychological, financial and other existential problems which a woman has to face as part of her punishment for leaving her husband. After divorce while a man feels free from all moral, social and financial responsibilities, a woman feels as if her inner self "has gone to pieces" (51) or like "a person thrown out of a train in the night and forced to find his way home in the dark" (51-52). Gail Putney Fullerton remarks that the final separation is bewildering: "It is like pushing against a door that suddenly gives way".[6] Even after divorce or separation which a woman mainly seeks for her peace, freedom and independence, she finds herself in troubled waters again. The male jealously and cruelty operate even after divorce.

In *The Day in Shadow* Sahgal exposes the inhumanity of a husband towards his estranged wife and his own children. Som Raman, a business magnate, agrees to divorce his wife for ultimate commercial benefits. Also, in order to rake revenge on his wife Simrit, he imposes cruel divorce terms on her in a satanically shrewd way. Simrit out of ignorance and good faith signs the consent terms without really reading them. Simrit's efforts to get rid of these unfair, unjudicious terms—"the document [that] trapped and maimed her" (39)—mutually and amicably, fail. Simrit is a woman who is "bleeding to death with taxes" (146). She has been "used as convenience" (168). Even after divorce her husband, in order to save his own income tax, thrusts cruel consent terms on her according to which she has to pay "huge taxes" (55) on the shares worth six lacs, which are presently in her name but will go to her son Brij, aged sixteen, after nine years, i.e., when he attains the age of twenty-five. Simrit pleads with Som's lawyer: "I don't want the shares left in my name. As long as they are, I'll have to pay this crippling tax and whatever I earn will just be wiped out by the tax" (56). The answer in response to her request overtly reveals that narrow, money-minded male attitude: "Because, Mrs. Raman, there would be a big gifts tax if we made a trust" (56). The lawyers believe that these terms are quite reasonable and were drawn with the consent of both the parties: "I must remind you, Mrs. Raman," Moolchand continues in the same formal vein, "that this was negotiated settlement to which you gave your consent" (60).

Simrit meets Som to appeal to his conscience and to find some way out but he proposes a fresh agreement, which is more cruel than the previous one. Simrit is horrified his irresponsible suggestion: "What we can do is make a new agreement. Let's say you can use the income from those shares—if you don't marry—and until they're transferred to the children. Of course I'd have to stop the support you're getting now. And you'd have to pay the taxes on the Corpus, but since you'd be using the income that would be quite fair" (221).

Simrit rejects the fresh terms outright and thus the problem remains unresolved. Raj, her friend and well wisher, also could not understand the motive behind such an agreement:

> "Whatever made Som stick a document like that on you? Revenge for what?"
> Simrit frowned. "It wasn't revenge. It was just Som."

> "Just Som is what I've been trying to get at," said Raj. "What was Som like?"
> "Well he liked to have the last word. The terms were his parting shot, like his not sending the car for Merriwether" *(225).*

Simrit continues to be in a state of agony till Raj angelically emerges to protect her and later marries her. While Som belongs to the artificial and material world of rat race, Raj's world is different. Opposed to the attitude of banal calculations is the spirit of humanism that Raj, a Christian, embodies in his relationship with Simrit. Simrit does not leave Som for Raj's sake; she only shares his friendliness and helping attitude though later both are tied in matrimonial knot. While Som never tried to fathom her depth, with Raj she has a more satisfying and absorbing relationship. Raj not only shakes her benumbed mind to awakening but makes her shed her shadows and live as a bold, assertive woman. But ironically, somewhere deep down, the patriarchal attitudes are embedded in Raj too. Raj very suddenly announces his marriage to Simrit before his elderly friend Ram Krishan, without even consulting her or giving her time to think over. Simrit is surprised at the abrupt announcement, but then accepts it silently (231-32).

Sahgal here effectively reveals the predicament of a woman after divorce. She purposely chooses an intelligent, sensitive and aware woman, who is a writer and a free lance journalist, but who is very shrewdly trapped in a brutal divorce settlement, to show that a woman can be easily used by a man for his convenience. In her essay "Of Divorce and Hindu Woman," Sahgal writes:

> I wanted to show how even in a free country like ours where women are equal citizens, a woman can be criminally exploited without its creating a ripple. Again, I am not speaking of any recognizable form of exploitation against which most people will naturally raise a cry. If a man beats his wife, for instance, hardly anyone will condone the fact. But if at divorce he inflicts a financial settlement on her that enslaves her with taxes and makes it impossible for her to make a decent living, no one will take any notice because this is a kind of beating where blood and bruises don't show. But in addition, and this is the crux of the matter—nobody

> bothers about it even when they do. Simrit in this story finds she has to serve as a tax convenience for her ex-husband all her life, and that tied up in this way, she will never be able to make an adequate living for herself.[7]

It is evident that through Simrit's divorce, Sahgal makes a strong plea for change and revitalisation of the Indian society.

Fear of loneliness, insecurity, emotional vacuum, financial pressures and unjust division of responsibility make the divorcees realise better than the single persons that married life, at large, is satisfying, and this consciousness makes than plan to return to it by remarriage. Remarriage or settling down again in marriage is not anti-feminist; it rather amounts to maturity and better understanding of the ideals of marriage which insists in life-long "till death do us part" commitment arising from mutual love and selflessness.

Despite the fact that in India remarriage is not very popular, Simrit in *The Day in Shadow* remarries as she can resume her life anew with Raj. The practice of remarriage is more prevalent in the West where "women feel more uncomfortable about answering 'divorced' to questions of marital status than about answering 'housewife' to questions of occupational status...For whatever combination of reasons, divorced women have the highest marriage rate of any group in the United States."[8]

Sahgal brings out that even after achieving cherished freedom in all spheres, women are not truly free and happy as they envisage, and have to pay a heavy price for their independence. A free woman feels lonelier and unprotected in a sexist society which is ready to crush her identity and individuality at every opportunity. The realisation thus dawns on her that while divorce provides one kind of freedom, i.e., freedom from oppression and exploitation by the husband, it creates new forms of sufferings and problems as well.

References

1. Marilyn French, *Beyond Power: On Women, Men and Morals,* 1985; rpt. London: Abacus, 1986, p.504.
2. Quoted in Promila Kapur, *Marriage and the Working Women in India,* Delhi: Vikas, 1970, p.9.

3. Gail Putney Fullerton, *Survival in Marriage*, Illinios: Dryden Press Hinsdale, 1977, p.395.
4. Rama Mehta, *Divorced Hindu Woman*, Delhi: Vikas, 1975, p.168.
5. Nayantara Sahgal, *The Day in Shadow*, New Delhi: Vikas, p.2. The subsequent citations have been incorporated in the text.
6. Fullerton, Gail Putney, *op.cit.*, p.446.
7. Nayantara Sahgal, "Of Divorce and Hindu Woman", *The Hindustan Times*, 18 December 1971, p.7.
8. Fullerton, Gail Putney, *op.cit.*, p.125.

11 Loneliness in Anita Desai's Female Characters

— Smita Jha

Anita Desai is an eminent Indian English novelist, and it is an accepted fact that she has made significant contribution to the growth and development of Indian fiction in English. It is quite understandable that she is ranked apart from such other female writers, her contemporaries, Kamala Markandaya and Ruth Prawar Jhavbala, because while the other novelists are interested primarily in the economic, political, cultural or domestic situation of our society, she is preoccupied with the interior weather, the inner climate, the sensibility of her female characters. Naturally so, her novels are inward looking and require sustained and profound consideration. Her protagonists are persons for whom aloneness alone is the sole natural condition, aloneness alone the treasure worth treasuring and that they are mostly women who, though they have reached different stages in life, are all fragile introverts trapped in their own skins.

Anita Desai has written a large number of novels and is writing still; however, for the purpose of the present paper only those novels have been taken up for analysis as were written till 1984. These novels are *Cry, the Peacock* (1963),*Voices in the City* (1965), *Bye-Bye Blackbird* (1971), *Where Shall We Go This Summer?* (1975), *Fire on the Mountain* (1977), *Clear Light of Day* (1980) and *In Custody* (1984). The female characters that we encounter in these novels are Maya in *Cry, the Peacock,* Monisha and Amla and their mother in *The Voices in the City,* Sara in *Bye-Bye Blackbird,* Sita in *Where Shall We Go this Summer?*, Nanda Kaul, her great granddaughter Raka and Nanda's friend Ila Das in *Fire on the Mountain,* Bimla or Bim and Tara in *Clear Light of Day,* and Sarla and Bibi in *In Custody.* At this point, however, we have to keep in mind three things that have their own bearing on our consideration of Anita Desai's novels. In the first place, here is a novelist who writes about the Indian situation and characters in her fiction as an insider. Secondly, though we come across several important phenomena of the present-day Indian society in her novels, she is interested principally and primarily in her female characters. Lastly, her task as a writer of fiction is far more difficult and delicate than that of Kamala Markandaya and Ruth Prawer Jhabvala, for trying to map out the inner world of sensibility is bound to be much more difficult and delicate than describing the outer world of action.

In *Cry, the Peacock* the central character, the protagonist of this novel is Maya, and it is she who does naturally dominate the scene from the beginning to the end. In other words, we may say that she is at once the centre and circumference of this world and it hardly matters whether she is sane, hysterical or insane. Maya is a young, sensitive and highly strong woman who is sorely obsessed by an early prophecy of disaster in her life only four years after her marriage. This, she is told, is a kind of disaster which can in no case be averted, and it is this feeling of panic, of mortal apprehension that completely grips her whole self.

The way Maya thinks and conducts herself is indeed something far from the natural and normal human practice of looking at things, objects or people. She is brought up tenderly by an indulgent father; she is a well protected and privileged child, and lives all the time in her own world of fantasy. She is married to a person named Gautam, a lawyer by profession, who is not only twice her age but also unsentimental and matter of fact in his approach to problems. The irony of the situation is that while Maya is haunted all the time by the prophecy of impending disaster, Gautam accuses her of living in an unreal world, and looks upon her as a pretty by tiresome and wayward infant, the spoiled daughter of a rich father.

Maya compares herself to the peacock which mates only after fighting, and 'peacock' is indeed the symbol central to the story of this novel. There is none to look after her; she is totally isolated, alienated and lonely character. It is in a state of psychological phrenzy that she pushes down Gautam from the parapet of the roof, the fall leading to his death and she herself, perhaps landing in an asylum. Maya's case is representative of people with distorted psychic condition.

In *Voices in the City* we meet Monisha, Amla and their Mother. Monisha is different from other Bengali women in the sense that she is an intellectual and that instead of saries and ornaments we find her wardrobe stocked with books by Kafka, Dostoevsky and Hopkins, besides French and Sanskrit books. It is important to note that we come to know of Monisha's psychic condition through her diary. It is on being married to Jiban, a person economically well off, that Monisha comes from Kalimpong to Calcutta. It is really unfortunate that she is a lonely individual, and that her life is all empty. She does indeed try to discover some meaning or purpose out of her life, but finds absolutely nothing to sustain her, and feels sorely frustrated.

Monisha's case is unenviable. The absence of the element of love from her life; her near-complete estrangement from her husband, her all-engulfing depression, and the suspicion of her in-laws—all these, in quite a substantial way, force her to realize the futility of her life, and finally drive her to suicide.

Amla, Monisha's unmarried sister, is seemingly a gay and lively woman, and, after having received necessary training in Bombay, comes to Calcutta to work as a commercial artist with a firm there. Even she does not like Calcutta. However, behind this façade of cheering engagement, she does have a growing feeling of the futility of life.

The mother is a complex figure, beautiful, rich, and well-settled and a dominating character. However, her children do not look up to her for help in times of distress. She is a soulless mother. In *Voices in the City* the Mother is projected as an agent of rejection or destruction. Monisha and Amla are incorrigible introverts, of course gifted with sharp sensitivity.

In *Bye-Bye Blackbird* we find Sarah, Adit's English wife, takes to self-weaving in order to be able to know her real identity. Adit's attitude towards England and English people undergoes a change, and his Anglophilia turns into Anglophobia. It is in view of this changed perspective that we have to consider Adit's observations in respect to Sarah. There develops a gap between Adit and Sarah.

And, finally, when Adit decides to leave England and get back to India, Sarah, who is expecting her first child, expresses her regrets. Sarah is caught in the painful cultural crosscurrents, and in spite of all her efforts Sarah continues to face a crisis of identity.

The only female character who claims our attention in *Where Shall We Go This Summer?* is Sita, a middle-aged woman, above forty, and married to a Bombay businessman named Raman. Sita does already have four children, and is expecting her fifth child, and yet the theme of this novel is that of husband-wife alienation. The discord between Raman and Sita arises out of their opposed temperament and differing viewpoints, for while Raman is practical and worldly kind of person, irrational and a conformist, Sita is a non-conformist, a sensitive and emotional character. This novel is a projection of her inner life, her loneliness; it is a probe into her agony, into her feelings of boredom and torment. She goes away, along with two of her children to the small island of Manori, off the West Coast. In spite of her escape from Bombay, she does seem to have a semblance in life still and it is on this island that she tries to find a way out of her spiritual predicament. She realises that her children are fast growing up and it is for this reason that with all inwardness, she seeks a solution to the problems of life. It is really gratifying to see that at the end of the novel she tries to arrive at a positive view of human life.

In her next novel, *Fire on the Mountain,* Anita Desai deals with three important female characters, namely, Nanada Kaul, her great grand daughter Raka, and her old friend, Ila Das. These three live in their own separate worlds of loneliness, although they also try to establish a bridge of understanding among themselves. Nanda Kaul is an old lady who, except for her servant, lives all alone in her house in Kasauli. She has discharged all her duties and obligations as wife, as mother and as the lady of the house, and it is only after having fulfilled her mundane commitments, when her husband is dead and her children are settled, that she lives like a recluse out of vengeance, holding herself religiously aloof. Raka is keen on going to Kasauli to regain her lost health there, and she hopes to receive herself with all the physical and spiritual comfort that she hopes to get from Himalayan beauty. Raka's feeling of loneliness, of withdrawal has been aggravated by the unhappy lives of her parents. Raka is a lonely figure because of her unhappy childhood, and it is because of this psychic condition that she speaks all the time of forest fire. Ila Das is Nanda Kaul's friend; she had seen a good deal of the world's glory, but it is because of the disintegration of her family that she feels all lonely and helpless. She is appointed lecturer at the Home Science college, and still she does not see any ray of hope in her life because of the shattering away of all that she had hoped for. It is really unfortunate that Ila Das has to meet a very humiliating death.

In *Clear Light of Day* the two female characters that claim our closest possible attention are Tara and Bim who are sisters and who do offer a sharp study in comfort. It is really interesting to see that while as a school student Bim takes her studies to be a challenge or as an opportunity, Tara looks upon going to school as a terror. Bim is dynamic and intelligent, Tara is dull. Tara is married to a successful diplomat and is the mother of two charming daughters, and yet she is afflicted with a sense of failure because she has been of little help to her problem-ridden parental home. On the other hand, her sister, Bim, unmarried, lecturer in a Delhi college, has sacrificed herself to the drudgery of looking after a mad aunt and a brother who has refused to grow up. Tara develops a sense of guilt and helplessness for the reason that she finds it difficult to cope with the existing situation and turns into lonely character. Bim is able to organise herself with great competence and skilfulness and yet there is a feeling of vacancy in her life.

The two female characters who need being referred to in the novel entitled *In Custody* are Sarla and Imtiyaz Begum. Sarla is a committed character, and she wants to put her own life in the right perspective. However, since she has not been Deven's choice and since she has been selected by his mother and aunt, she develops a feeling of anxiety, bitterness, inferiority, and looks the very picture of abandoned wife. Sarla is a typical Indian wife who has her own dreams of future, and in spite of all her sufferings she represses her feelings for the sake of domesticity and becomes a psychic and lonely character. Imtiyaz Begum is Noor's second wife who has been picked up from a brothel. She is an irritable, imperious and inconsiderate character. She is a terrifying woman in certain ways; all the same we do feel that here is a woman who has been maligned, mocked, ignored and neglected.

Anita Desai's female characters, it is not at all difficult to see, are striking and impressive individuals. They are not and cannot be types. They are the people who remained involved in self-introspection, in a searching analysis of their own psychic state. At this point it would be highly pertinent to refer to two or three different things that have their own relevance and value in any consideration of Anita Desai's female characters. In the first place, the mothers in her novels are not traditional or conventional figures; they are strikingly different from our usual, normal idea of mothers, for the simple reason that we find them involved in themselves, caring little or practically nothing for their children. This is the image of mothers that Anita Desai projects in such of her novels as *Voices in the City, Fire on the Mountain* and *Clear Light of Day*. In other words, we may say that Anita Desai has divested the mothers in her novels of their love and affection, greatness and glory, and has indeed debunked them. Secondly, quite a few of Anita Desai's female characters are wives, but, as we find them, they are fundamentally different from usual, normal wives. These characters are solitary people, and we see that they are, for one reason or another, alienated from their husbands.

Anita Desai's female characters are mostly educated individuals, and that what is really important about them is that they are highly sensitive, withdrawn and lonely people; they do not receive any positive help either from their surroundings or from life itself. Loneliness is a state of mind; it is a reflection of what goes on inside and as such it is really difficult for an ordinary writer to deal with this psychological phenomenon. Anita Desai is a gifted artist, and she has taken up this particular aspect of human existence because she finds decay, disintegration, disorder and death hitting life all around.

To a question regarding human relationships and female loneliness by Jasbir Jain in the course of an interview Anita Desai said: "I think all human relationships are inadequate, I have never worked this out. Basically every one is solitary. I think involvement in human relationship in this world invariably leads to disaster."

Works Cited

Desai, Anita. *Bye-Bye, Blackbird,* Orient Paperback, 1971.

– *Clear Light of Day,* New Delhi, 1980.

— *Cry, the Peacock,* Orient Paperback, 1980.
— *Fire on the Mountain,* New Delhi, 1977.
— *In Custody,* Penguin edition, 1984.
— *Voices in the City,* Orient Paperback, 1969.
— *Where Shall We Go This Summer?,* Delhi, 1975.
Jain, Jasbir. *Stairs to the Attic: The Novels of Anita Desai,* Jaipur, 1987.
Krishnaswamy, S. *The Woman in Indian Fiction in English,* New Delhi, 1984.

12 Dialectics of Philosophy, Spirituality and Desire in Nargis Dalal's *The Inner Door*

— Ashoo Toor

The Indian literary scenario, dotted with women writers, has experienced a meteoric rise. Yet Indian English literary scene bristles with amazing anomalies and curious contradictions. While some writers have gained excessive critical attention, others have been neglected and overlooked. Nargis Dalal is one such writer who seems to have suffered unjust critical neglect. Although Dalal's creative output has not been very prolific, yet her novel *The Inner Door* with the guide motif of enforced sainthood launched her as a versatile genius. It can undoubtedly be called her masterpiece with no artistic lapses as such. She certainly has no slogan to raise, no message to offer and no flag to her credit, yet she is a writer of socio-economic realities. *The Inner Door* is not only an attempt to uphold the spiritual heritage of our country and to insist on the importance of Yoga, but is also a sincere attempt to project the protected world of an individual, a world which illuminates subtle and complex emotions and passions, delicate memories, fragile fancies and evanèscent moments.

There seems to be a unique post-feminist streak in Dalal's approach to her protagonist, Rahul in *The Inner Door*. It is also an honest attempt to face the crucial question of identity. Making a distinct departure from the predominantly feminist stance of most of her contemporaries, the writer casts a male hero in the central position and reviews him with a genuinely concerned outlook. Her novel stresses the need for self-discovery and self-identity, which has become an archetype in post-feminist literature In the impersonal and threatening social milieu, she portrays an alienated individual's odyssey for attaining integration of the self by either assimilating or discarding social values of the community. Like Gita Mehta's *A River Sutra*, which is a treatise on metaphysics, *The Inner Door* also deals with intuitive feeling, a vision and a revelation of an ascent through spiritual planes. Both the writers re-interpret philosophy, spirituality and desire with holy rivers Ganga and Narmada as a backdrop. If Gita Mehta weaves her delicate, tragic stories evoking a profound presence of tradition and desire along the banks of the holy Narmada, Nargis Dalal brings her protagonist to the banks of Ganga which serves as a panacea for all sins and evils. Though the idea of escape may appear puerile and vain to many, yet many are the instances wherein the soul articulates a path for deliverance. Dalal's hero, Rahul, is delivered through yoga and achieves a complete inner calm. Rahul gains his soul and through a long process of realisation accumulates within him a silent power. The radiance of an inner illumination on his visage and the enormous serenity of his persona go ahead to prove that his soul is not crippled and cramped to the measure of some finite doctrine. The seer in him has glimpsed the contours of ultimate possibility, the mystic poet has hymned his glorified fields of trance, the philosopher has sought to interpret the vision in terms of reason, while the yogi has formulated a method, a multiform technique for achieving the desired total change in consciousness (Iyengar 171).

Dalal seems to augment a significant release into another state of consciousness through mystic and yogic experiences. The journey of Rahul from a fake yogi to an actual one is also a flight of thought from the material plane onto the illumined and intuitive zone, where the self becomes complete and ego is dead. Just like the Indian metaphysical thinkers of yore—be it Yajnavalkya, Sankara or Ramanuja, all have been both yogis and rishis and have armed their philosophy "with a practical way of reaching to the supreme state of consciousness" (Ibid.); so also the protagonist Rahul follows the trance of practical yogic exercises to escape into a higher mental plane. Writers—both Anglo-Indian as well as Indo-Anglican—have always showed an interest in presenting India as a country replete with curiosities and contraries, beggars and princes, yogis and dhongis. Yoga as a discipline has both physical and spiritual dimensions. Charlatans as well as authentic seekers for obvious diverse reasons pursue it. The author is keenly aware of the possibility of co-existence of such opposites as fake fakirs and genuine sadhakas, spurious sanyasis and genuine seekers after truth, hypocrites and authentic souls. Also, Dalal is aware that a sinner may become a saint or he may continue to parade himself as a saint even while remaining a sinner in essence. Clearly, she snipes at both the Western New-Agers and the Indian Gurus. The former are criticised for being blindly naïve in their search for salvation in India; the latter are denounced in their manipulation of naïve foreigners for their selfish interests.

The novel begins with a bus ride to Rishikesh. Rahul, a delicate and handsome young boy, quite spectacular in his appearance and hailing from a poor family is overcome by grief over the sudden death of his father. Accompanied by his widowed mother, he is on his way to meet his maternal uncle, Swami Jagdish, who runs a yogic ashram at Rishikesh. It is during this journey that Rahul is interface with the American couple Chris and Myra Stuart, who are also on their way to the same destination to seek spiritual instruction and inner life meditation. Disciples of a cultural revolution, they proclaim that the magic and mystery missing from their lives was to be found in the East. Over introductions, the American couple fathom the penury of young Rahul and his widowed mother, besides being all appreciation for his film star looks and his remarkable hold of the English language. Rahul's attractive appearance is a source of investment for them. Thus the stage is all set for an interaction with the oriental Rahul and the aggressive forces of western, occident culture representing a materialistic outlook. Chris and Myra plan to impart elementary yogic training to Rahul and consequently open their own yogic ashram, thus spinning easy money. They arrive at Rishikesh, which is noted for its ashrams, hermits, quacks and "the special smell of Rishikesh—a smell, compounded of river water, incense and corruption" (Dalal 14).

Rahul's gradual re-christening into Guru Sukhanand is a pointer as to how spirituality is commercialised in India. The authoress has no banners to flag about the traditional causes rather she derides the so-called spiritual obsession of a mighty nation. Rahul, alias Guru Sukhanand's school is called the Sukhanand Ashram, which has been constructed out of generous donations forwarded by philanthropists such as Govind Das. The ashram is an ultramodern piece of architecture boasting of modern amenities like posh accommodation, liquour, non-vegetarian food and to top it all, the provision of sex. Dalal appears to bring to light the hollowness of Indian religious sentiment which is blissfully oblivious to logic and reason. It is indeed a refreshing welcome change to have women writers taking up other significant issues besides the over-hyped feminist agenda. The authoress keenly takes up the issue of fake sainthood and the exalted status of fakirs and sadhus in India.

In the novel, plain hero, Rahul, pretending as a sadhu, undoubtedly eyes the comforts associated with sainthood in addition to the fat amount of remuneration, which could not be fetched from any other career. The materialistic aggressive American forces are ecstatic as their plans of minting money through Rahul's yogic prowess are on the verge of fulfilment. To further boost up the effectiveness of the yoga causes, training in sex is also arranged with Goldie. Rahul too is aware of a diffused sense of sensual pleasure at her sight. Strangely enough, Goldie is confronted with an unanticipated experience. She becomes emotionally involved with Rahul, whereas Rahul, most surprisingly, is detached from her. In addition to this detached emotion, a gradual change begins to overcome Rahul: "Rahul discovered his own method of inducing into his consciousness the intensity moment. He was left in a state of psychic emptiness, which was then filled by revelation and a new spiritual certainty" (Dalal 85).

As the protagonist reaches higher states of consciousness, the river, the sky and the temples around become for him a series of vibrations. His love for the hordes of monkeys and compassion for beggars and all living creatures becomes manifest. Rahul begins to slip into higher spiritual planes. He has begun a journey towards the "corridors of light." Mysticism makes him transcend the rational, intellectual mind to a state where words, thoughts and ideas exist only as surface forms of a deeper consciousness. Meanwhile crowds throng the ashram to seek admission since the word has spread that Swami Sukhanand performs miracles, reads the thoughts of people with a mere look at their countenances and also exhibits great spiritual prowess. Ironically his own mother, his uncle and the Stuarts fail to recognise the transition of Rahul from a fake guru into a genuine yogi. For them, Rahul's spiritual acts are acting. It is the Western novelist Carl Hanes who discovers

Rahul's newly acquired aura of spiritualism, much to the disappointment and bewilderment of all those who have pinned hopes on Rahul's success as a fake guru. Ironically, the so-called spiritual Gurus like Ramananda and Jagdish fail to realise that Rahul has slipped out of their control. At a later stage his mother bows and touches his feet but regrets as well that Rahul was not corrupted early enough. Rahul undergoes a self-transcendence and renounces all material desires; thereby moving to the peace and solitude of the mountains for spiritual attainment. The Stuarts admittedly come for spiritual enlightenment but they stoop to material ambition with Rahul as the tool in their enterprise. They have invested much but eventually lose everything. On the contrary, Rahul, who was earlier consumed with mundane desires, ultimately takes to spiritualism. Ironically enough, he (Chris) could never imagine that while he had thought of creating a fake saint, he had ended up creating a real saint to the ruination of his own business.

American mass-marketing sure has entered into the Indian interior real fast. While postcolonialism challenges forms of oppression, intelligent women writers such as Nargis Dalal and Gita Mehta (*Karma Cola*) remind us how the material west seeks to market the mystic east, adopting India as its newest spiritual resort. Six thousands years of spiritual and cultural history becomes a commodity in the hands of the Western, white male who stacks spiritual oriental tradition into the Western super market. Both Dalal and Mehta train their razor insight to ridicule the post-colonial marketing of the margins.

No character in the novel is sure as to when and how Rahul crosses over from being a charlatan to an actual yogi. The *Vedas*, the *Upanishads* and the Buddhist scriptures agree that it is impossible to describe accurately a mystical state because the mystical state is a level of consciousness different from the level of consciousness in which humans normally operate. Though Rahul had tasted the elixir of sexual satisfaction with Goldie, yet, the same act can draw him no more. Goldie gets entangled in an emotional attachment with Rahul, whereas Rahul grows indifferent; the snares and lures of earthly connections, relations and pleasures sink into insignificance and nothingness. The gay and charming Rahul relinquishes everything. Reason and logic appear inappropriate tools for describing the strange transition from material entrapments to spiritual attainment, quite in tune with the philosophy of Martin Heidegger who argues the limitations of mere reason.

Obviously, there are more things in this world than science and reason can account for. Thus, Rahul, who is trained to pretend as having powers with which he can open the inner door for the rich foreigners, most surprisingly opens the door for himself. Here Rahul can almost be likened to Raju in R.K. Narayan's *The Guide*, wherein Raju is transformed from a tourist guide to a spiritual guide. Raju, who is earlier content with the role of a holy man thrust upon him, later unselfishly with great danger to his life fasts to wipe out the drought and collapses, feeling rain falling in the hillside. So also Rahul wipes out the facade and mask of a fake fakir and is strangely transformed. An actual saint replaces the guise of a yogi; and yoga becomes a way of life for him. Consequently, Rahul resolves to teach the religious meaning of yoga to his followers.

Rahul, the nucleus of the novel, justifies the title of the story by no longer pretending as a god man, but one who has realised the ultimate spiritual truth. Yoga, which began as a business for him, becomes a means of flight from material bonds and helps Rahul to realise introverted mysticism wherein "the mystic turns inwards and finds the Ultimate One at the bottom of the self (atman)" (Boreham 3).

Both Narayan and Dalal propagate Oriental Hindu philosophy wherein realisation of truth comes after going through the acid test of illusion or maya. Reality exists only through experience and it must be a personal experience. The novel is also a far-off echo of T.S. Eliot's poetic drama *Murder in the Cathedral* wherein the main thrust of the play is the internal struggle of Archbishop Thomas Beckett who elects not to seek sainthood but to accept his death as inevitable and part of a better whole. Again, both writers deal with the theme of progression from conflict to pathos, suffering and finally to the glorification of God.

In the making of the novel, Dalal acts neither as an apologist nor a scoffer. Where she indicts the depravity in our saffron-clad prophets, she is equally forthright in her affirmation of the vital discipline of meditation and yoga. The novel is not just an expose of our spiritual fetish and moral obliquities, but is also an endorsement of that truth which the phoney soul searchers can never comprehend. It is this balanced treatment of an endemic theme that sets apart this novel as an enduring piece of creative exploration.

Works Cited

Boreham, Noel. A. *Mysticism in the Indian Tradition*, New Delhi: Indological and Oriental Publishers, India Book Centre, 1989.

Dalal, Nargis. *The Inner Door*, New Delhi: Orient Longman, 1976.

Iyengar, Srinivasa K.R. "The Life Divine" in *Indian Writing in English*, New Delhi: Sterling Publishers, 2003.

13 The New Woman in Shashi Deshpande's *Roots and Shadows*

— Anuradha Gaur

> If we have the habit of freedom and the courage to write exactly what we think.... If we face the fact that there is no arm to cling to, but that we go alone and that our relation is to the world of reality and not to the world of men and women, then the opportunities will come.
>
> —Virginia Woolf: *A Room of One's Own.*

Shashi Deshpande, a prominent figure in the contemporary Indian English fiction, makes gender central to her writing. She admits "I am a woman and I do write about women, And I am going to say it loudly. I don't want to dissociate myself."[1] She takes us into the realm of the female psyche with all its hidden motives, feelings, fears and frustrations—the job which no writer of the previous generation had dared so far. She is a modern writer with a new consciousness who records the changes that are taking place in a woman's life. She rejects the ideal picture of women and insists upon a little more space for women. In a personal interview taken at her residence, she proclaimed, "Being mother, daughter, wife is important for woman but that is not to be the all and end of her existence."[2] She captures with honesty the traits of revolt against gender discrimination that are evident in the new generation of educated women. She notices the subtle changes that are visible in the priorities of modern woman and reveals them without any hesitation.

The present paper is an attempt to analyses the traits of a progressive new woman who struggles to overcome the constricting dilemmas of present norms and pre-fixed rules in a male dominated society. She fights for freedom and emerges at last as a mature woman with a clearer vision of life.

Roots and Shadows, the second important novel of Deshpande, is the story of a highly sensitive, educated and enlightened girl who lost her mother at birth. She belongs to a middleclass orthodox Brahmin family where she is expected to follow the traditions of a patriarchal society. She is looked after by Akka who is a childless widow and head of the family. In her joint family full of Kakas, Kakis, Atya and many cousins there is a clear dividing line between male and female domain. The women of the family spend their whole time slaving for others without expecting even a single word of appreciation. Men are associated with power and decision making. There is a strict list of do's and don'ts in matters of conduct that circumscribed the girl-children. Girls were schooled in the thought that they have to keep away from boys, that they ought to put others' needs before theirs. They were taught to consider their preferences last. This was to prepare them for their marital life. The fact that they did not belong to their parents.' Home was drilled into them very early in life. Even in the matters of her marriage a woman had no free will of her own.

Indu is an awakened girl. She is different. She is inquisitive by nature. She questions the conventions which define different patterns of behaviour for girls and boys. She rebels against dictatorial Akka, refuses to follow her rigid rules and discards her old values and morals. Her rebellious nature is first seen in her reaction to Akka's indecent comment about her dead mother. She gets furious and at once decides to go to the hostel for studies. The crude way in which her sexuality is introduced to her makes Indu resent it. The impurity attached to a girl's puberty shocks her. Her rational mind can not accept all this. She feels suffocated in the conservative environment of her family. She confesses later on that, "I resented my womanhood because it closed so many doors to me."[3] When she is scolded by Akka for standing with a boy in the library of her college, Indu reacts bitterly: "We were just talking. Is that wrong? ... I haven't done anything wrong. Nothing I need be ashamed of"(74).

Indu develops hatred for Akka's dominating attitude. She resents her authoritative tone. She argues with her and questions the propriety of customs in a traditional setup. She cannot believe in superstitions like calling your husband's name shortens his life: "Such rules are just to frighten the women. To keep them in their places. What connection can there be between a man's longevity and his wife's calling him by name" (39). The ladies of her family pray to the tulsi plant to increase the life span of their husbands. Indu finds no sense in this. In her rejection of such rituals Indu reveals to see her life as independent. It is in indication of her autonomy. She leaves home and takes an oath, "I would never go back." After studies she becomes a journalist and achieves financial independence too. She rebels against Akka, her world, her values and much against Akka's wishes, she marries Jayant who is from a different caste and speaks a different language. This bold decision to marry a man of her own choice shows her free will and courage.

Indu hoped to attain her own identity, peace and happiness through marriage but ironically marriage seems to be just another cage not much different from the trap of parental home. Very soon after marriage she realises that Jayant's expectations were the same as those of any stereotyped male. Contrary to her romantic fantasies, he turns out to be a typical man like any other. Indu confesses: "And I was so proud of my logical and rational thinking. But there was my trap waiting for me after all" (82). She realises the futility of her marriage. "Jayant and I...I wish I could say, we have achieved complete happiness. But I can not fantasize" (23). After marriage Indu does all such activities which her husband would like. She notices: "When I look in the mirror, I think of Jayant, when I dress, I think of Jayant, when I undress, I think of him. Always what he wants, what he would like, what would please him...And one day I had thought...Isn't there anything I want at all? Have I become a fluid, with no shape, no form of my own" (53).

The thought of becoming an ideal woman who loses her identity in that of her husband frightens Indu. She discovers that in order to avoid conflict in her marriage she has started neglecting her own wishes. Perhaps marriage has taught her the things like deception and silence. She has unconsciously started imitating traditional women of her family whom she had laughed at calling them "martyrs, heroines or just stupid fools" (68).

Indu is a born writer who has a natural urge for creative writing to articulate her feminine voice, to forge moments in art that are original and arresting. To this Jayant says 'No' because they need money and have a long way to go in their marital life.

The process of self-negation makes Indu uncomfortable and discontented where as Jayant sees no problem in their marriage. Indu fails to establish emotional rapport with Jayant for it shocks Jayant to find passion in a woman. His views are coloured by age old traditions which have visualised woman as a means to satisfy man's physical needs. He does not appreciate Indu's demonstration of her emotions. Indu admits: "It shocks him to find passion in a woman. It puts him off. When I am like that, he turns away from me. I have learnt my lesson now. And so I pretend I am passive. And unresponsive. I'm still and dead" (82). She grows scornful of love and marriage. Her sexual situation forces her to go for extra-marital relationship which is a very bold step and seems to give her a sense of sexual autonomy. "Marriage itself is a difficult enough business" (98), feels Indu.

Making enormous sacrifices with regard to her profession, the protagonist begins to understand that marriage obstructs her growth as an individual. However she is not an average ordinary girl. She finds that the role of an ideal wife restricts rather than promote the development of her personality firstly by taking away her freedom of thought and expression and secondly by denying her the full play of her artistic genius. She wants to be a 'whole self'. But Jayant won't let her do so. She indulges in selfexploration and broods: "Sometimes I wonder if I leave him (Jayant) one day and live by myself. The only way in which I can be myself, my whole self again" (89). This quest for 'wholeness of being' is an entirely modern issue unknown to the women of older generation.

After this realisation Indu ceases to be a 'Pativrata' type. Her entering into a close relationship with Naren reveals her desperate attempt to achieve a kind of fulfilment that's lacking in her marriage with Jayant. Her affair with Naren represents the assertion of her sexual identity that was so indifferently crushed by her husband. This is a step far removed from the conservation concept of woman. Naren provides Indu true companionship. She confides in him freely. She finds it possible to talk to him on subjects which she could rarely discuss with anyone else. She introspects: "I thought of Jayant and how vulnerable he was... And so, I had to pretend, to cover my reactions, act out a pleasant willingness that grated on me. With Naren, I would never have to pretend"(86).

With Naren Indu experiences a freedom — freedom to be honest to herself. He becomes her true friend and does not demand any change in her original personality and advises her to write her own stuff. He admires her writing skills. The remarkable thing about this affair is that Indu has no guilt or shame about her sexual encounter with Naren. What happened between her and Naren does not concern Jayant. This indicates that Indu is aware of her autonomy. She realises that she is a being, and not a dependent on Jayant. Indu exhibits a detached objectivity while analysing her relations with Naren and suffers no misery, no remorse. She begins to evolve a now code of sexual ethics. She learns to accept her feelings without embarrassment. Indirectly it leads Indu to have a finer perception of her own life as well as human life in general.

Indu achieves self-knowledge. She realises what her roots are as an independent woman and a writer; and what her shadows are — a daughter, a wife and a commercial writer. She decides not to disclose to Jayant anything about Naren because "that was not important, that had nothing to do with the two of us and our life together" (168). After passing through a lot of emotional crisis Indu realises that she has to develop in herseif a fortitude to overcome the phantoms that are constantly haunting her. In order to live a meaningful life she has to stick to her roots. She takes firm decision: "That I would at last do the kind of writing I had always dreamt of doing. That I would not, could not enrich myself with Akka's money. That I would on the other hand, pay for Mini's marriage" (168).

The woman who resolves all her conflicts totally by herself and knows what to do and what not to do in her life, is definitely a rejuvenated, emancipated, unconventional and integrated woman. She represents the image of a New Woman. She is truly an embodiment of feminine strength and undaunted spirit. We admire her because she does not try to escape reality. On the other hand, with new freedom and courage she is ready to face her future responsibilities. We have every reason to hope that new opportunities are waiting for her.

The novel ends with a triumph of the independence of women and also the principle of life which is endless. Indu has learnt to see not only her own life as full of possibilities for growth and expansion but the very meaning of life itself: "I felt as if I was watching life itself…endless, limitless, formless and full of grace" (166).

References

1. Sue Dickman, "In conversation", *The Book Review,* 19.4, p. 13.
2. Shashi Deshpande, "An Interview with Rashmi Sahi in *Shashi Deshpande: A Critical Spectrum* ed. T. Indramohan, New Delhi: Atlantic Publishers, 2004, p. 22.
3. Shashi Deshpande, *Roots and Shadows,* Chennai: Orient Longman, 1983, p.78. Subsequent references to the text are from this edition and have been indicated by page number in parentheses.

14 Marital Discord in the Short Stories of Jhumpa Lahiri and Shashi Deshpande

— Madhavi Nikam

Short story is in existence since times immemorial. The primary purpose of a short story is to instruct, entertain, guide and inform the readers. Short stories in Indian English literature appeared a century ago. It flourished under the influence of the British writers. The British and French short story writers, like O'Henry, John Galsworthy, Somerset Maugham, Rudyard Kipling and Maupassant greatly influenced short stories in Indian English literature. Many Indian short story writers in English made their presence felt in the literary world with their outstanding creative works. Women writers like Ruth Prawer Jhabvala, Anita Desai, Nargis Dalal, Dina Mehta, Gita Hariharan, Vera Sharma, Ruby Gupta, Manjula Padmanabhan, Ritu Bhatia, Jai Nimbkar, Shashi Deshpande, just to name a few, have added glory and dignity to the genre. Diasporic writers, like Jhumpa Lahiri, Bharati Mukherjee, Uma Parameswaran, Mena Abdullah, Salman Rusdie, V.S.Naipual are outstanding.

Indian English short story flourished in the hands of Shashi Deshpande who has to her credit more than ninety short stories. Her stories deal with the lives of typical middle class Indian women trapped in socio-cultural roles. The stereotypical women models play a dominant role in her work. A native writer, Deshpande writes about Indian society in general and women in particular. On the other hand a diasporic writer, Jhumpa Lahiri shares her experiences, memories of India, especially Calcutta. She writes about the Indian immigrants, their loss of identity, dislocation, and feeling of being uprooted and so on. At present she has in her account two volumes of short stories and a novel. The present paper makes an attempt to delineate the theme of marital discord in the stories written by both the writers as they also share the same ties, same grouping of Indian writers in English.

Marriage is an institution in which all the family members are involved. It is the most sacred and virtuous part in life. Marriage is the union of not only two people but of two families. It is a human experience in which one shares emotions, feelings, joy, sorrow etc. A blissful marriage is stable and peaceful whereas disagreement and discord are also the harsh realities of the same relationship. It has its own pros and cons. Marriages arranged among same class, caste, culture is thought to be everlasting where as the inter-caste, inter-religious marriages are thought to be a doom. Marriage as an institution blooms with love and understanding, and fades with suspicion and non communication. It is a bliss if there is trust, an understanding in the relationship otherwise it is not less than a curse. Bacon says marriage makes men do better in certain spheres of work and has a detrimental effect in other spheres.

Jhumpa Lahiri's *Interpreter of Maladies* is also called *Stories of Bengal, Boston and Beyond*. The first story in the collection "A Temporary Matter" deals with the life of a young couple Shukumar and Shoba. The two feel alienated and isolated in the foreign land. The inability to communicate and express feelings of love, concern and care widens the gap between them. Non-communication in the relationship leads to silent warpath. Fortunately nature, rather modernity gives them a chance to unite. The electricity would be cut off for an hour for five days. They decide to while away time by telling one secret to each other. Darkness helps them confess as there is no restriction of guilty consciousness, no eye contact and no inhibition. Shoba reveals the truth that she needed some time alone and informs, "I've been looking for an apartment and I've found one."[1] Shukumar is shocked and reveals a harsh reality to her. He tells her the deadly secret of their lost baby that it was a male child. He kept it a secret as he thought that it might shock her. The sad incident of the child's death did not indicate that she would not be able to have children in future. Lahiri conveys the inability to communicate in the story. Caring, temporary emotional bonding in spite of the fact of non-communication is seen in the acts like Shukumar's plan of buying 'Malai' for Shoba, by not telling her the truth of the born dead baby.

Lahiri's title story "Interpreter of Maladies" is set in Puri, India. An Indian American couple visits India. Mr. and Mrs. Das and their children Tina, Ronny and Bobby are guided by a tour guide Mr. Kapasi. When he declares that he is not a doctor, but works as an interpreter, Mrs. Das reacts, "Interesting. I've never heard of anything like that."[2] Kapasi is happy as Mrs. Das feels that his job is full of challenges. She takes his address, takes a close snap with him, calls him to have lunch with them and thus becomes quite friendly. He fantasizes about their relationship and wants the tour to last a little longer. He suggests them to visit the hills of Udaygiri and Khandagiri. On reaching there Mrs. Das refuses to accompany her husband and stays back in the car. She requests the guide to stay back. When he praises Bobby as "a brave little boy," Mrs. Das comments, "It's not so surprising. He is not his."[3] She opens the floodgates and discloses that he is her son born out of the extramarital affair she had with her husband's friend. The truth is concealed for eight long years. She wants Mr. Kapasi to say something, comment on the relation and her son Bobby as an interpreter. The difficulty in communicating emotional pain is seen in the story. Extramarital affair, non-communication, lack of understanding in relation causes ocean of problems in marital life.

Shashi Deshpande's story "It was the Nightingale" reflects the life of Jaya who faces the problem of communication in her marital life. Doing things separately, remaining aloof, isolated, creates problems in her life. Jaya cannot share her feelings and emotions with her husband. She develops the habit of talking to herself as she realizes that there is no outlet to her feelings and no one has time to discuss, share and communicate with her. As a result of the distress, she decides to go abroad for two years. She runs from herself, her husband, her isolation and boredom. When Jaya comes late from her office, her husband keeps the dinner ready. For a moment the husband seems to be a stranger but the next moment she decides to break the silence by complementing on his beautiful eyebrows. Jaya knows that going abroad will widen the gap between them. The two years of separation is extremely troublesome. Jaya is very well aware that, "I'm putting two years between us. A fearsome period. Two years of experiences we will not share. And each one a brick that can ultimately become a wall between us. It isn't quarrels that shatter a marriage, its doing things apart. Can we stand two years of separateness?"[4] After a tug of war with the self and her husband, she sets out to go abroad. Her desire to have her separate identity makes her choose the path of isolation and separation. She leaves her husband without any tears.

Deshpande's other story "A Day Like Any Other" is the tale of a wife, who controls her emotions and feelings of anger for being cheated by her husband. She is aware that it takes minutes to destroy what takes years to build. The husband pretends to feel guilty of the act and there are explanations, justifications, and accusations. His false behaviour comes to the front but she accepts life without questioning as she knows, "After all, a man needs some fun, some entertainment. And he can't go alone."[5] She accepts the reality and engages herself in the family. Communication partially solves the problem. Confession and communication are two pillars of marital bliss. Sense of guilt, non-communication and infidelity are elements that crush marriage. Marital fidelity, especially for women, is taken for granted as an accepted traditional Indian value.

In Jumpa Lahiri's "A Temporary Matter" it becomes a permanent problem. Non-communication, misunderstanding, emotional detachment, keeping secrets creates problem in marital life. Lahiri visualises and writes about the Indian institution of marriage which survives on trust, emotions, feelings, understanding, sharing, caring etc. Marriage is a bond of understanding, love, respect and care. Social and domestic norms set for a wife are different in India and abroad. Shoba wants freedom and sometime wants to be alone which is not even thought of in India. Shoba wants liberty, both economic and personal. She plans accordingly by saving her bonus and searching for an apartment. One definitely remembers Ibsen's Nora in *Doll's House* and Kate Chopin's Edna Pontellier in *The Awakening*. Though the story ends on an optimistic, open end it is doubtful whether they will remain together forever, share and communicate, accompany each other forever. Will the temporary matter become permanent? Will the end be everlasting? In "Interpreter of Maladies" Lahiri portrays the husband-wife relation which is full of deceit, deception, dark deeds, non-communication, lack of trust and understanding. Fear, guilt captures the mind and soul of Mrs. Das. She is unable to share the secret, confess her adultery like Hester in Hawthorne's *The Scarlet letter*. Mrs. Das doesn't confess for the sake of self-security, for the family and her own self-respect. Lahiri's story shows Mrs. Das, a modern woman, who is tempted and in a spur of a moment loses her chastity. Mrs. Das who involves in extramarital affair gives birth to a son from the same relation which is not acceptable nor is permissible in Indian society.

Shashi Deshpande portrays the wife as emotionally, spiritually and morally one with the husband. She forgets and forgives the biggest crime of infidelity committed by the husband but as revenge never indulges herself in the wrongdoings for the sake of the family. The stereotypical role models of Sita and Savitri are still followed in Indian society. Lahiri brings to the forefront modern Indian women through her stories. She looks from a diasporic writers view at India and Indians. The family set-up is more or less similar in Jhumpa Lahiri and Shashi Deshpande. Shashi Deshpande's character Jaya is sure to return to her husband after two years. There is a come back on her part which is most probably missing in Shoba. In Deshpande's "A Day Like Any Other" the wife is ready to accept the infidelity in her own stride but one is in doubt of Mr. Das's reaction. Lahiri must be sure that Mr. Das will not forgive his wife's adultery but leaves it for the readers to analyse. Modern life, guilt, deceit is seen in Mrs. Das. Mr. Kapasi is a typical Indian male who misunderstands Mrs. Das's frankness as love. Mr. Das no doubt is liberal enough to tell his wife to move closer to Kapasi for a snap but the closeness that she had with his Punjabi friend would destroy the relation which took years to build.

Lahiri's stories are an amalgamation of Indian and Foreign culture. She never forgets India and Indian attitude towards life. Shashi Deshpande very aptly portrays Indian culture, tradition, norms followed by the Indians. In "It was the Nightingale" Jaya is sure to return. She is not like Nora, Edna nor like Shoba who might never be one with their husbands who are firm and emotions are no more vital for them. Jaya feels vulnerable at the time of departure. The wife in "A Day Like any Other" very obediently looks after the family and children. She does not quarrel or burst open like Mrs. Das would in the case of her husband's deceit. Trivial things also create a tiff amongst them.

Deshpande's character accepts the reality silently and the same silence becomes a punishment for her husband.

Shashi Deshpande is one with India and Indian culture but Lahiri being a diasporic writer is one with India but different when it comes to culture. A mixture of both cultures is seen in her stories. Human nature, tendencies, behaviour and problems are same everywhere which can be clearly seen from the stories of both Lahiri and Deshpande. The contribution of the native and diasporic writer is definitely noteworthy and appreciable. With various similarities and differences they offer interesting insights to the complexities of marital harmony.

References

1. Jhumpa Lahiri, *Interpreter of Maladies: Stories of Bengal, Boston & Beyond*, New Delhi: Harper Collins India, 1999, p.23.
2. Ibid., p.50.
3. Shashi Deshpande, *Collected Stories*, Vol.1, New Delhi: Penguin Books, 2003, p.64.
4. Ibid., *Vol. 2*, New Delhi: Penguin Books, 2003, p.184.
5. Ibid.

15 Feminist Thread in Anita Nair's *Mistress*

— Gunjan Chaturvedi

"I think of the butterfly I caught and pinned to a board when it was still alive, its wings spread so as to display the markings, oblivious that somewhere within, a little heart beat, yearning to fly. I am that butterfly now" (*Mistress*: 2005:54). This agonised cry, more or less, sums up the life of Radha, the female protagonist of Anita Nair's third novel, her *magnum opus, Mistress*. Feeling constrained in her marriage of convenience with Shyam, a materialistic and boorish fellow with lowbrow aesthetic tastes, Radha really pines for her individuality. "For Shyam," Radha confides, "I am a possession. A much cherished possession. That is my role in his life. He doesn't want an equal. What he wants is a mistress. Someone to indulge and someone to indulge him with feminine wiles" (*Mistress*: 53). She feels irritated when Shyam goes about regulating her universe. She feels a swell of rage when Shyam buys even sanitary napkins for her: "Why can't he let me breathe and bleed on my own?" she shouts. "I am your wife. Your wife. Do you hear me? But you treat me as if I am a kept woman. A bloody mistress to fulfil your sexual needs again and again," (*Mistress*: 73) she reiterates.

At this vulnerable point, there arrives a young American Christopher Stewart in her life. He is a journalist who has ensconced himself in the resort compound owned by Radha's husband. He has arrived in India with the intention of interviewing Radha's uncle Koman, a Kathakali dancer, about his illustrious career. It, however, is Radha who fatefully captures his interest. The attraction between them is immediate and immense. It stands in stark contrast to the thinly disguised revulsion that Radha feels for Shyam. Radha and Chris are, in fact, clever updates of the iconic Hindu lovers Radha and Krishna. Chris, the anglicised version of Krish or Krishna, causes Radha's latent vibrance to erupt with a volcanic fury of emotions. The young woman must, now, choose whether to stay in her marriage or to flaunt custom and risk ostracism to find what she perceives as true love.

Anita Nair categorically declines being a feminist writer. "I am not happy with the term feminism," she observes, "Why?" you ask. Well, firstly it is outdated. Secondly, the word 'feminism' implies a striving to be equal, a desperation almost, to get equal with men, while it is important to know that you are equal and exercise that equality. To experience that equality, "knowing it is yours, naturally." She similarly dismisses the word 'liberated woman'. "I don't like these labels. I don't need these words to introduce myself to another person or to make myself understood" (Nair: *The Hindu*: 2001: 4). She herself hails from a very traditional household in Kerala and revels in her role as a homemaker. But the fate of the suffocated and stifled women in the patriarchal set-up of Indian families always disturbs her. "Traditionally," she blurts out, "our women are projected as doormats". This image is reemphasized in TV serials. It is giving the woman a kind of template of how to behave.

Contemporary Indian woman has to cope with tradition, with being a good wife, mother and daughter. But the Indian male wants her to place her desires on the backburner. "I can't think of many men who can smile after a gruelling date at work...Indian women," she continues, "have a core of steel that does not rust or corrode. They are like silk knots" (in Sharma: *Metro Plus*: 2007:3). She may refuse to admit being a feminist but she has certainly taken upon herself the task of asking questions that nobody else dares to ask. In her attempt to do so she even challenges Indian mythology.

In *Mistress* she makes a pointed reference to the story of Ahalya, the wife of Saint Gautama. Ahalya was discovered by her husband in bed with Indra, the king of Gods. Indra had taken the form of her husband and slipped into her bed. Even though Ahalya was not responsible for the adultery, she was converted by her husband into stone and had to wait for many epochs to be freed of the curse. Indra had also been punished. He had a thousand vaginas imprinted on him so that everyone knew that he had been philandering. Hearing the tale Chris very meaningfully comments: "Indra managed to get away with little more than embarrassment. It was poor Ahalya who bore the brunt of the curse" (*Mistress*: 58). And actually it is the plight of these poor Ahalyas that has always caught Anita Nair's eye and attention.

Anita's first novel *The Better Man* (1999) is basically the story of Mukundan Nair, an escapist who runs away from responsibilities and is afraid of society. His path crosses that of Bhasi, who, practising a folk version of psychotherapy, manages to exorcise all the ghosts and restores Mukundan's self-confidence. But here also we hear of Mukundan's tyrannical father and constantly suppressed mother who has to deal with her violent, adulterous husband. Anita's heart also seems to go out to the plight of Anjana, a beautiful young school teacher, not fully divorced yet, with whom Mukundan has an affair and later betrays. In her second novel *Ladies Coupe* (2001) Nair shows great understanding and compassion for women and for the choices and regrets they can not avoid. It is a sensitive exploration of the tension of self actualisation vs. familial responsibility in a society with traditional values. Here Anita has delved deep into Akhila's personality and analysed the guilt of a woman living off her desires and has very boldly asked a question, "Can a woman remain single and be happy?"

In her third novel *Mistress* she has even more strongly brought forward the fate of a suffocated female through the character of Shyam, a rather hoary, unlovely personality, who deeply loves his wife but also believes, "Women like to be made to feel like women, dominated and put in their place" (*Mistress*: 164). He wants to lay his imprint on everything including his wife and will not hesitate even raping her in order to assert his power. Anita herself confessed: "Shyam – all what I detest in a man, I made him" (Nair: *Metro Plus*: 2007). Radha complains again and again, "You seem to want to rule me. You won't let me breathe" (*Mistress*: 203). And again, "His (Shyam's) walls, his people, his ruthlessness, they press in on me" (*Mistress*: 169). Shyam is shown as a typical male chauvinist who believes that men can never be infertile. Fathering of children is a symbol of manhood and Shyam can not digest the fact that he is incapable of that. "When Radha looked at me I wanted her to see a full bodied, red–blooded alpha male capable of fathering a hundred and one children" (*Mistress*: 2003). He does not disclose the fact regarding his infertility even when his wife has to bear the stigma of being a barren woman—a 'macchi' – and is not allowed to attend the festive occasion of the celebration of a woman's pregnancy coming close to full term. At the time what Radha feels is only a freezing within.

Shyam, however, is not alone in the novel to think that "women's lives didn't need to go beyond the kitchen and pretty trinkets" (*Mistress*:274). There are others also who love to see a woman only as "a helpless shrieking female" (*Mistress*:288). While reflecting upon his past, Radha's uncle Koman, allows us ample opportunity to catch definite glimpses of women living a stifled life in a traditional, closed, Muslim community. Koman's mother Saadiya, living in Arabipatnam, pines for "Life. Life in so many colours and shapes. Life that breathed and walked. Life that chewed and spat. Life that screamed and shouted. Life that mumbled and tumbled, hissed and crawled. Life that waited. Life that would never be hers" (*Mistress*: 102).

Saadiya's father, in accordance with the conservative thoughts of his community, believes that women are incapable of understanding "the nuances of freedom" (*Mistress*: 130).

The women in the family, as in the society outside, are not allowed to lead a normal life, fettered as they are to the agonizing customs and traditions of the patriarchal community. There are even separate alleyways for males and females in that city. "Twenty feet by thirty feet. That was the measure of her (Saadiya's) sky, the peripheries of her life" (*Mistress*: 99).

What Saadiya wants is just "a sky that was not bound by grey walls" (*Mistress*: 130), "a glimmer of the sky, a lungful of life, a breath of escape" (*Mistress*:102). The life outside the four walls of her world, beyond the constraints of 'burqua', beckons her again and again, "There is a singing in my head that says there is so much to see, so much to do, so much to know. It isn't fair that you men get to go wherever you want, see and do whatever you like, and I am expected to be content with this patch of blue and this maze of alleys" (*Mistress*: 99). She longs to go and enjoy life on the seashore. She feels suffocated and can not stop thinking of the moments of freedom. Consequently she ventures out to the general alley, if only to catch a fleeting glimpse of open life there. When she is caught by Zuleika (her sister), her vaapa (i.e. her father) has an iron rod heated till it blazes a fiery orange and lays it on Saadiya's calf, not once, not twice but three times, in order to still the restlessness inside her. He loves his daughter but feels compelled to warn her, "The next time you feel the need to break your reins, remember how your flesh melted and how my heart broke" (*Mistress*: 130).

Sethu, a doctor's Hindu associate, rekindles the dead hope in her heart and she, now, has to choose between the weight of her ancestry and the miracle of Sethu's love. She runs away from her father's house and hopes to have a good and free life with Sethu. But then their cultural and religious differences crop up unthought of barriers between them. Now Saadiya is overtaken by an unexpected fear: "This was the fear of another hunger. To be with her sister and ummama, Suleiman and Zuleika. To be with *vaapa*" (*Mistress*:193). But her *vaapa* would never accept a daughter who has destroyed the purity of his bloodline. Saadiya is now confused. She is reluctant to bring a child in the world who will be the result of her 'unholy' love and who will have no ancestry to speak of, not even a religion or a god to call his own. When the child is born, she vies with Sethu and tries to make the little baby imbibe all the muslim prayers and rituals. Torn between her ancestry and her life as it is now, she feels a great longing to lie in the embrace of the waters of the sea, never to know a moment's confusion, to be free from life forever, to just rest. Her body washes up three days later.

Sethu's second wife, the legally wedded one, Devyani, also finds her life to be no different. She is allowed to share nothing of her husband's life except his bed. Her marriage is merely a 'sambandham'—"a bond, a sexual bond and no more" (*Mistress*: 235). Devyani proves to be a "good enough wife, loving and considerate, and not given to emotional excesses. She smiled easily and seldom lost her temper. She ate well, slept well and loved well" (*Mistress*: 237-238). In the patriarchal Indian set-up this is what is expected of a woman even today.

When her husband suddenly brings Koman, Saadiya's son, before her, as if out of the blue, she is expected to accept him without any complaint. "Better a past wife than a mistress in the present," (*Mistress*: 263) says Paru Kutty to Devyani consoling her. Koman also derives relief from the fact that rejection of wives and beloveds was an accepted thing for males—"So this was something men did. Discard the past and step into a new future—

even if the past held wives and children. The owner of the clogs had, and so had my father. It had nothing to do with my mother. It was what men did" (*Mistress*: 264).

It is easy enough for a male to discard the past, follow his whims and start life afresh but not so for a woman. When Radha faces a similar dilemma, she finds her past sticking fast to her heels. Even though her marriage was already 'fractured' 'dead'—even before she met Chris, even though she felt nothing but despise and derision for Shyam, who treated her like a bloody object, she feels overwhelmed by a sense of guilt for having robbed her husband of his pride. In her misery Radha begins to understand her mother also though she has all the while hated her for having an affair with one brother and marrying the other, "I am beginning to know what my mother must have felt like, trying to divide her life between two men, each of whom seemed to have staked a claim to her" (*Mistress*: 214).

But this does not mean that Anita Nair glorifies females and is here trying to tell us that they are endowed with higher emotional sentiments and feelings or they are superior to males in any way. If Shyam is overbearing and haughty, Radha is also, by turns, spirited, stubborn and spoiled. Anita has injected equal amounts of likeability and self-destructiveness into her character. If Radha feels suffocated due to Shyam's arrogant and dominating self, Koman, her uncle, is shown as undergoing similar problems in his relationship with Angela, an English Kathakali student. First, it is Angela who complains being treated like a "parcel" or "a mere diversion" (*Mistress*: 336). And later in England Koman complains, "I felt beholden to her. I depended on her for every thing and I did not like to feel beholden. I was a kept man who had been robbed of everything including my dignity..." (*Mistress*: 386). Their alliance fails to give them happiness because theirs was not a matrimony of two equals. In India, it is Koman who is unable to comprehend Angela's desires and doubts, and in England, it is she who, though unintentionally, makes him feel like an "invalid....old, incapacitated man...stripped of everything...pride, maleness and virility. Shrunken, useless and impotent" (*Mistress*: 387).

In his relationship with Maya (a woman married to someone else) Koman experiences an alliance of not only the body but also the heart. In the curves of her body, in the undulations of her mind, Koman seeks a partner who is his equal and the relationship is successful. They are both, comfortable with each other and experience 'Shaantam'—"Detachment. Freedom. An absence of desire. A coming to terms with life" (*Mistress*: 397).

When the initial fury of passion is spent, Radha comes to confront a "masterful Chris" (*Mistress*: 290) who dislikes his opinion being questioned, be it on their beliefs or ideals or on their politics or principles. Realisation dawns upon Radha that her love affair with Chris was perhaps no more than an act of defiance against her domineering husband: "He may be a daddy, but I refuse to be the trembling, penitent child" (*Mistress*: 105). She now decides to leave Chris, even though she is now pregnant with his child. "I am a country," she muses, "that has to rebuild itself from nothing. I am a country that has to face recriminations and challenges and I don't know where to begin. Worst of all, I don't even know if you will be there to hold my hand through the rebuilding process. So wouldn't it have been best to leave me alone?" (*Mistress*: 293). She does not even stay with her husband: "All my life I have stumbled from one thing to another, persuading myself that this is how it should be. I have never behaved as if I have a mind of my own. I have never made a decision. I have let myself be swept along. Isn't it time I assumed some responsibility for my life?" (*Mistress*: 402). This new, self-actualised woman now decides to take the reins of her life in her own hands, to fight her own battles, to prove her mettle to her own self, to finally stop being a mere appendage and to evolve as an autonomous being.

But as a feminist would expect, the story of this woman does not conclude here. As Anita herself admitted in an interview, she has redeemed Shyam in the end, "I gave him a dimension that no one expects" (Nair: *Metro Plus*: 2007). Shyam makes a move in the positive direction. He realises that he had left no breathing space for his wife. He expected her to love him as he needed to be loved. He decides, "I will give Radha the time she wants. I will not force her or ask her for more than what she is prepared to give...All that is lost I will regain...Radha, I will say to her, this child, your child, will be mine" (*Mistress*: 403-425). The mutual understanding of each other's emotions and desires brings the story to a happy conclusion. Radha also realises that Shyam could not entirely be blamed for the failure of their marriage. She had married Shyam only to save herself from social ostracism as, at the time, she was carrying the child of her much-married boss in her womb. (This child, incidentally, she had miscarried later). "I," she says, "have not done right by Shyam. I have played wife all this while, despising him. For this I know remorse. I went to him broken, and expected him to heal me. When he couldn't, I began to despise him and I knew sorrow" (*Mistress*: 426).

The great yearning felt by Radha in the end to lean back on a male shoulder and feel comforted, may raise certain critical eyebrows. Questions may be asked: Is Anita Nair, here, suggesting that a female cannot survive without a male by her side? Does she want to say that even though well educated, independent, strong-minded and self-actualised, a woman can not think of her life beyond the embrace of a male? Does a woman need a man to feel complete? I, for one, do not think that we are justified in asking such questions after Anita has so strongly voiced her opinion in *Ladies Coupe*, which has been celebrated as "one of the most important feminist novels to come out of South Asia" (*Daily Telegraph*: Amazan.com).

This wonderfully warm novel is the story of a group of women who find comfort and strength in sharing the details of their lives with one another. No doubt, in that novel also, in the end, the heroine gives a phone-call to her dear boyfriend. But we have to remember that the kind of aggressive feminism that advocated the radical view of 'Amazon Utopia', i.e., female realm where men will be relegated to secondary roles, has never taken root in India. The anti-male stance, the anti-phallic campaign has never been accepted here.

Anita Nair takes into account the cultural moorings of our women. She is certainly against the patriarchal establishments and practices that cripple women. Her Radha, Saadiya and Angela are not really upholders of patriarchal virtues of self-denial or visible images of self-sacrificing services but she believes in the nurturance of family ties. Her female protagonist in *Mistress* is an initial rebel but finally a compromiser. During suffering and psychic disturbance she moves for self-introspection and later self-discovery which evinces a fresh perception of life and movement in positive direction to maximize her potential. Anita Nair, in all her novels, including *Mistress,* articulates the hopes and oppressions, the concerns and tensions of womankind and gives voice to her need of freedom, self-respect and autonomy. What she pleads for is the necessity of having knowledge, courage and determination to face the turbulent waves of the sea of relationships, specially the one between a man and a woman. The openness that she displays in the discussion of the topics like menstruation, sexual intercourse, etc., is also noteworthy. She evinces a clear inclination to say the unsaid, to encourage women to claim their full humanity which means acknowledging the shadows as well as the lights. As such she is able to develop a feminist ideology which is very close to the anti militaristic, holistic, humanistic and most practical postmodern approach to feminism. And she deserves all the praise for doing so in such a lucid manner.

Works Cited

Nair, Anita. *The Hindu: Literary Review,* Sunday, Dec.2, 2001.

Nair, Anita. *Mistress,* New Delhi: Penguin Books, India, 2005. References to the text are from this edition and have been indicated by page number in parentheses.

Review of *Ladies Coupe. Daily Telegraph*: Amazon.com.

Sharma, Priyadarshini, "Mistress of Tales Finely Told", *The Hindu: Metro Plus,* Chennai, Aug. 24, 2007.

16 Feminine Psyche in the Novels of Anita Desai

— Dipti Vanjare & Ashish Gupta

The scene of Indian writing in English today is marked with a rare creative energy which has been making waves in the literary world. Till the decades of the fifties and early sixties, Indian writing was more or less an imitation of the West. The highbrow and the elite were the main subjects of library deliberations. The environment was purely aristocratic and the writers either ignored or overlooked the middle and the lower classes of society which were and are the pulsating realities of India. The reason, perhaps, was insufficient exposure to the creative artists dominating the scene in those days. Moreover, the literary background of the writer was profoundly influenced by British and American literatures. Not that the influence of the Western world was in any way detrimental to the growth of Indo-Anglican writing but the writer of the day could not get effectively involved with the basic issues of society and naked realities of life.

Probably the growing social and intellectual awareness in Indian society created a suitable climate for a native approach to literature. The writer, instead of looking for inspiration outside his country, now began to look around himself. The people on the streets, in fields, in households and offices gave the writer much food for thought and the literary metaphor was deeply underlined with native considerations Moreover, the easily available facilities for mass communication gave the writer an access to the fast-changing social, economical and political atmosphere at home as well as abroad. It is in this active and creatively bustling environment that we find serious and committed artists like Anita Desai and others working to depict the subtle nuances of human behaviour.

Anita Desai has emerged as a powerful interpreter of the deeply underlying forces of human beings. Her writings significantly underscore the complexities of human relationships particularly that of man and woman. Her portrayal of intense emotions almost reach a philosophical height when she becomes acutely concerned about human existence.

Desai has been making significant contribution to contemporary Indo-Anglican fiction in experimenting with the themes of inner consciousness. Primarily interested in exploring the psychic depths and loneliness of her female characters, she may be said to be doing something unique among the contemporary Indo-Anglican fiction writers. Her preoccupation is with the inner world of sensibility rather than the outer world of action.

Srinivasa Iyengar observes that in Desai's novels: "the inner climate, the climate of sensibility...is more compelling than the outer weather."[1] Her primary interest lies more in "the interior landscape of mind than in political and social realities."[2] Without getting into any language controversy, Desai employs "the language of the interior" to deal with the "inner climate" or the "interior landscape" of her character's minds. Through this language she has recorded the stream of consciousness of her main characters.

Desai has accepted that when she first began to work seriously and consciously on her novels, it was D. H. Lawrence, Virginia Woolf, Henry James and Marcel Proust who influenced her most and she discovered that the technique used by them suited her purpose. Like these novelists, her forte is also the exploration of interior world, plunging into the limitless depth of the mind and bringing into relief the hidden contours of the human psyche. It is depth which attracts her. She remarks: "it is depth which is interesting, delving deeper and deeper in a character or situation rather than going about it."[3]

Desai is concerned exclusively with the personal tragedy of the individual and has tried to portray the tragedy of human souls trapped in adverse circumstances of life, and the tragic effect is intensified because the external conditions not only oppress the protagonists from outside but also flaw their nature from within. Her novels are about human fate, bewilderment, suffering and loneliness. They deal with the terror of facing single handed, the ferocious assault of existence. She believes in death as the ultimate fact of life and the prime impulse behind her fiction is the existential predicament rooted in the awareness of death.

The four major themes, persistently used by Desai are: death and violence, East-West encounter, man-woman relationship, and loneliness. Her first two novels, *Cry the Peacock* and *Voices in the City*, deal with death and violence while the third novel, *Bye-Bye Blackbird*, is the only one dealing with the theme of the East-West encounter. The rest of her books deal with the themes of man-woman relationship and loneliness, her most favourite subject.

Desai's popularity is not so much due to the choice of her themes as to their treatment by her. By writing about the miserable plight of women suffering under their insensitive and inconsiderate husbands, she has given a new dimension to the Indian novel in English by turning from outer to inner reality. Solitude is necessary for an inward turning. She feels privacy needs to be fiercely protected for all else is linked to it: contemplation, intuition, visionary sense, and finally critical faculty. "Only the individual, the solitary being," she says, "is of the interest, one must be alone, silent in order to think or contemplate or write."[4] It is necessary for a while to live without words if words are to acquire any meaning, to use the language of silence if the speech is to be made effective. She strongly believes: "all human relationships are inadequate, and basically everyone is solitary."[5]

The involvement in human relationships in this world invariably leads to disaster and the loneliness of her characters is the outcome of this inadequacy of human relationships. Her protagonists are mostly lonely women who have reached different stages in life and are fragile introverts "trapped in their own skins." They are hyper-sensitive introspective. Loneliness is present in its varying shades and meaning in her work and there is a striving at a more authentic way of life than the one which is available to them. There is a need to be loved — almost all her heroines desire this above all else, but they resist surrender and involvement.

Desai's concern with the portrayal of psychological reality makes her characters peculiar and eccentric rather than general.

In an interview she stated: "I am interested in characters who are not average, but have retreated or been driven into some extremity of despair and so turned against, or made to stand against the general current."[6]

For Desai, each character is an embodiment of some unexplained mystery which the novelist wants to peel and unravel layer by layer. The innermost psyche of her protagonists is revealed to us through their interaction with those who are emotionally related to them on the basis of kinship for the purposes of fiction. No human relationship is more fertile and potential than that in the family and specially among the kins. She knows this crucial fact and that is why her novels depict such relationships as they are based on emotional idealism. She is not an idealist; she is simply a recorder of the situations, but the emotional crises among kins are born of the realisation that the kins fall short of the ideal in such relationships. This fact is substantiated by almost all of her novels.

Her novel, *Cry the Peacock* is concerned with the dissonance and disharmony that disrupts the marital relationship between Maya and Gautama. *The Voices in the City* depicts the disintegration of Nirode's, Monisha's and Amla's lives caused by imbalances in familial ties. *Bye-Bye Blackbird* shreds to pieces the hypothesis that East and West can never meet to form lasting equations. Sarah and Adit care for each other's happiness even at the cost of being marginalised and condemned to live in two societies and in two, not merely different, but antagonistic cultures. *Where Shall We Go this Summer?* emphasizes the universal need for human ties with Sita awakening to the fact that even sky and earth try to meet each other near the horizon. *Fire on the Mountain* conveys the message that running away from human contacts or one's kin is not a desirable proposition. Thus the above references indicate the nature and the thematic thrust of Desai's novels.

Anita Desai thus tries to introduce a modern psychological vein and projects a sensibility generally not encountered in other Indo-Anglican writers of fiction. As a novelist her distinguishing qualities are many, the chief among them being the subordination of the background to the characters and the deft handling of language, imagery and syntax in order to convey an intimate expression of the inner world of her characters. The moving description of loneliness leaves a lasting impression on the reader's mind: Maya, Nirode, Amla, Monisha, Sarah, Sita, Nanda Kaul — all suffer from a sense of isolation that is not merely physical but also psychic.

A writer dealing with the psychological aspects of characters has to employ a certain design by which the inner working of the protagonist's mind is unfolded to the readers gradually with the progress of the narrative. As in the case of her themes and her characters, Anita Desai's plots too are not repetitive. Each book has an individual structural pattern of its own. However, all the mechanisms she employs lend the work a unique harmony where incidents, people, situation combine to produce an artistic whole.

One can say that Anita Desai's plots are not so much deliberate contrivances as natural and inevitable outgrowths of the themes and perspectives. As the story advances in each of her novels, she seems to be quietly sliding in her scenes, setting and characters, without much of an advance preparation. As her forte is the psychic presentation of individual human beings, the narrative is rightly allowed to move freely and not clogged by blocks and patterns artificially imposed from outside. But it is not as if there is no subtlety or control in plot structure. The plot is always simple and neat enough so as not to impede the psychological revelation, and it is always well defined enough to present her vision clearly. Her plot structure, therefore, shows a splendid fusion of form and expression, contrivance and spontaneity.

In Desai's stories action is subordinated to psychology. The central themes revolve around the mental and spiritual developments of the 'dramatis personae' and not on their physical adventures. She has explored the psyche of both the childless women, as of Maya in *Cry the Peacock*, of Monisha in *Voces in the City* and also of women with children, like Sita in *Where Shall We Go this Summer* and Nanda Kaul in *Fire on the Mountain*. The interesting thing to note is that Anita Desai has portrayed also the psyche of "unwomanly women in the sense that they don't want children. Certainly they are not as "unsexed" as lady Macbeth was.

In different novels, Anita Desai has portrayed different facets of feminine psyche. Her range of characters in this regard is quite wide as we have seen above. Her characters cover women of almost all age groups. In Raka we have a child going to girlhood. Maya is a married woman, Lotte a middle aged woman while Nanda Kaul and Ila Das are old women. Not only are they women of different age groups but they are also of different types and traits. If Monisha is an intellectual type, Maya is hypersensitive. Sarla in *In Custody* is a character who cannot look beyond the four walls of her house. Even though the wife of a Hindi lecturer she has absolutely no interest in literature, or her husband's profession. She is so ignorant that she attributes her husband's frequent visits to Delhi to interview the poet as a ruse for meeting his girl-friend. In *Voices in the City*, we also find subtle suggestions of adultery between the widow mother of Monisha and the retired Major Chadha.

Thus, it may be said that Anita Desai's novels unravel various facets of feminine psyche from the viewpoint of an author who records her observations with a mind that is endowed with the capacity to feel intensely.

References

1. K. Srinivas Iyengar, *Indian Writing in English,* New Delhi Sterling Publishers 1962, p.464.
2. M. K. Naik, *A History of Indian English Literature,* New Delhi Sahitya Academy Publication 1982, p.241.
3. Anita Desai, "Interview" by Jasbir Jain, *Rajasthan University Studies in English,* Vol. XII, p. 69.
4. "Anita Desai at Work: An Interview" by Ramesh Shrivastava in *Perspectives on Anita Desai,* Ghaziabad: Vimal Prakashan, 1984, p.212.
5. "Interview" by Jasbir Jain, 67.
6. Ibid.

17 The Incipient New Woman in Manju Kapur's *Difficult Daughters*

— Pramila S. Chawla

Manju Kapur is a post-modern Indian novelist writing in English. In her novels as well as short stories, she has evolved her own stream of feminism. A bold writer, she gives a realistic portrayal of the characters whose lives she describes in her stories. With thorough research on her subject, inside knowledge of the people, times and places she describes, she gives her readers an almost anthropological chronicle of Indian society as if she wants the world to understand her India of a particular phase in its history: pre-partition, partition and post-partition years.

In Kapur's novels the men are pre-occupied with their work outside home, caught in the melee of political upheaval and economic disaster, in re-establishing business or the father is deceased before quite settling the children. The men have little time to spare for the day-to-day problems of their women folk. Rather, it is the elder woman, a mother or a mother-in-law who is in the controlling position while the young or the new woman tries to fight tradition and carve out her life as an independent person.

But even as men are in ultimate control and society is still cast in the patriarchal mold, it is the Punjabi north-Indian psyche that is less rigid, allows changes such as education of women, their entrepreneurship in business, foray into school-teaching, painting, poetry-writing and political and social activism. So the women in Manju Kapur's novels are not as rigidly bound by society as in other parts of India. Other factors responsible for their relative freedom have been the influence of the Arya Samaj in women's upliftment, education and resulting freedom, political circumstances needing women at the forefront of action, the role of women in helping and educating people living in slums through NGOs. This then is the new woman of Manju Kapur's novels, trying to stand on her own feet, stumbling, falling, suffering but making her mark in life, succeeding in getting liberated even at the cost of her own happiness, forfeiting her secure life in the family and at home. The pitfalls are many but better a vibrant society than a stagnant one. This paper attempts to show the evolvement of the Indian middle class woman in her first novel, *Difficult Daughters*.

The search for control over one's destiny, surely the key theme of *Difficult Daughters*, refers to the independence aspired to and obtained by a nation, but also to the independence yearned after by a woman: Virmati, the heroine, who seeks human relations that will allow her to be herself and to exercise the degree of control over her life, which, as an educated woman she knows she deserves. Her mother Kasturi puts on her the responsibility of tending to her ten siblings as the eldest of the lot. Kasturi wants her to discontinue her studies after B.A. and to prepare herself for marriage by learning household chores such as cooking, stitching, knitting, weaving etc. since "...it is the duty of every girl to get married". (*DD* 15-16). This was said for Shakuntla, the independent, educated and unmarried cousin of Virmati by Virmati's mother. But for Virmati herself, her cousin Shakuntla is her inspiration. Like her, she wants to be independent, to shoulder responsibilities that go beyond husband and children: "...it was possible to be something other than a wife. Images of Shakuntla Behenji kept floating through her head...who having done her M.Sc. in Chemistry, had gone about tasting the wine of freedom.... She too had to go to Lahore, even if she had to fight her mother who was so sure that her education was over" (Ibid.)

Shakuntla encourages her young cousin Virmati to comprehend the meaning of freedom: "These people don't really understand, Viru, how much satisfaction there can be in leading your own life, in being independent.... Here we are fighting for the freedom of the nation...I wish you could see what all the women are doing in Lahore [going to jail with Gandhiji, conducting political meetings and demonstrations, joining rallies]. Times are changing, and women are moving out of the house so why not you?" (Ibid. p.15). But mere efforts, without clear objectives, strong will power and planned action are not enough. Virmati's flight from one mode of life and plunging into another of pre-marital sex, abortion and marriage with a married man (Prof. Harish), despite her education, status and intelligence is her undoing. When Virmati marries according to her own choice, she spoils her prospects in both the worlds — the one that she revolts against and the one she embraces. Though she dares to cross the patriarchal threshold, she is caught into another, where her free spirit is curbed and all she does is adjust, compromise and adapt. She could have put her foot down doing what she had said to herself, "she (Virmati) will be her own mistress and relate to him (Harish) with dignity or not at all" (*DD* 235-6).

Only for a very brief time, Virmati shows marvellous strength of mind when she decisively and coolly shuns the Professor on learning that even as he professed to love her he had got his wife Ganga with a child. But in spite of her initial revolt against the double standards of the Professor, she succumbs to his implorations and passion in Lahore. She had come to broaden her horizons, but instead she gets involved in a useless love, doubtful marriage and unwed pregnancy.

Just for a short while in Sirmaur, as the head mistress of a girls' school, Virmati achieves control over her life, a near-exemplary level of female autonomy. But her lover's clandestine visits result in her being forced to leave the place. She tries to go to the far off Shanti Niketan but her plans are foiled by her break journey in Delhi while waiting for the connecting train to her destination. She visits a common friend who sends for Harish and a reluctant Harish is forced to marry her. Thus the initial tenacious and assertive self gradually wanes away into a pawn whom, the Professor tells just what to look, what to admire and what to criticize. Undergoing a gradual process of self-effacement, her energies are directed towards pleasing him while she herself remains parched. However there are other 'difficult daughters' in the novel so titled who succeed better than Virmati in their parallel struggle for independence in their lives: Shakuntla, her cousin and Swaran Lata her room-mate in Lahore. Both are representatives of a certain female type that recurs in Indian literature: the emancipated woman militant, like Daisy, the militant of *The Painter of Signs* by R. K. Narayan, who prefers to remain single, or Malti Trivedi, the progressive activist of *A Suitable Boy* by Vikram Seth.

Thus in Virmati, we see the incipient new woman, who is conscious, introspective, educated, wants to carve a life for herself, to some extent she conveys a personal vision of womanhood by violating current social codes, yet she lacks the confidence, self control, far sightedness and is physically imprisoned with an underlying need to be emotionally and intellectually dependent on a superior force – Professor Harish and it is precisely this knowledge through which the patriarchy works. Consequently, she fails to break the dependence syndrome.

Works Cited

Kapur, Manju. *Difficult Daughters*, London: Faber & Faber Publication, 1998. References to the text have been indicated against the abbreviation *DD* by page number in parentheses.

– *Home*, London: Faber & Faber Publication, 2006.

– *Married Woman*, London: Faber & Faber Publication, 2003.

Rollason, Christopher, "Women on the Margins: Reflections on Manju Kapurs *Difficult Daughters*", *The Atlantic Literary Review* 5.1: 2 Jan-Mar and April-June, 2004.

18 The 'New Woman' and Contemporary Indian English Women Novelists

— **Hemlata Srivastava**

'Woman' has been the pivotal theme of literature all over the world. Women, who are also creators of Literature, constitute a major part of contemporary fiction by focusing generally on the role of women in society. This is true of Indian English fiction too. Women writers in India successfully adopted the fictional mode to deal with the 'woman-subject': their role, position and status in society. These 'women novelists' raised their voice on such themes by psychologically probing into the psyche of their characters. Hence, the woman presented in contemporary literature is different from the earlier one in terms of physical and psychological needs of woman as an 'individual.' Contrary to the presentation of 'Sadyovadhu' or traditional type of women of Vedic period there emerged a new type of woman who had become aware not only of her own identity, self-dignity and individuality but also her rights.

Factors responsible for the emergence of the 'New Woman' were: (a) Advent of education. (b) Reformists movements. (c) Freedom movements. (d) Promotion of institutions. (e) Feminist trends. (f) Economic independence.

What motivated the emergence of the 'New Woman' were: (a) Woman's position did not improve like man's position in society. (b) Necessity of woman's education made them reasonable and intelligent. (c) As woman gradually became aware of the basic weakness of the patriarchal society, she not only reacted against it, but also encouraged others to see and analyse the existing order. Thus, appeared the 'New Woman' on the social scene with new line of thinking that focused on the following factors:

a) It was the need of the time to rectify the fallible traditions prevalent in society as well as psychological views of femininity. Woman could now gather the courage to raise voice against the dual standard of the male dominated world. Thus, the protesting voices came on the surface. The steps taken by some of the women writers paved the way for the 'New Woman' to appear on the scene.

b) The necessity of woman's education helped woman to think independently with practical approach. Thus emerged the 'New Woman' who was not only practically independent but also confident and courageous.

However, the 'New Woman' of India is slightly different from her Western counterpart. Her struggle for survival is still going on. She is caught not only between the conventional values and fast approaching changes in life but also torn apart between the burden of the work place as well as the household duties. Nevertheless, this 'New Woman' was sure to preserve her own identity and individuality by getting herself equipped with education and knowledge. She realises the futility of her high status and position. However, she is full of resentment and assertion which sometimes becomes disastrous for her. The tyranny of male domination is so deeply felt by the 'New Woman' that she sometimes rejects marriage and prefers to remain unmarried.

There is no clear cut distinction between the old and the new woman. The 'New Woman' emerged from the old one. There are mainly two categories of this 'New Woman' in India:

a) The first category of the 'New Woman' belongs to those who are housewives, daughters, and mothers. These characters, no doubt wish to experience freedom yet at the same time they want to remain within the boundary of marriage.

b) The second type of the 'New Woman' is career oriented, economically independent and therefore she does not dependent on anyone for financial support.

The occurrence of the 'New Woman' in India was noticed from the post-Independence period. There was an awakening of the new consciousness in the modern women of India. Thus a 'New

Woman' appeared on the social horizon, manifestations of which were seen not only in public life but also in her writings. It was for the first time that women writers could explore even those experiences that were confined to women only.

The nineteenth century fiction contains only a few examples of strong and capable women who can be regarded as the antecedents of the 'New Woman'. With the second half of the twentieth century the 'New Woman' has come to the forefront. The adventure made by the 'New Woman', her physical and mental capacity and her social freedom have become the fresh stuff for the women writers. This 'New Woman' is projected vividly and efficiently by the second generation of women writers of Indian English fiction. The prominent women novelists like Nayantara Sahgal, Shashi Deshpande, Anita Desai, Kamala Markandaya, Rama Mehta, Attia Hossain etc. represented this 'New Woman' in their respective novels. The 'New Woman' projected in their works is rational as well as emotional. She is no longer a blind follower and believer but questions her surroundings as well as her existence.

The liberated modern woman of Nayantara Sahgal belongs to the first category of the 'New Woman'. Her women want freedom and are aware of their identity. However, they still want to remain within the boundary of marriage. According to Sahgal a woman is not to be taken as sex object or glamour girl, lulled into a passive role that requires no individual identity, but as an individual in her own right. She should be accepted as equal to her male counterpart in rights, position and status. Her woman is determined and leads a life of self-respect. She is courageous and willing to risk the unknown. She sometimes even leaves her home and takes a new partner. Few women do without men like Devi in *A Situation in New Delhi* and Sonali in *Rich Like Us*, Saroj, Gauri and Mara in *Storm in Chandigarh*, Simrit in *The Day of the Shadow*, Laxmi, Devika, Kusum and Maya in *A Time to be Happy*, Rashmi and Nita in *This Time of Morning* — all are moving depictions of the New Women struggling to retain their selfhood to breathe freely in the suffocating environs of loveless, unfulfilling marriages. Woman's struggle to retain her individuality was unconsciously started by the character of Kusum in Saghal's novel *Time to Happy*. Afterwards it was done deliberately by Saroj and Simrit in the later works of Nayantara Sahghal.

The next important woman novelist is Shashi Deshpande. Her female characters belong to the second category of the 'New Woman'. Her women cannot reject the network of relatedness within which she has to find her own space. If we focus on her, the same quest for selfexpression and identity can be discovered in the emerging class of the 'New Woman'. Deshpande takes her women mainly from the middleclass society. Jaya in *That Long Silence*, Saru and her friend Nallu in *The Dark Holds No Terror* represent the 'New Woman'. They are credible and moving embodiment of the modern Indian woman seeking for an honest understanding of her own individual self.

The 'New Woman' of Anita Desai is in fact the poignant portrait of the intelligent woman who is trapped in relationship which denies her the freedom, emotional involvement and self-respect she craves for. She does not seek fulfilment through a challenging career but seeks it within sustaining meaningful human relationship. In the process of this quest, Anita Desai's woman displays a sensitive and subtle awareness of the forces working to repress her and questions the inequalities of such system. Maya, Sita, Monisha, Nanda and Tara are all women of deep emotion and fine sensitivities. There is an incipient feminist consciousness present in the simmering anger of Maya or Sita and studied indifference of Monisha or Nanda.

Kamala Markandaya, another contemporary woman novelist, portrays a large repertoire of women in a changing Indian society. The 'New Woman' of Markandaya is modern and educated. Both Mira and Roshan Merchant in *Some Inner Fury* are brought up in the Eastern and the Western ways of living but are finally caught between these two ways of life. They symbolise the modern progressive Indian women. They are the best examples of enlightened women. Other enlightened women, for example, Mohini, Usha and Ansuya, are all carbon copies of Roshan. However, it is sad to note that Kamala Markandaya's portraits of emancipated modern women are images of those who are either divorcees or concubines or willful waywards that cannot fit in the traditional Indian society and end up as unsatisfied women with no hearth or home. There are few Western characters like Caroline in *Possession* and Mrs. Pickering in *The Nowhere Man* who are examples of the 'New Woman'. They have more freedom, and are intelligently superior. They possess an identity of their own, gaiety of spirit and wholeness of vision.

Apart from the voices in contemporary Indian English fiction by women discussed above, writers like Raji Narsimhan, Rama Mehta, Attia Hossain, Kiran Desai, Namita Gokhale, Shobha De, Geeta Mehta, Arundhati Roy, Manju Kapoor, Sagarika Ghosh, Anita Kumar, Meera Syal, Meena Alexander, Bharati Mukherjee, Nargis Dalal, Veena Paintal and others are seriously engaged in sketching the picture of the 'New Woman' in terms of her innate need for affirmation of selfhood, a selfhood vibrant with endless possibilities.

19 Diaspora Woman in Bharati Mukherjee's *Wife*

— Ruchi Singh

Transformations in the world scenario engendered large movements of people all over the world. The world gradually transformed into a 'global village'. Movement across the world posed myriad dilemmas. With this, cross-cultural consciousness has also assumed great significance in the present world of globalisation, speaking of consequent tensions of adaptations and assimilation. The painful experience of isolation, sense of exile, crisis of identity and efforts to bond with adopted lands equips English literature with cross-cultural narratives. These narratives are brought together into a unified whole, generally referred to as 'Diaspora' writings. The narratives of cross-cultural clashes have established 'Diaspora studies' as an academic field in the late twentieth century. In literature, the term 'Diaspora studies' is allied with works produced by globally dispersed community of writers inexorably writing on their experiences abroad. Contemporary literature is enriched by a legion of Indian English writers of international eminence like Salman Rushdie, V.S. Naipaul, Ved Mehta, Geeta Mehta, Farrukh Dhondy, Haneif Kureshi, Shashi Tharoor, Jhumpa Lahiri, Bharati Mukherjee and others.

The term 'Diaspora', originally mentioned in the context of Jews scattered in exile outside Palestine, is now applied to expatriates, exiles, refugees and other immigrants across the world. Precisely, it explains the dispersal of any ethnic group or community outside the country of its origin. Literally, the meaning of 'Diaspora' is "to sow over or scatter." Today, the construction of Diaspora involves movement from an ancestral land, settlement in new land and sometimes resettlement. The Diaspora carries with it socio-cultural ethos, which consists of a pre-defined social identity; a set of religious beliefs and practices governing family and kinship; food habits and dress; and a language. They share an emotional attachment to native soil, are cognizant of dispersal, oppression and alienation in the country of residence. Tambiah attributes the origin of Diaspora to two different sources, voluntary and involuntary migration. The 'push' factors favoring migration from East-Asian countries are strong, but so are the 'pull' factors drawing people to the lands of opportunity. The various concepts related to Diaspora are Identity, Intensity, Externalities, Genesis, Citizenship, Temporality, Localisation, Homeland, Transnationalism, Religion, Language and Culture. Existence of Diaspora cultures is a key element of cultural multiplicity today across the globe. The intricacy and convolution associated with redefining and revising home in relation to Diaspora discourse present a challenging topic for discussion.

The Diaspora sensibility comes through in the writings of Bharati Mukherjee. She has established herself as a powerful member of American literary scene. Her novels and short stories have been steadily winning acclaim in literary circles. The main theme throughout her writings revolves round the condition of Asian Diaspora with particular attention to the changes taking place in South Asian women in a new world. The ordeals and struggles of the immigrants in America form the literary agenda of Mukherjee. Her works deal with issues emanating from the encounter with the world outside the homeland.

As the title suggests, the novel *Wife*, published in 1975, is the story of an Indian wife, Dimple Mukherjee, torn between the need to play the role society expects of her and her own need for self expression. The author delves deep into the psyche of Dimple as she evolves from being single to a wife, from her existence in the household backdrop of Calcutta to the cosmopolitan world of America. The focus is on an Indian wife who is keen to take a plunge in the thrilling life of America but who is also being pulled back by her Indian ethics and values.

Dimple Dasgupta, married off to an engineer, soon finds herself in America. She had thought extraordinarily about America while in Calcutta. On her very first day in New York, "she felt like a star collapsing inwardly"(*Wife* 109). On her visit to a party, she expected to see apartments in America resembling the sets of Raj Kapoor's movies. On the contrary, the apartments are barely the size of her house in Calcutta. She goes out shopping but it turns out to be a sad experience. Dimple does not know what to buy and how to ask for it at the store. Dimple feels, "She was caught in the crossfire of an American communalism she couldn't understand"(*Wife 60*). The rebuff she gets is enough to discourage her from trying similar forays in future. She decides not to venture again all by herself. Dimple discovers in her first shopping experience that it is difficult to do even the smallest chores in an alien culture. This setback and rejection leads to holdups in course of assimilation.

Life in America allows Dimple to seek ways out of the role reserved for a wife in her community and to explore methods of breaking out of the traditional moulds. She comes to America ready to be transformed and willing to seek out an identity that would take her away from the wifely ideals exemplified by 'Sita', yet she fails to break away from her Indian Bengali community and connect with the conventional American society. Dimple believed that she would be free to experience a life distanced from that which she left behind in India. On the contrary, she finds her existence in a nebulous, undefined social space that reinforces her indigenous cultural moorings. Marginalised by the patriarchy of Indian culture, Dimple is equally perturbed in her adopted culture.

Migration towards America also disintegrates the marital bond between Amit and Dimple. Dimple feels temporary joblessness has made her husband frail and flimsy, losing his erstwhile infallible position in family. Back home in India she held him in high esteem. The commendable comments of her friends and relatives drew Dimple's attention to her husband's persona. No longer confined to the social and cultural patterns of her past while in America, Dimple gradually loses faith in her husband.

Dimple suffers from alienation in a culture the codes of which she is unable to decipher. Even before Dimple landed in New York, she had heard friends talking of America as a place where one can have fun but one would have to be a foreigner for all his life. At a farewell party in India, Dimple was told by a woman that America may be thought of as an imagination, but a person from another land is a resident alien. In New York, Meena, Dimple's friend, confesses how inadequate she feels outside her community because she has such a hard time understanding American humour and the English language. At times, Dimple thinks of talking to one of the American woman she keeps meeting on the streets but decides that there are things she just could not ask them. Such thoughts inevitably lead to frustration and make her wonder how she could keep on living in a country where every other woman is a stranger, where she felt different, ignorant, and exposed to ridicule even in the elevator. Nevertheless, Dimple keeps trying in her own confused and uncertain manner to put out feelers to see if she could immerse herself in this strange but exciting world. Dimple is helplessly caught in gripping quest for a new female American identity. For Dimple a happy guiltless amalgamation seems impossible. What goes inside her is a simultaneous fracturing and evolving of identity. If she had remained a housewife living with her extended family in India, she probably would not have asked herself questions regarding her happiness, freedom, identity and liberation. In India she experienced a comfortable but restricted existence. For Dimple the loss of old culture is not an exhilarating experience. Freedom from the bonds of caste, gender and family instead of turning her free, leave her utterly lonely and desolate.

Social position largely dictates women experiences. Controlled by their traditions, women are accepted if they concur with tradition and rejected if they dissent. They belong to home, they should be 'pavitra', and they obtain identity, first from their fathers and then their husbands. The Indian ghetto in New York reminds Dimple of a community that puts premium on a woman's ability to sacrifice herself for her family. Her sense of loss is heightened by her seduction by Milt Glasser, a moral lapse that is as inimical to her status and self-identity as it is insidious to her role as a wife. Mukherjee indicates the dilemma of the Indian woman whose social role is defined by tradition and a patriarchal encoded culture. Marriages are arranged by parents, the husband assumes authority and the wife is expected to subsume her individual identity into the social and cultural context. It is her feminine duty to subjugate her desires to the will of her husband. She is brought up to defer to her father and husband's final authority to judge her every emotion and behavior. The act of murder stems from Dimple's resistance to male ideology. It liberates her. Her final analysis is to be seen as a denial of her identity as a victim of cultural displacement and patriarchal discourse. If Dimple continued to live in Calcutta she would have reconciled to her fate or else she would have committed suicide. In a foreign environment she is trapped in a dilemma of tension between American culture and the traditional constraints surrounding an Indian wife, between the desire to be assertive and independent and the Indian need to be diffident and self-effacing. There is in Dimple a craving to stick to traditions. At the same time the influence of American notion of freedom inculcates in her the desire to protest against the strict norms of traditions. However, she finds herself in a flux because she is unable to determine any clear-cut priority. After a few wretched attempts to merge into the new culture, she experiences rupture from herself and her surroundings. She is caught in the whirlwind of traumatic emotions, her traditions questioning her outrageous adultery, her current baffled identity wishing to become American by any means. It is not easy for a young woman like her, born and bred in a very different environment, to adjust to the American ways.

An attempt to immerse herself in a strange but exciting world gives rise to a host of questions in Dimple's mind. This causes misunderstanding, incomprehension and confusion. She confronts a different set of conditions that pose a challenge and adventure. She becomes a prisoner of the ghetto in Flushing, Queens. Unable to accept the contradictions of this existence, Dimple descends into depression, madness and murder. She also finds that it is not easy for a young woman like her, born and bred up in a very different environment, to adjust to the American ways. The cultural and social gulf dividing the two worlds is too vast and deep for her to bridge over. The frustrations of her lonely and dull existence in the apartment makes her depressed and neurotic. Thinking she is ready to venture forth in America, she finds that she is not really prepared for it and in no time gets depressed and dejected. In spite of all her attempts, she experiences total estrangement from herself and her surroundings. The multicultural reality leads to a variety of new exposures in new world but does not deny the past affiliations. She tries to reconcile the Bengali ideal of perfect, passive wife with the demands of her new American life. She takes a drastic step at the end to get away from the cultural maladjustment that enmeshes her. She is driven to aggressive behaviour after becoming conscious that she is a misfit in both the cultures, the adopted Western culture and the Bengali culture which she was desperate to leave behind. The Indian woman, when facing an unfamiliar cultural environment, has problems that take unpredictable turns. Having nothing and nobody to fall back upon, she has to tackle her problems by herself. Dimple, caught up in a cross-cultural dilemma, has to be her saviour. In trying to adapt to American society she is portrayed as rootless. She belongs to nowhere at the end of the story.

Through Dimple, Mukherjee comments on the lives of immigrants from Third World countries and their attempt to adjust to a fast-paced American society. A close experience of the Western and Eastern worlds gives her an authentic and unbiased perspective of these cultural codes. An attempt to immerse in a strange but exciting world gives rise to a tumult of questions in the human mind. This causes misunderstanding, confusion and incomprehension in the mind of the Diaspora. Diaspora is confronted with different sets of conditions that pose a kind of challenge and adventure. The colliding worlds of their exile and immigration spawn a number of psychological glitch that merge into one another to form a curious blend of cross-cultural consciousness. Mukherjee's novel *Wife* exhibits this cross-cultural consciousness.

Works Cited

Bhabha, Homi K. "Cultural Diversity and Cultural Differences", *Post-Colonial Studies Reader,* Ed. Bill Ashcroft, Gareth Griffith and Helen Tiffin. London: Routledge, 1995.

Gabriel, Sharmani Patricia. *Between Mosaic and Melting Pot: Negotiating Multiculturalism and Cultural Citizenship in Bharati Mukherjee's Narratives of Diaspora,* http://postcolonial.org/index.php. 15 January 2006.

Ghosh, Nibir K. *Multicultural America: Conversations with Contemporary Authors,* Chandigarh: Unistar Books, 2005.

Iyengar, K. Srinivas. "Introduction", *Indian Writing in English,* Bombay: Asia Publishing House, 1994.

Maini, Cookie. *Fleeing The Cage Has Its Pains Too,* http://www.tribuneindia.com. 10 January 2006.

Mukherjee, Bharati *An Interview with Bill Moyers,* http://www.pbs.org/now/transcript/transcript mukherjee.htm. 10 January 2006.

— *Wife,* New York: Fawcett Books, 1975.

Nelson, Emmanuel S. Ed. *Bharati Mukherjee: Critical Perspectives,* New York: Garland Publishers, 1993.

20 Reconstructing the Self: A Reading of Bama's *Sangati*

— C. Sharada

> Dalits, who have for so long been treated as commodities owned by others must shout out their selfhood, their "I", when they rise *up*.
>
> —*Raj Gautaman*

Bama is the pen name of a Tamil Dalit woman from a Roman Catholic family. Her main works are *Karukku* (1992), an autobiography, *Sangati* (1994): a novel and *Kisumbukkaaran* (1996): a collection of short stories. Bama, for the first time in the history of Tamil literature, speaks about the experiences of Dalit women. She draws her energy and strength from the Dalit movement in Tamil Nadu. Her works are a source of inspiration to the sidelined women of her community. Her famous work, *Karukku* (1992), is the first autobiography of its kind. The tension throughout *Karukku* is between the self and the community (of a religious woman to join another community as a Dalit woman). *Sangati* is the autobiography of that community. The Tamil version was translated into English by Lakshmi Holmstorm.

Bama's *Sangati* throws light on Dalit women's consciousness, their status, their struggles, and their selfhood. It is an autobiography of Dalit women community. *Sangati* is a string of events, memories, happenings and stories of the Dalit women. It is the semblance and the sameness of their experiences and understanding that holds them all together as a community. Sharan Kumar Limbale observes in *Towards an Aesthetic of Dalit Literature*: "Dalit writers assert that their literature conveys the life that they have lived; experienced and seen. Since the experience contained in Dalit literature is articulated out of a desire for freedom, its character is collective rather than individual" (32).

Bama reiterates this observation of Limbale by saying, in the Preface to *Sangati,* that she wrote the novel with a definite purpose, to let the world know about them and their lives. She says: "*Sangati* grew out of the hope that the Dalit women who read it will rise up with fervour and walk towards victory as they begin their struggle as pioneers of a new society" (Bama 16).

The stories, memories of personal experiences are narrated by a young girl in the early chapters of *Sangati* but later they are narrated by a middle-aged woman. These two narrators seem to be exploring, reflecting, pondering doubting and questioning the experiences. They engage themselves in self-search to achieve self-respect. Quest for 'Self-search' and 'Self-respect' are the main themes that run through *Sangati*, other themes being: status of Dalit woman at her own home, in her own community and outside her community, domestic violence and sexual exploitation by her man at home and outside, by the landlords at her workplace. Though she is crushed, stifled and smothered under these mighty forces, she rises against all odds with great gusto and zeal for life. She tries to strike a fine balance between these two scales and affirms and asserts her position to scale new heights. The tension and conflict that arises in this mêlée forms the structure of this novel.

This paper focuses on the many issues concerning Dalit women, like their life, their celebrations, their hardships, cruelty meted out to them, physical and psychological pressures and finally their courage and strength to recollect themselves, assert their status and reconstruct their 'self' by means of self-respect, self-confidence and spirit of individuality.

The novel begins with the young narrator's grandmother Vellaiyamma, a single woman who stood as a strong fortress and braved and weathered the tough conditions of life. She was like a role model to many women of her community who were forced to be on their own, yet remained strong and self-sustained. Life for a single woman to raise her family is challenging, but the women of Dalit community emerge stronger with each experience, which stands as a test of their fortitude. Vellaiyamma says: "She told herself she had become a corpse without a husband, and struggled single-handedly to care for her two children" (Bama 5). There are many references to married women who can handle any unforeseen situations single handedly; they are so brave, so sensible, and practical at times that they even can deliver babies on their own. Once a woman, in full term of her pregnancy went into labour, and delivered the child right there: "She cut off the umbilical cord with the sickle she had taken with her to cut the grass, dug a hole and buried the placenta, and then walked home carrying her baby and her bundle of grass" (Bama 6). The young narrator after listening to this experience raises questions that how can a woman in such a state be sent to work. Pat comes the reply from Velliamma: "If they stay at home, how are they going to get any food? We have to labour in the fields as hard as men do and then on top of that, struggle to bear and raise our children" (Bama 6).

This statement of her grandmother actually launches the themes of the novel. Women are into hard labour, they slog at work place equally with men; when they come back home, men go out to assemble and gossip away and burn their money, where as women have to fetch water, firewood and cook the evening meal; men come at the time of eating and eat until they cannot eat anymore, and women being the bread earners and makers should shove into their mouth, the leftovers? They innocently feel that it is written down in the books that women should eat only the leftovers. There is a reference to a song about the plight of a pregnant woman who ate first:

> I waited and waited for him to come home
> And began to eat as he came through the door.
> He came to hit me the hungry brute
> He pounced at me to kill me...(Bama 30).

Men beat their wives at the slightest provocation. Domestic violence is a glaring theme. They humiliate, beat and abuse them both physically and psychologically as they see wife beating as a symbol of pride and authority. Some women succumb silently as there is no escape but some women find their ways out to escape the hard blows. They have schemes and strategies to overpower and cope with the open beating and humiliation. They use obscene language to mitigate their husband's anger or run into the streets to get support from the neighbours. One woman, who is being battered mercilessly by her husband, actually shames him by threatening to lift her sari, "If I hadn't shamed him like this, he would surely have split my skull in two" (Bama 62). Bama asks: why should the Dalit women bear the brunt both outside and within?

The Dalit woman is pushed to the margin at her home, in her community and outside her community. She has to put up with the violence and sexual exploitation under her own husband and at her workplace under the landlords. As Prahlad Gangaram critically observes: "Women from lower castes were considered so lowly and degraded in life that their body was a free terrain for colonization" (6).

Bama empathizes, sees through, analyses, studies and gives answers to many problems the women of her community face. Why do women quarrel at the time of dusk, why do they use obscene language, why are they possessed by evil spirits and see hallucinations? "When they come home after an arduous day's toil, there is only more and unending work. From all sides they have to deal with the pestering of children and the anger and unfair domination of their husbands" (Bama 68).

The bottled up frustration, helplessness, unsettles them so much that all the bitterness is vented out in the form of aggressive behaviour. These women are beaten and battered emotionally and physically from dawn to dusk by breaking their backs in the fields. At night they have to give in to their husband's pleasure. They are crushed under monotony, despair, disgust, depression and despondency. They are so exhausted that mentally they become weak and feeble. They succumb to mental ill-health and as a result see hallucinations and act as if they are possessed by evil spirits. Caste, class and gender, all join to crush her freedom. They are afraid of invisible forces like *bhoots*, evil spirits.

Bama also focuses on the freedom and privileges that the women enjoy. Widows and divorcees can remarry without having to face social stigma, and above all they have no dowry system. The women open up and participate in community festivals and they have songs for every occasion: on the fields, at the time of birth, at marriages, betrothal ceremony, girls coming of age ceremony and dirges. The female characters in Dalit literature are dynamic and not static. Bama writes, "From birth to death, there are special songs and dances; and it is only the women who will sing them" (xx). Yet, their talent goes unnoticed and kept under wraps, as they are never given a chance to display their mettle outside, but limit it within the domestic periphery.

The female narrators in *Sangati* are truly dynamic, self-motivated and forceful. They raise questions against the system and structure of the society. Once a young girl was accused of misbehaviour and was punished after a biased trial at the community assembly. The young narrator who sees that the punishment is unjustified, seethes with anger and says: "People won't consider whether the accusation is true or not, nor will they allow the woman to speak out" (Bama 42). She feels that had the assembly allowed the woman to speak the truth, she would have been acquitted. Bama wonders: "Why were women pushed aside always and everywhere? The question kept on churning me inside"(28). The women are voiceless, space less and are pushed to the margins. It is so disheartening to see that women are so conditioned to this system, that they accept it as if it is made only for them. Caught in this complex maze of norms and rules set aside for them, women lose their self. They cannot think for themselves, speak for themselves, and eat the food they like, or do anything on their own. They are not only marginalized at home but also self-marginalised and lead their lives in self-denial and self-abnegation.

The middle-aged narrator is more practical, and realistic towards addressing the problems. She says that to combat the ills and evils in the social structure and to empower, emancipate and liberate women from the shackles of subservience and submission. Education is the only weapon and instrument. It helps the woman to etch an identity and give her the spirit of individuality and freedom. She no longer needs to remain in shadow of somebody 'else' she can be her own 'self: "We should educate boys and girls alike, showing no difference between them as they grow into adults. We should give our girls freedom we give our boys. If we rear our children like this from the time they are babies, women will reveal their strength" (123).

Women themselves should learn not to retreat and recoil, instead flare the hood and reassert and reconstruct their 'Self'. They should wake up and change the very make up of the society. If the system and structure of the society are reconstructed on the foundations of gender equality and liberty, then one day men and women can live together as one, with no differences, no violence, and no inequalities.

Works Cited

Bama. *Sangati*. Translated into English by Lakshmi Holmstorm, New Delhi: Oxford University Press, 2004. References to the text are from this edition and have been indicated by page numbers in parentheses.

Gangaram Jogdanand, Prahlad. Ed., *Dalit Women in India: Issues and Perspectives,* New Delhi: Gyan Publishing House in collaboration with University of Poona, Pune, 1995.

Gauthaman, Raj. "We have no need for haloes", *India Today Annual,* 1995.

Limbale, Sharankumar. *Towards an Aesthetic of Dalit Literature: History, Controversies and Considerations,* New Delhi: Orient Longman, 2004.

21 Women's Issues in Shobha De's *Starry Nights*

— Atima Adhikari

In the contemporary world the status of woman is a question that has to be studied as a fundamental part of the socio-economical structure in which the woman lives. Shobha De is among the first to explore the world of the urban woman in India. In her novels, she heralds the arrival of the new Indian woman, eager to rebel against the intense moral orthodoxy of the patriarchal social system. She re-defines feminine archetypes and the societal power game. As she writes: "Eventually, every relationship is a power struggle either on an overt or subliminal level."[1] The power struggle between man and woman is evident in Shashi Deshpande's *A Matter of Time*, Anita Desai's *Clear Light of Day*, Margaret Atwood's *The Handmaid's Tale* and Alice Walker's *The Colour Purple*. Dé's novels can be called the representation of the dynamics of such a power struggle.

Certain women's issues have been stressed by De. Sexual harassment and rape are practices of female victimisation. Rape is a violation of one's human rights; it is a deliberate defeat of one's possession of one's body; in fact it is a physical invasion with drastic emotional and mental trauma, and yet for rape, the victim is condemned and not the victimiser.

Indian marriages are considered to be one of the most sacred institutions of social norms. Here also, women are often victimized through various kinds of domestic violence and bondages. A girl-child and a woman are subjected to a greater degree of domestic violence. Prostitution of women is another aspect of female victimisation. Women are bought and sold for sexual gratification of the males. The monetary benefits are not transferred to the victim but is handed over to the victimizer.

De has painted these burning issues related to women in all her novels.

Today, woman's literacy and education is an important issue. It is through education that she gains confidence, self-awareness and can taste real freedom. It also allows her to enjoy economic freedom, which according to De, is very important to create a worthy space in society. Unfortunately, De has also revealed that despite education woman is not always successful in discarding the various dwarfing influences of society.

De's viewpoints in relation to women's issues are strongly demonstrated in her novel *Starry Nights*. She in her novels mainly represents the woman's role in society. Socialisation plays an important role in the construction of gender roles and bears the link between social values and the overpowering male domination. In fact, during the past few centuries, the place of woman in the tradition bound, male dominated society has been very unenviable. Annis Pratt in her book *Archetypal Patterns in Women's Fiction* says that "the female quest is distinct from a male quest in that the latter is a quest outward for the Holy Grail, while the former is a journey into the inner self."[2] Pratt divides the quest further as spiritual and social and avers that "the spiritual quest is for self-awareness while the social quest is for social integration."[3] Both the quests are presented in De's novels.

Shobha De has dealt very minutely and delicately with the problems of upper middle class educated women. Her female characters react radically whereas Shashi Deshpande's women, with a voice and identity of their own, handle the problems diplomatically. In De's novels the role of family is very significant. There are four basic functions that a family performs in all societies. They are the universal functions and are termed as sexual, reproductive, economic and educational. The sexual function also helps to stabilise the society. It is thus the family that provides both control and expression of sexual drives and in doing so performs important functions both for its individual member, for the family as an institution and for society as a whole. Culture plays an important role in structuring the personality of its members. Culture is not simply learned but internalized as a part of personality structure. Family normally attempts to resolve the tensions and conflicts within its structure. In the process the children may become the scapegoats. Shobha De has tried to portray Aasha Rani in *Starry Nights* and Mumtaz in *Socialite Evenings* as the emotionally disturbed innocent children who are caught between the conflicts of their parents.

Marital breakdown is also considered as one of the women's issues in the novels of Shobha De. Marital breakdown is divided into three main categories: divorce refers to legal termination of marriage; separation which refers to the physical separation of the spouses; they no longer share the same dwelling and the so called "empty shell" marriages, and lastly where the spouses live together, remain legally married, but their marriage exists in name only. Some of the factors for a marital breakdown are values attached to marriage. In De's novels marriage, motherhood and wifehood are central issues. Their success or failure affects the life of women diversely.

The Indian woman in general carries the burden of the family. She slaves for her husband, children and family whether it is nuclear or extended. A patriarchal joint family system consolidates the position of the man forever by damning that of the woman. In an Indian society the son/brother plays a major role, The sister/daughter is believed to be weak. One of the greatest virtues of women is considered to be "silence." It is the man who is powerful and likes to demonstrate his superiority over the woman, and tries to control her life, actions and her behaviour. An Indian woman is taught to keep her husband in perfect comfort because for a stable marriage and family it is a necessity. This traditional idea is presented in *Socialite Evenings* and *Starry Nights*. The conventional husband considers her to be a 'mule' (as in Alice Walker's *Colour Purple*) and never tries to communicate with her. The woman longs for a son because he will give her a prominent position in the family hierarchy. This view is accepted by many educated women though a few think that they can be happy without marriage.

Educated or otherwise, women still continue to be 'givers' and not 'takers'. It is only as a mother and wife that she plays a major role. If a daughter, wife or mother takes employment due to economic necessity, her freedom ends as soon as she returns home.

The six duties and characteristics of a wife are: to serve as a slave, counsel like a minister, look like Lakshmi, endure and feed like mother earth and be a practitioner of good acts in bed, act like Rambha, the celestial prostitute. An Indian wife's silent suffering is common and very few men realise that they are humans with weaknesses and strengths. Kamala Markandaya's Rukmani in *Nectar in the Seive* is a *pativrata* (a wife who is dedicated to her husband like Savitri) who never forgets that a woman's place is with her husband. She is the ideal.

Shobha De has changed this very traditional image of women. She tries to get into the emotional and psychological aspects of her protagonist and tells a woman's story from a woman's point of view. She tries to trace the impact of the early happenings in the life of the female characters. The impact of these are invariably psychological in her novels. Indian women in the modern times seek self-realisation, wage continuous wars on existing misconceptions, and modify their attitudes towards marital relationships. Her characters are very confident and they try to discard the traditional image of women subjected to the superior power of man in marriage. She writes about the conflict between tradition and modernity in relation to women in the middle class society. A woman's desires, efforts and failures and her achievements are the main concerns in her novels. At times, in her world, not men but women disturb their own world and invite suffering and trouble. Her creation of women is authentic, realistic and convincing though they belong to a particular class and with a particular bent of mind. Men often play a minor role. The confrontation is not always between the opposite sexes. It is more frequently within the sexes. The women's issues are directly projected through the female characters that either obey or protest against the norms of society.

In all literary works, authored by women, the search for identity, the establishment of selfhood, have not only been popular themes but also the central issue. Shobha De with her varied experiences and unusual exposures in the film world, could not remain chained to the humdrum story of a conventional woman's life, and thus in her second novel, *Starry Nights* (1991), she explores the dazzling world of a female film star. This novel created strong waves in the literary world because of the unorthodox picturization of the murky film world of Bombay and also because it seemed to be a *roman a-r clef*, a fictional presentation of a very popular star's true life story.

Starry Nights (1991) revolves around Aasha Rani, a very average young girl who comes to Bombay from a small town near Madras, and after struggling for sometime becomes a star, the "Sweetheart of millions."[4] This novel of De shows the rise and fall of a star struggling for survival in this sex dominated ravenous society. In fact, she specifically reveals how moral values are eroded in the professional world of show business. Aasha Rani's rise to a great extent is based on her relationships with a large number of men and occasionally women who either exploit her or she surrenders willingly before them. Her connection with the blue film producers and underworld dons initially gives her the required thrust forward.

Aasha Rani is a daughter of an insecure mother who has been abandoned by her husband, a renowned film producer of Madras. The mother, Geetha Devi, known as amma has to prostitute herself in order to support her two daughters. Amma's financial insecurity and ambition are the key factors that make Aasha Rani a dazzling star but never the ideal woman of Indian tradition. The game of power is initiated by amma and thus, she patterns a path for her daughter to reach stardom. De presents such a picture of the mother because she clearly feels that economic concerns are subsumed below the social exploitations of all kinds. She says: "Eventually, everything boils down to money—that great leveller. There can be no independence for women, without economic self-sufficiency. An independent mind of free spirit, is meaningless so long as the body and soul are being kept together by somebody else.

The mother-daughter relationship is one of the most important factors in the development of a child, especially a girl-child. In this novel, Shobha De highlights this aspect but does not portray an image of a self-sacrificing noble mother; instead, she is human, mundane and quite mean. It is the mother who propels her daughter into the world of blue films and yet, the daughter achieves her selfhood, identity and becomes the dream girl of the millions. Amma emotionally blackmails her and never allows Aasha Rani to forget her struggle. The ill-treatment of amma by appa, and Aasha Rani's own exploitation by males since her childhood, also has something to do with her shocking behaviour: "Perhaps it had something to do with *appa* and the way he'd mistreated her mother. Or maybe she felt soiled, used, exploited by them— she often told him bitterly: "All of you are just the same, but wait, I will show you. I will do to men what they try to do to me. I will screw you all—beat you at your game"(8).

Geetha Devi was not always like this. Once she was a traditional housewife who believed that her husband was a "real movie-moghul"(68). Later her husband leaves her and the children for another woman who calls her a "common prostitute"(68). Her husband's betrayal is a shock to amma who is suddenly cut off from all money, she had to sell her jewellery and clothes and subsequently prostitute herself. The change brought about in her nature is due to a deep psychological impact.

Amma exposes Aasha Rani in the world of blue films and to the reluctant daughter she says, "Don't be stupid these films will not be shown in the theatre. There is a lot of money involved. I've committed on your behalf"(53). It is shocking to see a mother/ woman exploiting another daughter/woman. Financial insecurity is the root cause of such exploitation. Shobha De's comments are very vocal and clear on such situations. She affirms that women's destinies have been determined largely in that context alone. It is time they were made aware of the own potential and power. Shakti needs to be harnessed, directed and explored for the furtherance of overall human development.

In her different novels De has stressed that woman surrenders to physical exploitation mostly due to monetary problems. Financial insecurity is a serious issue. Kishenbhai introduces Aasha Rani to the world of sex and cinema. He transforms a simple girl named Viji into Aasha Rani the leading actress of Bombay. Aasha Rani had been first seduced by her uncle in her childhood and then Kishenbhai uses her. She surrenders; one feels sympathy for her as she tells Kishenbhai: "You don't know about my childhood," she'd tell him hugging a doll. "I never had anything to play with ... no toys nothing. The poverty, deprivation, the struggle"(4).

Traditional issues of womanhood, chastity, sacrifice etc., are no issues for De's protagonist in this novel. Aasha Rani's life moves on with contacts with new males. During her struggle for survival Kishenbhai is her first mentor and seducer. Next comes Seth Amirchand, a member of parliament who keeps a 'Godfather image' and calls himself a protector of the weak. His assertion is ironic. Seth Amirchand takes a keen interest in Aasha Rani and discovers that she is not all desire but substance also. It is only under his tutelage that Aasha Rani learns to manipulate the world in her own terms and is empowered. He helps her to recognise her potential and tells her: "Smart woman. You will go far. Fame will come to you if you have any talent, which I believe you do. I will watch you, watch your every move"(62). A similar situation is to be found in *Socialite Evenings* when Karuna's literary achievement is appreciated by her male friend Ranbir Roy. In Aasha Rani's world, power has greater meaning than honesty, chastity or morality.

Aasha Rani and Akshay Arora episode in the novel paints another aspect of Aasha Rani's life. The episode is a medium tc voice De's views on the institution of marriage. It also points out the double standards of society. Her reasons for clinging to Akshay are: firstly, she is infatuated and secondly, he is the ladder to climb the ramp of Bollywood and society and thirdly, she wishes to enjoy the social respect granted to a married woman and lastly because she wishes to experience motherhood like all women. But she realises that her desires for a normal life cannot be actualised because Akshay's brother and her own mother are there to disrupt it. A person's dreams remain unfulfilled because society invariably interferes. Karuna's mother in *Socialite Evenings* opines how a woman cannot live alone for she would always need a man's protection. Aasha Rani tries to live a normal life. But when she fails she thinks like Karuna and says, "[...] why does security rest with a man? I feel confident now that I can look after myself."(75). Woman leading a single life, is a possibility according to De. This is an important issue in a woman's life.

Shobha De through Aasha Rani advocates free thinking for women. A woman in a traditional society thinks like Malini. Aasha Rani turns out to be an emancipated woman, thinking and acting with authority, hope and desire. Often women are made powerless by brutal force. Domestic violence is often perpetrated against woman. At one point of time, frustrated, betrayed and humiliated Aasha Rani tries to commit suicide but fortunately escapes death. Escape through death is a common solution to end woman's agony. But De is not inclined to present the story of a powerless woman. She is keen to project the power inherent in a woman. She is a champion of *Stree Shakti* projection. A woman's weakness is a conspiracy of the male hegemony.

Aasha Rani's meeting with Abhijit Mehra, the son of a top industrialist, is a coincidence. Their first meeting is only due to her popularity and her appealing personality. All through the novel, Shobha De tries to give justice to Aasha Rani, where she can live her life, conforming to her choice. Women's freedom is an important issue for De and all enlightened women. But Aasha Rani is trapped because of her own emotions and her image on the silver screen. She rightly tells Abhijit: "you are not making love to me. You are screwing my image—my screen image. Get out of here, Abhijit. Go back to your wife and make a man of yourself. I have my own life to lead"(97). Mutual trust and loyalty in marriage is demanded by all women because these issues play important roles in their life and in bringing up a family. The issue of betrayal in marital relationship is raised by De repeatedly. Again and again she projects the infidelity of men and yet, it is women who are condemned.

Economic independence is very important in one's life but to lead one's own life is even more important. Aasha Rani had always been a dutiful daughter but on account of the constant interference of her mother she dislikes her for insisting that she should work without any holiday. Amma says, "Now is the time to make money"(106). Aasha Rani retorts in anger: "Money, money, money. That's all you think of. Well I'm fed up of being your money machine. I've done enough for everybody...you, Sudha and others... now, I want to live for myself and enjoy my life" (106). According to De, A woman's demand to live for her own self is much against the traditional idea of self sacrificing woman. Financial self-sufficiency has different meanings for the mother and the daughter. The mother is afraid to go back to the days of deprivation. She knows like De, that an independent mind or free spirit is meaningless so long as the body and soul are being kept together by somebody else. Aasha Rani is never a home-breaker and she always wants a home, a family that would be her own world. Because of Akshya's betrayal, in rebound, she falls for Abhijit which is very temporary. Frightened of her loneliness, desperately in search of happiness, she sleeps with many men. But happiness still eludes her. Ultimately in Jammy Philips (Jay), an old time admirer of Aasha Rani, she finds happiness and marries him. Far from her own world, she begins a life of a farmer's wife and she feels contented and happy with her present. Her happiness reaches the high point when she becomes a mother of a beautiful little baby girl, Sasha. Her life is filled with complete happiness. "Marriage," says Simone de Beauvoir, "is the destiny traditionally offered by society."[5] De also fails to go beyond this tradition in this novel but in *Socialite Evenings* the boundaries are crossed boldly.

Shobha De has shown through Aasha Rani that marriage for women has great significance because it provides security. The ultimate happiness of a woman, according to Dé is localized in a good faithful husband, children and a family where mutual trust is the key value. This concept is nurtured and preserved in *Manusamhita* because this is how society can flourish under male control and supervision. Aasha Rani promises her husband, "you are a good man Jay. And I promise you I'll be a good mother to Sasha"(129). She keeps her promise but at a later stage, it is not reciprocated by her husband. It is obvious that De never negates the values of motherhood and wifehood.

Aasha Rani comes to India for a short visit and is surprised by the changes in her family: her sister Sudha had emerged as a famous star; the people had not forgotten her; her father was back home and was quite ill; her mother had lost the dictator-like image and was living at Sudha's mercy. An invitation from an old friend to a mahurat party, takes her once again near the flashbulbs of filmdom and everything comes back to her. She is touched by the moment. She realises that this was her world and she had missed it all. For the sake of her family, she had killed her dreams and ambition. This is, of course, expected from a woman. She had sacrificed her identity. But after all these years, she feels deceived.

This was hers. It was her home. She wanted to stay back. She wanted to enjoy the liberty of action, thought and "authentic selfhood." She feels pain for the missed opportunities.

On her husband's insistence Aasha Rani stays back but she is shocked to find that the gap of five years had demolished her heroine image for now she was being offered the role of a mother or a mother-in-law. Her marital status and her age were against the image of a heroine who is always a sex-object. She is disturbed by the change, and her world is further rocked by Sasha's call that tells her about her husband's affair with the nanny. Shattered Aasha Rani remarks: "Whichever way one looks at it, there was always a man in the picture. A man using, abusing and finally discarding a woman"(157).

Shobha De etches the picture of women who are consistently abused and experience great pain. A man seems to have the right to discard a woman under any pretext. Betrayed Aasha Rani reaches Wellington and she comes to know that her marriage is over. Her daughter rejects her and is not ready to accept a sari-clad Indian woman as her mother. Despite her best efforts, Aasha Rani is rejected from the role of a wife and a mother. The banishment of women from the domestic life and the ensuing problems are major issues of an Indian woman's life. She confronts the problems of survival boldly. Her inner strength compels her to fight a second battle. In India, marriage is the ultimate fate of a woman's life where the she is supposed to dedicate her life for the family and marriage till her death. Aasha Rani's failure in marriage is not due to her shortcomings. She is compelled to break her marriage not because her husband reflects her but it is she who has to pay. The attitude of men is summarised by her friend: "We demand communication, attention, pampering, Arrey baba forget it. We should be happy if they don't beat us, burn us, torture us, insult us, discard us. That is all"(117). This is the truth of a woman's life. It is women who have to make all compromises. Many of Shashi Deshpande's novels also reveal the same fact.

Aasha Rani returns to the film world with greater vengeance. She returns as a liberated queen. Helene Cixous in *The Laugh of the Medusa* has much to say about similar situations: "When the 'repressed' [women] of their culture, and their society returns, it's an explosive, *utterly* destructive, staggering return, with a force never yet unleashed, and equal to the most forbidding of suppressions."[6] For liberated and emancipated Aasha Rani sexual encounters and compromises become routine affairs. She creates her own value system. She meets Shonali. With her, she experiences a totally different lifestyle where all that matters is money. Shobha De, through Shonali, has shown the importance of financial independence and how women are driven into the life of sexual encounters.

De's women are fighters despite many odds Aasha Rani reopens appa's studio and dreams to make her daughter Sasha, "The Golden Girl of the silver screen"(234). With support, strength and courage she begins her life afresh. Now free, she has existence, belongingness and an opportunity to do something creative in life. She realises that she can succeed only on this soil of India and specially Madras to which she belongs.

In her portrayal of Aasha Rani, Dé in a way has followed the vamp school of feminism proposed by Sandra Gilbert and Susan Gubar in "The Mirror and the Vamp: Reflections on Feminist Criticism." In it they state, "The Vamp is glamorous, an actress in a kind of guerilla theatre, but the drama of seduction and betrayal that she enacts in her foray [...] may end up being as seductively treacherous to women as to men."[7] It is true that Aasha Rani is considered to be a vamp by many, but she is not so. She becomes a vamp due to circumstantial pressures. Her frustration, desperation seeks an outlet through sexual activity and there are many males who are ready to take advantage of her temporary weakness. She is also constantly betrayed. Many issues and problems of a woman's life is reflected through Aasha Rani's life story.

Malini, the wife of Akshay Arora, a typical traditional housewife, abandons her career as a ghazal singer and accepts to become a doormat. But her sacrifice has no value for Akshay who plays with other women. She is totally devoted to her husband and fools herself when she says: "It proves that he is my man. My husband. He may sleep with dozen of prostitutes like you. But I am the one he respects; whose home he regards as his own"(49).

In this male dominated society there are many women who stay behind the four walls and keep themselves happy with whatever they have. In fact, they have no choice. Patriarchy has preached that having been given a husband, home, children and some financial security women have no reason to complain. Satisfaction of their physical, emotional, psychological and financial needs can be ignored legitimately by the masters. Like beggars, they cannot be choosers. The issue of wifehood is projected through the story of amma and Malini. Both are betrayed factually, but amma is totally abandoned while Malini is rejected metaphorically.

Through the character of Rita, Shobha De has portrayed a woman who can find a solution for the betrayed wives like Malini. Rita is the efficient wife who makes compromises to live a happy married life. To her, romance in marriage is an illusion and it "finishes the morning after the wedding night"(50). It is followed by a painful and long dragging period of "boredom" for women because all men like "variety"(50). But this variety is not permitted to women. Shobha De through Rita projects a practical and clear picture of marriage: "Most women shared their husbands—it's a fact. They hate marriage. That's also a fact. But what else they can do? What is the choice? The only way to make a marriage work is true sex—and most women hate that too. But the day a man feels that his woman has lost interest in sex and therefore in him, the relationship is finished and he starts looking elsewhere. Aasha Rani and her kind are always waiting"(50). Shobha De's observations on the institution of marriage expressed through Rita are practical and true: "A wife is acting all the time - this is the world's best kept secret ... Everything is decided by the bed. On the bed...no woman should be foolish enough to be honest with her husband where sex is concerned"(50).

Many of De's women characters act according to their own will and live happily in the social system. Issues and problems are there, but women have learnt to manipulate them. She seems to suggest in the novel that the institution of marriage, love, family, trust etc, are all illusions but in personal interviews her opinion is quite different. In an interview given to Malavika Sanghvi she says, "[...] even though it [marriage] has become fashionable to degrade it, the system is unbeatable."[8]

De has touched upon the issue of lesbianism. Through Linda a journalist friend of Aasha Rani. Shobha De has dealt with lesbianism as a very natural phenomenon and logically has treated it with sympathy. It is very difficult for the traditional society to accept this kind of relationship but she has attempted to change this outlook. Simone de Beauvoir has observed that a lesbian relationship is based on a mutual glorification and love for the other: "Between women love is contemplative; caresses are intended less to gain possession of the other than gradually to recreate the self through her; separateness is abolished, there is no struggle, no victory, no defeat; in exact reciprocity each is at once subject and object, sovereign and slave; duality becomes mutuality."[9]

De in the novel has not given much importance to lesbianism but the implications are very much present. Aasha Rani's lesbian experience in this novel is a way to freedom that nurses, nourishes, and guides a broken soul and body. Bonding between women is often depicted by women writers. Women's issues are related with women's rights and empowerment. De has empowered women with lesbian relationships also. She views it not as an aberration but as a means of acquiring women's independence from men. Women are often manipulated to oppose each other. This is an attempt by patriarchy to divide and rule. De sabotages the attempt by unifying the opposing forces.

Most of the female characters in this novel are exploited, suppressed and crushed and these are the major issues of a woman's life. Anita Desai, the great Indian novelist and a pioneer of feminism reveals the grinding suppression of women in India: "Even if in reality she is nothing but a common drudge, first in her father's house and then her husband's—a beast of burden bearing an endless string of children, putting up with any brutality or disloyalty or failing of her husband—she has no alternative: she must live as Sita did, as Draupadi did; she is Durga incarnate."[10] Desai's last four words are ironically stated. Women are used and abused in the name of tradition and mythology.

De's female characters are different. They protest against the massive oppression and exploitation that is carried through historical, philosophical, cultural and ideological constructs. But the path of liberation, chosen by her protagonists is closely dotted with frustration, pain, depression, many existential disasters and failure. De convincingly transforms Aasha Rani from a simple, ordinary girl to a successful career oriented practical business woman.

In the course of the novel several issues have been discussed. A woman's role as mother and wife, her need and desire for sexual freedom, her economic independence, the problems of mother-daughter relationship, her search for identity and her placement in the equation of power struggle are some of the issues that have been highlighted. It is very difficult to create a platform in this male dominated society where things are easily acceptable. A woman's dream is always looked down upon because her image is of a "permanent giver." Her ambition is condemned as selfishness. She is expected to remain always passive and acted upon. But Aasha Rani, the protagonist of De, wins her battles through great sacrifices and achieves success. De has also illustrated Aasha Rani's use of her sexuality as a mode of defiance, and a show of power. She has revealed the hypocrisy, double standards of people in the filmdom.

References

1. Shobha De, *Shooting from the Hip: Selected Writings,* New Delhi: UBS, 1994, p.113.
2. Annis Pratt, *Archetypal Patterns in Women's Fiction,* Bloomington: Indiana University, 1981, p. 135.
3. Ibid.
4. Shobha De, *Starry Nights,* New Delhi: Penguin Books, 1991, p.24. All subsequent textual quotations are from this edition and have been indicated by page numbers in parentheses.
5. Simone de Beauvoir, *The Second Sex,* trans. and ed. H.M. Parshley, London: Penguin, 1974, p.55.
6. Helene Cixous, "The Laugh of the Medusa", trans. Keith Cohen and Paula Cohen (OUP,1976), p. 246. Originally published in French in *1975);* reprinted in New French Feminisms, ed. Elaine Marks and Isabelle de Courtivron, University of Massachusetts Press, Cambridge, MA, 1981, pp. *245-264.*

7. Sandra M. Gilbert and Susan Gubar, "The Mirror and the Vamp: Reflections on Feminist Criticism", in *The Future of Literary Theory*, ed. Ralph Cohen New York: Routledge, 1985, p. 154.
8. Malavika Sangghvi, Interview with Shobha De, "De One and Only", *The Times of India*, Delhi: 10 April 2005.
9. Simone de Beauvoir, *op.cit.*
10. Anita Desai, "Secret Connivance", *Times Literary Supplement*, 14 September 1990, p. 972.

22 The Changing World of Women in Rama Mehta's *Inside the Haveli*

— Sudhi Rajiv

In the post-independence period women are gradually occupying the centre-stage along with the other oppressed groups. It is natural, therefore, that women writers and even male writers should treat them in diverse aspects. Their novels reflect the varied features of contemporary Indian society on the threshold of awakening and change.

Rama Mehta's *Inside the Haveli* (1977) which won the Sahitya Akademy Award in 1979 depicts the lives of women inside a haveli in Udaipur, Rajasthan. Mehta skilfully describes the hopes and despair, superstitions and beliefs, joys and sorrows of the women inside the haveli. My paper examines how traditional values and practices are negotiated in the present times by different classes of women inside the haveli.

Geeta, an educated girl from Bombay where there was "free mingling of men and women", is married into an aristocratic family where women "remained in purdah". This juxtaposition of different worlds: the urban modern world *vis-à-vis* the traditional conservative world, the world of the poor *vis-à-vis* the world of the rich and the joint family *vis-à-vis* the individual provide for a variety and complexity of human relationship within the family. Her marriage to Ajay Singh is a marriage into a family dominated by patriarchal feudalism. Geeta has to live in "a constricted atmosphere of world of women" where men are regarded as Gods. But the male dominated world is confined only to the men's section. Rama Mehta wants us to see the haveli which has "no shape from the outside, but inside there is a definite plan" (6). It is the women who are at the centre of the novel. The onslaught of the collective will of the women of the haveli does not completely efface Geeta's individuality, although it does restore communal values. Though in the beginning she is irritated and angry at the loss of her individuality she later, to some extent, internalises the discipline of the haveli. The life inside the haveli is regulated by a strict code of conduct, reducing relationships to a fixed pattern. Any violation is resisted and frowned upon. Those who are inducted into this closed world are indoctrinated in such a way that they are made to accept it as the only way of life worth living. The desire for change is suppressed. The apparent homogeneity and togetherness are deceptive but they are accepted in the name of tradition, custom and family values which give the haveli a distinct character. Men interact with the outside world but women remain within the closed system and are supposed to preserve the values. Women are not expected to speak, question or reveal their emotions to any one outside the confines of the haveli. Geeta is supposed to obey the commands of her grandmother-in-law, mother-in-law and even Pari, the oldest maid servant of the family. These matriarchs control the environment in the haveli. "This hierarchical weave of generations of mistresses and generations of servants complex in its patterning of personal loyalties and power rivalries, is the synchronic pole of communal identity, for the book shows repeatedly the emotional investments everyone has in everyone else's lives" (Siegle 23).

It takes almost fifteen years for Geeta to adjust herself to the life of haveli. It is her mother-in-law's love and concern that wins her heart and draws her into the life of haveli. Thus we see Geeta growing into the "web of relations" herself. Though she has accepted the discipline of the haveli without protest, there are many times "when she [feels] the crushing weight of the walls that shut off the outside world" (88). Her resentment of 'male privileges' of food, separate and more comfortable section in the haveli and also their 'remoteness' wherein they do not allow wives to go alone with their husbands, is more forceful than her submission to the traditions of the haveli. She expresses her frustration at living within the confined gendered space of the haveli: "I know the men have no problems in the world of Udaipur; you are all pampered. You lead your lives and think women are mere chattels" (53). The dream of leaving Udaipur dies in her heart. At the same time she feels relieved for at last she is sure that her life was to be in the haveli.

It is she who induces the inhabitants of the haveli into a silent transformation that is provided by education and awakening. It is interesting that the changes in human environment are brought about by a woman. She is not a rebel nor is she a radical feminist – but in her own quiet way she brings about changes in the lives of young girls in the family and outside. She does not completely conform to the old mores of the haveli but she absorbs some of its values. That is why the resistance to it is not violent. She starts teaching women from all classes of society. Initially there is a lot of resistance (the maid servants think that an educated girl would be a total misfit in the community) but their criticism does not deter her and she is determined to empower the servants and their children through education. With the support of her in-laws and her husband she is able to send Sita (the daughter of a run-away maid) and Ravi (a bright servant boy) to school. She herself runs her own 'school' and teaches servants, their children and the daughters of the haveli.

For those who find it impossible to read and write, Geeta starts sewing classes and engages a woman to teach them to cut and embroider. The tangible effect of all these efforts is that they get economic independence. "Binniji [has] changed the lives of these girls... most of them now can read and write; they can get work"(191). Women from other havelis complain that education is "making rebels of our servants"(165). Pari recognises the undertone of the complaints: "their own daughters and daughters-in-law come and sit for hours with Binniji. It's only the poor that they prevent from coming" because they no longer have to "depend on the havelis"(191). Geeta is instrumental in changing the lives of these girls.

Geeta achieves another victory when she does not consent to the engagement of her very young daughter, Vijay with a well-bred, educated young man from another haveli. "If I have ruined my life, the children are not going to ruin theirs" (206) and she tells her husband that she cannot "be fooled again. I know nothing matters more than money and prestige to you all"(207). She thinks that the union of two havelis through marriage was more important than the fact that Vijay "would languish in the vast haveli"(220). Her daughter becomes "one locus" of her resistance. She does not accept the proposal in spite of the persuasion of her in-laws though she does rethink about it towards the end of the novel. It is with determination and humility that she tackles the problem of child marriage. In Geeta we find a harmonious blending of the positive phase of tradition and modernity.

Often in my reading of the book I feel disturbed with the fact that Geeta refuses to the engagement of her daughter at such an early age but she agrees with her mother-in-law (after a little resistance, of course) to get Sita married and stop her schooling. "Binniji, you have made Sita's life... But now we must accept their condition"(188). She is forced to accept that marriage is the only security for women. As the children and women learn to read and write Geeta gets a deeper understanding of poverty. She consents to the marriage because she comes to understand that for the poor it was important to abide by family customs otherwise they would lose the family's approval.

As a woman belonging to Rajasthan I have a first-hand knowledge of its tradition-bound system, its hierarchal social and familial structure especially for the poor which is very difficult to do away with. It is Geeta who has made it possible for Sita to be married into a family with land, a well, a house and bullocks. It is from her that we can learn not to define ourselves definitively but in constant contextualisation. Geeta, the new mistress of the haveli, has transformed traditions, fought her battles, achieved her victory and made the "gift of learning" to posterity.

In post-independence India, patriarchal hierarchy co-existed with a developing democratic ethos. A new class of women emerged who were shaped by old traditions and strengthened by the power of education they had acquired. These women liberated themselves from the hold of conformism and male domination. They tried to control their own environment and to improve women's educational and economic opportunities.

Geeta is a humanist in action who is able to modify tradition and reorganise the social forms. She herself undergoes change and brings about a change through her action. This modern educated woman belonging to the upper echelons of society schools the other women and is responsible for the arousal of "humanist consciousness" in both the men and women in the haveli.

There is a subliminal message in the novel. Though hers was a struggle for independence, she would never have been able to achieve anything without the support of her husband and father-in-law. Her struggle, therefore, is not so much against patriarchy as against a social system that denied women their due. For me Geeta finally emerges as a humanist who has opened the way for the other women to free themselves from the circumscribed reality of their lives. She offers the way for a positive change by means of education, protesting against child marriage and differential treatment of boys and girls. She has opened up new horizons of possibilities arousing a sense of self-worth and self-esteem in women. It is through education that such a change is effected. Once the girls begin to perceive things for themselves they begin to question and change. In words of T.L. Vasvani, "Education must be illuminated and re-illuminated in the light of the soul... The new community of girls and women in India must be a community of Light. And Light knows no distinction or creed or community" (Ruhela 167). It is into this world of Light that Geeta has moved the women of the haveli.

Works Cited

Mehta, Rama. *Inside the Haveli,* New Delhi: Penguin Books, 1977. Subsequent references to this work are marked in the text in parentheses.

Ruhela, Saryu. *Understanding the Indian Women Today: Problems and Challenges.* Delhi: Indian Publishers' Distributors, 1999.

Siegle, Robert B. *Mirror to Mirror : Post Modernity in South Asian Fiction,* Online. Centre for Digital Discourse and Culture at Virgina Tech., 2002. Internet. 29 July 2005. Available www2.cddc.vt.edu/mtm/four.htm.

23 Celebration of Women's Sexuality in Eve Ensler's *The Vagina Monologues*

— Ujjwala Tathe

It is said that history repeats itself. Well, history has repeated itself but with a significant difference. Eve has once again entered the forbidden zone. This time not innocently but deliberately and cautiously; without any inhibitions, awkwardness, shame, and guilt. The forbidden fruit is nothing but her exploration of women's 'self' and their sexuality. Eve has taken a bold step to awaken women to celebrate their "down there" in all its complexity and mystery. Her giant step is towards the reclamation of womanhood and her own humanity. No doubt, the fall has turned out a boon in disguise. Let us salute this Eve who is strong and courageous enough in revising and/or refuting the age-old conventions, prejudices, ideas, misconceptions regarding female sexuality.

The modern revolutionary Eve, Eve Ensler, an American feminist, has challenged the male bastion by giving a call to women across the world to fight the violence directed against them. In fact, the need for this call is deeply rooted in the ideology of feminism in understanding the world and changing it to the advantage of women. Though today some women occupy covetous positions as prime ministers, administrators, scientists, and many more, the feminists still assert that there is a need to overthrow social practices that lead to the oppression and victimisation of women. The last few decades of feminism were marked by a deep anger as the truth of violence against the female body was revealed in the form of rape, childhood sexual abuse, anti-lesbian violence, physical abuse, sexual harassment, terrorism against reproductive freedom, or the international crime of female genital mutilation.

Unfortunately, though the learned world today is progressing with an awesome hi-tech speed, women still have to demand and fight for their right to live. They still are miserable victims of horrifying atrocities. This is the reason why a woman like Eve Ensler comes forward to awaken in them a joyous consciousness to realise their own power, the possibility of unprecedented personal growth and the strength to release the energy long suppressed. Well, the time has come for women to realise their precious 'self' and an importance of their meaningful emancipation. The woman should gain, as Barbara Berg says, "freedom to decide her own destiny; freedom from sex-determined roles; freedom from society's oppressive restrictions; freedom to express her own thoughts fully and to convert them freely to actions".

Being an idol for both women and men for her unflinching efforts to run an anti-violence campaign for women, Eve Ensler, in fact needs no introduction. However, in India, except for some activists and literaties, she seems invisible for the masses. Hence, this attempt to introduce her. Ensler is an American award-winning playwright, performer, and feminist activist best known for the play *The Vagina Monologues.* Ensler's other works comprise plays titled *Conviction, Lemonade,The Depot, Floating Rhoda etc.,* and books like *V-World, I Am An Emotional Creature* and *Vagina Warriors.* She has also been involved in several films like *Fear No More: Stop Violence Against Women* (2002),*The Vagina Monologues* (2002), *Until the Violence Stops* (2003), and *What I Want My Words to Do to You: Voices From Inside a Women's Maximum Security Prison* (2003).

As a prominent anti-violence activist, Eve Ensler has devoted her life to stopping violence and envisioning a planet in which women and girls will be free to thrive, rather than merely survive. In February 2004, she, alongside Sally Field, Jane Fonda and Christine Lahti, protested to have the Mexican government re-investigate the slayings of hundreds of women in Ciudad Juarez on Mexico-Texas borders.

Eve Ensler's seminal play *The Vagina Monologues* was written in 1996 as a response to the guilt and embarrassment that many women still connect with their bodies and/or their sexuality. It is written in episodic manner and translated in 45 languages. It gives voice to women's deepest sentiments, hidden fantasies and fears. With humour and grace, the play celebrates women's sexuality and strength. The play is born out of Ensler's interaction with a vast crosssection of women covering religion, language, country and culture. She interviewed over 200 women: young, old, married, single, lesbians, college professors, actors, corporate professionals, high-powered businesswomen, sex workers, and many women across the globe, making them talk about their vaginas. The play is thus what she calls "vagina interviews." While interacting with the women, she found: "At first the women were reluctant to talk. They were a little shy. However, once they got going, you couldn't stop them...They got very excited, mainly because no one's ever asked them before." The strange experiences of these women created a strong urge in her to address their suffocated and suppressed feelings through the play. On hearing the heart-rending experiences, she comments. "...the desecration of women indicated the failure of human beings to honor and protect life and that this failing would, if we did not correct it, be the end of us all.... When you rape, beat, maim, mutilate, burn, bury, and terrorize women, you destroy the essential life energy on the planet. You force what is meant to be open, trusting, nurturing, creative and alive, to be bent, infertile and broken."

In order to reach people, Ensler began her show by reading out the memoirs, desires, and humiliating events of victimised women. It was her attempt to share very personal stories that had been told to her. After every show, she would meet hundreds of women wanting to talk to her about their lives. She heard the same stories — women being raped as teenagers, as little girls, as elderly women; women who finally escaped being beaten to death by their husbands; women who were taken sexually before they were even conscious of sex, by their step fathers, brothers, cousins, uncles, mothers, and fathers. Ensler was being told the things she was not supposed to know. In one of her interviews she says, "by talking about them, they made themselves more real, more present and more legitimate." Ensler has turned these intimate narratives into poetry that celebrates women's strength and individuality.

The Vagina Monologues is made up of a varying number of monologues read by varying number of women. Every monologue in this episodic play relates to the vagina, be it through sex, love, mutilation, menstruation, masturbation, birth, orgasm, the variety of names for the vagina, or simply as a physical aspect of femal body. Every monologue has the power of saying the unsayable. With the monologues, Ensler's use of language is more of an examination of what the word 'vagina' is and why people are afraid to say it.

The monologue "My Vagina was My Village" is dedicated to the women returned from the rape camp in Bosnia. Ensler appreciates the spirit of one of the victims who now says:

> They invaded it. Butchered it and burned it down.
> I do not touch now.
> Don't visit.
> I live someplace else now.
> I don't know where that is.

In "My Angry Vagina", a woman humorously rants about injustices wrought against the vagina, such as tampons, douches, and the tools used by gynaecologists.

"The Little Coochie Snorcher" is about memories of traumatic sexual experiences of a woman in her childhood and a positive healing sexual experience in her adolescent years. Another monologue "The Flood" gives a heart-rending account of a girl who was humiliated and made ashamed of her own vagina. She reflects on asking: "What would it wear?" She says, "It would wear a big sign: Closed Due to Flooding." And when asked, "What would it say?" Regretfully she says: ...It's a place you don't go. It's closed up."

Ensler recounts her own experience regarding the birth of her granddaughter in "I Was there in the Room". Awestruck by the capacity and power of the vagina, she finds great resemblance between heart and vagina. She says:

The heart is capable of sacrifice.
So is the vagina.
The heart is able to forgive and repair.
It can change its shape to let us in.
It can expand to let us out.
So can the vagina.
It can ache for us and stretch for us,
die for us and bleed for us into this difficult,
Wondrous world. So can the vagina.

"I was Twelve. My Mother Slapped Me" echoes the fear, confusion, enthusiasm, curiosity, guilt, and a pleasurable realization of being a woman. The women interviewed echo "a kind of wild collective song." The monologue talks about the first experiences of menstruation. When asked how they felt, the women as well as girls articulate their intimate feelings: "I associated my periods with inexplicable phenomena;" "(It) Changed my whole feeling about myself;" "I'm a woman;" "(I was) Terrified." The woman in "The Vagina Workshop" reveals her intimate interaction with her vagina. For her it was "a mystical, magical thing" and recognition of "me," "the essence of me." Also included in the special edition are testimonials from young women who have performed the monologues successfully at their colleges for V-Day as part of a nationwide campaign to stop violence against women. Ensler also gives an account of mixed reactions *The Vagina Monologues* earned from TV channels, newspapers, common people, high schools, colleges, feminists and critics.

First performed in the basement of the Cornelia Street Café in *SoHo*, New York, in 1996, *The Vagina Monologues* has been performed in 76 countries. After the initial hiccups, the performances have succeeded in opening a window showing new perspective of women's sexuality to men. In these performances, Ensler is joined by celebrities like Whoopi Goldberg, Cate Blanchett, Kate Winslet, Meera Syal, Jane Fonda, Oprah Winfrey, Glenn Close, Susan Sarandon, Donna Hanover, New York City's first lady and many more. Today it is running in theaters all over the world, including sold-out runs at both Off-Broadway's Westside Theatre and on London's West End. Eve Ensler has written the play with such a might that its reading and viewing makes sure that no one will ever look at woman's body or think of sex in quite the same way again. Gloria Steinem in her Foreword writes: "It offers an encouragement to both men and women to emerge from the pages not only feeling more free within themselves and about each other but with alternatives to the old patriarchal dualism of feminine/masculine, body/mind, and sexual/ spiritual that is rooted in the division of our physical selves into 'the part we talk about' and 'the part we don't.'"

The book concludes with an account of an emergence of the V-Day. Ensler's experience performing *The Vagina Monologues* inspired her to create one of its kinds V-Day—a catalyst, a performance that simply demands that the violence must end. Every year it is celebrated on February 14, Valentine's Day. Began in 1998, this global, grassroots movement has spread its roots in many countries. Funds are raised through benefit performances of *The Vagina Monologues* staged at college campuses and communites around the world. The benefit goes to rapist crisis centres. The "V" in V-Day stands for Valentine, Vagina and Violence, linking love and respect to ending violence against women and girls. What started as a play has become an international phenomenon!

While in a country like India, the message of the work needs to penetrate into the masses, especially when incidents of gang rape, female child abuse, domestic violence and marital violence are on the rise. The word "vagina" is still a taboo and hence faces immense reservations not only among orthodox, uneducated women folks but also among the educated class. Only one performance in Mumbai is insufficient to educate a billion odd population of this country. Director-actor Mahabanoo Mody-Kotwal whose production of the play created quite a stir in the metropolitan cities says: "Only now is the Indian woman experimenting with and discovering her sexuality. It's funny that we use sex to sell anything from cars to vacuum cleaners but don't talk about it." Ironically, though this June the play is set to celebrate its 300th show in India, it has failed to reach to the grass root level where the exposure is really needed. However, in India, the concept and Ensler's objective behind using the word 'Vagina' needs to be put through. Then only we can join our hands and blend in our voices with what Sojourner Truth says:

> If the first woman God ever made
> Was strong enough to turn the world
> Upside down all alone,
> These women together ought to be able
> To turn it back, and get it right side up again!

Work Cited

Ensler, Eve. *The Vagina Monologues,* New York: Villard Books, 1998.

24 Unpeeling the Layers of Draupadi

— Archna Sahni

The revival of mythological themes witnessed on the Indian cultural scene since the 1980's, and the ongoing debate on the woman question, are obviously related. Myths in India are not "vestiges of the wishful fantasies of whole nations",[1] as Freud defines it, but constitute a living cultural idiom that orders and re-enforces reality. This paper is an attempt to understand and explain why five mythological or epic women celebrated in our culture have been clubbed together as the *panchakanyas,* and why remembering them is said to be redemptive. The paper focuses mainly on Draupadi but in order to understand why the term *kanya* is used to describe the five women, I will on occasion touch upon the other four.

The source of the *panchakanya* concept in question is a supposedly popular *shloka* of obscure origin celebrating the redemptive value of the *panchakanyas* or five maidens—Ahalya, Tara, Mandodari, Kunti, Draupadi: *"ahalya draupadi kunti tara mandodari tatha / panchakanya smaranityam mahapataka nashaka//"*.[2]

It is not a straightforward *shloka,* as it calls five full-grown 'women' as 'kanyas', and moreover, says that their daily invocation can redeem us of our sins. Why are these five married women called *kanyas*? Who is to be redeemed by the recollection of the *kanyas,* and why is remembering the *kanyas* redemptive? These two interrelated issues shall also be considered.

According to the *Shabdakalpadruma,* an eight-year-girl is called *gauri,* a nine-year-old *rohini* and a ten-year-old *kanya. Kanya* is defined as a virgin or unmarried girl. But we find that in the *panchakanya shloka* the term *kanya* is applied to women who are not only not *kanyas* in the former sense, they all have also sexually co-habited or had a sexual encounter with more than one man. This includes even Mandodari, as there are traditions such as the Bengali Krittibas, *the Ramayana* and the Oriya Balaramdas *Ramayana* that refer to Mandodari marrying Vibhishana. In the case of Ahalya and Kunti, the man in question is other than her husband.

Our interpretation is helped by the fact that all the *kanyas* except Kunti have been included in a *shloka* celebrating the five *pativratas*. Kunti has been replaced by Sita. The *shloka* occurs in an article titled "Pativrata"[3] written by Shuchivrat Lakhanpal Shastri: *"ahilya draupadi tara sita mandodari samah/dharma ritini baddhastah sarvah santi pativrata//"*.

All the *kanyas* of the *panchakanya shloka* are also *pativratas* except for Kunti. It seems that Draupadi, on account of being 'married' to five men, was allowed entry into *pativrataloka* while Kunti who 'slept' with her four god-husbands and accepted the pre-marital embraces of Surya, was banished from the same. Kunti is the odd woman out, as she is apparently the most transgressive of the lot. But is she really transgressive? After all, she only follows the orders of Pandu to produce offspring via *niyoga,* an occurrence which has been allegorised as Kunti's summoning of gods to father sons on her.

Kunti's replacement by Sita as a *pativrata* hints to us that what is at work in the usage of the term *kanya* is nothing but patriarchy's age-old preoccupation and fascination with the idea of virginity for women. To understand why these five have been called *kanyas* or why Draupadi has been called a *kanya,* we have to consider the place of virginity within patriarchal society. Let us unpeel the layers of Draupadi, by unpeeling the layers of meaning contained in 'kanya'.

Layer One: Untouched by Man: Virginity as Chastity

Virginity as an ideal for women was instituted and popularised during the consolidation of patriarchy. The cornerstone of patriarchy is the notion of woman as property and the stipulation of monogamy for women. Chastity in a woman is symbolised by the condition of virginity before marriage. Virginity before marriage ensures the marriageability (read sale value or exchange value) of woman. Within the marriage, virginity translates as chastity, or sexual and emotional fidelity to her lawfully wedded husband, and makes it possible to identify the paternity of the child. This in turn secures inheritance to legitimate offspring. It is to perpetuate the stability of patriarchy through producing legitimate offspring on chaste wives that the ideal of *pativrata* and *sati* has been glorified through the ages.

Can Draupadi be called a *kanya*? In the ordinary or literal sense of being a virgin or untouched by a man, we could say that prior to her polyandrous marriage Draupadi is a *kanya*.

Layer Two: Ever-chaste Women: Virginity as Expediency

It is interesting to observe the manner in which the *Mahabharata* voices its confusion over sexual morality. The method Kunti adopts to obtain sons from various gods in none other than *niyoga*, one that Vyasa himself practiced with Ambika, Ambalika and a Shudra maid to father Dhritrashtra, Pandu and Vidura respectively. Yet in Kunti's case it is not openly admitted and therefore allegorised. It is for the same reason that Vyasa—as a character in the epic—intervenes to provide justification for Draupadi's polyandrous marriage. Despite the fact that he regards the practice as "old and eternal" and "quite conformable to virtue,"[4] he feels compelled to narrate numerous tales in support of the practice.

Scholars have testified that the *Mahabharata* contains accretive layers as it developed over the centuries. Sarva Daman Singh's *Polyandry in Ancient India*[5] marshals ample evidence from the epics and other ancient texts to prove that polyandry was widely known and practiced in ancient India including the time contemporaneous with the action of *Mahabharata*. It is probable that later redactors uncomfortable with practices such as *niyoga* and polyandry which seemed to them morally reprehensible, attempted to explain them away by recourse to mystification, allegory, and the miraculous. Hence in the epic, Gods and revered *rishis* grant boons of virginity to women when it is required that they either satisfy their lust or when the husband commands the wife to beget sons via *niyoga* to keep alive the family line.

The *Mahabharata* is clearly aware that monogamy as an institution has evolved over time, and the origin of monogamy is clearly mentioned. It is stated that it was the promulgation of Svetaketu, son of Uddalaka, who introduced the patriarchal form of marriage with monogamy for women. The epic acknowledges sexual morality to be relative with time and place. Co-existing with the kingdom of Hastinapur, Panchala and the Yadavas were regions whose marriage laws were different from those that are upheld in the *Mahabharata,* namely, monogamy for women, and within it, the ideal of *pativratya.* The epic itself says that the women of Vahikas, Madrakas and Sindhu-Sauviras had sexual freedom. Madradesa, which might have had a communal marriage system with the concomitant much greater freedoms for women, is therefore derided by Karna for the promiscuity of its women. Uttara-kuru is spoken of as a paradise of plenty where women make love with whomsoever they choose. It is in this context that we must understand the preoccupation with virginity in the *Mahabharata.* The preoccupation with the idea and ideal of virginity or a woman's *kanyabhava* is the result of a dual effort. It reveals the narrators' attempt to counter the seemingly strange and sinful sexual laws co-existing with the "Kuru-Pancala cultural complex,"[6] and at the same time to consolidate the idea of virginity as a moral and social value.

In the *Mahabharata* the concept of *kanyabhava* or virginity in a woman seems to be a double-edged sword. On one hand it is set up as an ideal for women within monogamy. On the other hand, and ironically, the virginity of women is seen as a non-issue or one that can be regained after her monthly bath in case her person is required to be lent or exchanged. Thus, it is not surprising to hear that "women, gems, and rivers can never be soiled". Madhavi, who is gifted with renewable virginity, is willfully sold by her father over and over again to perpetuate four royal lineages that would have otherwise ended childless. This is an instance of virginity treated at its most expedient in the *Mahabharata,* wherein we see how a woman becomes a mere pawn in the world of masculine action, where notions of purity and impurity are continuously modified to suit the ends to be achieved.

In the case of Draupadi we are told the fantastic story of how she retained her *kanyabhava* or virgin status after consummating each consecutive marriage with the Pandava brothers.[7] That Draupadi could be thought capable of retaining her virginity after marriage with each Pandava, and Kunti thought to preserve hers even after giving birth to Karna, tells us that the idea of virginity was not conceived as an irreversible event after the initial defloration of the woman. The loss of virginity persisted for some time after an encounter with a man, and it was something that could be re-attained through a boon or purification ceremony. Such an expedient treatment of virginity in the *Mahabharata* should not be surprising, for as we have seen, the editors and redactors of the epic were beset with having to make sense of varying sexual mores and marriage customs in synchronous time, and at the same time establish the pre-eminence of virginity as an ideal for women within the patriarchal institution of monogamy.

The notion of Draupadi persisting as a *kanya* or virgin despite consummating her marriages with the Pandavas is meant to testify to her chastity, and hence suitability for marriage or marriages. Whereas the various stories narrated by Vyasa stem from a desire to rationalis e the practice of polyandry, the conferring of the boon of virginity on Draupadi is an attempt to accommodate the idea of virginity or chastity outside the boundaries of monogamy for a woman.

Layer Three: Kanya: the Goddess in Woman

Could the expedient treatment of virginity be a carry-over of an attitude from a previously matriarchal age in which women had much more freedom and the notion of sin was not linked to sexuality, and in which 'promiscuity' as a concept did not exist? What would the notion of *kanya* have been in such an age where women possessed much greater freedom? Leonie Caldecott's reading of the esoteric meaning of Goddess Durga is relevant here:

> Durga's name means "Beyond Reach". This to me is an echo of the woman warrior's fierce, virginal autonomy.... This is

> not meant in the limiting sense understood by the patriarchal order, but rather in Esther Harding's sense: she is "one-in-herself"... part of the reach she puts herself beyond so adamantly is the reach of society's attempt to describe her to herself. The more repressive the images available to women, the more the virgin condition becomes a defence against these. In extremis, women will reject womanhood itself, if the condition "unable to move around freely", both physically and psychically, is seen necessarily to accompany it.[8]

Caldecott's reference to the analytical psychologist, Esther Harding, in the above quote is from Harding's book, *Woman's Mysteries,* which attempts to present certain archetypal foundations to feminine psychology through a study of the inner life of woman as portrayed in religious myths and rituals. The phrase "one-in-herself" occurs in the chapter "The Virgin Goddess" where Harding explains the concept of virginity within the context of moon goddesses in ancient myths. "The chief characteristic of the goddess in her crescent phase", she points out, "is that she is virgin;"[9] her divine power does not depend on or derive from her relation to a male husband-god, she bears divinity in her own right. Applying this idea to real-life women, Harding explains, "the woman who is a virgin, one-in-herself, does what she does—not because of any desire to please, not to be liked, or to be approved... but because what she does is true."[10] Such a woman, whether married or unmarried, whose actions might indeed appear to be unconventional, possesses an inner attitude of 'psychological virginity', which does not make her dependant on someone or something outside her own psyche. We might add to this explanation the observation that to this day *kanya* is used as an epithet for Goddess Durga. This seems to convey the idea that a woman becomes truly autonomous or truly her own person only when she realises the Goddess within herself; realising her own Goddess-energy or *shakti* within, she herself becomes Goddess-like.

Is Draupadi a *kanya* in the sense of a woman who is "one-in-herself" or autonomous being? I'm afraid that the aforementioned explanation does not seem to fittingly describe any of the *panchakanyas*, including Draupadi. All of the women function squarely within the precincts of patriarchy, and do not challenge them in any way.

To my mind, Draupadi functions primarily as a narrative tool in the hands of Vyasa. Even Draupadi's thirst for revenge that fuels the main course of action eventually leading to the annihilation of the *kshatriya* race, is preordained. Draupadi's birth, her polyandrous marriage, even her ceaseless quest for revenge—all are preordained. She is merely an instrument for fulfilling a purpose that is not of her own choosing. Hence she does not appear to be "one-in-herself" or a woman who functions autonomously. In this regard we note that another epithet for her along with Krishna and Yajnaseni is Panchali, which besides meaning native of the kingdom of Panchala, also signifies 'doll' or 'puppet'. Her being gambled away by her husband is not the only way in which she is treated as a puppet. Throughout the entire canvas of the epic she is continuously manipulated for ends that were not her own but which she was nevertheless destined to fulfil. Draupadi as Panchali hints to us that for all her fire, she was never her own person. In the sense of Caldecott's or Harding's definition of a virgin, we could say that Draupadi is a woman who despite having the potential of becoming a *kanya,* is not allowed to become one.

Is Draupadi a *kanya* in the sense of being a Goddess? Draupadi is certainly likened to a goddess in the epic. But it is only as a spouse goddess that she is identified, not as a mother goddess. Her polyandrous marriage is justified on the grounds that she was an incarnation of Sri, and the five Pandavas, incarnations of former Indras. Only when links between the potential *kanya* Draupadi and the unspoused goddess Kali or Durga are forged, does Draupadi evolve into a *kanya* as described by Caldecott. We see this in a popular religious tradition of South India, the Draupadi Amman cult. In this cult Draupadi, having been assimilated to the Navaratri worship of Durga, is transformed into a primal goddess and worshipped as a primary deity.[11]

Layer Four: Going to the Root of *Kanya*: I Desire, Therefore I am

I suggest that the key to the deepest layer of meaning of *kanya* possibly lies in the root that governs the word. *Kanya* comes from the root *kam*, meaning 'to desire'. We get a glimpse into this level of meaning when Surya plays etymologist in his quest to seduce Kunti:

> Do thou listen to my words! It is because a virgin desireth the company of every one, that she hath received the appellation of Kanya, from the root kama meaning to desire. Therefore ... a virgin is, by nature, free in this world. Thou shalt not, O lady, by any means, be guilty of any sin by complying with my request .... That all men and women should be bound by no restraints, is the law of nature. The opposite condition is the perversion of the natural state.[12]

It is interesting to note that Sanskrit scholars of my acquaintance translated *kanya* in the above passage as 'one who is desired', which was not surprising, for this is a notion—or should we say interpretation?—enforced by patriarchy through the ages. It is possible that the interpretation of *kanya* as one who is desired seems to be the result of a patriarchal distortion, while its original meaning—or at least its 'other' meaning—seems to be that of 'one who desires', a meaning which views woman as her own agent, and harmonises with Leonie Caldecott's explanation of woman as virgin. The two interpretations of *kanya* are certainly not mutually exclusive. *Kanya* as a ten year old, after all, is a girl on the threshold of puberty, close to becoming a *rajasvala* or a menstruating girl/ woman; this is also a time when a girl becomes sexually aware; hence, the meaning of *kanya* as one who desires as well one who is desired, is sound. But to say that *kanya* means only 'one who is desired', evinces a bias.

Is Draupadi a *kanya* in the sense of 'one who desires'? It does not appear to be so. Instead, she fits in squarely with the staunchly patriarchal viewpoint of woman as sexual object and property. She is desired by all the Pandavas, a fact noticed by Yudhisthira and which motivates him to propose her as common wife to them all. But does Draupadi desire all the Pandava brothers? The epic does not care to tell us, and the central heroine remains silent on this crucial point.

That a *kanya* signifies 'one who desires' need not mean that the object of a woman's desire is a man—something we have become accustomed to assume. We are *what* we desire. We are *because* we desire. Indeed, what can be more profound than desire, the 'first seed of mind'? It was desire that came upon the One in the beginning when there was neither death nor immortality. Poet-seers searched their hearts and found in desire the link of existence with non-existence. This, in my view, is the deeper meaning of woman as a *kanya;* one who desires, and by virtue of doing so, is in touch with her mind, remains self-aware, and though a deepening self-awareness, acquires selfhood. *I desire, therefore I am.* It is only by remaining true to this primal impulse of desire that a woman can remain true to her mind, and, hence, to her self; and it is only by revering and nurturing such a self that she may discover the Goddess within.

Draupadi of the *Mahabharata* cannot be a *kanya* in the sense of woman as autonomous being (as discussed under Layer Three and Layer Four) and one who desires, for the simple reason that she is not allowed to desire. If desire were the seed of her mind, it must have lain dormant or been crushed, for it never ripens into the fruit of an individuated self.

II

It is difficult to imagine that the formulator of the couplet had access to deeper meanings of *kanya* as Goddess and one who desires. It is more likely that the *kanya* in the *panchakanya shloka* or concept carries the meaning of 'one who is desired', that is, women as objects of desire, and hence, viewed as having been manipulated by men for their own ends. That all the women, including Draupadi, have known more than one man is hardly transgressive, considering that those responsible for creating the situations the women find themselves in, were also men. On the surface, Ahalya and Draupadi seem to occupy gray areas. Ahalya is venerated, but she is also viewed as a fallen woman; the two are related. She fell because she was tricked by Indra,[13] and she is venerated because she was thought worthy of redemption by Rama, not because her transgression is being held up as a value or viewed as progressive. Vijaya Ramaswamy explains, "The seemingly contradictory images of Ahalya make sense only when you look upon her as a woman who lost her chastity without her knowledge but retained her *pativratya*."[14] Similarly, though Draupadi is mocked at for being 'shared' by five husbands, her wifely devotion towards her husbands redeems her from her anomalous marriage—which was not her own doing in the first place—in the eyes of posterity. In both cases it is the *pativratya* of both, and also of the other three *kanyas*—or the women found in variants of the *panchakanya shloka*—that 'redeems' the women from the shadow of (what appears to be) deviant sexual morality. Such an explanation shows how *kanya* in the *panchakanya shloka*, in fact, colludes with the concept of *pativratya*, which is what the five women are and have been lauded for. Even Kunti, who apparently slept with men other than her husband, was only carrying out the orders of Pandu; she was doing 'work', not indulging in pleasure.

The point to be noted, however, is that the *shloka* nevertheless views the women as having transgressed, for they have all violated the sexual morality of monogamy. The *shloka* seems to encode multiple messages in an effort to juggle and reconcile the current and older meanings of *kanya*. It voices discomfort with the idea of a woman's sexual experience outside the institution of monogamy. Further, seeing men as responsible for the apparent 'immorality' of these five women, it seeks to wipe clean the record of their transgression by admitting its own sin: the sin of complicity. In this reciprocal cleansing lies the key to understanding the conundrum-like *shloka*. The *panchakanya shloka* turns out to be a ritual to be enacted, and not just a verbal construct.

It makes good sense that it is men who would need to remember the maidens, for it is they who would benefit from such a reciprocal moral cleansing. The setting up of the pentad of *kanyas* serves as a constant reminder of the ongoing, eternal drama in which men transgress upon women and render them sinful in the eyes of society. The *shloka* does not distinguish between Indra who seduced Ahalya, Pandu who urged Kunti to beget offsprings via *niyoga*, Pandavas who divided Draupadi amongst themselves, Sugriva and Vali who fought over Tara, and Vibhishana who married Ravana's wife. It sees the agents as 'men' and the sufferers as 'women'. It is unlikely that the *panchakanya shloka* views the five *kanyas* as agents of their life's action or as desiring beings, for if this were the case and they were only doing what they wanted and pleased with it, the notion that remembering them allows one/ men to wash away his/their sins would not carry any meaning.

III

Coming back to Draupadi, the Draupadi of the *Mahabharata*, we have discussed, is not a *kanya* in the sense of an autonomous or desiring being. She serves, at best, as a bridge from the revered triad of Sita-Savitri-Parvati to further horizons.

Draupadi of the *Mahabharata* led an existence that was not active, but reactive. Her plight as *nathavati anathavat* is indeed full of pathos. But it only serves to remind us of her status as a wife, and seems to announce that the greatest disaster befalling a woman is to be many-husbanded yet husbandless. True, Draupadi does challenge the right of Yudhishthira to stake her in the game of dice with Duryodhana when Yudhishthira himself had lost to him; but she does not question the idea of ownership of a husband over his wife. In contrast to her epic counterpart, it is the contemporary incarnation of Draupadi that truly speaks to us, and has the courage to suggest that a woman's suffering might stem from patriarchy's institutionalization of different sexual mores for men and women. It is not the epic heroine but Pratibha Ray's Yajnaseni who wonders why monogamy is stipulated only for woman:

> If one woman married more than one husband she would be branded a sinner. Who had laid down this law? It must be some male god! Otherwise how could there be such a distinction of virtue and sin between male and female?[15]

It is P.K. Balakrishnan's philosophic Draupadi who poses a question that is its own answer: "Draupadi, were you ever loved for yourself, entirely for your sake?[16]

It is Sethu's radical and daring vision in *Pandavapuram*[17] manifested through his two visionary Draupadi—figures that bring together the deeper meanings of *kanya* as Goddess and one who desires. The primary Draupadi-figure, the protagonist of the novel, is appropriately named Devi and partakes of the fire and majesty of Goddess Durga with whom she is linked through imagery and ironical statement. Devi transforms the epic Draupadi's desirelessness into an all-consuming polyandrous desire of a Nair woman for paramours. The secondary Draupadi-figure is part of a sub-text that reworks epic Draupadi's relationship to her Pandava husbands. Casting aside her five quarrelsome husbands, Amba-like, the sub-textual Draupadi does penance in a forest and becomes deified in her own fire. She turns into a Goddess, a 'Devi'. Both the Draupadis are not defined in relation to a man; their concern is with formulating and realising their own vision, however imaginary it may be. It is in Sethu's *Pandavapuram* that we see the Draupadi of the *Mahabharata* transformed into a *kanya,* for it is here that she transforms herself into the primal Goddess by invoking the occult powers within her.

A woman needs to go from the epic Draupadi to her contemporary incarnation in order to discover the *kanya* within her. Perhaps we need to go beyond both, into the past, to re-discover epic women who provide far more interesting role models for the twentyfirst century woman than Draupadi and the other four *kanyas* with whom she comprises the *panchakanyas*. I propose a new set of *panchakanyas*: Shakuntala, who had the courage to enter into a *gandharava vivaha* with Dushyanta and assert her proud *apsara* ancestry when slighted by him in his pretended forgetfulness; Ganga, who had the assertiveness to put pre-conditions before accepting the marriage proposal of Shantanu; Hidimba, who actively courted Bhima; Madhavi, who chose the forest as her bridegroom; and Amba, who, when rejected by the man she loved, becomes a *tapasvini* in order to fulfil her goal of revenge against Bhisma whose abduction of her renders her soiled in the eyes of her paramour. She adopts the virgin condition as described by Leonie Caldecott and literally rejects womanhood itself in her protest against patriarchy.[18] Amba, to my mind, exemplifies *par excellence* the esoteric or spiritual meaning of *kanya*.

Women cannot entirely do away with patriarchy; what is significant is that their brush with it puts them on the path to self-discovery and self-realisation. This is what happens with Amba.

Let us keep Draupadi in view, but let us learn from Amba.

References

1. Sigmund Freud, "Creative Writers and Day-dreaming", in *Twentieth Century Literary Criticism: A Reader,* ed., David Lodge, London: Longman, 1972, p. 41.
2. Pradip Bhattacharya, "Panchkanya" endnote 1 email.
3. *Vedoddharnini* Jan-Mar, 1987, Vol.XV, pp.19-20.
4. Ganguli, *Mahabharata,* Adi Parva, p. 389.
5. Sarva Daman Singh, *Polyandry in Ancient India,* New Delhi: Motilal Banarsidass, 1978.
6. Shalini Shah, *The Making of Womanhood: Gender Relations in the Mahabharata,* New Delhi: Manohar, 1995, p.18.
7. Ganguli, *Mahabharata,* Adi Parva, p. 394.
8. Ajit Mookerjee, *Kali: The Feminine Force,* London: Thames and Hudson, 1988, Preface, pp. 8-9.
9. Esther Harding, *Women's Mysteries: Ancient and Modern,* London: Rider and Company, 1971,p.124.
10. Ibid., p.125.
11. Alf Hiltebeitel's pioneering work *The Cult of Draupadi: Mythologies, from Gingee to Kuruksetra,* Chicago: Univ of Chicago Press, 1988 provides ample information on this tradition.
12. Ganguli, *Mahabharata,* Vana Parva, p.595.
13. In the Uttarakanda, Ahalya takes Indra to be her husband, and therefore sleeps with him; in the *Kathasaritasagar* and Adikanda version, however, she knows it is Indra and therefore dissimulates when her husband asks who was inside, saying 'a cat' (*majjara*) but which can also mean 'my lover' (*ma-jara*).
14. Vijaya Ramaswamy, ed., *Researching Indian Women,* New Delhi: Manohar, 2003, p.18.
15. Pratibha Ray, *Yajnaseni: The Story of Draupadi,* English trans. of Oriya novel *Yajnaseni* by Pradip Bhattacharya, New Delhi: Rupa, 1995 p.92.
16. P.K. Balakrishnan, *And Now Let Me Sleep,* English trans. of Malayalam novel *Ini Njan Urangatte* by K.C. Sarasamma, New Delhi: Sahitya Akademi, 1999, p.72.

17. Sethu, *Pandavapuram*, Madras: Macmillan, 1995, trans. from the Malayalam original by Prema Jayakumar.
18. By Amba's literal rejection of womanhood I am referring to the penance she performs in order to win the boon of being reborn as a man (Shikandin) so that s/he may seek revenge by killing Bhisma in battle. As being a 'woman' is equated with weakness and the inability to fight in battle, she gives up her biological sex as well as the socially-constructed false notion of womanhood stemming from it.

25 Kamala Das: The Voice Within

— Piyas Chakrabarti

One of the most significant developments in post-independence India in the genre that has since then controversially come to be known as "Indian writing in English" is the advent of a band of women writers who have used the verse form to express the needs and desires of the female subject in a patriarchal society. The art form became for them a "room of their own" where free from the "senses" of a misfit world they could voice their deepest "sensibilities". Their works often sparked scandals and there was none more scandalous than Kamala Das when she started publishing. In such collections as *Summer in Calcutta* (1965), *The Descendents* (1967) and *The Old Playhouse and Other Poems* (1973), she created a furore with her bold subjects and her bolder handling of them. Her collection is a fascinating study of the entire gamut of female desire throbbing with a sense of immediacy rarely found in English poetry. Her poems stem mostly from her own experiences and the visible signs of herself are so evident in her works that they are often classified as "confessional poems".

Confessional poetry is often characterised by an intense study of very personal experiences, and as a study of Kamala Das's poetry and her autobiography *My Story* reveals, this was very true of her. However, her poetry is not just a confession but also a vigorous voicing of her identity: she establishes herself firmly as a desiring female subject searching for love in a world that rarely understands her and is even more rarely comfortable with what it finds.

During the days when she was still a Hindu and married to her Hindu husband, Kamala Das was constantly looking for love in a system where marriage was often for convenience with very little thought spared for such trivialities as emotional bonding. Her early remembrance of the Nalapat marital system clearly shows this:

> My mother did not fall in love with my father. They were dissimilar and horribly mismated. But my mother's timidity helped to create an illusion of domestic harmony which satisfied the relatives and friends.

Kamala Das lacked her mother's "timidity" and hence the blessing of seemingly peaceful cohabitation was denied to her in her first marriage. Her earliest experience of physical love has a strange violence attached to it:

> Again and again throughout that unhappy night he hurt me and all the while the Kathakali drums throbbed dully against our window... (MS 90).

It comes therefore as no surprise that her poems often question the limitations of a purely physical association:

> ...can this man with
> Nimble finger-tips unleash
> Nothing more alive than the
> Skin's lazy hungers...*("The Freaks")*.

Her many escapades into the fleeting world of carnal experience only mirror the restlessness of her soul and the desire to be loved and wanted. Even in her early years she was constantly searching for one who would treat her with more than just physical brutality:

> I was ready for love. Ripe for a sexual banquet....A cousin of ours grabbed me when I was climbing the stairs whispering, "You are so beautiful" and although I did not believe him, in sheer gratitude I let him hold me with his arms for a couple of minutes. He panted with his emotion. When he kissed me on my mouth I disliked the smell of his stale mouth (MS 95-96).

A deep sense of insecurity marks her sexual wanderings and often sex turns out to be a mask for her battered soul:

> I am a freak. It's only
> To save my face, I flaunt, at
> Times, a grand, flamboyant lust ("The Freaks").

Kamala Das makes judicious use of the eunuch symbol in "The Dance of the Eunuchs" to indicate the vacant ecstasy of their frenzied movement. The visible frenzy is only an effort to hide the loneliness within, and in their dance the poet finds an articulate parallel to her internal despondency.

My Story seems to indicate that her husband's homosexual inclinations increased her sense of inadequacy:

> At this time my husband turned to his old friend for comfort. They behaved like lovers in my presence. To celebrate my birthday, they shoved me out of the bedroom and locked themselves in (MS 104).

The controversial autobiography has at times been accused to be bordering on fiction and does at times seem an erratic mixture of fact and fantasy but it also is a valuable indicator of her firm desire to establish a space of her own. On rare occasions when she did find love in her husband it was cloaked in a homosexual fantasy:

> After bathing me in warm water and dressing me in man's clothes, my husband bade me sit on his lap, fondling me and calling me his little darling boy (MS 111-112).

Her writing has a bare-all-dare-do that no doubt shocked conventional Indian morality but probably was a necessary act of defiance on her part. Her poetry showcases the acute emotional struggles of a woman who abandons her passive role to discover and assert her individual liberty and identity.

Her quest for identity and love takes different turns which find reflection in her writings. In *My Story* there are references to her mild flirtations with lesbianism, the first symptoms of which are evident in her infatuation for her English teacher:

> Her voice was strange, fractured in the middle and I thought it was beautiful. It was easy for me to fall in love with her....I wrote a poem addressed to my teacher in which I likened her to *a rose* (MS 74).

Later when she was on a vacation with a large number of students she tasted her first lesbian physical experience with a fellow student in a railway compartment:

> Then she lay near me holding my body close to hers. Her fingers traced the outlines of my mouth with a gentleness I had not dreamt of feeling...(MS 79).

There is, of course, very little chance for us to validate any of her accounts given in *My Story*, but real or imagined they nevertheless provide a monitor for the yearnings of her heart. Her lesbian instincts chart a desire within her to be treated with tenderness and love. However, in her relationship with men she rarely achieved this. She approached them with all her feminine beauties and as is often the case in Kamala Das, there was no holding back: "...Gift him all,/ Gift him what makes you a woman, the scent of / Long hair, the musk of sweat between the breasts,/ The warm shock of menstrual blood, and all your / Endless female hungers..."("The Looking Glass").

But the unfolding of her body and soul was often met only by the unfeeling hunger of the body:

> That was the only kind of love,
> This hacking at each other's parts
> Like convicts hacking, breaking clods
> At noon...("Convicts").

She rarely achieved a satisfaction of both her carnal and emotional needs within her marriage and the resulting frustration is given voice in the "Captive": "My love is an empty gift, a gilded / empty container, good for show, nothing / else." Even her escapades into the domain of "adultery" remain a futile exercise: "To be frank / I have failed. / I feel my age and / Uselessness ("Composition"). Despite her frankness about sex, she reveals, at times, a deep disgust with her own body. She sought love with it, but often it was the impediment she could not transcend: "The silly female shape had again intervened to ruin a beautiful relationship, the clumsy gadgetry that always, always, damaged bonds." (p.183). Her sense of disgust of the mere bodily union is clearly presented in "A Request": "When I die / Do not throw the meat and bones away / But pile them up / And / Let them tell / By their smell / What life was worth / On this earth / What love was worth / In the end."

Her search for identity was even more difficult because she was, in a sense doubly displaced. She was not just a woman in a male-dominated society but also one who wrote in English. In her famous poem "An Introduction" she brilliantly employs the confessional and the rhetorical modes in order to raise relevant questions relating to a woman's or an Indian poet's identity. She unabashedly accepts her ignorance and lack of interest about the larger political/social issues surrounding her:

> I don't know politics but I know the names
> Of those in power, and can repeat them like
> Days of weeks, or names of months, beginning with
> Nehru... ("An Introduction").

Her poetry was primarily in English, and about her own experiences. She wrote in two languages, Malayalam and English, and she claims both of them as her own:

> ...Why not let me speak in
> Any language I like? The language I speak
> Becomes mine, mine alone. It is half English, half
> Indian, funny perhaps, but it is honest,
> It is as human as I am human, don't
> You see? It voices my joys, my longings, my
> Hopes... ("An Introduction").

Indian writers writing literature in the English language is at present a common feature, but Kamala Das had to actively claim that which is now unquestioningly accepted. A.K. Ramanujan probably provided one of the best answers to all the questions regarding whether Indian writers should at all write in English: "I think the real question is whether they can. And if they can, they will." He goes on to state, "It is not a matter of controversy whether people can, will, or should write in a particular language." However, for the people around Kamala Das, the ones who wanted her to "fit in", it was evidently a problem. She, with her "strange" ways disrupted a mode of life where to be able to merge silently into the social pool was considered a supreme virtue.

She claimed that it was her reading that provided her with the courage to be her own self. Against the "categorizers", she sustained herself through her voracious reading: "Ask the books that I read why I changed. Ask the authors dead and alive who communicated with me and gave me the courage to be myself (MS 152). However, the "books" and "authors" only echoed that which was already there in her heart, a deep desire to live life on her own terms.

She remains defiant all through her career, but there is also a constant quest to transcend the bodily limitations. At times she seeks escape from this claustrophobic existence through identification with the world:

> ...I met a man, loved him. Call
> Him not by any name, he is every man
> Who wants a woman, just as I am every
> Woman who seeks love. In him...the hungry haste
> Of rivers, in me...the oceans' tireless
> *Waiting...* ("An Introduction").

At other times she looks for escape in the mythical Hindu symbols of love, be it Radha-Krishna or Mira Bai-Krishna: "This becomes from this hour/ Our river and this old Kadamba/ Tree, ours alone, for our homeless/ Souls to return someday"("Radha-Krishna").

Her religious poems often show a deep distrust and disregard for the body. This desire to reach beyond her body can be seen even in some of her non-religious poems: " I throw the bodies out,/ I cannot stand their smell./ Only the souls may enter / The vortex of the sea. / Only the souls know how to sing / At the vortex of the sea" ("The Suicide").

The imperfections of her earthly lovers forced her to find solace in Krishna, the archetypal symbol of divine love. In the arms of her divine lover she gained, for a brief span, her moments of complete happiness: "Everything in me / Is melting, even the hardness at the core / O Krishna, I am melting, melting, melting / Nothing remains but / You..." ("Radha").

Amidst the emotional wilderness of an unfeeling world, Ghanashyam provided her with an image of permanence, an assurance that there is hope yet for the believer: "...Ghanashyam, / My life, until now a sleeping jungle / Is at last astir with music" ("Ghanashyam").

The same restlessness, which prompted her to the symbol of Radha-Krishna, resulted her in embracing Islam. This is found to be inconsistent by many critics but her soul's wanderings have not always been consistent. In life and poetry, consistency has not been her strength. She had always been governed by her heart's desire and on December 16, 1999 she finally embraced Islam. She claims to have deliberated for years about this, but as is often the case we do not know for sure. Her decision sparked major debates and was met with the same sense of shock that her writing often generated. She was sixtyfive years old at the time of her conversion and her decision might have been partly prompted by a desire for public spotlight that had for long been her companion but was slowly shifting allegiance. The anonymity of the burqa might have provided her with physical space but one doubts whether it can give her the emotional solace that was always the focus of her search. However, despite her inconsistencies Kamala Das's poetry remains a powerful statement from a woman who wanted to voice her desires in a largely unfeeling world.

Works Cited

Das Kamala, *My Story,* New Delhi: Sterling Publishers, 1988 pp. 4-5. All further references from this edition of the text have been indicated in parentheses with the abbreviation MS.

— "The Freaks", "The Looking Glass", "An Introduction", *Indian English Poetry Since 1950: An Anthology* ed. Vilas Sarang, Hyderabad: Orient Longman Limited, 1989.

— "A Request", *An Anthology of Indian English Poetry,* Hyderabad: Orient Longman Limited, 1989, pp. 56-57.

— "Convicts", "Captive", "Composition", "The Suicide", & "Radha", *The Descendents,* Calcutta: Writers Workshop, 1967.

— "Radha-Krishna", *Summer in Calcutta,* New Delhi: Everest Press, 1965, p.37.

– "Ghanashyam", *Tonight, This Savage Rite: The Love Poems of Kamala Das and Pritish Nandy,* New Delhi: Aronld-Heinemann Pvt. Ltd. 1979, p.18.

– A.K. Ramanujan, "Replies to the Questionnaire" in P. Lal ed. *Modern Indian Poetry in English: An Anthology and a Credo,* Calcutta: Writer's Workshop, 1969, p. 444.

26 *One Day in Ashadha*: Unacknowledged Epic of a Woman

—B.T. Seetha

The title of Mohan Rakesh's play in Hindi, *Ashadha Ka Ek Din,* suggests an emphasis on one particular day in the month of Ashadha. Translated into English as *One Day in Ashadha* by Sarah K. Ensley, the phrase suggests any day in the month of Ashadha. Perhaps *One Day of Ashadha* would have been a better choice for the title.

Ashadha, following the month *Jeshta* in the Hindu calendar, is the last month of the summer season or the *Grishma ritu and* it announces the coming of the rains. Thus a particular day of the month suggests a pattern in the movement from the particular to the general, from the microcosmic to the macrocosmic, from the day to the month to the season. *Ashadha* to *Aswayuja,* the *chaturmasa* period, is believed to be the time of Vishnu's rest when the goddesses take charge to fight sickness and disease, dirt and slush. *One Day in Ashadha* presents such a situation and calls our attention to the relationship between Man and Nature, Creation and Creativity. Analogously, if the artist is the creator/Bramha, the society is the creation run by Vishnu. The questions that the play raises are: What happens when Vishnu sleeps? What happens when the society responds to art not with feeling and emotion but with a superficial admiration only to satisfy one's own whims and fancies? Does art then become subdued by the forces of power and politics or can it be rescued by the sensitivity of the goddesses? How significant is time/season in this process of creativity? What is the role of *prakriti* or/and women?

The play opens with Mallika. Her name in Sanskrit means, "a Swan" or the month of *Magha* of *Sisir ritu*. In Tamil the name refers to jasmine, a fragrant white flower, some varieties of which blossom through summer and some bloom during the rains. As a swan, she is symbolic of purity and elevated consciousness; she is also the vehicle of *Saraswati*, the goddess of learning often depicted in a white attire. It is significant that the swan, *Saraswati* and the jasmine are all white, symbolising purity, peace and the complete range of colours. However, these characteristics in Mallika seem to contend with each other and Mallika herself becomes the object of contention. In contrast to *Ashadha, Magha* is the month of late winter and early spring, the rains of *ashadha* bring forth life which blossoms in Mallika. These rains are a prelude to the spring. Thus Mallika, in *One day in Ashadha* represents the goddess who evokes creativity, desire and acceptance in Kalidasa.

There is very little historical evidence available of Kalidasa's life. In literary history, tales of his transformation from a simple-minded uneducated foolish cowherd to a master-poet of Sanskrit bestowed with the grace of Goddess Kali have been told repeatedly. Mohan Rakesh subtly recreates this tale which has in it allusions to the power of speech and creativity. Mallika in *One Day in Ashadha* refers to the blue lotus, and Kalidasa while addressing the injured fawn, refers to Mallika's eyes and compares them to the eyes of the fawn. While red, pink and white lotuses are commonly known, the reference to the blue lotus is rare and has mystical and mythical connotations. Vararuci comes to take Kalidasa to the court of Ujjaini to honour him and appoint him to the position of Poet Laureate. This information does not seem to impress Ambika who betrays no emotion in spite of Mallika's excitement. The argument that follows is a poignant statement made about the reality of relationships that go beyond materialistic concerns and stress the need to be aware of the bitter facts of life.

Ambika tries to define the relationship between Mallika and Kalidasa. She asks Mallika to marry Kalidasa as they seem to understand each other so well. However, both Kalidasa and Mallika, in spite of their involvement with emotions and feelings do not lose touch with reality. It is perhaps their imagination that makes them aware of the demands of human existence. When Mallika justifies Kalidasa's lack of interest in marrying her due to poverty, Ambika's reaction is that If poverty is sufficient reason to avoid marriage, then the absence of poverty is all the more reason to avoid it! A mother's fears about the future of her daughter make her a cynic.

Kalidasa's childlike innocence becomes manifest when he brings in the injured fawn to be nursed by Mallika, assuring the fawn that it would meet someone who has eyes like a fawn and affection like a mother. Ambika as a mother seems to fail in her duties of expressing love and affection, whereas Mallika, young and passionate lives up to the image of a mother figure. Is it her power of imagination and creative abilities that have made her sensitive to pain and emotion or is it an inherent quality of womanhood that manifests itself in the presence of her beloved? Ambika, even as the name suggests, seems to work under the pressures of society and the impressions of the people around. She suppresses her affections with the fear that her daughter Mallika might tread on an unconventional path. The narrative of the play with its intertextual allusions to the works of Kalidasa, particularly *Ritusamhara* and *Meghadutam*, presents them as texts within the texts. The direct and indirect use of characters from the classical works and History gives the play complex form and structure. The action of the play during the month of *ashadha* encompasses the various seasons, moods and responses related to the creativity of Kalidasa, as both the classical poet and the character in the play, and it explores the basic concepts of art and creativity.

Both the beginning and the ending of the play refer to thunder and the first rains of the season which suggest a cyclic form and pattern in the play. If the play begins by evoking joy and happiness, the same setting in the end of the play promises neither joy nor hope. The same *prakriti* has different responses from the *purusha*. As Kalidasa says in *Meghadutam*, "The sight of rain clouds makes even happy hearts / stir with restlessness;" it is this restlessness that becomes the conflict in the play. Vilom appears whenever there is a crisis of situation and action. After Kalidasa leaves for Ujjaini and makes a name for himself, he stops by in his home town on his way to Kashmir but is unable to visit Mallika but when he returns to her he says: "I came for the very reason I didn't come before on my way to Kashmir.... Today I am free from everything that is binding me." Power and authority, politics and society bind him. If *Rithusamhara* is creativity of a free mind;

Meghadutam and *Shakuntalam* are an attempt to release himself from the shackles of power and politics. As Chandana Rajan in her introduction to *The Complete Works of Kalidasa,* says: "In *Ritusamharam* woman and nature borrow each other's attributes when they are not competing in a friendly manner; in *Meghadutam* woman and nature are one, the identification is complete; the landscape *is* the beloved"(16).

Rangini and *Sanjini,* who come to study the place and the environment of Kalidasa's poetry try to find the "herbs which emit light," are disappointed when Mallika simply dismisses off their search saying that, "Herbs do not give off light." It is the enlightened mind of the poet that is able to see the unseen." Kalidasa places himself in the ancient tradition of the Vedic poet-seers who saw themselves as speaking the word and uttering the Truth. Looking deep within, into the depths of their consciousness, they saw the light that never was on sea or land and expressed the vision they discovered there for all ages to come. The word reveals the unseen through the seen, using the language of metaphor and links the transcendent with the transient"(3).

Anunasik and *Anuswar* are the characters who present themselves as "the servants of Mantragupta." Both these pairs add to the play a comic dimension true to the role of a *vidushaka.* The names of Anunasik and Anuswar suggest the alphabets that have a characteristic nasal pronunciation. Anuswar added to a letter makes it an *anunasik.* In their attempt to reorganise Mallika's house and prepare it to receive the princess they betray ignorance and a shallow approach to the understanding of literature. They seem to be awed by the fact that semantic structures of Kalidasa's work are no different from the structures of the common man's language. This raises a question of what then makes Kalidasa's poetry so brilliant. Simultaneously it answers the question of how various people respond variously to literature.

Priyangu the princess is a sad combination of an artist who has a very superficial relation to art and a selfish ruler who makes no attempt to empathise with the others. She lives in a world of power and authority; she thinks she could transfer "some of the atmosphere of this place" to Kashmir. However, it is evident that she is unable to respond to the atmosphere in the same way as

Kalidasa or Mallika. With her power and authority she thinks she is serving the cause of art. Priyangu is a contradiction to Mallika; Mallika is eager to further Kalidasa's creativity whereas Priyangu wants him to move away from literature into politics. She even wants to remodel Kalidasa's past and changes his name to Mantragupta. She wants to remodel the house he spent his childhood in, if the present is the result of the past which shapes consciousness. Priyangu tries, therefore, to change not only Kalidasa's identity but also his consciousness. Mohan Rakesh once again exploits history using Mantragupta, a poet-king of Kashmir, a historical figure mentioned in *Tarangini* or the *History of Kashmir*.

The duality of the princess as a scholar and a ruler, found in the historical references, is presented by Mohan Rakesh in the play as Mallika, the connoisseur of art and therefore a scholar, and Priyangu, the princess symbolic of the power of the ruler. If for Kalidasa a woman is an objective correlative when both woman and nature borrow each other's attributes or they become one, in Mohan Rakesh the subjective nature of a woman plays a significant role. A woman's identity and the recognition of the self become one of the thematic issues. Mohan Rakesh reorganises history to emphasize how art and creativity over the ages have not been able to find relevant space for themselves nor for those who appreciate it. He subtly elaborates on the role of a woman as an artist / creator. In *One Day in Ashadha*, if for Kalidasa and Mallika artistic creativity is a source of joy and peace, Ambika and Vilom represent just the opposite; feeling and sensitivity according to them is a "sick (ness)".

When Mallika returns home full of joy and feeling she is snubbed by her mother. She feels dejected and disappointed by her mother's reaction. When Kalidasa walks in with the injured fawn she changes her expression and tries to empathize with Kalidasa. She is thus caught between impulse/instinct and reason/thought. The fawn being hurt with the officials' bow is symbolic of Mallika herself being hurt as a result of the official's announcement of taking Kalidasa away. The officials who come to take Kalidasa to the king's court to offer him the honour of poet laureateship, do not recognise him. They follow him to claim the fawn they have shot. The argument between Kalidasa and the official show the tender and innocent attitude of Kalidasa who cares for none and is immune to insult or injury. Unwittingly though, he makes a statement that describes the attitude of the officials when he says, "I'm surprised to find that the words are the property of the royal family." Kalidasa's only intention is to save the bleeding fawn. His own actions and speech reveal a very complacent, introvert individual who is blind to the emotions of Mallika yet is able to relate to the pain and suffering of the fawn. He could rely on Mallika to nurture the fawn but fails to get any support from others with respect to his feelings for Mallika. Ambika's indifference and Vilom's interference work as deterrents to further or strengthen his relationship with Mallika. His status, condition, and literary abilities are all described by Mallika and the other characters.

Although this play focuses on Kalidasa as the central character around whom the story and the plot revolve, characters like Mallika, Ambika, Matul and Vilom shape the play proper which becomes a statement on art and its value. The word Vilom means opposite. He is everything that Kalidasa is not. Vilom frequents Mallika's house only to gain her favour as a companion. However, Mallika recognising and enjoying Kalidasa's poetic ability, does not relate herself to Vilom. Vilom as the opposite of Kalidasa makes a mockery of people's interest in Kalidasa. H.s arguments come forth as powerful ironic statements on life and art. As Kalidasa says, "all opposites are close to one another… the passing years could not separate one opposition from another…." Vilom by way of his crude reasoning tries to provoke Kalidasa's conscience.

Is it then the fate of an artist to be judged and valued by those who have chosen other occupations? Is Mallika a poet at heart? If provided by proper support and encouragement could she have blossomed into a poet of repute and recognition? These are some of the questions that manifest themselves without finding a solution. Ambika and later even Mallika remain just women, taking care of children and fulfilling their duties toward them and society. Mallika who gathers palm leaves leaving on them marks of her tears writes an epic of woe; creativity suppressed manifests in the form of tears and torment. She could have been a poet if she was not snubbed and forced into marriage with Vilom. Instead of writing an epic with tears, flowers and the impact of changing seasons, she could have expressed herself in words, images, metaphor, metonymy and meter.

Kalidasa identifies Mallika as merely "one of these ties, as are the sky and clouds, the foliage, the fawns, the shepherds." Yet Mallika, without betraying her emotions, steadily encourages him to accept the court honours. Symbolic of *Prakriti,* Mallika displays a firm and sturdy nature. Her unquestioning surrender to his art and poetry leads her to a state of complete self-neglect. When he leaves without visiting her she is a broken woman. She sheds tears either for her own neglected self or for the fact that Kalidasa is destined to move away from poetry to politics therefore ultimately he would move away from Mallika towards Priyangu. She seems to give up all hope of any further relationship with him and surrenders herself to the circumstances.

Her marriage to Vilom and bearing a child thereafter makes her a mother figure that now needs to cater to the material comforts and physical needs of her child and her husband. Kalidasa returns after his experiments with poetry and politics which he is unable to keep together. He comes back with the hope that Mallika would remain the same, a source of inspiration. Although it is the same month of *Ashadha,* the room in Mallika's house is no longer the same, the walls bearing the designs of swastika and the lotus are in a dilapidated condition. Mallika's state of body and mind too "reflect(s) the broken-down condition of the room." These designs symbolic of well being and the seat of wealth and knowledge have faded.

Matul is now seen walking on crutches seeking shelter in Mallika's house from the heavy rain. He expresses his confidence in Mallika as the constant, when he says, "you are the same Mallika to me, even today." Matul's depiction of the royal palace as the most uncomfortable place (where his fall due to the slippery floor makes him a cripple) suggests the slippery ground that Kalidasa as Mantragupta had to tread on thereby crippling himself/his creative abilities. Matul's statement that "when I walked on two feet, I didn't have to worry about even the heaviest of rains," suggests Mallika and Kalidasa were his two feet; losing one in the precincts of the court, he has lost Kalidasa to the court. He further describes the court as a place where one has no freedom to be oneself; constantly being surrounded by the guards, he is distanced from nature, and he could see neither clouds nor fawns. Princess Priyangu was able to reorganize Matul's reality and consciousness by rebuilding his house by renovating it with marble. Matul's fear of the smooth slippery marble of the court haunts him even in his own house. He feels comfortable in Mallika's house which still has "the earthen floor" and "the same Mallika ...even today".

When Matul informs Mallika that he had heard the news about Kalidasa taking the vows of a sanyasi and going to Banaras, she is disturbed. Although between them they have a long conversation about the real and the unreal, truth and falsehood, both of them find themselves in a dilemma. Their beliefs are shattered. Mallika's reasoning and her effort to come to terms with reality are brought forth in the loud thinking presented by way of a dramatic monologue. She finds a sense of existence only through Kalidasa: "For in spite of my ruin, I felt that you were growing. I saw myself in you, not in me. Now today I hear that you are going to renounce everything and become a sanyasi? Are you going to be indifferent? Indifference...is it going to deprive me of my only sense of existence?"(183)

When Mallika hears about Kalidasa's marriage to Princess Priyangu she is hurt more at the loss of faith in her own commitment and in the loss of her identity. Even as she is contemplating, the same day in *Ashadha* as it was in the beginning with clouds and rain, brings back the tangible and the intangible, the familiar and the unfamiliar, the self and the other together. When Kalidasa comes to Mallika's house, during the first few moments Mallika is stupefied and "stares fixedly at him." He merely looks at her without ever registering the fact that there have been considerable changes in her appearance and the surroundings. Both of them seem to make an effort to grapple with the reality that strikes them. He says: "I have come to see reality as it is once again." He admits that he is no longer the same person: "I am someone that I myself do not recognize!" He declares that he was now free from his "love of power and authority" and that he would like to return and be Kalidasa again. Could he return in Time though he could in space? He could recollect the past but could he relive the same? Kalidasa's statement, "The jugs, tiger skin, kusha grass, the lamps, the designs on the wall...and your eyes. Until today the look that was in your eyes on the day of our parting has been imprinted on my heart. I kept trying to convince myself that whenever I would come back everything here would be the same"(185), ends with a knock on the door. Both Mallika and Kalidasa seem to lose themselves in trying to reason out the past; Kalidasa expresses his conflict between poetry and politics and the difficult choice he had to make to prove himself to "everyone who had insulted me and laughed at me." In an effort to gain worldly riches he had to impoverish poetry. He was unable to mould himself into this new image and divide himself "equally between two types of work, but instead (he) was shaped and controlled by the immediate situation." His selfcentred view completely negates the reality of Mallika's situation. He says: "The Himalayas are the backdrop for *Kumarasambhavam* and you are the austere Uma. The pain of the yaksha in *Meghadutam* is the pain I felt at being separated from you and the pain of the yaksha's wife is your pain, though I imagined myself here and you in Ujjainni"(187). He does not realise that Mallika had read all his works paying a good price for them and spending very little on her own comforts. With this realisation he comes to terms with his inadequacies and he accepts that "I should have returned years ago to get drenched in the rain, so that I could write what has remained unwritten, what has been inside me for several years pent up like the rain clouds of Ashadha..."(188).

Kalidasa could at least mention his feelings about his unwritten works but Mallika who gets drenched in the same *Ashadha* rains year after year could not quench her thirst of emotions, so she leaves the blank pages sewed together unwritten: "I thought that if you would come from the capital, I would give it to you as a gift. I would ask you to write your greatest epic on these pages"(189). His perception, hitherto preoccupied with the concerns within himself, seems to now recognize the pathos in the unwritten work of Mallika. He says, "Where are those pages empty Mallika? There is an epic of infinite chapters written on them." It is an epic written he says "with (her) tears," "drops of sweat," colours left behind by the "flower petals," "scratches" left by the "finger nails," "marks made by the biting teeth," "the light and shadow of the summer sun," "the dust of autumn leaves" and the dilapidated "house" (189).

If Kalidasa, in spite of the support he has from Mallika, Matul and Nikshep, struggles with the forces of society and politics in the process of creativity, Mallika has neither support nor succour from either her family or the society, even to expresses her feelings – to be herself. In the absence of Kalidasa she had to accept Vilom. When Vilom returns home, and finds Kalidasa, he questions the latter's presence in his inimitable crude manner. He wonders if Kalidasa is "back to claim the land which you abandoned years ago? Because you have a permanent right over it?" (192).

Is Mallika then the land that takes the burden of man/ mankind? Is she the goddess who could have saved art and the artist? Is the goddess too powerless in the flow of time? However Vilom's questioning and Kalidasa's reasoning bring about a realisation in Kalidasa about the power of time over desire. Mallika merely remains a carrier of creativity, time subsumes all: "Possibly it was a struggle between desire and time. I see that time is more powerful because...Because it does not wait." He surrenders to Time and concludes, after all "the epic on these pages had not been written"(193).

Works Cited

Rakesh, Mohan, *One Day in Ashadha* from *Modern Indian Drama: An Anthology*, Ed. G.P. Deshpande. Delhi: Sahitya Akademi, 2000.

Rajan, Chandra, Tr. *The Complete Works of Kalidasa*, Vol. I, Delhi: Sahitya Akademi, 1997.

27 Self-agony as a Mode of Protest in Jainendra Kumar's *Tyagpatra*

—Sunita Rani Ghosh

In the post-Premchand era in Hindi literature, Jainendra Kumar occupies an undisputed place of prominence. He is probably the first writer of fiction in Hindi who ventured out of the limited circle of idealism and morality to encompass within his expansive vision a sense of reality which can be called down-to-earth. Yet, for his characters the battlefield is not the world of action but an inner world of their own self. Characters and not events lend to his fiction both strength and authenticity. Mixing philosophy of life and psychology of perception with his fictional ingredients, he succeeds in transforming the elemental reality of the human predicament, especially the plight of women, into something decidedly conspicuous.

Tyagpatra, Jainendra's magnum opus, has been translated into fourteen international languages. This short novel enjoys enormous historical significance in Hindi literature. Exposing the contradiction that exists between human values and the so-called socio-moral beliefs, the novel seeks to reveal the reactionary possibilities of the human mind.

At the centre of the novel is Mrinal. Losing her parents in childhood, Mrinal lives with her brother's family. She develops a sense of closeness with her nephew Pramod who, in turn, is affectionately drawn towards her. In her adolescent stage she feels close intimacy with the brother of her friend Sheela but for certain reasons she is unable to marry him. After some time when this affair is discovered, her brother quickly marries her off to a widower. Although she is reluctant to enter into this marrriage, she nevertheless feels impelled to demonstrate her total commitment to her husband. She sincerely confesses: "I cannot deceive. Deception is sin. What has happened has happened. A married woman must remain devoted to her husband. Only by being true can one be truly dedicated"(54).

She unhesitatingly discloses the story of her first love to her husband. The effect of this honest disclosure is disastrous. Unable to appreciate her honesty of intent, the male in him rises to the fore and he sends her out of his house. Forced by the turn of circumstances, Mrinal is compelled to seek refuge in a shabby dwelling provided by a coal merchant. A daughter is born to her out of this relationship. After sometime she is again left alone as this coal merchant deserts her and goes away. The daughter also dies shortly after. Her next encounter is with a doctor's family where she makes a living by teaching the children in the family. She soon learns that her nephew Pramod's marriage has been fixed with Rajnandini in this family and decides to leave this house. She then goes to live the rest of her life among the downtrodden and the so-called 'dirt' of society.

Pramod goes to meet her there and implores her to come back and live with him. She rejects his offer of compassion and tells him that if he wanted he could give her sufficient money which she could use for the upliftment of people like her in that surrounding. He evades the issue under the pretext of incomprehension and returns home. She finally dies of some dreadful disease. Pramod, the narrator as well as spectator to the grim tragic life of his 'bua' (aunt), is so deeply affected by a sense of guilt that he resigns from his judgeship. The novel derives its title 'Tyagpatra' (resignation) from this action.

From the standpoint of individualism *Tyagpatra* can thus said to be a great revolutionary novel delineating an individual's reaction against social orthodoxy. Society never accepts the primacy of individual aspirations over social mores and norms.

Through the character of Mrinal, the novelist questions the false morality of a society bound by traditions. Mrinal, who is endowed with sensitivity and compassion, fully understands that the foundations of society rest on double standards and hypocrisy rather than on logic or honesty of purpose and intent. On account of her failure to find fulfilment in her adolescent love relationship, she is prepared to accept the consequences of an ill-matched matrimony. Deprived of love as well as of a healthy relationship in marriage, and unable to take cudgels against a hostile world, she decides to suffer in silence rather than take recourse to the easy path of ending her own life through suicide. In the process of carrying out her silent rebellion against the orthodox traditions of society, Mrinal prefers to destroy her own self. Through her tragedy, Jainendra has tried to highlight the fact that subjecting oneself to pain and suffering in order to live for one's own convictions is an appropriate mode of protest: "This very accumulated suppressed pain is the gem of the soul whose radiance illumines man's path to progress"(41).

Self-satisfaction through suffering is the natural trait of Mrinal's character. On account of the death of her parents in her childhood she remains deprived of parental love and affection. The strict discipline and excessive control she is subjected to by her sister-in-law breeds in her a feeling of dissatisfaction for life. This feeling of helplessness gives her the strength to endure suffering and pain. She in fact finds fulfilment by torturing her own self.

Even in her school days she seemed to have derived a great deal of pleasure in accepting to be beaten by her teacher for a mischief committed by her friend Sheela. Similarly, her capacity for suffering is demonstrated when she quietly accepts to get married to a widower who is no match to her. When driven out of the house by her husband for her honest confession, she does not seek help from her brother but accepts with grace and equanimity the scorn and neglect accorded to her. The pain she is wary of causing others, she gladly accepts for herself. It is this inherent strength she is endowed with that renders the sympathy, idealism, and altruism of Pramod totally ineffective. She knowingly ignores the selfishness of the coal merchant and gratefully accepts him for helping her in her hour of need. She does everything in the true spirit of sacrifice rather than paying lip-service to sacrifice as most mortals do. Whenever Pramod meets her he always finds her afloat like the lotus flower untouched by the scum of society around her. At no stage of her life, apart from the genuine love she experienced in her adolescent stage, does Mrinal display any sign of weakness, either emotional or physical. She moves from one male to another in search of refuge but the essential strength of her character begets no hatred for her in the minds of the readers. She virtually lives for others with the remotest concern for her own good. As the protagonist of the novel, her life is in tune with her name which means: 'stem of the lotus'. Like the lotus stem, Mrinal withstands and weathers the most severe storms of fate as well as the pressure of the waves of social circumstances but continues to strive to keep intact the lotus of the social system even at the cost of her own life: "I don't want to wreck society. If society breaks where shall we be? That is why all that I can do is keep on breaking myself for the well-being of society"(62).

Mrinal's personality is an ideal of self-sacrifice and the sad saga of her life becomes an epitome of struggle between a woman and her fate. Her relentless fight against adversities of life, which ultimately destroy her, helps her touch the heights of tragic grandeur. Her poignant tale may not evoke any revolutionary feeling against the established traditions of society but there is a faint glimmer of hope that the sympathy, compassion and respect which her life and personality generate in the minds and hearts of the readers would persuade them to look at the likes of Mrinal, perhaps with a little less contempt.

Work Cited

Kumar, Jainendra, *Tyagpatra* (1937) rpt. New Delhi: Purvoday Prakashan,1998. References to the text are from this edition and have been indicated by page numbers in parentheses.

28 स्त्री अस्मिता, स्वातंत्र्य और भूमिका

—हेतु भारद्वाज

नयी सदी का पहला वर्ष महिला सशक्तीकरण का वर्ष घोषित हुआ। इस बहाने नयी सदी की स्त्री को पुनर्परिभाषित करने का प्रयास किया गया। स्त्री को पुनर्परिभाषित करने की आवश्यकता है, क्योंकि 20वीं सदी में स्त्री प्रश्नों को लेकर बराबर बहस चलती रही है तथा स्त्री को परिभाषित करने के लिए विश्व भर में अनेक वैचारिक आन्दोलन भी हुए हैं। भारत में भी स्त्री की पहचान को लेकर अनेक स्तरों पर विमर्श और संघर्ष चलता रहा है। मोटे तौर पर आधुनिक मनुष्य की पहचान को हम तीन प्रतिमानों में समझ सकते हैं। अस्मिता, स्वातंत्र्य और उसकी सामाजिक भूमिका या सहभागिता। वस्तुतः ये तीनों प्रतिमान पुरुषों के ही रहे हैं। जब तक पुरुष स्त्री को अपनी दासतां से मुक्त नहीं करता तब तक स्त्री की स्वतन्त्र पहचान बनने का प्रश्न ही नहीं उठता। इसलिए यह जरूरी है कि पुरुष आत्मालोचन करें तथा स्त्री पर अपने वर्चस्व को आरोपित रखने की मानसिकता से मुक्त हों। इसलिए स्त्री को नयी सदी में पुनर्परिभाषित करने का मूल अर्थ है- पुरुष दासता से स्त्री की मुक्ति जिसके लिए पुरुष को पहल करनी ही होगी। नयी सदी में यह पुरुषों का दायित्व है कि वे स्त्री को उनकी पहचान बनाने की सामर्थ्य देने के लिए उसे आगे बढ़ने का अवसर दें।

इतिहास साक्षी है कि पुरुषों ने स्त्री को आगे बढ़ने से रोका है। उसके विकास के मार्ग में अवरोध पैदा किये हैं, जिनसे स्त्री जीवन में अनेक जटिलताएं पैदा हुई हैं। स्त्री की पहचान के सन्दर्भ में पुरुष की अब तक की भूमिका की पूरी तरह से कलई खुल गयी है-उसने स्त्री की अस्मिता को दबाये रखने के लिए अनैतिक और बेईमान तरीके अपनाए तथा पाखण्ड किये हैं। सामाजिक,

आर्थिक तथा संस्कृति के सैकड़ों स्तर ऐसे हैं जिनसे स्त्री को वंचित रखा गया है। हमने स्त्री होने को पारिवारिक कोटि में सीमित रखा है और उसके लिए सकीर्ण आचार-संहिता लागू कर रखी है। संहिताबद्ध सामाजिक कोटि में हमने उसे शूद्र के साथ रखा है। इतिहासकार रामशरण शर्मा ने अपने 'शूद्रों का इतिहास' नामक ग्रंथ में ऐसे अनेक श्लोकों का उल्लेख किया है जिनमें स्त्री और शूद्र का नाम साथ-साथ आता है, साथ-साथ नाम रखने का अर्थ है कि हम दोनों को हेय समझते हैं, दोनों से घृणा करते हैं और दोनों के स्वतन्त्र अस्तित्व को नकारते हैं। पितृसत्तात्मक समाज व्यवस्था में हमने वर्ण, जाति, धर्म, व्यवसाय आदि के नाम पर अनेक कोटियाँ बना दीं किन्तु स्त्री इन्हीं कोटियों में उपश्रेणी बनी रही। स्त्री को 'मिस' और 'मिसेज' के बीच में बाँट दिया गया। इसी आधार पर हमने स्त्री को नाम दिये किन्तु यह नामांकित करने की एक भ्रम भरी प्रक्रिया (फेलसी - ऑफ नेमिंग) है। वस्तुतः 'मिसेज शर्मा' या 'मिसेज सिंह' नाम नहीं होते-ये पुछल्ले भर होते हैं और हम सभी को इस पुछल्ले से ही भ्रमित करते रहे हैं।

इसलिए जब हम स्त्री की अस्मिता की बात करते हैं तो सबसे जरूरी यह है कि पहले पुरुष स्वयं पितृसत्तात्मक संस्कारों से मुक्त हो, पुरुष स्त्री का स्वामी है, इस रूढ़ि से मुक्त हो, क्योंकि 'स्वामी' का भाव आते ही स्त्री को हम लगभग एक पालतू पशु में परिवर्तित कर देते हैं और उसे पालतू पशु की कोटि में डाल देते हैं; वह इस पूर्वग्रह से मुक्त हो कि पुरुष स्त्री से श्रेष्ठ है। स्वामी होने, श्रेष्ठ होने जैसे भ्रमों ने स्त्री की अस्मिता को दूसरे दर्जे की नागरिकता प्रदान की है, इसलिए स्त्री की अस्मिता को स्वतन्त्र गौरव प्रदान करने के लिए जरूरी है पुरुष की पितृसत्तात्मक संस्कारों से मुक्ति। स्त्री की मुक्ति से पूर्व पुरुष की मुक्ति आवश्यक है, यदि वह अपने पूर्वग्रहों से मुक्त हो जाता है तो स्त्री स्वयं मुक्त हो जायेगी। उसकी मानसिकता स्त्री के विकास मार्ग में सबसे बड़ा अवरोध है यदि वह स्त्री के आगे बढ़ने के मार्ग से हट जायेगा तो वह स्वयं आगे बढ़ने का प्रयास करने लगेगी।

स्त्री की अस्मिता को स्वतन्त्र समझने के लिए हमें अर्थशास्त्री अमर्त्य सेन के चिन्तन से मदद मिल सकती है। यदि हम स्त्री

तथा पिछड़ों को आगे बढ़ाना चाहते हैं तो हमें उन्हें आगे बढ़ने के अवसर देने होंगे तथा नये-नये विकल्प देने होंगे। यदि हम इनको समानता प्रदान करते हैं, तो वह हवा में लहराने वाली समानता नहीं बल्कि व्यवहारिक स्तर पर 'स्टेटस' देने की प्रक्रिया से आरम्भ होगी। 'मिस' और 'मिसेज' की कोटि से निकाल कर उसे किसान, व्यवसायी, ब्यूरोक्रेट, राजनेता आदि की कोटियाँ प्रदान करनी होंगी। जब तक हम स्त्री को 'स्टेटस' की गरिमा नहीं देंगे तब तक उसकी अस्मिता को समानता की गरिमा भी नहीं दे पायेंगे। दरअसल हम देने वाले भी कौन होते हैं-यह 'दाता' की मुद्रा भी तो हमें खण्डित करनी होगी तथा उपयुक्त विकल्प के साथ समान अवसर देने की सामाजिक संरचना ही विकसित करनी होगी। जरूरत एक नयी सामाजिक व्यवस्था के विकसित करने की है जिसकी अन्तःरचना में ही स्त्री के लिए समानता का स्पेस हो-भले ही उसके लिए हमें स्त्री की अतिरिक्त सहायता करनी पड़े, कभी उसके साथ चलकर, तो कभी उसके पीछे चलकर। जरूरी है कि यह सारा परिवर्तन समाज की अन्तःरचना (इन्फ्रास्ट्रक्चर) का हिस्सा बने तभी स्त्री को उसकी सच्चीं अस्मिता का अहसास हो सकता है। यह सब कुछ कर पुरुष ऐतिहासिक 'प्रायश्चित कर सकते हैं।

स्त्री सशक्तीकरण का दूसरा मुद्दा स्वातन्त्र्य है। स्वतन्त्रता की कामना एक सहजात कामना है, किन्तु यह एक ऐतिहासिक सत्य है कि स्त्री की स्वतन्त्रता को हमने इरादतन सीमित करके रखा है। कहीं हमें भय भी है कि यदि स्त्री को अधिक स्वतन्त्रता दे देंगे तो वह उच्छृंखल हो जायेगी, इसलिए स्त्री की स्वतन्त्रता को हमने सामाजिक मर्यादा से जोड़ दिया है, स्त्री की अस्मिता से उसका नैतिक सम्बन्ध स्थापित कर दिया है। किन्तु हमें यह नहीं भूलना चाहिए कि नारी-स्वातन्त्र्य का यह नैतिक प्रत्यय हमारे मन के 'स्वामी भाव' से जुड़ा हुआ है। जहाँ स्वामी भाव है वहाँ दूसरे की स्वतन्त्रता को छीनने का भाव निहित है किन्तु दूसरे की स्वतन्त्रता को छीनकर हमारी स्वयं की स्वतन्त्रता समस्याग्रस्त हो जाती है। पुरुष की स्वतन्त्रता भी तभी पूर्ण होती है जब वह स्त्री की स्वतन्त्रता को भी सुनिश्चित करे। वह स्त्री के मूल-अधिकारों की रक्षा करे, उसे स्वतन्त्र चेतना का अधिकार दे, उसे चयन की स्वतन्त्रता का अधिकार भी दे, खुद

की देह के मामले में स्त्री को स्वतन्त्रता का अधिकार बहाल हो। स्वतन्त्रता के जितने आयाम हो सकते हैं उनको स्त्री के लिए सुनिश्चित करने का दायित्व पुरुष का है और उसी निस्संग स्वतन्त्रता में पुरुष की स्वतन्त्रता निहित है। प्रकारान्तर से पूरे समाज तथा पूरे मानव समुदाय की स्वतन्त्रता निहित है। स्वतन्त्रता का यह भाव भी समाज की अन्तःरचना का अनिवार्य और स्वाभाविक अंग बने, तभी इसकी सार्थकता है।

यहाँ एक सवाल उठता है। मान लीजिए कि स्त्री को पूरी स्वतन्त्रता मिल जाती है, उसे समाज की अन्तःरचना का सामाजिक अंग बना दिया जाता है तब क्या स्त्री को उसका अभीष्ट मिल जायेगा? नहीं, स्त्रियों को भी यह नहीं भूलना चाहिए कि स्वातन्त्र्य अधिकार ही नहीं एक चुनौती भी है, एक बहुत बड़ा जीवन मूल्य भी है जिसकी रक्षा करना सरल नहीं होगा, यह स्त्री का दायित्व होगा कि वह स्वातन्त्र्य का प्रयोग किस तरह करती है। उसे स्वतन्त्रता का उपयोग करना आना चाहिए तथा नये समय की चुनौतियों का सामना करने के लिए स्त्री को तत्पर रहते हुए अपनी अस्मिता को नयी अर्थवत्ता प्रदान करने का प्रयास करना चाहिए। अपनी स्वतन्त्रता का उपयोग करते हुए उसे अपनी प्रतिभा और संघर्ष के रास्ते आगे बढ़ना है। यदि वह संघर्ष के बिना सिर्फ अपनी देह के बल पर आगे बढ़ती है तो बाजार के स्वार्थों में प्रयुक्त होने में उसकी अस्मिता तथा स्वतन्त्रता खो जायेगी और उसकी अस्मिता की उपलब्धियों को एक खतरनाक और नकारात्मक मोड़ मिल जायेगा। बाजारवादी शक्तियाँ आज नारी देह का किस तरह उपयोग कर रही हैं, यह किसी से छिपा नहीं है।

और यहीं से उसकी सामाजिक सहभागिता की भूमिका आरम्भ हो जाती है। दरअसल अस्मिता, स्वतन्त्रता, सहभागिता, सक्रियता, चेतना सभी समाज सापेक्ष कारक हैं तथा इनके सही अर्थ समाज में ही खुलते हैं। अपने आप में ये मूल्य अमूर्त हैं किन्तु सामाजिक संबोधनों में ही वे अपनी सार्थकता पाते हैं। इस दृष्टि से अस्मिता, स्वतन्त्रता तथा सहभागिता के सन्दर्भ में स्त्री की भूमिका और भी महत्वपूर्ण हो जाती है। सामाजिक स्तर पर सब कुछ पाने के बाद उसकी भूमिका दुहरी होगी–सामाजिक विकास में अपना सकारात्मक

सहयोग देना तथा निजी जीवन में संघर्ष तथा प्रतिभा के रास्ते आगे बढ़ने का विकल्प स्वीकार करना। यहाँ हमें स्त्रियों की स्त्रियों के प्रति दृष्टि पर भी विचार करना होगा। हम देख रहे हैं कि समाज में स्त्रियों का बहुत बड़ा वर्ग ऐसा है जिन्हें वर्गीय-समृद्धि की सुविधाएं प्राप्त हैं। स्त्रियों की समृद्धि क्या उनके लिए ही सुरक्षित रहे? चेतना तथा साधन दोनों स्तरों पर समृद्ध स्त्री का दायित्व और बढ़ जाता है। यह किसी से छिपा नहीं है कि हमारे समाज में स्त्री और दलित होना अभिशाप है, किन्तु दलित स्त्री होना सबसे बड़ा अभिशाप है। समृद्ध स्त्रियों की सक्रिय सामाजिक सहभागिता का अर्थ होगा- पूरे स्त्री समुदाय को नये समाज की चुनौतियों के अनुरूप प्रशिक्षित करना।

ये सारे मुद्दे इतने सरल नहीं है कि इन्हें बड़े स्थूल तरीकों से हल किया जा सके, क्योंकि समाज की अन्तःरचना में बड़े बदलाव लाने के लिए लम्बा संघर्ष करना होता है। दुर्भाग्य से हमारे समाज में स्त्री-संघर्ष की परम्परा बड़ी क्षीण है। अतः इस परम्परा को ठोस आकार देना इस सदी की बहुत बड़ी जरूरत है, किन्तु जहाँ आकर आज नारीवाद ठहर गया है उससे अनेक जटिलताएं सामने आ रही हैं। नारी स्वातन्त्र्य के ऐसे आयाम भी खुले रहे हैं जिससे नारीवाद के समक्ष अनेक सवाल पैदा हो रहे हैं। स्त्री-अस्मिता तथा स्त्रीत्व से ही जुड़ा एक सवाल है अकेली स्त्री को मान्यता का। अर्थात् कुछ विमर्शकार चाहते हैं कि अकेली स्त्री को बिना पुरुष के स्वतन्त्र इकाई के रूप में मान्यता मिले। देखा यह भी गया है कि कुछ स्त्रियाँ अकेलेपन को वरण कर जीवन जीने का साहस दिखा रही हैं, किन्तु अध्ययन इस तथ्य को भी रेखांकित करते हैं कि बिना पुरुष के जीवन जीने वाली अकेली स्त्रियाँ उम्र की ढलान पर हताशा के कारण असामान्य हो जाती हैं। रचनात्मक कार्यों में व्यस्त अकेली स्त्रियाँ फिर भी अपने सृजन सुख के कारण असमानता के दर्द से कुछ-कुछ बच जाती हैं। इसका कारण यह भी हो सकता है कि उन्नत प्राणी जगत में जोड़े बनाकर रहने की एक नैसर्गिक प्रवृत्ति देखी जाती है और स्त्री का खुद चुना अकेलापन शायद इस नैसर्गिक प्रवृत्ति को बाधित करता है।

इस प्रसंग में स्त्री विमर्श का एक अन्य मुद्दा है-स्त्री समलैंगिकता (लैस्बिनिज्म) का, जिसके पक्षधर कहते हैं कि स्त्री पुरुष से मुक्ति चाहने लगी है तथा पुरुष के विकल्प के रूप में वह दूसरी स्त्री के साथ का वरण करने लगी है। समलैंगिकता के पक्षधर यह भी सोचते हैं कि यह सीधी चयन की स्वतन्त्रता से जुड़ा सवाल है तथा पुरुष के विकल्प के रूप में स्त्री का साथ चुनना उसकी 'जोड़े में रहने' की नैसर्गिक प्रवृत्ति की भी रक्षा करता है। किन्तु तत्सम्बन्धित विमर्शों तथा अध्ययनों से यह भी पता चला है कि अकेलेपन के अपने खतरे तथा उनकी भयावह परिणतियाँ देखने को मिलती हैं। साथ ही समलैंगिकता से भी विभिन्न जटिलताएं उत्पन्न होती हैं। देखने में यह आया है कि साथ-साथ रहने वाली दोनों स्त्रियों में से एक का पुरुषीकरण हो जाता है और परस्पर सम्बन्धों में वह अपना वर्चस्व स्थापित करने लगती है। व्यवहारिक तौर पर तो एक स्त्री पुरुष का चरित्र ही धारण कर लेती है तथा एकाध उदाहरण तो ऐसे भी मिले हैं कि एक स्त्री दूसरी स्त्री की पिटाई भी कर देती है। पुरुष समलैंगिकता (होमो सैक्श्युलिटी) में भी यह देखा गया है कि दोनों में से एक पुरुष स्त्रैण हो जाता है और वहाँ भी जटिलताएं उत्पन्न होती देखी गयी हैं। दरअसल इस समलैंगिक विकल्प में सम्बन्धों का स्थापत्य तो सामान्यतः स्त्री-पुरुष का ही रहता है। वैसे कोई भी वह सम्बन्ध व्यवस्था जो कुण्ठाओं और जटिलताओं को जन्म देती है, सामाजिक निकष पर मानवीय नहीं हो सकती। इस तथ्य से भी इंकार तो नहीं ही किया जा सकता है कि यह विकल्प अप्राकृतिक है। स्त्री विमर्श का ध्यान स्त्रीत्व से नैसर्गिक रूप से जुड़े मातृत्व के सवाल की ओर भी गया है। मातृत्व के क्षेत्र में नयी-नयी प्रवृत्तियाँ जन्म ले रही हैं। परखनली शिशु की तकनीक कुछ स्थान पाती जा रही है, पर उसकी सीमाएं भी साथ-साथ उजागर हो रही हैं। दरअसल मातृत्व प्राकृतिक अधिकार से जुड़ा एक नैतिक प्रश्न है जिसमें पुरुष की भूमिका लगभग नगण्य है।

किन्तु बच्चों की रक्षा में माता-पिता दोनों की भूमिका बराबर की होनी चाहिए। उधर भ्रूण हत्याएं नैतिक दृष्टि से ही नहीं वैधानिक दृष्टि से स्वीकृति पा रही हैं। जबकि भ्रूण हत्या को अनैतिक ही कहा

जायेगा। किन्तु परखनली शिशु की अवधारणा तो एक तकनीकी जैविक व्यापार है जिससे सामाजिक जैविकी के ध्वस्त होने की पूरी संभावनाएं हैं। यही स्थिति किराए की कोख द्वारा उत्पन्न बच्चों की भी होगी। इस प्रक्रिया से विकसित संतति के समक्ष यह समस्या तो रहेगी ही कि वह किस विरासत से अपने आपको जोड़े तथा परस्पर सम्बन्धों की कौन सी श्रेणी में अपने आपको रखे। क्या इस प्रकार की संतति को सम्बन्धित परिवार की स्वाभाविक विरासत में स्थान मिल पायेगा? क्या उन्हें समाज में परस्पर सम्बन्धों की गर्माहट का अहसास हो पायेगा? कमोबेश यही स्थिति किराए की कोख द्वारा प्राप्त बच्चों की भी होगी। इसमें सन्देह नहीं कि सभ्यता के जिस पड़ाव पर हम आ पहुँचे हैं वहाँ किराए की कोख के खरीददार भी मौजूद हैं तो आर्थिक विषमताओं के कारण कोख बेचने वाले भी तैयार हैं। किन्तु यहाँ भी समस्या सामाजिक एवं पारिवारिक सम्बन्धों की विरासत को लेकर ही होगी। किराए की कोख से पाली गयी संतति के समक्ष अपनी उस पहचान का संकट बना ही रहेगा जो उसे परिवार की विरासत से अपने आप मिल जाती है। परिवार और समाज में पारिवारिक सम्बन्धों का संकट चाहे जिस रूप में हो, घाटे में तो बच्चे ही रहते हैं तथा उन्हें ही सारे कष्ट सहने पड़ते हैं। अनाथ बनते हैं तो बच्चे बनते हैं, विरासत से बेदखल होते हैं तो बच्चे होते हैं। जबकि बच्चों के लालन-पालन का नैतिक दायित्व माँ-बाप दोनों का होता है। यदि माँ-बाप (स्त्री-पुरुष) स्वतन्त्रता चाहते हैं तो बच्चों की स्वतन्त्रता की रक्षा भी तो उनका ही दायित्व है क्योंकि एक की स्वतन्त्रता से दूसरे की स्वतन्त्रता बाधित नहीं होनी चाहिए। सामाजिक सम्बन्धों की व्यवस्था में बच्चों की स्वतन्त्रता और सुरक्षा को आश्वस्त किये बिना कोई भी विकल्प सामाजिक स्तर पर नैतिकता के दायरे में नहीं आ सकता।

मातृत्व से जुड़ा एक आयाम प्रजनन का भी है जो स्त्री के लिए नैसर्गिक के साथ ही सामाजिक रूप से विशेष दायित्व है जिसमें पुरुष की भूमिका लगभग नगण्य होती है। मातृत्व का दायित्व स्त्री के लिए एक पवित्र सामाजिक दायित्व है जिसके निर्वहन में उसे अनिर्वच आनन्द से युक्त पीड़ा भोगनी पड़ती है। इस आनन्दपूर्ण पीड़ा की कोई कीमत नहीं आँकी जा सकती। यह पीड़ा सर्जन

की पीड़ा होती है जिसे सम्पूर्ण प्राणी जगत भोगता है। वनस्पति जगत में भी प्रजनन की प्रक्रिया है तो जीव-जन्तु जगत में भी। पता नहीं जीव जन्तुओं को प्रजनन की पीड़ा का आनन्द कैसा मिलता है किन्तु देखा यही गया है कि उन्नत किस्म के जीवों में भी प्रजनन एक नैसर्गिक जैविक क्रिया है, भले ही उनमें यह क्रिया मौसमी है। मनुष्य जगत में प्रजनन की क्रिया का कोई मौसम प्रकृति द्वारा निर्धारित नहीं है। किन्तु इसमें सन्देह नहीं कि स्त्री प्रजनन की नैसर्गिक जैविक क्रिया की पीड़ा को एक अवर्णनीय आनन्द के साथ सहती है। सृष्टि की यात्रा को अनवरत रखने के लिए प्रकृति ने यह व्यवस्था की है तथा इस नैसर्गिक चक्र से पूरा जीवन जगत आह्लादित होता है। इसी चक्र को बनाए रखने की दृष्टि से प्रकृति ने नर और मादा में अलग-अलग हारमोन्स की सृष्टि की है तथा प्रजनन के लिए प्रकृति ने स्त्री को ही अधिक अनुकूल माना है। इसलिए स्त्री को इस नैसर्गिक चक्र से मुक्ति नहीं मिल सकती। इस नैसर्गिक चक्र से मुक्ति के जितने भी उपाय-समलैंगिकता, अकेले जीवनयापन, परखनली शिशु, किराए की कोख आदि मनुष्य ने निकाले हैं वे समाज को उन्नत बनाने के बजाए समाज को विकृतियों की ओर ले जाने वाले हैं। व्यक्तिगत स्वतन्त्रता के नाम पर हम कहीं मानव जीवन की सम्बन्ध-नैतिकी और सामाजिकी का ही निषेध तो नहीं कर रहे हैं? कहीं हम अपने सामाजिक दायित्व से पलायन तो नहीं कर रहे? कहीं हम एक-दूसरे प्रकार के व्यापार-तन्त्र को प्रश्रय तो नहीं दे रहे? ये सारे नैतिक प्रश्न हैं जो स्त्री अस्मिता, स्वतन्त्रता और उसकी भूमिका से जुड़े हैं।

स्त्री तथा नारीवादी सक्रिय संगठनों को भी इन प्रश्नों पर गम्भीरता से विचार करने की आवश्यकता है और नारी की अस्मिता तथा स्वतन्त्रता को सुनिश्चित और अक्षुण्ण बनाने के लिए सकारात्मक प्रयत्न भी करने हैं तभी समाज में उसकी सहभागिता की अर्थवत्ता प्रमाणित हो सकेगी।

29 स्त्री-विमर्श : इस सदी के साहित्य का रुपहला पक्ष

—त्रिभुवननाथ शुक्ल

स्त्री-विमर्श साहित्य-विमर्श का बीज भाव रहा है। बीज के बिना जिस प्रकार वृक्ष की कल्पना असंभव है, वैसे ही स्त्री और उसके समशील के बिना साहित्य की कल्पना असंभव है। दुनिया की सभी भाषाओं के साहित्य में यह अपृथक तादात्म्य के रूप में विद्यमान है। वर्तमान सदी में यह विमर्श बहुत रुपहला हो चला है। अब मैं भी इससे बिदकता नहीं हूँ। कारण कि अगर कोई विचार सदी के चिन्तन का पक्ष बनता है तो उस पर अपना पक्ष रखना ही चाहिए।

वेदों, स्मृतियों, पुराणों, रामायण और महाभारत से लेकर कालिदास आदि तक के साहित्य में यह विषय अंगभूत के रूप में व्यक्त हुआ है। हिन्दी के आदिकालीन साहित्य से लेकर समकालीन साहित्य तक में यह अपने यथासमय रूप में स्थान पा सका है।

छान्दोग्य उपनिषद में अश्वमति का कथन है:-

> "मेरे राज्य में कोई स्वैरिणी स्त्री नहीं है। नारी जाति में स्वैरिता न फैले इस दृष्टि से राज्य का कर्तव्य पुरुषों को कामाचार से बचाना था। शासन में स्त्रियों को 'अबध्य' माना गया था। जिन अपराधों के लिए पुरुषों को कड़े दण्ड दिये जाते थे, स्त्रियाँ उनके लिए साधारण दण्ड पाकर छुटकारा पा जाती थीं।"

स्पष्ट है कि हमारा भारतीय समाज उनके प्रति सदाशयी रहा है। भारतीय परम्परा में विद्या की अधिष्ठात्री सरस्वती, धन की लक्ष्मी, पराक्रम की दुर्गा, सौन्दर्य की रति और पावित्र्य में गंगा को अपना मानक स्वीकार किया गया है। मनुस्मृति में व्यक्त है कि "ईश्वर ने अपने शरीर को दो भागों-नारी और पुरुष में विभाजित

कर सृष्टि की रचना की।" (1-32) वहीं ये वाक्य भी उद्धृत पाए जाते हैं "स्त्री कभी स्वतन्त्र नहीं होती, स्त्री को मंत्रादि नहीं जानने चाहिए, स्त्री को धन सम्पदा का अधिकार नहीं है, जहाँ स्त्रियों का सम्मान है, वहाँ देवता निवास करते हैं। कन्या ही कुल का जीवन है (कालिदास); कन्या के स्वरूप में परिवार की लक्ष्मी का निवास होता है (महाभारत), स्त्रियाँ अस्थिर वृत्ति की होती हैं (रामायण), पुरुषों का भाग्य और स्त्री का चरित्र देवता भी नहीं जानते, मानव की सामर्थ्य कैसे हो सकती है (ऋग्वेद)।"

शिव पुराण में कहा गया हैः-

क्लीवं च दुखस्थ च व्याधित वृद्धमेव च।
सुखितं दुखितं चापि पतिमेंकं न लंघयेत।।

(अध्याय 54, पार्वती खण्ड)

अर्थात् न तो सुख में और न ही दुख में अपने बुरे, कमजोर, बीमार और वृद्ध पति की आलोचना करनी चाहिए अन्यथा नरक में दुख भोगने पड़ते हैं। तुलसीदास ने नारी को अवगुणों की जड़ तथा दुखों की खान कहा है। 'अपगुण मूल सूलप्रद, प्रमदा सब दुख खानि'। वहीं मनु कहते हैंः- "शोचन्ति याम यो यत्र विनश्यत्याशु तत्कुलम" अर्थात् जिन घरों में स्त्रियाँ शोक करती हैं, उस घर का विनाश शीघ्र होता है। स्पष्ट है कि नारी की स्तुति और निन्दा की एक दीर्घ परम्परा रही है। मगर ये सभी मत एकांगी प्रतीत होते हैं। यह सब पुरुषों के दृष्टिकोण पर निर्भर रहा है।

पाश्चात्य परम्परा में भी नारी की ऐसी ही स्थिति पाई जाती है।

'विलीव ए वूमैन ऑर एन एपिटाफ
आर एनी अदर थिंग दैट्स फाल्स' (बायरन)

अर्थात् नारी अथवा अन्य किसी वस्तु पर विश्वास नहीं करना चाहिए क्योंकि वे झूठे होते हैं। एम.एम. पियावे ने नारी के अस्तित्व को नगण्य माना है। 'वूमैन इज ऐज फाल्स ऐज ए फीदर इन द विंड' अर्थात् नारी का अस्तित्व वायु में उड़ते पंख के समान है, जो कि असत्य है।

'ए वूमैन ए डॉग एण्ड ए वालनट ट्री।
दि मोर यू बीट दैम दि बेटर दे बी।।' (थामस फिलर)

अर्थात् नारी, कुत्ता और अखरोट को जितना तुम पीटोगे वे उतने ही उत्तम हो जाते हैं। शेक्सपियर का कथन है–'फ्रैलिटी दाई नेम इज वुमन' अर्थात् नारी तू अबला है।

वहीं दूसरी ओर गौरवमय स्थान भी दिया गया है। गेटे ने कहा 'द एटर्नल फेमिनिन ड्रॉज अस अपवार्ड' अर्थात्, शाश्वत नारीत्व, हमें सामान्य स्तर से उठाकर ऊँचाई की ओर ले जाता है। ओटवे ने कहा है:-

'ओ वूमैन। लवली वूमैन। नेचर मेड दी टू टैंपर मैन,

वी हैड बीन बीस्ट बिदाउट यू'

अर्थात् ए नारी! सुन्दर नारी! प्रकृति ने तुझे पुरुष को शांत करने वाला बनाया अन्यथा हम (पुरुष) तुम्हारे बिना पशु ही रहते। नेपोलियन ने उत्तम राष्ट्र में स्त्री की भूमिका को स्वीकार किया है। 'गिव मी गुड मदर्स, एण्ड आई विल गिव यू गुड नेशन' अर्थात्, मुझे अच्छी माताएँ दीजिए और मैं आपको अच्छा राष्ट्र बनाकर दूँगा।

स्पष्ट है कि दोनों परम्पराओं में दोनों दृष्टियों (मान एवं अपमान) से नारी के व्यक्तित्व को रेखांकित किया गया है। हमारे वैदिक युग में नारियों को पूर्ण स्वतन्त्रता थी। समय के अनुसार स्थितियों में परिवर्तन आता गया। स्त्री देवी के स्थान से सन्तान उत्पादन की वस्तु मात्र बनकर रह गई। मैं इस विमर्श के कुछ शाब्दिक साक्ष्य को भी यहाँ रखना उचित समझता हूँ। पतंजलि ने माना है:-

'शब्द, स्पर्श, रूप, रस और गन्ध का समुच्चय स्त्री है। पुरुषों के ज्ञानेन्द्रियों की तृप्ति नारी से होती है इसलिए उसे स्त्री कहा जाता है।'

हिन्दी के रासो साहित्य में स्त्री विमर्श का दूसरा ही रूप है। इस युग में नारियों में वीरता के प्रति आकर्षण है। एक सखी अपनी दूसरी सखी से कहती है:-

भल्ला हुआ जु मारिया बहिणि महारा कंतु।

लज्जेजं तु बयंसिअहु जइ भग्गा घरु एंतु।।

अर्थात् युद्ध में भागने वाले पति के प्रति उसके मन में कोई सम्मान नहीं है। इसलिए वह कहती है कि हे बहिन, अच्छा हुआ

कि मेरा पति मारा गया यदि वह भागकर घर आता तो मैं अपनी समवयस्काओं से लज्जित होती। चन्दबरदाई की 'संयोगिता' में नारी की पवित्रता, पतिव्रता पत्नी और सौन्दर्य आदि गुणों की अभिव्यक्ति हुई है। 'वीरसतसई' में नारी का शक्ति रूप व्यक्त हुआ है। कवि कहता है– 'उस कविता को धूल में फेंक दो जिसमें नारी के शक्ति रूप की वन्दना न हो।'

वस्तुतः स्त्री विमर्श का जैसा स्वरूप समकालीन महिला कथा लेखिकाओं में पाया जाता है, वैसा हमारे पूर्व विवेचित साहित्यिक पक्षों में नहीं मिलता। कारण कि पहले के रचनाकार अपने समय में कम और पिछले युग में अधिक रमण करते थे। हमारा समकालीन रचनाकार अपने समय में अधिक स्थिर होकर गहराई से सोचता है। मैत्रेयी पुष्पा की 'तुम किसकी हो बिन्नी?' में व्यक्त है कि आज के समाज में पुत्र को अधिक महत्व प्राप्त है। उससे वंश चलता है, अर्थात् वह वंशवाहक है। पुत्र की प्राप्ति प्रत्येक परिवार की महत्वाकांक्षा है। यही कारण है कि पुत्र की जगह पुत्री का जन्म होता है तो उसके साथ दुर्व्यवहार किया जाता है। स्वयं माँ भी पुरुष-प्रधान समाज के संस्कारों के कारण उसके साथ अमानवीय व्यवहार करती है। इस कहानी में आरती ने दो बेटियों को हताशा और निराशा के साथ स्वीकार किया। बाद में पुत्र की चाह में उसने तीन बार गर्भपात करवाया। इसके बाद उसने पुनः गर्भधारण कर लिंग परीक्षण कराया और इस बार 'मेल चाइल्ड' की रिपोर्ट आई थी परन्तु लड़की का जन्म हुआ। बेटी के जन्म की खबर मिलते ही पूरे घर में मातम सा छा गया। इस अनचाही, अवांछित बेटी की ओर न माँ ने देखा और न ही उसे दूध पिलाया। यहाँ तक कि उसका नामकरण भी नहीं किया, नर्स का दिया हुआ नाम 'बिन्नी' ही प्रचलित हो गया। यहाँ रहने के दौरान पहले दादी ने और फिर बाद में महरी ने उसे सँभाला था। बिन्नी जैसी कई लड़कियाँ आज इसी मानसिकता की शिकार हुई हैं और हो रही हैं।

मंजुला भगत की 'रसप्रिया' कम उम्र में विधवा हुई स्त्री की कहानी है। नमिता सिंह की 'उबारने वाले हाथ' में स्त्री अपनी

शक्ति को पहचान कर पूरे परिवार को उबारने का निर्णय लेती है। मेहरून्निसा परवेज की कहानी 'विद्रोह' की नीना प्रौढ़ा कुमारिका है। परिवार की दयनीय स्थिति के कारण वह परिवार की बागडोर थामती है। राजी सेठ की 'स्त्री' कहानी ग्रामीण स्त्री की संवेदना को व्यक्त करती है। इस कहानी की नायिका कमली, एक अनपढ़ एवं गँवार महिला है। उसकी अपनी कुछ निजी समस्याएँ हैं। उसका सहनशीलता का स्वभाव परम्परागत पत्नी के ही चरित्र को प्रदर्शित करता है। मालती जोशी की कहानी 'ढाई आखर प्रेम का' प्रेम सम्बन्धों पर केन्द्रित है। जयंती अपना सम्पूर्ण जीवन मृत प्रेमी और उसके माँ-बाप के लिए समर्पित कर देती है, केवल ढाई आखर के लिए। शशिप्रभा की 'गुंबद' कहानी नारी मन की व्यथा को सशक्त रूप में अभिव्यक्त करती है। उषा प्रियंवदा की 'जिन्दगी और गुलाब के फूल' अर्थ के कारण बदलते पारिवारिक सम्बन्धों के सूक्ष्म विवेचन की कहानी है। उषा वर्मा की कहानी 'मैं क्या बताऊँ' बेटे-बेटी को समान मानकर चलने वाली विचारधारा से प्रभावित है। मन्नू भण्डारी की 'ऊँचाई' विवाहोत्तर सम्बन्धों को सहज और नैतिक बोध के रूप में अभिव्यक्ति देने वाली कहानी है। मृदुला गर्ग की 'हरी बिन्दी' दांपत्य जीवन की एकरसता से ऊबी एक युवती की मनोव्यथा को व्यक्त करती है। क्रांति द्विवेदी की कहानी 'नहीं बधूँगी' दांपत्य सम्बन्धों की नई व्याख्या करती है। मृणाल पाण्डे की कहानी 'यानि कि एक बात थी' एक सफल स्त्रीवादी कहानी है। यह कहानी स्त्री के स्वतन्त्र व्यक्तित्व की परिचायक है। चित्रा मुदगल की कहानी 'शून्य' दाम्पत्य की टूटन और उससे उपजी समस्याओं को अभिव्यक्ति देती है। इन्हीं की कहानी 'लाक्षागृह' पुरुष प्रधान समाज में नारी शोषण के विविध आयामों को प्रस्तुत करती है। कमला सिंघवी की 'एक टुकड़ा धरती' स्त्री स्वावलंबन और उसकी अस्मिता की महत्ता को प्रदर्शित करती है। कृष्णा अग्निहोत्री की 'बया का घोंसला' एक आधुनिक, आत्मनिर्भर स्त्री की कहानी है। सुधा गोयल की 'ठूँठ' स्त्री के शरीर और उसके मन को विशिष्ट पहचान देती है। अरुणा सीतेश की 'अनुत्तरित' मन की अतल गहराइयों को व्यक्त करने वाली मनोवैज्ञानिक कहानी है। ममता कालिया की 'जिन्दगी सात घण्टे की' उच्चपद पर कार्यरत महिलाओं

की अवस्था, उनकी मनःस्थिति, एकाकीपन की समस्याओं आदि पर केन्द्रित कहानी है।

इन सभी समकालीन महिला कहानीकारों की कहानियों में अभिव्यक्त नारी अपनी अस्मिता, अपने व्यक्तित्व और अपने आत्मसम्मान और उसकी रक्षा के प्रति सजग हैं। नारी मन की सूक्ष्मातिसूक्ष्म संवेदनाएं इन कहानियों में व्यक्त हुई हैं। यही नहीं ये कहानियाँ पुरुष सत्ता को चुनौतियाँ भी देती हैं। इन कहानियों में यौन सम्बन्धों के प्रति नए दृष्टिकोण अपनाए गए हैं। परम्परागत मान्यताओं के विरुद्ध विवाह पूर्व और विवाहोत्तर यौन सम्बन्धों को उचित माना गया है। यद्यपि यह बात आज भी आदर्श भारतीय पाठकों के गले के नीचे उतरने वाली नहीं है। कहीं यह भी आश्चर्य होता है कि स्त्री विमर्श या स्त्रीवादी लेखन को केन्द्र में रखकर जो बहस चल रही है, उसमें केवल विकृतियों पर ही हमारी दृष्टि क्यों केन्द्रित हो जाती है? उसका सतपक्ष भी तो है, जहाँ हमारी दृष्टि को विश्राम मिलना चाहिए। परम्परागत भावुकता के स्थान पर बौद्धिक एवं तार्किक दृष्टिकोण इन नारी पात्रों की विशेषता बनकर उभरे हैं। नारी अब बौद्धिक और तार्किक दृष्टिकोण के साथ जीना चाहती है। इन कहानियों के अधिकांश पात्र अत्याधुनिक विचार और जीवन शैली को स्वीकार करने लगे हैं। पश्चिमी विचारों के प्रभाव के कारण भी उनकी जीवन शैली में परिवर्तन होने लगा है। वे अपने जीवन को आधुनिक जीवन शैली में बदलकर जीना चाहते हैं। बंगमहिला (राजेन्द्र घोष) की कहानी 'दुलाई वाली' (सरस्वती 1907) से आधुनिक महिला कथा लेखन की जो परम्परा प्रारम्भ हुई, वह निरन्तर विकसित होते हुए गौरव शिखर पर पहुँच रही है।

कहानियों के अतिरिक्त समकालीन हिन्दी उपन्यास लेखिकाओं में यही भावबोध दृष्टिगत होता है। यहाँ इस भाव बोध के कुछ उपन्यासों का उल्लेख करना आवश्यक होगा। उषा प्रियंवदा के 'पचपन खम्भे लाल दीवारें' उपन्यास में सुषमा सुशिक्षित, सुशील, संवेदनशील, अंतर्मुखी तथा आत्मपीड़क महिला है। कृष्णा सोबती की 'मित्रो मरजानी' उपन्यास में मित्रो नामक युवती की कथाव्यथा है। मेहरूनिसा परवेज के उपन्यास 'आँखों की दहलीज' में निजी

जीवन की कड़वाहट का व्यापक अनुभव अभिव्यक्त हुआ है। ममता कालिया का 'बेघर' उपन्यास हमारे समाज में व्याप्त संकीर्णता और दकियानूसी के विपरीत एवं विनाशकारी परिणामों को व्यक्त करता है। मंजुल भगत का 'अनारो' एक सशक्त नारी चरित्र प्रधान उपन्यास है। सूर्यबाला का 'अग्निपंखी' उपन्यास सातवें दशक की रोमांटिक भरमार से हटकर सामाजिक सरोकारों से जूझता है। नासिरा शर्मा का 'ठीकरे की मंगनी' उपन्यास हालात के मार से पैदा हुई एक लड़की महरुख की कहानी है। ॠता शुक्ला का 'अग्निपर्व', पद्मा सचदेव का 'अवन बनेगी देहरी', प्रभा खेतान का 'छिन्नमस्त्रा', मैत्रेयी पुष्पा का 'इदन्नमम', नमिता सिंह का 'अपनी सलीबें', राजी सेठ का 'निष्कवच', सुषमा बेदी का 'लौटना', चित्रा मुदगल का 'आवां', जया जादवानी का 'त्वमसि', मृणाल पाण्डे का 'रास्तों पर भटकते हुए', अलका सरावगी का 'शेष कादम्बरी' आदि उपन्यास नारी मन की अतल गहराइयों को अभिव्यक्ति प्रदान करने के साथ-साथ पुरुष सत्ता के एकाधिकार को भी चुनौती देते हैं। ये उपन्यास स्त्री को केवल करुणा के पात्र के रूप में न प्रस्तुत कर उसे शक्ति, सामर्थ्य से युक्त रूप में हमारे सामने प्रस्तुत करते हैं। यही कारण है कि इन उपन्यासों में स्त्री के विशिष्ट अनुभवों की अभिव्यक्ति हुई है।

इस प्रकार समकालीन स्त्री लेखन ने स्त्री की मूक, बधिर और अंधदर्शक छवि को तोड़ दिया है। समकालीन स्त्री विमर्श ने स्त्री के गूँगेपन को स्वर दिया है। उसने तो नारी को अबला मानने की जगह सबला मानने पर मजबूर कर दिया है।

30 'मित्रो मरजानी': नारी स्वातंत्र्य और परिवार

—सुनीता रानी

कृष्णा सोबती ने स्त्री के जीवन एवं चरित्र को अपने उपन्यासों का केन्द्रीय भाव बनाया है। उनके उपन्यासों के नारी चरित्र सामाजिक आचार संहिता एवं पारिवारिक मर्यादा के अलौकिक उदाहरण नहीं वरन् नैतिक-अनैतिक की अपनी धारणाओं से मुक्त जीती-जागती स्त्रियाँ हैं जो केवल स्त्री जाति का ही प्रतिनिधित्व नहीं करतीं बल्कि वे व्यक्ति के रूप में, एक ईमानदार मनुष्य के रूप में समाज में अपनी पहचान चाहती हैं।

'मित्रो मरजानी' की मित्रो यानि समित्रावंती स्त्री के पुराने आदर्शों, थोथी मान्यताओं, सनातन कर्त्तव्यों के साथ-साथ उसके परम्परागत बिम्बों को विनष्ट करती हुई एक नवीन आकर्षण एवं जिज्ञासा जगाती है। संवेदना के स्तर पर मित्रो उस जाति का प्रतिनिधित्व करती है जो स्त्री-पुरुष सम्बन्धों की विसंगतियों, परिवेश से विलगता एवं सामाजिक मान्यताओं के पालन की विवशता के चलते एक अजीब-सी घुटन महसूस कर रही है और इस घुटन से निकलने के लिए हाथ-पैर मारती प्रतीत होती है। ऐसी मित्रो को सामाजिक सम्बन्ध अर्थहीन प्रतीत होते हैं और नैतिक मान्यताएं खोखली। 1967 में पहली बार अक्षर प्रकाशन से प्रकाशित लघु परन्तु स्त्री चरित्र की पूर्णतया नवीन उद्भावना करने वाले इस उपन्यास का कथानक लीक से हटकर है। मित्रो को अपने पति सरदारी लाल से वैवाहिक जीवन की सन्तुष्टि नहीं मिलती और अपने पति से असन्तुष्ट हो वह उसका सरेआम मजाक उड़ाती है। मित्रो एक पूर्ण संवेदनशील नारी है जो अपनी इच्छा, भावना, आवेग तथा मनोवेग का सम्मान करती है और अपने अधिकार तथा आवश्यकताओं की पूर्ति का हरसंभव प्रयास करती है। उसके व्यक्तित्व में बनावटीपन नहीं है। मित्रो आज की स्त्री है जो अपनी आवश्यकताओं यहाँ तक कि शारीरिक

आवश्यकताओं को भी महज नैतिकता के नाम पर अनदेखा नहीं करती, खुलकर उनके बारे में बोलती है। यौन-सम्बन्ध शरीर की आवश्यकता है और स्त्री-पुरुष के सम्बन्ध की स्वाभाविक प्रवृत्ति। स्त्री शरीर की जरूरतों को व्यक्त करती मित्रो के लिए पति केवल परमेश्वर नहीं है और न ही परिवार धर्म का पालन जीवन का एकमात्र लक्ष्य। मित्रो एक सामान्य नारी है और उसकी दैहिक आवश्यकता भी स्वाभाविक है किन्तु उसकी निर्भीक अभिव्यक्ति एवं बुलन्द माँग असामान्य प्रतीत होती है और उसके चरित्र को असाधारण बनाती है:-

> "देवर तुम्हारा मेरा रोग नहीं पहचानता। बहुत हुआ हफ्ते-पखबारे और. मेरी इस देह में इतनी प्यास है, इतनी प्यास कि मछली-सी तड़पती हूँ।"[1]

इस सन्दर्भ में राजेन्द्र यादव लिखते हैं:-

> "मित्रो हिन्दी की अकेली कथा नारी है जो सदियों से लादे गये संस्कार सम्बन्धों, सुन्दर-सुन्दर उपमाओं को ललकारती मुँह चिढ़ाती और उन्हें झुठलाती हुई अपनी मूलभूत जरूरत और जबान के साथ हमारे सामने आ खड़ी है छिन्नमस्ता काली की तरह मानो हम उसके तेज को बर्दाश्त नहीं कर पाते।"[2]

मित्रो काम की पूर्ण तृप्ति चाहती है और उसका पति जीवन में अन्य कामों को भी महत्व देता है। यही दोनों के बीच संघर्ष का कारण है। मित्रो अपने सौन्दर्य के प्रति, अपने प्रति अपने पति का आकर्षण चाहती है:-

> "फिर पड़छती पर रखे आइने में अपना मुखड़ा देख हँस पड़ी मेरा यह बेअकल मर्द-जना यही नहीं जानता कि मुझ-सी दरियाई नार किस गुर से काबू आती है। मैं निगोड़ी बन-ठनके बैठती हूँ तो गबरू सौदा-सुल्फ लेने उठ जाता है।"[3]

स्त्री-पुरुष के बीच यह तनाव सनातन है किन्तु उसकी निर्द्वन्द्व अभिव्यक्ति सर्वथा नवीन है। मित्रो घर-परिवार की मर्यादा के नाम पर सब चुपचाप नहीं झेलती वरन् अपने सच को अभिव्यक्ति देने का साहस रखती है। दैहिक असन्तुष्टि के सच को बखानती मित्रो को हर रोज अपने पति की पिटाई खानी पड़ती है।

"जिठानी, तुम्हारे देवर-सा बगलोल कोई और दूजा न होगा। न दुःख-सुख न प्रीति-प्यार, न जलन-प्यास बस आए दिन धौल-धप्पा लानत-मलामत!"[4]

लेकिन मित्रो सामाजिक मर्यादाओं एवं पारिवारिक अंकुशों से अपने को मुक्त रखती है। दैहिक असन्तुष्टि ही उसके व्यक्तित्व में असामान्यता एवं विसंगति उत्पन्न करती है। उसका व्यक्तित्व उद्दाम बन जाता है। एक हद तक उद्दण्ड मित्रो का व्यक्तित्व पिटाई से आहत नहीं होता। वह पति के पीटने पर भी उसके आँखे नीची करने के आदेश को पूर्णतः अस्वीकार कर देती हैः-

"मँझली बहू ने ऐसा सब कुछ नहीं किया। बड़ी-बड़ी भूरी आँखों घर वाले का सामना किए रही।"[5]

और यहाँ तक कि वह उसके लिए सजा की भी उद्घोषणा कर देती हैः-

"माँजी, बेटे की चिन्ता में तन न सुखाओ इसकी करनी आप ही इसे काले पानियों भिजवाएगी।"[6]

पति का ठण्डापन और दुर्व्यवहार मित्रो को कटुभाषी बना देता है। पर-पुरुषों के साथ हँसने-बोलने में उसे कोई बुराई नजर नहीं आती और अपनी पारिवारिक पृष्ठभूमि तथा बाल्यकाल में वैश्या माँ द्वारा पढ़ाए गये पाठों को वह सहज-भाव से स्वीकार करती हैः-

"मित्रो झिझकी हिचकिचाई नहीं। पड़े-पड़े कहा-सात नदियों की तारू तवे-सी काली मेरी माँ और मैं गोरी-चिट्टी उसकी कोख पड़ी। कहती है इलाके के बड़भागी तहसीलदार की मुहादरा है मित्रो। अब तुम्हीं बताओ जिठानी तुम-जैसा सत बल कहाँ से पाऊँ लाऊँ?"[7]

अपने अधिकारों के विषय में वह भारी-भरकम शब्दों में सैद्धान्तिक बातें नहीं करती परन्तु सहज रूप में ही अपने व्यक्तित्व को उपेक्षित नहीं होने देती है। उसकी उपस्थिति के अहसास से कोई चाहकर भी अछूता नहीं रह पाता। पूरी तरह बेफिक्र मित्रो के चरित्र में कोई दोहरापन नहीं है, कोई उलझाव नहीं हैः-

"मित्रो ने ओंठ बिचकाए-चिन्ता जंजाल किसको? मैं तो चिन्ता करने वाली के पेट ही नहीं पड़ी।"[8]

उसका यह बेफिक्र खुला व्यवहार परिवार की इज्जत धूल में मिल जाने की समस्या को जन्म देता है, क्योंकि वह एक सभ्य एवं परम्परागत परिवार की बहू है। उसके परिवार द्वारा उस पर अनैतिकता का आरोप लगाया जाता है। फलतः उसे परिवार के पुरुषों के समक्ष कठघरे में खड़ा होना पड़ता है। वहाँ भी वह बेझिझक अपने चरित्र पर लगे आरोपों को बड़ी चतुरता से स्वीकार भी करती है, नकारती भी है:-

'सरदारी की बहू को मुँह-माँगी मुराद मिल गयी। कटोरी-सी दो आँखें नचाकर कहा "सोने सी अपनी देह झुर-झुरकर जला दूँ या गुलजारी देवर की घरवाली की न्याई सुई-सिलाई के पीछे जान खपा लूँ? सच तो यूँ जेठ जी, कि दीन-दुनिया बिसरा मैं मनुक्ख की जात से हँस-खेल लेती हूँ। झूठ यूँ कि खसम का दिया राजपाट छोड़ मैं कोठे पर तो नहीं जा बैठी?"[9]

वास्तव में मित्रो की यह स्वीकारोक्ति आधुनिक भारतीय स्त्री के मन का यथार्थ है। मित्रो के माध्यम से कृष्णा सोबती ने इस सत्य का उद्घाटन किया है कि भारतीय समाज में आदर्श, सदाचार, नैतिकता एवं मूल्यों का बखान करने वाले परिवारों की वास्तविक स्थिति क्या है, वहाँ मित्रो जैसे नारी रूप चलते-फिरते देखे जा सकते हैं:-

"किसी भी घर-गृहस्थी के आँगन में मित्रो की आदिम महक सूँघी जा सकती है।"[10]

मित्रो दृढ़ इरादों वाली स्त्री है। वह अपने ऊपर, अपनी शक्ति पर विश्वास करती है, किसी धर्म या ईश्वर में नहीं। वह उन ईश्वरीय परिकल्पनाओं, कर्म सिद्धान्त एवं मान्यताओं का विरोध भी करती है जिनके नाम पर आज तक स्त्री ठगी जाती रही है। वह सदियों से चढ़ाये आदर्श भारतीय नारी के लुभावने मुखौटे को उतार कर फेंकती है। उसे अपनी दैहिक संरचना एवं सौन्दर्य पर विश्वास है जिससे वह ईश्वर को भी मुग्ध करने का साहस अथवा दुस्साहस रखती है। इसीलिए ईश्वर से नहीं डरती:-

"मित्रो ने सदा की तरह आँखे नचाईं–काहे का डर? जिस बड़े दरबार वाले का दरबार लगा होगा वह इन्साफी क्या मर्द-जना न होगा? तुम्हारी देवरानी को भी हाँक पड़ गई तो जग-जहान का अलबेला गुमानी एक नजर तो मित्रो पर भी डाल लेगा।"[11]

यह मित्रो का अद्‌भुत आत्मविश्वास ही है कि वह पुरुष रूप परमात्मा को भी अपने सौन्दर्य से रिझाने की ताकत रखती है। मित्रो समाज से सीधा-साधा गणित चाहती है। वह समाज के रवैये से कहीं-कहीं क्षुब्ध भी दिखायी देती है:-

"जिन्द-जान का यह कैसा व्यापार? अपने लड़के बीज डालें तो पुण्य, दूजे डालें तो कुकर्म।"[12]

ऊपरी तौर पर निराले रंग-ढंग वाली मित्रो एक पूर्णतया संवेदनशील नारी है। वह अपनी जिठानी सुहाग के पातिव्रत का सम्मान करती है तो अपनी सास के लिए कुछ भी कर सकती है। उसके मन में किसी के लिए कटुता नहीं। दैहिक तृप्ति की माँग करने वाली मित्रो इतनी समझ भी रखती है कि स्त्री-पुरुष के सम्बन्ध केवल देह तक ही सीमित नहीं वे सुख-दुःख के साथी हैं। तभी तो मित्रो खीझ उठती है कि उसका पति सरदारी लाल क्यों नहीं उसके साथ अपने दुःख-दर्द बाँटता। मित्रो के मन में कसक है कि उसका पति उसे मन की बात नहीं बताता। उसे इस योग्य ही नहीं समझता, क्योंकि वह पुरुष है वह तो यही मानता है:-

"क्यों सिर खपाने बैठी है? मर्दों के फिकर मर्दों के लिए।"[13]

परिवार पर संकट की स्थिति में मुँहफट दिखने वाली मित्रो भी जबान पर काबू रखना जानती है:-

"सुनकर एक बार तो जी हुआ घरवाले को एक करारी सुना चित कर दे; पर जुबान पर काबू पा, मित्रो बोली-महाराज जी, न थाली बाँटते हो न नींद बाँटते हो, दिल के दुःखड़े ही बाँट लो।"[14]

परिवार पर आए आर्थिक संकट की इस घड़ी में मित्रो अपनी जमा-पूँजी बिना किसी सोच-विचार के निकाल कर दे देती है:-

> "मित्रो ने एड़ियाँ उठा पड़छत्ती पर से टीन की सन्दूकची उतारी। ताली लगा लाल पट्‌ट की थैली निकाली और घरवाले के आगे रख बोली-यह दमड़ी दात परवान करो लाल जी कौन इस नाँवे के बिना मित्रो की बेटी कुँवारी रह जायेगी।"[15]

परिवार के प्रति इस हद तक उसके लगाव को देखकर उसका पति भी हक्का-बक्का रह जाता है। और मित्रो अभी भी सहज, मस्त, उसे यह तनिक भी गुमान नहीं कि उसने परिवार की लाज बचाने के लिए अपनी सारी दौलत लुटा दी है।

उसकी संवेदनशीलता तथा भावप्रवणता उसमें माँ बनने की तीव्र इच्छा जगाती है। सुहागवती के गर्भवती होने की खबर सुनकर वह खुश है परन्तु अपने विषय में सोचकर वह उदास हो जाती है। वह माँ न बन पाने पर न तो घुट-घुटकर समाज के भय से मरी जाती है, न रो-रोकर अपने भाग्य को कोसती है, न ही अपने सुन्दर शरीर को चिन्ता में जलाकर राख करती है। वह तो सीधे-सपाट शब्दों में अपने पति को ही उत्तरदायी ठहराती है। इसलिए सास द्वारा पुत्रवती होने के आशीर्वाद को सुनकर वह बिफर उठती है:-

> "मेरा बस चले तो गिनकर सौ कौरव जन डालूँ पर अम्मा अपने लाड़ले बेटे का भी तो आड़तोड़ जुटाओ! निगोड़े मेरे पत्थर के बुत में भी कोई हरकत तो हो।"[16]

मातृत्व के प्रति अनुराग ही उसे परिवार के प्रति आस्थावान बनाता है।

मित्रो के चरित्र को देखकर कुछ प्रश्न अवश्य कौंधते हैं-क्या मित्रो की स्वाभाविक दैहिक कामना और उसकी सहज अभिव्यक्ति समाज विरुद्ध है? क्या पति पर उदासीनता का आरोप लगाना ठीक नहीं? इन प्रश्नों पर विचार करते समय मित्रो के पालन-पोषण तथा उसके विवाह पूर्व के सामाजिक-पारिवारिक परिवेश को ध्यान में रखना आवश्यक हैं। मित्रो बालो वैश्या की पुत्री है जो एक सभ्य परिवार की बहू बनती है। मित्रो की माँ बालो तथा मित्रो के माँ-बेटी के संबंध अजीब हैं। मित्रो की माँ बालो बुढ़ापे में अपनी बेटी के गृहस्थ जीवन से ही ईर्ष्या करने लगती है। बालो वह माँ है जिसने वैश्या

के रूप में राग-रंग में जीवन बिताया है और अन्त में उसके जीवन में खोखलेपन के सिवाय कुछ नहीं रहताः-

"मित्रो का हाथ पकड़ रो-रो कहती चली- न न, री, अब इस ठटरी ठण्डी भट्ठी का कोई वाली-वारस नहीं। कोई मरे मनुक्ख का नाम भी नहीं... तेरी अकेली माँ को अब यह घर काटने दौड़ता है, री।"[17]

मित्रो अपनी ही माँ द्वारा पति को छीनने की बात सोचकर दहल जाती है और जिस कमरे में उसका पति सरदारी लाल सो रहा था उसकी कुण्डी चढ़ा देती है। जो मित्रो सरदारी लाल से सदैव असंतुष्ट रहती थी वही मित्रो अपने पति के प्रति पूर्ण समर्पण के भाव से युक्त हो जाती हैः-

"फिर बाँहों से अँगड़ाई ली, हाथों को चटका मुटका उठ बैठी। सैंया के हाथ दाबे, पाँव दाबे, सिर-हथेली ओंठों से लगा झूठ-मूठ की थूकर बोली-कहीं मेरे साहिब जी को नजर न लग जाए इस मित्रो मरजानी की।"[18]

अन्ततः मित्रो की सजगता देखते ही बनती है। वह अपने अधिकारों के प्रति पूरी तरह सजग है। अभी तक वह अपने पति से अपने स्त्रीत्व का अधिकार चाहती थी और अब वह अपने पत्नीत्व का अधिकार खोना नहीं चाहती। यहाँ मित्रो अपने होने का पूर्णतः बोध कराती है कि वह दिशाहीन नहीं है, उसे अपना लक्ष्य पता है। बालो की तरह मित्रो का लक्ष्य मात्र दैहिक धरातल तक सीमित नहीं है। मित्रो तो पूरे उपन्यास की वह धुरी है जो शारीरिक सुख खोजते-खोजते इस शाश्वत सत्य का ज्ञान प्राप्त करती है कि अपने जिस दैहिक सौन्दर्य के बूते पर वह ईश्वर तक को चुनौती दे रही थी, वह देह पानी के बुलबुले की तरह क्षणभंगुर है, इस देह की वृद्धावस्था में वही परिणति होती है जो विशालकाय भवन के खण्डहर में परिणत होने पर। अन्ततः हरदम चहकने वाली मित्रो का जीवन के प्रति दृष्टिकोण ही बदल जाता है। उसकी वैचारिक क्षमता चैतन्य हो उठती है। देह की व्यर्थता का आभास मित्रो की अनुभवजन्य कमाई है जो उसे अपनी माँ की तबाही तथा अपने भविष्य की आशंका से प्राप्त हुई है।

उपन्यास के अन्त में मित्रो के चरित्र के इस उदात्त पक्ष को उभारकर कृष्णा सोबती घर तथा परिवार की महत्ता प्रतिपादित करती हैं। व्यक्ति संसार में अकेला आता है, अकेला जाता है।

समाज में कुछ लोग नाम कमा जाते हैं, समाज उन्हें याद भी रखता है, शेष आते हैं और चले जाते हैं, समाज में उनका कोई चिह्न शेष नहीं रहता। लेकिन घर-परिवार में हर व्यक्ति का अपना स्थान होता है। वहाँ उसकी उपस्थिति मायने रखती है। वहाँ मृत्यु उसे मार नहीं पाती, स्मृति के रूप में वह सदैव जीवित रहता है। उसकी उपस्थिति चिरकाल तक महसूस की जाती है। इसलिए जिस मित्रो को देखकर लगता था कि वह तो परिवार-समाज को जूते की नोंक पर रखती है, वही मित्रो दृढ़ता के साथ अपने बूते पर अपने पति के प्रति दायित्व बोध एवं प्रेम से युक्त हो अपने परिवार को बचाती है। नारी के व्यक्तित्व, उसकी अधिकारों के प्रति सजगता, दायित्व बोध, समाज एवं परिवार के प्रति उसके रवैये पर जब भी हिन्दी साहित्य में चर्चा होगी, मित्रो मरजानी वहाँ जरूर उपस्थित होगी, जो किसी भी स्थिति में निराश नहीं होती, अपने तरीके से जीवन जीना जानती है।

सन्दर्भ:-

1. कृष्णा सोबती, मित्रो मरजानी, राजकमल प्रकाशन, नई दिल्ली, 1999, पृष्ठ-19।
2. राजेन्द्र यादव, औरों के बहाने, अक्षय प्रकाशन, नई दिल्ली, 1979, पृष्ठ-44।
3. कृष्णा सोबती, मित्रो मरजानी, पृष्ठ-30।
4. वही, पृष्ठ-17।
5. वही, पृष्ठ-11।
6. वही, पृष्ठ-12।
7. वही, पृष्ठ-19।
8. वही, पृष्ठ-17।
9. वही, पृष्ठ-35।
10. कृष्णा सोबती, सोबती एक सोहबत, राजकमल प्रकाशन, नई दिल्ली, 1989, पृष्ठ-388।
11. कृष्णा सोबती, मित्रो मरजानी, पृष्ठ-79।
12. वही, पृष्ठ-61।
13. वही, पृष्ठ-46।
14. वही, पृष्ठ-46।
15. वही, पृष्ठ-47।
16. वही, पृष्ठ-72।
17. वही, पृष्ठ-93-94।
18. वही, पृष्ठ-95।

31 अमृता प्रीतम के उपन्यासों में व्यक्त भारतीय नारी के जीवन-सन्दर्भ

—संतोष गाबा

साहित्य अकादमी और फिर ज्ञानपीठ पुरस्कार से सम्मानित अमृता प्रीतम पंजाबी भाषा की वह सशक्त लेखिका हैं जिनके साहित्य का अनुवाद प्रायः सभी भारतीय भाषाओं के साथ-साथ विदेशी भाषाओं में भी हुआ है। उनका व्यक्तिगत जीवन भी किसी क्रान्ति से कम नहीं रहा और उसका स्पष्ट प्रतिभास उनके द्वारा लिखित उपन्यासों में अंकित नारियों के चरित्र में दृष्टिगोचर होता है। उनका स्पष्ट मानना है कि-

> "नारी की शारीरिक और मानसिक दासता संसार के सब देशों का दु:खद इतिहास है पर साथ ही एक संग्राम का इतिहास भी है जो संसार की प्रत्येक संवेदनशील नारी ने अपने-अपने क्षेत्र में अपने-अपने आँसुओं से लिखा है।"[1]

सम्भवतः इसी कारण उनके स्त्री पात्र मानसिक धरातल पर अत्यन्त सशक्त हैं। वर्तमान नारी सशक्तीकरण के दौर में वे इसलिए भी प्रासंगिक हैं कि जहाँ उनके उपन्यासों के स्त्री-पात्रों में प्राचीन भारतीय नारी के आदर्शों को पूरी गरिमा के साथ संजोया गया है, वहीं पाश्चात्य नारी-मुक्ति आन्दोलनों से जनित चेतना का वहन भी उनमें दिखाई देता है। नारी-मन की विभिन्न सरणियों से होती हुई इस क्रान्तिचेता नारी की गति में अवरोध कहीं नहीं है। वहाँ है तो बस निर्बाध आगे बढ़ने की ललक, ललक और बस ललक। उनके प्रायः सभी उपन्यास 'कच्ची सड़क', 'डाक्टर देव', 'जलावतन', 'औरत', 'अशू', 'पिंजर' सभी में भारतीय नारी के विभिन्न जीवन सन्दर्भों का चित्रण मिलता है।

'डाक्टर देव' में नारी और पुरुष के एकान्तिक प्रेम को सहज धरातल पर प्रस्तुत करते हुए इस ज्वलन्त प्रश्न को उठाया गया

है कि समाज नारी को क्यों बाध्य करता है कि वह हृदय किसी को देकर शरीर किसी अन्य को समर्पित कर दे। इस उपन्यास में उठाया गया यह प्रश्न आज भी ज्वलन्त है। समाज के लौह-श्रृंखलात्मक हाथों के समक्ष सदैव नारी को ही अपनी इच्छाओं की बलि देनी पड़ती है। जो पुरुष उसे स्वीकार्य नहीं, उसे पति के रूप में वरण करना पड़ता है और जिसे हृदय वरण करता है, समाज और कानून उसे पति स्वीकार नहीं करते।

उनके उपन्यास 'अशू' में एक कलाकार स्त्री अशू की कथा है जिसने जीवन की आन्तरिक उलझनों का सामना करते हुए "नवीन भारत की विधात्री नारी का मुक्ति मार्ग प्रशस्त किया है।"[2] अशू प्रेम में आकण्ठ डूबी उस नारी का भी प्रतिनिधित्व करती है जो प्रतिदान में कुछ नहीं माँगती। ऐसा लगता है जैसे अमृता का हृदय ही अशू के हृदय में प्रविष्ट होकर भारतीय नारी की प्रवृत्ति को पढ़ रहा है-

> "औरत जब किसी से प्यार करती है, कितना प्यार करती है निरे पूरब के कालिदास की शकुन्तला ही नहीं बल्कि पश्चिम के हार्डी की टैस भी जब पानी के बरतन में अपने दोनों हाथ डालकर अपने प्यारे के हाथों से खेलती है और वह अपनी अंगुलियाँ उसकी अंगुलियों में डालकर पूछता है, बताओ तो तुम्हारी कितनी अंगुलियाँ हैं और मेरी कितनी? तो वह कहती है-'सभी तुम्हारी हैं'।"[3]

इसी उपन्यास का दूसरा स्त्री-चरित्र तारा है जिसका विवाह निश्चित बेला में नहीं हो पाता लेकिन वह हारती और टूटती नहीं बल्कि परिस्थितियों का सामना दृढ़ता से करती है। आज भी भारत की कितनी कन्याएँ कई-कई कारणों से विवाह वेदी तक पहुँच नहीं पातीं और हताश होकर मृत्यु का आलिंगन कर लेती हैं। ऐसी स्त्रियों के लिए तारा का यह कथन कितना प्रेरणादायी, कितना प्रासंगिक और कितना महत्वपूर्ण है-

> "जब तक ब्याह का समय नहीं निकला था, मैं रोती रही थी पर जैसे ही फैसले की घड़ी बीत गई, मेरे आँसू सूख गये। मैंने अपनी माँ को सम्भाला। मैंने अपने हाथों से

> बिखरे हुए दहेज को सम्भाला। मैंने अपने हाथों से लगी हुई वेदी को हटाया। जितनी देर मुझे लगता रहा कि वह मेरा कुछ लगता है, मैं रोती रही थी। उस घड़ी कितनी ही बार मेरा मरने को जी किया पर जैसे ही वे लोग चले गये, मेरे अन्दर के सारे सम्बन्ध टूट गये। फिर मैंने मरना नहीं सोचा मैं किसके लिए मरती? कोई मरता तो उसके लिए है जिसके लिए जीना चाहे और जी न सके मैं तो उसके लिए जीना नहीं चाहती, फिर मैं उसके लिए क्यों मरूँ।"[4]

अमृता का बहुचर्चित उपन्यास 'पिंजर' भारतीय साहित्य की अन्यतम कृतियों में से एक कहा जा सकता है। इसका कथ्य भारत-पाक विभाजन की विभीषिका पर आधारित है। विवाह से पूर्व ही पूरो का रशीद द्वारा अपहरण करने के बाद तो मानो उसकी दुनिया ही बदल जाती है। उसे रशीद से निकाह करना पड़ता है पर उसके बाद की कथा विवश नारी के जुझारूपन की वह गाथा है जो परिस्थितियों का न केवल निर्भीकता से सामना करती है, बल्कि उन्हें अपने अनुसार मोड़ने में भी सफल रहती है। वह हिन्दू स्त्रियों को मुसलमानों के घर से निकाल कर उनके परिवार वालों के पास पहुँचाने में अपने जीवन की सार्थकता समझती है। इस कार्य में रशीद उसका सहायक बनता है। उपन्यास के अन्त में स्वजनों को तिलांजलि देकर रशीद के साथ रहने का पूरो का निर्णय उसके लिए अत्यन्त कठिन होने पर भी रशीद की सहृदयता के कारण पूरो को उचित लगता है जो अन्ततः यह भी सिद्ध करता है कि नारी के लिए हृदय के सम्बन्धों के सम्मुख प्रत्येक बन्धन अमान्य हैं चाहे वह धर्म का ही क्यों न हो? विभाजन के दंश से पीड़ित भी पूरो अस्तित्व की सार्थकता खोज ही लेती है-

> "लाजो अपने घर लौट रही है समझ लेना इसी में पूरो भी गई। मेरे लिए तो अब यही जगह रह गई है चाहे कोई लड़की हिन्दू हो या मुसलमान, जो भी लड़की लौटकर अपने ठिकाने पहुँचती है, समझो कि उसी के साथ पूरो की आत्मा भी ठिकाने पहुँच गई।"[5]

अमृता प्रीतम के उपन्यासों में ही नहीं, उनकी अनेक कहानियों, भेंटवार्ता संग्रह 'कड़ी धूप का सफर' और आत्मकथा 'रसीदी टिकट' में भी नारी की जीवन यात्रा के चेतना के स्तर पर अनुभूत अनेक सत्यों का प्रकाशन हुआ है। किसी भी स्तर पर वे हताश, निराश नहीं होती हैं।

संदर्भ:-

1. अमृता प्रीतम, 'कड़ी धूप का सफर', भूमिका, पृष्ठ-6।
2. अमृता प्रीतम, 'अशू', भूमिका।
3. अमृता प्रीतम, 'अशू' पृष्ठ-12।
4. वही, पृष्ठ-10।
5. 'पिंजर' पृष्ठ-138।

32 आधुनिक हिंदी काव्य में नारी चेतना के स्वर

—भारती पारिजात

सृष्टि की अप्रतिम भेंट नारी, पर्याय है संवेदना की, ममता की, करुणा की और औदार्य की। जीवन के हर पड़ाव पर नारी शक्ति की अहमियत है और उसकी सहभागिता है इसीलिए उसे सर्वोपरि स्थान दिया गया। देवी की संज्ञा दी उसे, सच्चे मायनों में देवी माना भी पर अफसोस कि समय की धारा इस शब्द की आत्मा बहा ले गई और यह शब्द अर्थहीन हो गया। परिणामतः स्त्री को बाध्य कर दिया गया बन्धनों की अनचाही आज्ञा को शिरोधार्य करने के लिए। लेकिन समय बदला और नारी का दबा सहमा व्यक्तित्व बन्धनों को तोड़ने के लिए विद्रोह कर उठा, हालाँकि उसे दबाने के हर सम्भव प्रयास किए गए पर नारी-चेतना खोखले संबोधनों की भ्रमित आख्या से सन्तुष्ट नहीं हुई और स्वयं की अस्मिता को अभिव्यक्त करने का सैलाब घर से साहित्य तक जा पहुँचा। साहित्य के आधुनिक काल में सर्वप्रथम श्री प्रसाद ने सच्चे अर्थों में नारी की गरिमा को, उसकी शक्ति को जाना-समझा और उसे अपने साहित्य में दृढ़ इच्छा शक्ति का पर्याय मान सम्मानित किया। सुप्रसिद्ध कवयित्री महादेवीजी ने इसे आगे बढ़ाया। इस श्रृंखला में मैं हिन्दी काव्य की कुछ नवीन कवयित्रियों की कविताओं का उल्लेख करना चाहूँगी जिसमें नारी चेतना के स्वर मुखरित हैं।

आधुनिक काव्य की शीर्ष कवयित्री स्नेहमयी चौधरी का काव्य निजता और नारी अस्मिता से सराबोर है 'पूरा गलत पाठ' कविता संग्रह के समर्पण में नारी के लिए उनका कहना है:-

नौकरी या घर
कहाँ है उसका अस्तित्व
भ्रमित हो गयी वह
चकित हो गयी वह

'कविता के लिए' रचना हर नारी को यह सोचने के लिए विवश करती है कि आखिर वह है कहाँ? स्वयं कवयित्री का मानना है– "मुझे पता नहीं ये कविताएं हैं, या वक्तव्य हैं जिनमें औरत की आजादी के सही बिन्दु की खोज है।"

इसी प्रकार डॉ. मधुरिमा सिंह की कविताएं नारी चेतना से जुड़ी हुई हैं। कवयित्री को विज्ञापन में बिकती नारी पर बेहद खिन्नता है, क्योंकि उसने अपनी अस्मिता को नहीं पहचाना है। उनका विचार है:-

खतरे में है
उस राष्ट्र की संस्कृति
जिसकी बेटियाँ
ज्ञान और प्रतिभा से रहित
विज्ञापन में बिकने वाली
देह मात्र हैं।

मधुरिमा जी का मानना है कि बीत चुका वह समय और वह त्रासदी जब स्त्री शक्ति चुप रह जाती थी, झूठ को ओढ़ लेती थी और सच से मुँह छिपा लेती थी, अब तो वह अडिग है अपने निश्चय पर कि चाहे कुछ हो जाए झुकना उसकी विवशता नहीं होगी:-

लग जाए आग चाहे, पर सच नहीं झुकेगा।
आँखों के आगे उनकी, जलते रिसाले रखना।।

कवयित्री सुनीता जैन नाम है अलग सोच, अनूठी अभिव्यक्ति और स्वतन्त्र चिन्तन का। उनका काव्य नारी मन के उस सूने कोने से जुड़ा है जब माँ की जरूरत व अहमियत जाने कहाँ गायब हो जाती है और बेटों की नजर में उसकी माँ 'कलह प्रिय', 'लालची' व 'दकियानूसी' बन जाती है। ऐसे बेटों को कवयित्री समझाना चाहती है।

माँओ को
मखमल पे रखो

झुला दो
फूलों पे
वे हैं आज
मगर कल होंगी न
सोचो तब
क्या-क्या खो जायेगा
जीवन से।
सोचो, फिर से सोचो।

संवेदनशील कवयित्रियों की श्रेणी में प्रभा ठाकुर का नाम अग्रगण्य है। उनकी कोमल व सहज अनुभूति मन की गहराइयों को अन्दर तक छूती है। नारी चेतना के स्वर मन की पीड़ा, अकुलाहट, बेचैनी व स्थितियों के दंश के साथ एवं पूरी सक्षमता के साथ उनकी कविताओं में उजागर हुए हैं वे कहना चाहती हैं:-

मैं औरत नहीं हूँ मात्र।
एक इंसान हूँ मैं
एक मनुष्य हूँ
सिर्फ औरत होना
मेरी पहचान नहीं
केवल औरत होना, मेरा परिचय नहीं
मैंने, देखी हैं
इस शब्द के साथ जुड़ी दयनीयता
विवशता, एक निरीह आर्द्रता।
सदियों से, चली आती इस इमेज को
अब तोड़ना चाहती हूँ मैं।
चाहती हूँ, तुम मुझे
औरत से अलग, व्यक्ति के सन्दर्भ में देखो
व्यक्ति के सन्दर्भ में सोचो।

सहज आदमकद, पाने की चाह
दौड़ रही मेरी शिराओं में।
ललकारते हुए मेरे समूचे वजूद को।
मेरे सहज बढ़ते कद पर
अब नहीं लगा सकते, तुम विराम
मन है, अब खुली आँखों से देखूँ, यह दुनिया
पुरुषों की नहीं, ईश्वर की दुनिया
एक औरत बनकर नहीं
एक इनसान बनकर।

ये हैं आधुनिक काव्य में नारी जागृति के सशक्त चैतन्य स्वर जिनकी खनक काव्य में गूँजती रहेगी और हिंदी काव्य में नारी के योगदान पर प्रश्नचिह्न नहीं लगाया जा सकेगा।

33 नारी चेतना के विविध रूप : समकालीन हिन्दी कथा साहित्य के आईने में

—मुकुल शर्मा

स्वतन्त्रता प्राप्ति के पश्चात् भारतीय समाज व्यवस्था एवं परिवार के पारम्परिक ढाँचे में आरम्भ होने वाले परिवर्तनों का परिणाम हुआ कि इक्कीसवीं सदी तक आते-आते शिक्षा तथा नौकरी के नये-नये उभरने वाले साधनों और उनसे जुड़ी हुई तथा उत्पन्न होने वाली नयी स्थितियों तथा नये परिवेश से नारी के मन में नये अधिकारों की माँग तथा बराबरी के दर्जे के प्रति हद दर्जे का आग्रह बढ़ गया। वैधानिक प्रावधानों ने भी उसे पहले से अधिक स्वतन्त्र, अपने अधिकारों के प्रति सचेत, अधिक साहसी, आत्मविश्वासी और आत्मनिर्भर बना दिया। आज वह केवल पुरुष और परिवार के लिए त्याग और बलिदान की प्रतिमूर्ति या अपनी इच्छाओं को दबाकर, घुट-घुट कर, सिसक-सिसक कर जीने वाली नारी न रह कर जीवन के सभी क्षेत्रों में पंख फैलाये अपनी नयी आकांक्षाओं को समेटे जीने को आतुर है। इन बदलते प्रतिमानों का प्रतिबिम्ब समकालीन साहित्य विशेषतः कथा साहित्य में प्रतिबिम्बित होना स्वाभाविक है और ऐसा हुआ भी।

समकालीन हिन्दी कथा साहित्य में श्री राजेन्द्र यादव की कहानी 'जहाँ लक्ष्मी कैद है' नारी की कैद की ही नहीं, उस कैद में निहित छटपटाहट और घुटन, उस कैद से जुड़े हुए इतिहास, और उस कैद से मुक्ति पाने की प्रबल आकांक्षा एवं विद्रोह की कहानी है। इसे मूल्यों के नाम पर लगाए गए अर्थहीन बन्धनों और वर्जनाओं के विरोध के साथ नारी समानता का उद्घोष करती नवीन चेतना का आरम्भ कहा जा सकता है। समकालीन कथा साहित्य में घर, परिवार, समाज तथा व्यवस्था से विद्रोह करने वाली नारियों की संख्या बहुत है। श्रीमती चित्रा मुद्गल की 'प्रेतयोनि' की नायिका

स्वयं को कायर तथा कमजोर लड़की कहलाने को तैयार नहीं है क्योंकि "जब वह एक से लड़ सकती है तो पाँच से क्यों नहीं लड़ सकती।"

आधुनिक परिवेश ने नारी को जो साहस दिया उसका उदाहरण है मोहन राकेश की कहानी 'एक और जिन्दगी' की बीनू जो अपनी बुद्धि और क्षमता के प्रति पूर्ण विश्वास रखती है, और जब पति से वैवाहिक सम्बन्ध बनाये रखना सम्भव नहीं होता, एक ही झटके में उन्हें तोड़ देती है और अपने किये पर वह कभी पश्चाताप् नहीं करती, क्योंकि अपने निर्णय पर उसे पूर्ण विश्वास है। नारी के बदलते हुए यथार्थ एवं व्यवहारिक रूप का एक और उदाहरण श्रीमती मन्नू भण्डारी की 'यही सच है' की नायिका दीपा भी है, जो भारतीय युवती की सारी भावनात्मक कमजोरियों के बावजूद पुरानी कहानियों की प्रेमिकाओं के समान देर तक घुटन या अवसाद में अपने आपको सालती नहीं रहती वरन् जो नया सामने आता है, उसे साहस एवं सहजता से अपना लेती है। नारी के नवीन साहस की जीवन्त मिसाल मन्नू भण्डारी की 'ईसा के घर इंसान' कहानी की नायिका एंजिला भी है, जो अन्याय के विरुद्ध विद्रोह करके चर्च और फादर का भण्डा फोड़ती है, और धर्म के नाम पर होने वाले नारी शोषण के विरुद्ध आवाज उठाती है। कमलेश्वर की 'तलाश' कहानी आज के नये बदलते सम्बन्धों में एक शिक्षित युवा लड़की सुमि और उसकी विधवा माँ के पारस्परिक सम्बन्धों को और बेटी की एक नयी साहसी भूमिका को प्रस्तुत करती है, जो माँ के नये जीवन के लिए उसके रास्ते से हटकर होस्टल चली जाती है।

त्रिकोणात्मक प्रेम अब पुरुषों तक सीमित नहीं रह गया है, वरन् पुरुषों की भाँति नारी भी एक से अधिक समानान्तर सम्बन्ध बिना किसी अपराधबोध के बनाने लगी है। मन्नू भण्डारी की 'ऊँचाई' कहानी की नायिका शिवानी शिशिर के साथ आठ साल तक सुखी दाम्पत्य जीवन भोगते हुए भी अपने पूर्व प्रेमी अतुल के साथ शारीरिक सम्बन्ध स्थापित करके किसी भी प्रकार की ग्लानि या पश्चाताप का अनुभव नहीं करती है। राजेन्द्र यादव की 'प्रतीक्षा' कहानी

की एक ही कमरे में रहने वाली दो वयस्क अविवाहित लड़कियाँ नन्दा और गीता आधुनिक युग में उभरते हुए समलैंगिक सम्बन्धों की मिसाल हैं।

समकालीन कथा साहित्य में कुछ ऐसी भी नारियाँ हैं, जो भारतीय नारी के पारम्परिक रूप एवं विचारों का ही प्रतिनिधित्व करती हैं। उदाहरणार्थ भीष्म साहनी की 'चीफ की दावत' की माँ, 'नशा' कहानी की शराबी पति को ही परमेश्वर समझने वाली आनन्दी, मन्नू भण्डारी की 'जीती बाजी की हार' कहानी की आशा, उषा प्रियम्वदा के उपन्यास 'पचपन खंभे लाल दीवारें' की नायिका नारी के परम्परागत रूप का ही प्रतिनिधित्व करती हैं। इस कालखण्ड के साहित्य में मन्नू भण्डारी की 'एक कमजोर लड़की की कहानी' की नायिका जैसी कुछ नारी सृष्टि भी हैं जो वैचारिक दृष्टि से तो विद्रोह करती हैं पर परम्परा और संस्कार के कारण कमजोर पड़ जाती हैं।

'नारी मात्र देह नहीं है' जैसी घोषणाएं भी नारी की स्थिति में वास्तविक तौर पर कुछ सुधार नहीं ला सकी हैं। आज भी नारी दैहिक शोषण का शिकार है। नारी शोषण की इन्तहा दिनेश पालीवाल की 'बंजर' कहानी में देखी जा सकती है, जहाँ पुलिस का दरोगा एक ग्रामीण लड़की की हत्या कराकर उसकी लाश के साथ रात भर थाने में ही बलात्कार करता है और अन्त में भेद खुलने के डर से उसे जलवा देता है। लड़की होने की सजा तो नारी हमेशा भुगतती ही आ रही है। पुरुष सत्तात्मक समाज में नारी दोयम दर्जे की नागरिक ही है। मृणाल पाण्डे द्वारा लिखित 'लड़कियाँ' कहानी की नन्हीं लड़की की माँ की व्यथा मुखरित है- "इस बार लड़का हो जाता तो छुट्टी होती, बार-बार की मुसीबत से" यह कथन जहाँ एक ओर लड़की और लड़के के भेदभाव का बोध प्रदान करता है वहीं भारतीय स्त्री की पुत्र के लिए बार-बार गर्भधारण करने की बाध्यता को भी प्रदर्शित करता है, पता नहीं कब संसार इस सत्य को समझेगा।

"बेटी के पैदा होते ही माँ सदाजीवी हो जाती है। वह कभी नहीं मरती। हो जाती है वह निरन्तरा। वह आज है, कल भी

रहेगी, माँ से बेटी तक बेटी से उसकी बेटी, उसकी बेटी से अगली बेटी। अगली से भी अगली, यही सृष्टि का स्रोत है।"

कृष्णा सोबती के 'ऐ लड़की' उपन्यास में माँ नारी की पुरानी स्थिति के विषय में कहती है- "पहले शादी में लड़की का सिर ऐसे गूँथा जाता था, ज्यों दुनिया भर की पाबन्दियाँ दुल्हन के बालों पर ही लगा देनी हैं।" और शादी के बाद तो शोषण ही शोषण है- "हाँ शादी के बाद औरत पूरे परिवार के लिए शिकारे की माँझी बन जाती है। उन पर सवार परिवार मजे-मजे में झूमते हैं और चप्पू चलाती है औरत। उम्र भर चलाती ही जाती है।" सूर्यबाला जी की 'रक्षा कवच' कहानी की नायिका के मन की बात सुने बिना सम्भवतः समकालीन हिन्दी कथा साहित्य में नारी की पहचान यात्रा पूरी नहीं हो सकती- "यों अपने को महसूस करने से अब बहुत कतराती हूँ। पर जब भी देखती हूँ, लगता है यह जिन्दगी एक सपाट सीधी सड़क है, जिस पर से अहसासों के काफिले गुजरते जा रहे हैं। गुजरते जा रहे हैं। सब मुझ पर होकर कहाँ से कहाँ पहुँच रहे हैं और मैं? वैसी की वैसी पड़ी हुई हूँ। गुजरते अहसासों के निशान लिए।" इसी के बाद वह अनुभव करती है कि "रक्षा कवच की सार्थकता अब नहीं रही है या झूठी पड़ती जा रही है।"

इसके अतिरिक्त उषा प्रियम्वदा की 'सम्बन्ध', कमलेश्वर की 'प्रेमी-प्रेमिका', कृष्णा सोबती की 'मित्रो मरजानी', निर्मल वर्मा की 'परिन्दे', मृदुला गर्ग की 'कितनी कैदें', रघुवीर सहाय की 'प्रेमिका', ममता कालिया की 'जिन्दगी सात घण्टे बाद की', दीप्ति खण्डेलवाल की 'विषपायी', शिवानी की 'स्वयंसिद्धा', 'अपराजिता', 'सती' जैसी अनेक रचनाएं नारी यथार्थ के विविध आयामों को समेटे हुए हैं। इस तरह समकालीन हिन्दी कथा साहित्य वह आईना है, जिसमें नयी चेतना और अपने समय की नयी भूमिकाओं के साथ नारी के नये-नये रूप पूरी विविधता तथा वैशिष्ट्य से उभरते दिखाई देते हैं, जिनमें अनेक आयाम हैं, नयी चेतना है, नयी भावना है, नयी दृष्टि है, नयी सृष्टि है, नये विचार हैं और नयी अवधारणा

है। सच तो यह है कि समकालीन कथा साहित्य में नारी चेतना के इतने विविध रूप हैं कि सीमित कलेवर में उनको प्रस्तुत करना सम्भव नहीं है।

सन्दर्भः-

1. डॉ. रघुवीर सिन्हा, आधुनिक हिन्दी कहानीः समाजशास्त्रीय दृष्टि
2. मृणाल पाण्डे, स्त्री देह की राजनीति से देश की राजनीति तक
3. चित्रा मुद्गल, चर्चित कहानियाँ
4. कृष्णा सोबती, ऐ लड़की
5. अनीता राजुरकर, कथाकार मन्नू भण्डारी
6. मृणाल पाण्डे, चार दिन की जवानी तेरी
7. सूर्यबाला, रक्षाकवच
8. ममता कालिया, प्रतिदिन
9. मन्नू भण्डारी, मैं हार गई
10. मन्नू भण्डारी, श्रेष्ठ कहानियाँ
11. शिवानी, स्वयंसिद्धा

34 आधुनिक संस्कृत नाट्य-साहित्य में महिला नाट्यकारों का योगदान

—बीना कुमारी गुप्ता

महिलाओं ने अपनी प्रतिभा तथा कलात्मक अन्तःप्रवृत्तियों से अनेक पारिवारिक, सामाजिक एवं राष्ट्रीय उत्तरदायित्वों का निर्वाह किया है, साथ ही संगीतकला, नृत्यकला, चित्रकला, काव्य लेखन में भी अपना वैशिष्ट्य प्रतिपादित किया है। काव्य रचना में मानव मन को संस्कृत करने की अभूतपूर्व शक्ति है और नाट्य में जीवन और समाज के विविध रूपों एवं भावों की यथार्थ एवं सजीव अभिव्यक्ति की सामर्थ्य अन्य विधाओं की अपेक्षा अधिक है। नाट्यशास्त्री ए. निकॉल ने साहित्य की अन्य विधाओं की अपेक्षा नाट्य को अति विशिष्ट एवं मोहक विधा कहा है। यह प्राकृतिक शक्तियों के विरुद्ध मानव के संकल्पनिष्ठ संघर्ष की कहानी है, जिससे मनुष्य को अपनी सीमा और प्रतिबद्धता का आभास होता है। कीथ महोदय ने संस्कृत नाट्य को भारतीय काव्य की उत्कृष्टतम सिद्धि स्वीकार किया है।

पुरुष नाट्यकारों के समान महिला नाट्यकारों ने भी अपनी नाट्य रचनाओं द्वारा संस्कृत साहित्य को समृद्ध किया है और अनवरत रूप से कर रही हैं। आधुनिक संस्कृत साहित्य में डॉ. रमा चौधरी, श्रीमती लीलाराव दयाल, श्रीमती कमलारत्नम्, डॉ. वनमाला, श्रीमती देवकी मेनन, डॉ. रत्नमयी देवी दीक्षित, डॉ. वीणापाणि पाटनी, डॉ. नलिनी शुक्ला, डॉ. मिथिलेश कुमारी मिश्रा, सुश्री भगवती देवी, डॉ. चिन्मयी माहेश्वरी, सुश्री आशा, सुश्री अर्चना, श्रीमती भक्तिसुधा आदि महिला नाट्यकारों का महत्वपूर्ण योगदान नाट्य कृतियों की रचना तथा नाट्य-कथ्य दोनों ही दृष्टियों से अभूतपूर्व है।

डॉ. रमा चौधरी ने संस्कृत भाषा में पच्चीस रूपकों का प्रणयन किया। 'यतीन्द्रम्' इनका पहला नाटक है, जो बारह दृश्यों में निबद्ध है। 'शंकरशकरम्' चौदह दृश्यों में निबद्ध है। इन दोनों ही नाट्यकृतियों में आध्यात्मिक भावों को दर्शाया गया है। 'देशदीपम्' देश के लिए आत्मोत्सर्ग की घटना से युक्त आठ दृश्यों वाला नाटक है। 'पल्लीकमलम्' नायक-नायिका के प्रेम एवं विवाह को प्रस्तुत करने वाला नाटक है तथा 'कविकुलकोकिलम्' महाकवि कालिदास के जीवन की चारुचरितावली से सम्बन्धित है। 'मेघमेदुरमेदनीयम्' नाटक में 'मेघदूत' की कथा को आधार बनाया गया है। 'कविकुलकमलम्' नाटक कालिदास की उत्तरकालीन जीवनगाथा से सम्बन्धित है। 'युगजीवनम्' में स्वामी रामकृष्ण परमहंस की जीवन गाथा है। 'निवेदित-निवेदितम्' में स्वामी विवेकानन्द से प्रभावित मार्गरेट (बाद में भगिनी निवेदिता नाम से प्रसिद्ध) के भारत आने तथा भारत के लिए अपना जीवन समर्पित करने की घटनाएं रूपायित हैं। 'भारताचार्यम्' में भारत के द्वितीय राष्ट्रपति सर्वपल्ली डॉ. राधाकृष्णन् के जीवन की प्रमुख घटनाएं चित्रित की गई हैं। 'भारततातम्' महात्मा गाँधी के जीवन की झाँकी प्रस्तुत करता है। 'भारतपथिकम्' में राजाराममोहन राय तथा 'चैतन्य चैतन्यम्' में महाप्रभु चैतन्य के आविर्भाव से लेकर समाधिस्थ होने तक की प्रमुख घटनाएं नाट्यीकृत की गई हैं। 'नगरनूपुरम्' में मेखला नामक अपूर्व सुन्दरी गणिका के भोग एवं ऐश्वर्य सम्पन्न जीवन को दर्शाया गया है। 'रसमयरासिमवि' में विधवा रासमणि के आदर्श कार्य एवं महासमाधि की घटनाएं प्रमुख हैं। 'अभेदानन्दम्', 'रामचरितमानसम्', 'लेनिनविजयम्', 'भारतवीरम्', 'तानतनुः' तथा 'गणदेवतानाटकम्' का भी उल्लेख डॉ. रमा चौधरी के नाटकों में किया जाता है।

श्रीमती लीलारावदयाल संस्कृतज्ञ स्व. क्षमाराव की पुत्री हैं। संस्कृत के प्रचार-प्रसार के लिए इन्होंने अनवरत प्रयास किये। इसके लिए इन्होंने अपनी माँ की रचनाओं की कथाओं का संस्कृत में नाट्य रूपान्तरण किया। इन्होंने चौबीस रूपकों का प्रणयन किया। 'होलिकोत्सवम्' रूपक के तीन दृश्यों में होली के दिन सुरापान से एक मत्स्यजीवी परिवार की दुर्दशा का भावुकतापूर्ण प्रस्तुतीकरण किया गया है। 'कटुविपाकः' में गाँधी के सत्याग्रह से प्रभावित रेखा

एवं वीरमा द्वारा देश के लिए सर्वस्व त्याग की कहानी है। 'मिथ्याग्रहणम्' में दो सखियों के मध्य उत्पन्न भ्रान्ति का निवारण मनोरंजक रूप में प्रस्तुत है। 'तुकारामचरितम्' में तुकाराम के चरित्र का वर्णन है। 'क्षणिक-विभ्रमः' में ग्रामीण अध्यापक की दरिद्रता एवं दुर्दशा का वर्णन है। 'गणेशचतुर्थी' में गणेश चौथ के दिन चन्द्र-दर्शन में होने वाले मिथ्या कलंक के प्रति जीवन-बीमा के महत्व को स्पष्ट किया गया है। 'श्रीमती ज्ञानेश्वर चरितम्' में महाराष्ट्र के सन्त ज्ञानेश्वर का वर्णन है। 'असूयिनी' में मछुआरे की सन्तानहीन पत्नी की असूया तथा पश्चाताप को दर्शाया गया है। 'वश्त्तशंसिच्छत्राम्' मे यूरोपीय रीति नीति पर एक दामाद का अपनी सास से प्रेम, दुर्घटना में स्मृति भ्रंश तथा त्यागी बाबा के रूप में एक विधवा से प्रेम प्रदर्शित है। 'वीरभा' में वीरमा नारी के द्वारा सत्याग्रह का नेतृत्व करने तथा क्रूर ग्रामीणाधिपति के हृदय-परिवर्तन की कथा है। 'स्वर्णपुरकृषविलाः' में गाँधीवाद से प्रभावित नायिका रेखा के नेतृत्व में 'स्वर्णपुर' के किसानों द्वारा भूमिकर न देने का निर्णय करके ग्राम छोड़ने का इतिवृत्त है। 'मीराचरितम्' में कवियित्री मीरा के बाल्यकाल से अन्त तक की कथा को १३ दृश्यों में दर्शाया गया है। 'बाल-विधवा' में एक बाल विधवा की दीन हीन दशा का वर्णन है। 'मायाजाल' में बांग्लादेश के विभाजन के समय अपने परिवार से वियुक्त चार महिलाओं की त्रासदी का वर्णन है। 'अनूप' में कुष्ठव्याधि के कारण अपने परिवार के परित्याग करने वाले युवक अनूप का वृतान्त है। 'कृपाणिका' में पति के मरणासन्न होने पर पत्नी की कातरता का वर्णन है। 'क्षमाचरितम्', 'नाट्यचन्द्रिका', 'विठालाचरितम्' आदि रूपकों की रचना का श्रेय भी श्रीमती लीलाराव को है।

संस्कृत प्रेमी तथा कालिदास एवं रामायण को विदेशों में लोकप्रिय बनाने में प्रमुख भूमिका निभाने वाली श्रीमती कमलारत्नम् हैं। 1963 में 'अखिल भारतीय कालिदास परिषद्' की स्थापना की। मैक्सिको में आयोजित महिला पत्रकारों के सम्मेलन में यह भारत की प्रतिनिधि बनीं। इनके पाँच संस्कृत रूपक उपलब्ध हैं। 'गणयछागः', दो दृश्यों का बालरूपक है। निरक्षरों को साक्षरता की प्रेरणा देता है। 'नचिकेतो यम संवादम्' में नचिकेता एवं यम के प्रसंग के आध्यात्मिक पक्ष का प्रस्तुतीकरण

है। 'विवेकानन्दविजयम्' में स्वामी विवेकानन्द का चरित्र वर्णित है। 'विक्रमवेतालनाटिका' में वेतालपंचविशंति की एक कथा का नाट्य रूपान्तरण है। 'विवेकानन्द स्मृतिः' एक रेडियो वृत्तचित्र है। यहाँ वाचक-गायिकाओं के स्वर के प्रभावी उतार-चढ़ाव द्वारा विवेकानन्द के जीवन-घटनाओं की सूचना दी गयी है।

डॉ. वनमाला मवालकर ने दिल्ली के युवा महोत्सव के लिए 'बैसाखी' नामक रेडियो एकांकी लिखा-उसी का संस्कृत रूपान्तरण 'पाद-दण्डः' है। 'रामवनगमन' एवं 'पार्वतीपरमेश्वरम्' का मंचन कालिदास समारोह में हुआ। 'सीताहरणम्' तथा 'अन्नदेवा' आपके द्वारा ही लिखे गये हैं। इनके रूपकों की विशेषता इनका अभिनेयत्व है।

श्रीमती देवकी मेनन मूलतः अध्यापन क्षेत्र को अलंकृत कर रही हैं। 'शारदा देवी चरित संग्रह' महाकाव्य के अतिरिक्त आपकी चार संस्कृत नाट्य रचनाएं हैं। 'कुचेलवश्त्तम' के सात दृश्यों में सुदामा का कृष्ण के घर आना और कृष्ण द्वारा अतुल ऐश्वर्य प्रदान करने की कथा भारतीय रागों व तालों में निबद्ध करके प्रस्तुत की गई है। 'सैरन्ध्रीप्रेक्षणकम्' में ब्रज की एक कुब्जा सैरन्ध्री पर कृष्ण की कृपा तथा उसे अपूर्व सुन्दरी बनाने की घटना को प्रदर्शित किया गया है। 'कालीदर्शनम्' में रामकृष्ण परमहंस की सहधर्मचारिणी श्री शारदा देवी के उज्ज्वल चरित्र को प्रस्तुत किया गया है। 'सन्तान-गोपाल' नामक रेडियो रूपक भी उल्लेखनीय है।

डॉ. रत्नमयी देवी दीक्षित दिल्ली विश्वविद्यालय से सम्बन्ध मिरण्डा कॉलेज के संस्कृत-विभाग में रीडर व अध्यक्षा रहीं। 'Women in Sanskrit Dramas' विषय पर आपने पी.एच.डी. की। आपने मराठी भाषा में रचित 'भूमिकन्यासीता' नाटक का संस्कृत में रूपान्तरण किया।

डॉ. वीणापाणि पाटनी उदीयमान् महिला संस्कृत नाट्यकार हैं। इन्होंने संस्कृत गद्य में 'अपराजिता' की रचना की। इन्होंने 'मधुराम्लम्' की रचना की। 'निम्बपत्राणि' हास्यव्यंग्य प्रधान एकांकी है। इसमें गुरुकुल से स्नातक उपाधि प्राप्त सैद्धान्तिक ज्ञानयुक्त परन्तु व्यवहारिक ज्ञान से रहित चार ब्रह्मचारियों की कथा है। 'प्रतिबुद्ध' नामक

एकांकी में नौकरी करने वाली महिला की गृहकार्य एवं कार्यालय के कार्य में संलग्न रहने पर प्रारम्भ में दुखद अवस्था अन्त में समन्वय करने की प्रतिबद्धता को सिद्ध किया गया है। 'यथार्थ्यगरलम्' में एक महत्वाकांक्षी दरिद्र ब्राह्मण की धनार्जन के लिए नानाविषयगत प्रवृत्ति पर कटाक्ष किया गया है। 'नारददौत्यम्' में पृथ्वी पर हो रहे ग्रह-उपग्रह के अनुसन्धान पर स्वर्गस्थ देवताओं का सम्भ्रम तथा भारतवासियों के पारस्परिक राग-द्वेष का वर्णन है। 'कविकालिदासीयम्' में राजा भोज के दरबार में कालिदास के वाग्वैदग्ध आदि गुणों का वर्णन है।

डॉ. नलिनी शुक्ला का जन्म 8 जून 1940 में हुआ। पारिवारिक दायित्वों का कुशलतापूर्वक निर्वहण करते हुए आपने संस्कृत की विशिष्ट सेवा की है। आपने संस्कृत में तीन नाट्यकृतियों की रचना की है। 'राधानुनय' आधुनिक संगीत नाट्य है। इसके चार दृश्यों में कृष्ण का गोपियों के साथ नृत्य, राधा का मान तथा कृष्ण का अनुनय-विनय है। 'पार्वतीतपश्चर्या' तीन दृश्यों का संगीत प्रध ान रूपक है। इसमें शिव द्वारा मदन-दहन, रति का विलाप, शिव की प्राप्ति के लिए पार्वती की घोर तपस्या तथा शिव का प्रसन्न होना आदि प्रसंग है। 'मुक्तिमहोत्सव' तीन दृश्यों में विभक्त आधुनिक एकांकी है। इसमें स्वतन्त्रता दिवस के ध्वजारोहण के अवसर पर महिलाओं की स्वतन्त्रता के प्रश्न को उठाया गया है।

डॉ. मिथिलेश कुमारी मिश्रा का जन्म सितम्बर 1952 में फर्रुखाबाद जनपद में हुआ है। संस्कृत में काव्य, शतक, उपन्यास आदि के अतिरिक्त 'आम्रपाली' सरस नाटिका एवं 'दशमस्त्वमसि' दस एकांकियों की रचना की है। 'चराचरसंचितकर्मयान्त्रीतम्' 'भक्तराज' तथा 'संचाप्यस्तिरजकएव' एकांकी भक्ति का प्रतिपादन करते हैं। 'माता भूमिः पुत्रोऽहम् पृथिव्याः', 'न मुनिपुनरायातो न चासौ वर्धते गिरिः' तथा 'सत्यमेव जयते' देशहित के लिए स्वार्थत्याग की प्रेरणा देते हैं। 'अलक्ष्यं दूरदर्शनम्' में मूर्खतापूर्ण कृत्यों के दुष्परिणाम को प्रदर्शित किया गया है।

ब्रह्मचारिणी वेलादेवी सम्प्रति रामकृष्ण संघ द्वारा परिचालित आद्यापीठ कोलकाता की संचालिका हैं। आपकी तीन संस्कृत नाट्यरचनाएं हैं:- 'नचिकेतष्चरितम्', 'महीयसी गार्गी', 'विराड्गृहम'।

उपर्युक्त महिला नाट्यकारों के अतिरिक्त पाण्डिचेरी में संस्कृत विभाग की प्राध्यापिका डॉ. चिन्मीय माहेश्वरी ने 'चौरस्यचातुर्यम्', 'भारविः' तथा 'सद्वा सुदामा'—ये तीन बाल नाटिकाएं लिखी हैं। संस्कृत प्राध्यापिका सुश्री आशा भी संस्कृत भाषा की उत्कृष्ट गद्यकार एवं नाट्यकार हैं। इनके द्वारा 'महामुनिःदधीचि' तथा 'शठेशाठ्यं समाचरेत्' इन दो नाट्यों की रचना की गई है। श्रीमती भक्तिसुध ा द्वारा रचित 'सुकन्या' एवं 'मदनदहन' दो रूपकों की रचना की गई है। भारतीय वरखेड़कर द्वारा रचित 'वनदेवता', श्रीमती सुध ा सहाय विरचित 'परशुराम प्रतिज्ञा', निर्मला शुक्ला का 'यौतुकं पापकं परम्' तथा श्रीमती विजयलक्ष्मी त्रिवेदी का 'नचिकेताः कुत्रागतोऽसि', स्फुट नाट्य रचनायें हैं। इस प्रकार पौराणिक इतिवृत्तों का कायाकल्प करके चरित्रप्रधान नाटक तथा समसामयिक विषयों पर महिला नाट्यकारों ने अनेक रूपक लिखकर संस्कृत साहित्य में अपना अभूतपूर्व योगदान दिया है।

संस्कृत महिला नाट्यकारों की रूपक रचनाओं में स्थान एवं पात्रानुरूप वेशभूषा, आचार-व्यवहार आदि के वर्णन से रूपकों में यथार्थ बिम्ब उभरे हैं। वेशभूषा की दृष्टि से सर्वाधिक विविधता लीलाराव की रचनाओं में दृष्टव्य है। आधुनिक पेण्ट-शर्ट से विभूषित पात्रों से लेकर मछुआरे तक की वेशभूषा वाले पात्र रंगमंच में प्रविष्ट हुए हैं। प्रादेशिक विविधता भी दृष्टिगत होती है। यथा महाराष्ट्रीय ग्राम वातावरण—'अनूप', 'गणेशचतुर्थ', 'होलिकोत्सव' में है और 'असूयिनी' में बंग वातावरण है। ये नाटक बाल-विवाह, अनमेल विवाह, तिधवा विवाह, पर्दा प्रथा, नगरों की आवास समस्या पर प्रकाश डालते हैं। एक ओर बौद्धयुगीन नियमों-मान्यताओं को दर्शाया गया है और दूसरी ओर गाँधीवादी विचारधारा का व्यापक प्रयोग है। आधुनिक शस्त्र पिस्तौल, आवागमन के साधन मोटरयान, रेलयान तथा वायुयान साधनों का प्रयोग है। साक्षरता मिशन, नृत्यगान की बढ़ती प्रवृत्ति तथा पाश्चात्य प्रभाव का दर्शन आदि भी नाट्य कृतियों में दृष्टिगत होता है। आधुनिक पेय पदार्थों चाय, कॉफी, पाउडर के दूध से बनी चाय आदि का वर्णन है। आधुनिक महाविद्यालयों, विश्वविद्यालयी शिक्षा, विदेश शिक्षा आदि का वर्णन है। वर्तमानकालीन दहेज समस्या के साथ-साथ आधुनिक सुख

सामग्रियों टी.वी., फोन, कार, फ्रिज आदि का वर्णन है। लॉटरी का उन्माद तथा उससे उत्पन्न हताशा, मदिरा से बिगड़ते परिवार, भारत के पाश्चात्यीकरण आदि समस्याओं पर अपना दृष्टिकोण प्रस्तुत कर सामाजिक परिवेश के सुधारने में अपना योगदान प्रस्तुत किया है। इस प्रकार अर्वाचीन महिला नाट्यकार अपने रूपकों में आधुनिक जीवन के वैशिष्ट्य को प्रस्तुत कर स्वाभाविकता एवं सजीवता उत्पन्न करने में समर्थ रही हैं एवं उनके रूपक समाज के दर्पण सिद्ध हुए हैं।

अर्वाचीन महिला नाट्यकारों के रूपक एक ओर भरत आदि प्राचीन नाट्याचार्यों के द्वारा स्वीकृत पुरुषार्थ चतुष्ट्य उद्देश्यों की पूर्ति करते हैं, तो दूसरी ओर आधुनिकतम समस्याओं का निरूपण तथा समाधान प्रस्तुत कर समाजोत्थान का मार्ग प्रशस्त करते हैं। आधुनिक नाट्य-साहित्य की समृद्धि में संस्कृत महिला नाट्यकारों का अनवरत एवं प्रशस्त योगदान रहा है। नाट्य रचनाओं का समय-समय पर मंचन तथा आकाशवाणी से प्रसारण होने से उनकी नाट्य क्षमता एवं सामाजिक प्रतिष्ठा में वृद्धि हुई है। इन नाट्यकृतियों से इनकी समसामयिक विषयों एवं समस्याओं के प्रति जागरूकता एवं संवेदनशीलता प्रकाशित होती है, साथ ही संस्कृत की जीवन्तता तथा भारतीयता के प्रति निष्ठा प्रमाणित होती है। इस प्रकार नाट्यकृतियों की संरचना तथा नाट्य कथ्य दोनों ही दृष्टियों से अर्वाचीन महिला नाट्यकारों का योगदान अविस्मरणीय है।

सन्दर्भ ग्रन्थः-

1. पं. बलदेव उपाध्याय-संस्कृत साहित्य का इतिहास
2. डॉ. चन्दनलाल पाराशर-मंगल भारतम्
3. पण्डिता क्षमाराव-सत्याग्रह गीता
4. पण्डिता क्षमाराव-ग्राम ज्योतिः
5. पण्डिता क्षमाराव-वीरभा
6. पण्डिता क्षमाराव-कटुविपाक
7. डॉ. रमेश चन्द्र शुक्ल-बंग्लादेशम

35 समकालीन महिला हिन्दी उपन्यास : नारी मुक्ति बनाम पितृसत्ता एवं संस्कृति

—ऋतम्भरा शुक्ला

सामाजिक यथार्थ का संवाहक होने, मानवीय संवेदनाओं के विविध आयामों को व्यक्त करने में समर्थ होने के कारण उपन्यास आज साहित्य की सर्वाधिक लोकप्रिय एवं सशक्त विधा है। मनोरंजन का तत्व उसे लोकप्रिय और जीवन के व्यापक अंकन की शक्ति से सम्पन्न बनाता है। महिला रचनाकारों में से प्रायः सभी ने इस विधा को अपनाया है और अनुभूतियों की अभिव्यक्ति के लिए प्रामाणिक दस्तावेज के रूप में इसका प्रयोग किया है। व्यापक फलक के कारण महिला उपन्यासकारों को अपनी पीड़ा, संघर्ष, छटपटाहट, बैचेनी को उपन्यास के पर्दे पर उतारना अधिक समीचीन लगा है। महिला जीवन के सुखात्मक-दुखात्मक पक्ष, संवेदनाओं, अपने परिवेश के प्रति जागरूकता, अपनी स्थितियों की पहचान, अस्मिता बोध, परिवार और बाहर की दुनिया के अन्तर्विरोध, परम्पराओं की जकड़न तथा पितृक मान्यताओं से मुक्ति के विविध रूप महिला उपन्यासकारों में देखने को मिलते हैं। समकालीन महिला उपन्यासकारों की कृतियों में नारी मुक्ति के स्वर कहीं मन्द हैं, कहीं आँसू से भीगे हैं, कहीं विरोध की अनुगूँज से विवादित और कहीं तीखे तेवरों के साथ क्रान्ति का बिगुल बजाते हुए हैं जहाँ मुक्ति की कामना एक सतत् प्रक्रिया है और निरन्तर संघर्ष है।

नारी जिन अमानवीय हिंसक यातनाओं, सन्तापों, दुःखों और कष्टों के बीच सहनशील व समर्पिता का जीवन बोझ ढो रही है वह पितृसत्तात्मक वर्चस्व की ही देन है। पितृसत्तात्मक मानसिकता ने औरत को लेकर ऐसी तर्क व्यवस्थायें निर्मित की हैं जो अपने उद्देश्य को भली भाँति पूरा करती हैं। एक सत्ता व्यवस्था जब पूर्ण वर्चस्व की स्थिति में हो तो उसे जोर-शोर से अपना मंतव्य

जताने की जरूरत नहीं रह जाती है और वह बिना किसी शोर शराबे के सुनियोजित ढंग से अपना कार्य करती रहती है। भौतिक एवं शारीरिक नियन्त्रण की बुनियाद पर निर्मित यह वर्चस्व नियंत्रित समुदाय के मनोमस्तिष्क पर अपना नियंत्रण स्थापित करता है जिससे कि वह समुदाय अपनी हीनतर स्थिति को स्वाभाविक माने तथा वर्चस्व को स्वीकृति प्रदान करे। पितृसत्ता ने शताब्दियों के ऐतिहासिक विकास क्रम में वर्चस्व के ज्ञात-अज्ञात इतने रूपों का निर्माण किया है जिनका सम्यक उद्‌घाटन अभी भी सत्ता मीमांसक स्त्री-पुरुष विद्वानों द्वारा किया जा रहा है। अपने उपन्यासों के माध्यम से संवेदना एवं आनुभाविक प्रखरता से युक्त सृजनधर्मी महिला उपन्यासकारों ने भी सामाजिक सत्ता के विविध रूपों के साथ ही पितृसत्ता के जटिलतम रूपों तथा इसकी अन्तर्गुम्फित अभिव्यक्ति की अपनी रचनाओं के माध्यम से पड़ताल की है। यह पड़ताल नितान्त अकादमिक या बौद्धिक मात्र न होकर सर्जनात्मक है जो पाठक वर्ग को चेतना एवं अनुभूति के स्तर पर ही नहीं भावनात्मक एवं संवेदनात्मक धरातल पर भी इस वर्चस्व की सत्ता एवं उसकी विकृतियों से साक्षात्कार कराती है। उपन्यास इस अन्वेषणात्मक साक्षात्कार का सर्वाधिक सफल रचना रूप सिद्ध इसलिए हुआ है क्योंकि इसमें देश-काल, पात्रों, कथानक, अनुभूतियों के व्यापक धरातल का संस्पर्श सम्भव है। भारतीय सन्दर्भों में औपनिवेशिक नियंत्रण के उपरान्त उपन्यास अपनी इसी क्षमता के कारण प्रतिरोध का प्रमुख रचना रूप दिखाई देता है। उपन्यास में एक पूरे के पूरे समाज, रचना संसार का निर्माण सम्भव है जो रचनाकारों के अतीत एवं वर्तमान का रचनात्मक विवरण प्रस्तुत करते हुए उनके स्वप्नों एवं भविष्य के प्रारूप की अभिव्यक्ति संभव बनाता है।

पुरुष निर्मित पितृसत्तात्मक नियम, कानून, सिद्धान्त, अनुशासन इस तरह गढ़े गये हैं कि वे स्त्री को पराधीन व आया बनाने के लिए पूरी ताकत से कार्यरत रहते हैं। अपनी सत्ता को बनाये रखने के लिए स्त्री को अनेक नियमों के ढाँचे में ढाला गया है। महिला उपन्यासकारों ने स्त्री की पराधीनता के कारणों, पितृ सत्ता और वर्चस्व को पहचान कर, उसमें जीते हुए भी उससे मुक्ति

पाने के रास्तों पर अपने लेखन के माध्यम से पैर बढ़ाये हैं। मुक्ति कामना के लिए उठाये गये उनके कदमों की धमक उनके उपन्यासों में मौजूद है। कृष्णा सोबती एक ऐसी महिला उपन्यासकार हैं जिन्होंने अपने लेखन में स्त्री की बदलती हुई स्थिति, उसकी यातनाओं, संघर्षों को विद्रोही तेवर में प्रस्तुत किया है। कृष्णा सोबती के लेखन में स्त्री की एक अलग ही छवि उभर कर सामने आई है जो पितृसत्तात्मक नैतिकता, हिंसा, यौनाचरण का अनुकरण नहीं करती अपितु अपनी स्व की पूर्ति हेतु पितृसत्तात्मक अनुशासन को तोड़ती नजर आती है। 'डार से बिछुरी', 'मित्रो मरजानी', 'ए लड़की', 'सूरजमुखी अंधेरे के', 'समय सरगम' में नारीवादी चेतना प्रखर रूप में मौजूद है। इन उपन्यासों में औरत कतरा-कतरा जिन्दगी जीती, पिसती अपनी अस्मिता के लिए संघर्ष करती है।

आज तक स्त्री के साथ मानवीय ढंग से व्यवहार नहीं किया गया है और न ही उसे पूर्ण मनुष्य के रूप में स्वीकृति दी गयी है। इसलिए उसके साथ अमानवीय व्यवहार होता रहा है। पितृ सत्ता की खोखली लक्ष्मण रेखाओं को तोड़ती, कृष्णा सोबती की नायिकायें यथास्थिति से बाहर निकलकर मुक्ति की तलाश करने वाली साहसी और निर्भीक हैं जो औरत के निर्मम शोषण और उत्पीड़न को नकारती हैं और सिद्ध करती हैं कि कैसे स्त्री के लिए परिवार एक खुली दासता है, जहाँ वह नियमों, कानूनों, सिद्धान्तों, रीतिरिवाजों, परम्पराओं के नाम पर पिसती है। वहाँ पितृसत्तात्मक समाज का बड़ा अनुशासन है, कठोर नियम बन्धन हैं जिसमें वह बँधी हुई है। परिवार स्त्री को कैसे अनुशासित, नियन्त्रित करता है इसकी समझ पितृसत्तात्मक समाज के अन्तर्विरोधों को जाने बिना नहीं हो सकती। सोबती के लेखन में इन स्थितियों का पूरे यथार्थ के साथ चित्रण हुआ है। 'मित्रो मरजानी' की 'मित्रो' का चरित्र सामन्तवादी पितृसत्ता के लिए बेहद चुनौतीपूर्ण है। मित्रो सजग नारी का प्रतीक है जो शोषण अन्याय को चुपचाप नहीं सहती। मित्रो अपने बूते पर घुटती है, लड़ती है, मसखरी करती है, टक्कर लेती है, सीनाजोरी भी करती है। पितृक प्रतिमानों में जकड़े पाठकों के लिए 'मित्रो' एक चुनौती बन जाती है।

माँ के प्रेम करने की सजा में रोज पिटती प्रताड़ित 'डार से बिछुरी' की नायिका पितृसत्ता के दायरे में नहीं बँध पाती और बार-बार बेची जाती है और एक ऐसे परिवार में बेच दी जाती है जहाँ वह 'द्रौपदी' बना दी जाती है। उसका कोई घर नहीं है। वह केवल एक देह है, खरीदने और बेचने की वस्तु की तरह, अस्तित्वहीन, अस्मिताहीन, बेनाम जिसे एक प्रतीकात्मक नाम दे दिया गया है। 'द्रौपदी' जो एक नाम ही नहीं है वरन वह सांस्कृतिक वर्चस्ववाद में पितृसत्तात्मक समाज का चिन्तन, प्रतीक भी है।

'सूरजमुखी अँधेरे के' की रत्ती बचपन के पारदर्शी काँच के टूट जाने से घायल वह नारी है जो सम्बन्धों की जमीन पर सुरक्षा के तम्बू नहीं गाड़ सकती। रत्ती जैसी औरत अपने सर्दपन में सिर्फ जान-पहचान के दावे कर सकती है। उसका सोचना, उसका अन्तर्द्वन्द्व सम्बन्धों के लिए नहीं, सम्बन्धों में नहीं, सम्बन्धों की लीक के बाहर है। प्रेम शब्द का उसके निकट कोई उपयोग नहीं। 'सूरजमुखी अँधेरे के', 'मित्रो मरजानी', 'यारों के यार' सभी में स्त्रियाँ सम्बन्धों की त्वरित लीक को तोड़ती नजर आती हैं। वे निरन्तर स्वयं से लड़ती हैं, औरत के एकान्त अन्तर्द्वन्द्व को प्रस्तुत करती हैं। पितृसत्तात्मक घेरे को तोड़ती हुई वे भी एक आजाद पंछी की तरह अपने पंखों को फैलाकर खुले गगन में उड़ना चाहती हैं। वे अनन्त दूरी को मापना चाहती हैं। ये स्त्रियाँ क्षत-विक्षत हैं, अँधेरे के सूरजमुखी हैं, जो घने अंधेरे से लड़ते-लड़ते लहूलुहान हो चुकी हैं। पितृसत्तात्मक लीक को तोड़ती हुई अपमानित हो रही हैं लेकिन अपनी अस्मिता व स्वतन्त्रता की तीव्र आकांक्षा तो उनमें है ही, वे अपने स्वत्व, अस्मिता तथा स्वतन्त्रता के प्रश्नों को लेकर जबरदस्त संघर्ष कर रही हैं।

'पचपन खम्भे लाल दीवारें' में उषा प्रियंवदा ने परम्परागत नैतिक सामाजिक मूल्यों की टूटन तथा उसे तोड़ने की कोशिश करती सीमित आय वाले, मध्यवर्गीय परिवार में पढ़ी-लिखी नौकरीपेशा, अधिक उम्र तक अविवाहित रह जाने वाली लड़की के मानसिक तनावों, संघर्षों को व्यक्त किया है। चन्द्रकिरण सौनरैक्सा ने अपने उपन्यास 'चन्दन चाँदनी' और 'वंचिता' में नारी विषयक सामाजिक

रूढ़ियों से ग्रस्त मध्यमवर्गीय परिवार की धुँआती, रुद्ध प्रवाह छटपटाती जिन्दगी का चित्रण किया है। पितृसत्ता की घुटन भरी जिन्दगी से मुक्त होने, परम्परागत जड़ मूल्यों को नकारने और तोड़ने की विद्रोहपूर्ण आकांक्षा उपन्यास के नारी पात्रों में स्पष्ट है। 'चन्दन चाँदनी' में 'गरिमा' और 'शान्ता' के रूप में उपन्यास लेखिका ने दो प्रकार की स्त्रियों का चित्र प्रस्तुत किया है। गरिमा आध ुनिक और प्राचीन मूल्यों के द्वन्द्व में पड़ी रहती है, जबकि शान्ता प्राचीन मूल्यों को सर्वथा नकारती हुई जिन्दगी जीती है। मध्यमवर्गीय 'हिप्पोक्रेसी', ढोंग, मिथ्याचार, मिथ्या प्रतिष्ठा तथा स्त्रियों की आर्थिक परवशता का चित्रण भी उपन्यास को प्रासंगिक बनाता है।

पितृसत्ता और वर्चस्व की अवधारणा ने स्त्री को, यहाँ तक कि परम्परागत भारतीय पत्नी को अपनी प्रताड़ना का विषय न बनाया हो, ऐसा नहीं है। 1968 में प्रकाशित शशिप्रभा शास्त्री के पहले उपन्यास 'अमलतास' में अभिजात्य वर्ग की उपेक्षित, अपमानित स्त्री परम्परागत भारतीय पत्नी की भूमिका ईमानदारी के साथ निभाने पर भी पति का प्रेम और सम्मान नहीं प्राप्त कर पाती और परित्यक्ता का जीवन व्यतीत करने को बाध्य है। शशिप्रभा के अन्य प्रकाशित उपन्यास 'नावें'; 1974, सीढ़ियाँ; 1976, 'परछाइयों के पीछे'; 1979, ककरेखा; 1985, 'परसों के बाद'; 1985 , 'छोटे-छोटे महायुद्ध'; 1988, 'उम्र एक गलियारे की'; 1989, 'मीनारें; 1992, 'हर दिन इतिहास'; 1995 आदि में भी स्त्री के विवश जीवन का चित्रण किया गया है जो पितृ सत्ता की तमाम शर्तों को स्वीकार करने के बाद भी जीवन में सुखी नहीं हो पाती। पढ़ी-लिखी और आर्थिक रूप से स्वावलम्बी होने पर भी वह मानसिक रूप में परम्परागत नारी चरित्र आचार संहिता से आक्रान्त है। स्त्री के चरित्र पर शक करना, उसे शारीरिक और मानसिक यातना देना पुरुष अपना अधिकार समझता है।

1971 में ममता कालिया का उपन्यास 'बेघर' प्रकाशित हुआ जिसमें पितृसत्ता के निर्धारित मानक 'यौन शुचिता' के क्रूर विरोधाभासों को बड़े ही सशक्त ढंग से प्रस्तुत किया गया। यौन शुचिता, कौमार्य और केवल पति से यौन सम्बन्ध परम्परागत रूढ़ नारी संहिता

के आवश्यक नियम हैं। जो भी स्त्री जाने अनजाने इनका उल्लंघन करती है उसे पुरुष समाज का कोपभाजन बनना पड़ता है। स्त्री को अपने भोग की वस्तु समझने वाला पुरुष इस बात को बर्दाश्त नहीं कर पाता कि विवाह के पूर्व कोई उसे जूठा कर चुका है। जाहिर है यह नियम पुरुष पर लागू नहीं होता। यौन शुचिता के रूढ़ संस्कार से ग्रस्त नायक परमजीत अपनी प्रेमिका संजीवनी को इस कसौटी पर खरा न पाकर उससे सम्बन्ध तोड़ लेता है और रमा जैसी 'साधारण', 'बेमेल' लड़की से विवाह कर अपने जीवन को ही नरक बना लेता है और मृत्यु को प्राप्त होता है। कस्बे से मुम्बई आया परमजीत संजीवनी के व्यक्तित्व से प्रभावित हो उसे प्रेम करता है और उसे हर हाल में पाना चाहता है। उसे पाने हेतु संजीवनी के प्रतिरोध की भी परवाह नहीं करता।

यौन शुचिता के पितृक प्रतिमानों पर खरी न उतरने पर आहत 'पुरुष' परमजीत संजीवनी से बिना मिले और उसकी कोई बात सुने बिना ही उससे सम्बन्ध विच्छेद कर लेता है। संजीवनी की त्रासदी द्वारा ममता कालिया ने नारी नियति को परिभाषित करते हुए स्पष्ट किया है कि विवशता की स्थिति में अपने कौमार्य की रक्षा न कर पाने का इतना बड़ा दण्ड सर्वथा अमानवीय ही कहा जायेगा। परमजीत के प्रति अपने गहरे संवेदनात्मक लगाव और सारी कोशिशों के बावजूद संजीवनी उसे उसके जड़ संस्कारों से मुक्त नहीं कर पाती। ममता कालिया के अन्य उपन्यासों 'प्रेम कहानी'; 1980, 'एक पति के नोट्स'; 1997 में स्त्री-पुरुष सम्बन्धों में मौजूद पितृसत्ता के विविध रूपों का चित्रण किया गया है। प्रेम के विवाह में बदलते ही उसकी चमक और खनक के खत्म होने, परम्परागत धार्मिक एवं नैतिक संहिताओं के चलते मध्यवर्गीय दाम्पत्य जीवन के नरक बनने, पुरुषों द्वारा अपनी पढ़ी-लिखी पत्नियों को घर की एक 'वस्तु' समझने, आत्मकेन्द्रित, पाखण्डी, परपीड़क संवेदनाहीन पतियों की कमीनी हरकतों आदि का अंकन उनके उपन्यासों का मुख्य विषय है।

मृदुला गर्ग के उपन्यासों में नारी की जटिल मानसिकता, उसकी अस्मिता का संघर्ष और मुक्ति की कामना को देखा जा सकता

है। 'उसके हिस्से की धूप'; 1975 में आधुनिक स्त्री के प्रेम का त्रिकोणात्मक संघर्ष बिल्कुल नये रूप में परम्परागत मूल्यों और भावुकता को नकारते हुए प्रस्तुत किया गया है। परम्परागत विवाह की एकरसता, पति की उदासीनता तथा सजर्नशील मन की बैचेनी से ऊबकर भावुकता के प्रवाह में प्रेम और विवाह के नये सम्बन्ध स्थापित करना और उससे भी ऊबकर प्रथम पति की ओर आकृष्ट होने के प्रभावी चित्रण से केन्द्रीय पात्र 'मनीषा' के मनोभावों, सोचों, प्रतिक्रियाओं और अवचेतन में सुप्त कामनाओं का विश्लेषण किया गया है। मनीषा के रूप में एक सर्जनशील व्यक्तित्व को भी उभारने का प्रयास किया गया है। 'चित्तकोबरा'; 1979 के केन्द्र में एक संवेदनशील लेखिका के नीरस, प्रेरणारहित, ऊब भरी, पति और बच्चों वाली दुनिया में सर्जनात्मक, नैतिक शक्ति के रूप में एक व्यक्ति के प्रवेश के फलस्वरूप उत्पन्न आवेगात्मक, नैतिक और रचनात्मक तूफान अवस्थित है। दोहरी जिन्दगी के तनाव से विखण्डित नारी के व्यक्तित्व, तन-मन के द्वन्द्व और रतिक्रम के साहसपूर्ण खुले चित्रण के कारण उपन्यास में नयापन है। पितृसत्ता नारी को इस प्रकार की सच्चाइयों के सही सटीक बयान की अनुमति नहीं देती तथा इसी कारण पुरुष आलोचकों की टेढ़ी नजर भी इस उपन्यास पर काफी पड़ी है।

नारी समाज का यथार्थ प्रस्तुत करने में समर्थ मंजुल भगत की नायिकाओं में पितृसत्ता के विरुद्ध विरोध व उनसे मुक्त होने की आकांक्षा कई रूपों में व्यक्त होती है। 'टूटा हुआ इन्द्रधनुष' में वह पत्नी होने के साथ केवल प्रेमिका बने रहने का ही नहीं अपितु अपने प्रेमी से पुत्र पैदा करने का अधिकार भी माँगती है। परम्परागत आचार संहिताओं को तोड़ती हुई 'अनारो', 'बेगाने घर' और 'गंजी' की नायिकायें अभिजात्य वर्ग की नहीं हैं अपितु चौका बरतन करने वाली हैं। वे बिना किसी दिखावे के नारी स्वातन्त्र्य के ऐसे नये आयाम खोलती हैं जो चेतना को झकझोरते हैं। 'अनारो' निम्नवर्गीय नारी के शोषण के साथ ही साथ उसकी जिजीविषा और स्वाभिमान का प्रतीक है। 'गंजी', अनारो के विषय का विस्तार मात्र है। 'गंजी' अनारो की पुत्री है जो अपने परिश्रम, विवेक

और लगन से नये जीवन का निर्माण करती है। वह अपने पति की उपेक्षा से रोती-टूटती नहीं आर्थिक रूप से स्वावलम्बी बन अपना ही नहीं दूसरों का सहारा भी बनती है।

यह नयी नारी का नया रूप है। इन उपन्यासों में पितृसत्ता और आर्थिक नियन्त्रण, दूसरे शब्दों में लिंग और वर्ग नियन्त्रण पर आधारित सत्ता के सम्पूरक सम्बन्धों का आख्यान है तथा लेखिकाओं ने स्त्री मुक्ति हेतु आर्थिक मुक्ति की प्रधानता को रेखांकित किया है। यह मुक्ति कामना कहीं-कहीं उन्हें संघर्षरत निम्न वर्गों की कतार में उनके साथ खड़ी करती है तो कहीं-कहीं वे वर्गीय मुक्ति की अवधारणा से मुक्त स्वतन्त्र आर्थिक आत्मनिर्भरता हेतु प्रयासरत दिखाई देती हैं। प्रभा खेतान के पास नारी को लेकर कुछ बोध प्रश्न और निष्कर्ष हैं। इसलिए उनके अधिकांश उपन्यासों में नारियाँ पितृसत्ता के चौखटे से बाहर निकल संघर्ष करती हुई अपने स्वत्व को पाने का प्रयास करती हैं। पितृसत्ता के पारम्परिक पुरुष आधिपत्य के खिलाफ 'छिन्नमस्ता'; 1993 की 'प्रिया' ऐसी नारी का आख्यान है जो निरन्तर शोषित है, समाज की जर्जर मान्यताओं से भी और पुरुष की आदिम भूख से भी। टूट जाने की हद तक, लेकिन वह टूटती नहीं बल्कि शोषक शक्तियों के लिए चुनौती बनकर एक नयी राह पर चल पड़ती है। उसके सामने एक लक्ष्य है समाज की जिन बर्बर मर्यादाओं और शक्तियों के सामने एक दिन वह मेमने की तरह मिमियाती रही थी; वे देखें कि नारी सदा ऐसी ही निरीह नहीं रहेगी। वह अपनी निरीहता से उभर कर अपनी अस्मिता को प्राप्त कर एक सबल नारी के रूप में उभरती है। वह भ्रमों में नहीं जीती और अपना रास्ता निर्धारित कर लेती है। 'छिन्नमस्ता' में प्रिया यह कहती तो है कि औरत कहाँ नहीं रोती, सड़क पर झाड़ू लगाते हुए, खेतों में काम करते हुए, एअरपोर्ट पर बाथरूम साफ करते हुए या फिर सारे भोग ऐश्वर्य के बावजूद पलंग पर रात भर अकेले करवटें बदलते हुए, हजारों साल से इनके ये आँसू बहते जा रहे हैं, पर वह अपने आँसुओं को अपनी कमजोरी न बनाकर क्रान्ति का बीज बना लेती है। प्रभा खेतान की 'पीली आँधी' में मारवाड़ी समाज

के व्यापक फलक पर तीन-तीन पीढ़ियों की औरतें हैं जो कोई 150 साल की यात्रा करते हुए अपनी-अपनी बात कहते हुए अपने जीवन का चुनाव स्वयं अपनी तरह करना चाहती हैं। इसमें स्त्री की सिर्फ बाहरी नहीं उसकी निहायत निजी, आन्तरिक और गोपनीय परतों को खोला गया है। परिवार की मालकिन ताई जी की खामोश प्रेम कहानी और छोटी बीड़नी सोमा का पारम्परिक रूढ़िग्रस्त परिवार में समलैंगिक पति के साथ यंत्रणामय जीवन, पुरुषों का 'कमीनापन', बदलते राजनैतिक सामाजिक परिदृश्य के बीच प्रभा नारी जीवन की त्रासदियों का उद्घाटन करती हैं। परम्पराओं में जकड़े परिवार की सोमा अपने पति की 'कमीनगी' से त्रस्त अपने प्रेमी से गर्भधारण करती है और इसके लिए उसके मन में कोई अपराध भाव नहीं है। नपुंसक पति की भार्या होने पर वह पारिवारिक प्रतिष्ठा पर बलि होने को अभिशप्त नहीं है और परम्परागत नारी मूल्यों के सारे नियमों को अपने पैरों तले रौंदती घर के बाहर निकल जाती है। तीन पीढ़ियों की स्त्रियाँ चाची, बड़ी माँ और सोमा अपनी-अपनी पीड़ा अपने ढंग से भोगती हैं।

मैत्रेयी पुष्पा ने भी परम्परागत पितृसत्तात्मक समाज द्वारा स्त्री पर होने वाले अत्याचारों को अपने उपन्यासों का केन्द्र बिन्दु बनाया है। 'स्मृति दंश' और 'बेतवा बहती रही' की भावुकता के बाद 'इदन्नमम' में मैत्रेयी की नायिका करुणा की सीमा का अतिक्रमण करते हुए 'जुझारू' हो गयी। 'इदन्नमम' की 'मंदाकिनी' वास्तविक अर्थों में एक जुझारू युवती है जो केवल परिवार और समाज द्वारा स्त्री के लिए निर्मित बन्धनों को ही नहीं तोड़ती वरन् उस शोषण के विरुद्ध भी तनकर खड़ी हो जाती है जो आज के नेताओं और माफिया ठेकेदारों द्वारा आदिवासियों और अन्य ग्रामीणों पर कहर के रूप में बरपाया जा रहा है। मैत्रेयी नारी चेतना को बुन्देलखण्डी परिवेश और ग्रामीण समाज के साथ उसके पूरे खुरदुरे यथार्थ को वैसी ही खुरदरी भाषा के सहारे जीवन्त रूप में प्रस्तुत करती हैं। चाहे मन्दाकिनी की 'बऊ' जी हों या ममहर परिवार के अक्खड़ किसान सभी अपने मौलिक रूप में प्रस्तुत हैं। मन्दाकिनी की माँ प्रेम और उसकी भाभी कुसुम की व्यथा नारी की परम्परागत नियति है।

'इदन्नमम' के बाद 'चाक'; 1997 और झूलानट'; 1999 में भी ग्रामीण परिवेश में व्याप्त पितृसत्ता के मध्य उभरती नारी चेतना हैं। 'चाक' में जाट समाज में पैतृक नारी संहिता की रूढ़ियों में जकड़ी पुरानी पीढ़ी के क्रूरता भरे हठ का चित्रण किया गया है जिसके तहत पितृसत्ता के नियमों का उल्लंघन करने वाली स्त्री से जीने का अधिकार छीन लेना मामूली बात है। कोई पुरुष इस अमानवीय कृत्य के विरोध में खड़ा होने की हिम्मत नहीं जुटा पाता। इसके विरोध में खड़ी होती है 'सारंग' जो ज्यादा पढ़ी-लिखी नहीं है पर जिसके संकल्प में गजब की दृढ़ता है। सारंग पैतृक रूढ़ियों को चुनौती देती हुई, श्रीधर से देह सम्बन्ध स्थापित करती है और पुरुष सत्ता को चुनौती देते हुए ग्राम पंचायत के चुनाव में प्रधान पद के लिए खड़ी हो जाती है। पति से लेकर सारा पुरुष समाज उसका विरोध करता है पर वह अपने खुद के निर्मित नारी संगठन के बल पर पुरुष सत्ता को चुनौती देने का साहस भरा कदम उठाती है और सिद्ध करती है कि जब तक सत्ता स्त्री के हाथ में नहीं आती, पुरुष समाज द्वारा उसका शोषण और उस पर होने वाला अत्याचार समाप्त नहीं हो सकता। 'झूला नट' की शीलो में भी अद्भुत जिजीविषा, अपना भाग्य स्वयं लिखने का संकल्प और समाज से अकेले ही लोहा लेने की क्षमता है। समाज के दबाब को नकारते हुए वह 'बछिया' की रस्म से मना कर देती है और निर्द्वन्द्व भाव से अपने देवर के साथ रहते हुए दूसरी औरत को रखने वाले अपने सिपाही पति की सारी हेकड़ी खत्म कर देती है। पितृसत्ता के विरुद्ध खड़ी ये औरतें उस चेतना से अनुप्राणित हैं जो उन्हें मुक्ति द्वार तक ले जाने की सामर्थ्य रखती है। उपन्यास के ये दृश्य नारी मुक्ति को समर्पित तपन सिन्हा के चलचित्र 'मिर्च मसाला' का स्मरण कराते हैं।

'एक जमीन अपनी' में चित्रा मुद्गल की नायिका उस परिवेश का यथार्थ प्रस्तुत करती है जिसमें स्त्री चाहे जितनी योग्य हो उसे योग्य वस्तु के रूप में देखा जाता है। स्त्री के अधिकारों के प्रति सजग चिन्तन की मान्यता है कि पुरुष सत्ता द्वारा निर्धारित नियमों, मान्यताओं और प्रतीक चिह्नों से मुक्त हुए बिना नारी अपनी बेड़ियाँ नहीं खोल पायेगी। चित्रा की नारी को पत्नी शब्द

में दासत्व की बू आती है। वह सहचरी बनना चाहती है। वह यह भी मानती है कि औरत बोन्साई का पौधा नहीं है, जब जी चाहा उसकी जड़ें काटकर उसे वापस गमले में रोप दिया। पितृ सत्ता के षड्यन्त्रों के प्रति इनके मन में विद्रोह तथा उनसे मुक्त होने की कामना है।

पितृसत्ता एवं संस्कृति द्वारा निर्मित रूढ़ियों व परम्पराओं ने नारी को पराधीन व उपेक्षित बनाने में सर्वाधिक महत्वपूर्ण भूमिका निभाई है। अतः सभी महिला उपन्यासकारों में इन परम्पराओं और रूढ़ियों के प्रति घृणा और विरोध के गहरे भाव हैं तथा प्रायः सभी महिला उपन्यासकारों ने अपने नारी पात्रों के माध्यम से इस विरोध को स्वर दिया है। कृष्णा सोबती, राजी सेठ, प्रभा खेतान, नासिरा शर्मा, उषा प्रियंवदा आदि महिला उपन्यासकारों ने पितृ सत्ता के सामन्ती रूपों का वर्तमान पूँजीवादी संक्रमण तथा उससे उत्पन्न विसंगतियों का चित्रण किया है। इस प्रक्रिया में उत्पन्न नैतिक एवं चारित्रिक ऊहापोह एवं अनिर्णय की स्थिति इन उपन्यासों का वर्ण्य विषय है।

सन्दर्भ ग्रन्थ

1. कृष्णा सोबती, 'समय सरगम' राजकमल प्रकाशन, नई दिल्ली, 2000।
2. कृष्णा सोबती, 'जिन्दगीनामा' राजकमल प्रकाशन, नई दिल्ली, 1979।
3. कृष्णा सोबती, 'दिलोदानिश', राजकमल प्रकाशन, नई दिल्ली, 1993।
4. कृष्णा सोबती, 'डार से बिछुरी', राजकमल प्रकाशन, नई दिल्ली, 1958।
5. कृष्णा सोबती, 'मित्रो मरजानी', राजकमल प्रकाशन, नई दिल्ली, 1967।
6. कृष्णा सोबती, 'तिन पहाड़', राजकमल प्रकाशन, नई दिल्ली, 1968।
7. कृष्णा सोबती, 'सूरजमुखी अँधेरे के', राजकमल प्रकाशन, नई दिल्ली, 1972।
8. कृष्णा सोबती, 'बादलों के घेरे', राजकमल प्रकाशन, नई दिल्ली, 1980।
9. कृष्णा सोबती, 'सोबती एक सोहबत', राजकमल प्रकाशन, नई दिल्ली, 1989।
10. कृष्णा सोबती, 'हम हशमत भाग-1, भाग-2', राजकमल प्रकाशन, नई दिल्ली, 2003।
11. कृष्णा सोवती, 'दिलोदानिश', राजकमल प्रकाशन, नई दिल्ली, 1993।
12. उषा प्रियम्वदा, 'पचपन खम्भे लाल दीवारें', राजकमल पेपर बैक्स लि०, नई दिल्ली, 1961।

13. उषा प्रियम्वदा, 'रुकोगी नहीं राधिका', अक्षर प्रकाशन लि., नई दिल्ली 1967।
14. उषा प्रियम्वदा, 'शेष यात्रा', राजकमल पेपर बैक्स लि., नई दिल्ली 1984।
15. शशिप्रभा शास्त्री, 'क्योंकि', नेशनल पब्लिशिंग हाउस, दिल्ली, 1980।
16. शशिप्रभा शास्त्री, 'ककरेखा', राजकमल प्रकाशन, नई दिल्ली, 1983।
17. शशिप्रभा शास्त्री, 'परसों के बाद', नेशनल पब्लिशिंग हाउस दिल्ली, 1985।
18. शशिप्रभा शास्त्री, 'हर दिन इतिहास', वाणी प्रकाशन लि., नई दिल्ली, 1995।
19. शशिप्रभा शास्त्री, 'मीनारें', किताब घर, नई दिल्ली, 1994।
20. शशिप्रभा शास्त्री, 'बेघर', राजकमल पेपर बैक्स, नई दिल्ली, 1985।
21. ममता कालिया, 'नरक दर नरक', लोक भारती, इलाहाबाद, 1975।
22. ममता कालिया, 'प्रेम कहानी', लोक भारती, इलाहाबाद, 1980।
23. ममता कालिया, 'लड़कियाँ', लोक भारती, इलाहाबाद, 1981।
24. चित्रा मुद्गल, 'एक जमीन अपनी', राजकमल पेपरबैक्स, नई दिल्ली, 1999।

36 समकालीन हिन्दी कथा साहित्य में नारी

—शिखा श्रीधर

हिन्दी साहित्य में नारियों के योगदान पर विचार करते ही जिस तेजस्वी व्यक्तित्व का नाम ध्यान में आता है, वह हैं- मीरा, जिन्होंने मध्यकाल के पितृसत्तात्मक सामंती समाज में विद्रोह का झण्डा बुलन्द किया और अपने समय को झकझोर कर रख दिया। मीरा ने समाज द्वारा स्थापित मूल्य, मान्यताओं को ललकारा और अपने विद्रोही तेवरों के सहारे अपनी अनोखी पहचान बनायी। मीरा के पश्चात् आधुनिक समय में जो अत्यन्त महत्वपूर्ण नाम सामने आते हैं, वे हैं:- महादेवी वर्मा और सुभद्राकुमारी चौहान। महादेवी जी ने जहाँ पुरुष समाज के बंधनों को अस्वीकार करते हुए स्त्री होने की करुणा को चित्रित किया, वहीं सुभद्रा जी ने स्त्रीत्व के उल्लास और कान्तिमयी तरलता को शब्द देते हुए स्त्रीत्व की गरिमा को नई ऊँचाई दी।

जैसे मनुष्य के सुख-दुःख देशकाल की सीमा में नहीं बँधे रह सकते, वैसे ही संसार भर में स्त्री होने की वेदना भी लगभग एक जैसी है। यूरोप में स्त्री-मुक्ति की लड़ाई जिस जुझारू लेखिका ने लड़ी है-वह है सीमोन द बुवा, जिन्होंने स्त्री के पक्ष में अपनी आवाज उठाई। हालाँकि उनसे पूर्व भी जॉन स्टुअर्ट मिल आदि अनेक लेखकों ने भी स्त्री पक्ष की पैरवी की, परन्तु सीमोन ने स्त्री पक्षधरता को अपने लेखन का लक्ष्य बनाकर समस्त यूरोप में एक व्यापक आन्दोलन खड़ा कर दिया। उनकी पुस्तक 'द सैकेण्ड सैक्स' ने विश्व में क्रान्ति ला दी।

समकालीन हिन्दी साहित्य में, विशेषतः कथा लेखिकाओं ने अपनी कहानियों और उपन्यासों के माध्यम से नारी की जिस स्थिति का चित्रण किया है, उसका बीज-वपन वर्षों पूर्व भारत में मीरा, महादेवी

और सुभद्रा कुमारी चौहान आदि एवं यूरोप में *सीमोन द बुवा* द्वारा किया जा चुका था। प्रस्तुत शोध-पत्र के सन्दर्भ में समकालीन हिन्दी साहित्य में नारी की स्थिति पर प्रकाश डालने से पूर्व यह अप्रासंगिक ही नहीं अनिवार्य भी होगा कि आधुनिक काल की नारी की सामाजिक हैसियत की पड़ताल भी कर ली जाए, क्योंकि लेखकीय रचनाकर्म और परिवेश का गहरा अन्तःसम्बन्ध होता है। जब हम इस ओर विचार प्रवृत्त होते हैं तो पाते हैं कि:-

> "19वीं शताब्दी में समाज सुधार के आन्दोलनों के कारण ही स्त्री मुक्ति के प्रश्न को महत्व मिला है। वस्तुतः प्राचीन भारत में स्त्रियों के महत्व के बाद मध्ययुग में उनकी अवस्था सामन्तकालीन नजरिये के कारण अत्यन्त चिन्तनीय हो गयी थी। सामाजिक, राजनीतिक, आर्थिक और सांस्कृतिक क्षेत्र में पुरुषों के वर्चस्व के कारण स्त्रियाँ अधिकारहीन थीं। उनका सामाजिक अस्तित्व संकट में था और वह शिक्षा के अधिकार से वंचित होकर, लिंगभेद की शिकार हो गयी थीं।"[1]

वस्तुतः स्वतन्त्रता के पश्चात् ही संवैधानिक अधिक.रों के तहत स्त्री को स्वतन्त्रता और समानता के अवसर मिले। शिक्षा, रोजगार और वैयक्तिक जीवन में उसे पुरुष के समान अवसर प्राप्त हुए। आधुनिकता के आदर्शों का अनुमोदन करते हुए मध्यवर्ग ने अपने परिवार की स्त्रियों के लिए उपर्युक्त सभी अवसर उपलब्ध कराये। स्त्री शिक्षा पर विशेष ध्यान दिया गया। शिक्षा से स्त्री में आत्मविश्वास, आत्मसम्मान और आत्मनिर्भरता का भाव उत्पन्न हुआ। सन् 1960 के आसपास हुए सर्वेक्षणों, अध्ययनों से स्पष्ट है[2] कि अब मध्यवर्ग स्त्री का नौकरी करना असम्मानजनक नहीं समझता। आगे चलकर आठवें दशक में स्त्री के विकास में राष्ट्र के विकास की सम्भावना टटोली गयी। स्त्रियों को पारम्परिक क्षेत्रों में बँधकर रहना अब पसन्द नहीं, वे उन क्षेत्रों में आना चाहती हैं, जो आर्थिक दृष्टि से अधिक लाभ के हैं और अब तक पुरुष वर्चस्व के अधीन थे। इस प्रकार असाधारण और निर्णायक भूमिका वाले पदों पर आई स्त्रियों ने एक नई स्त्री को जन्म दिया है, जो पिछले लगभग पन्द्रह वर्षों में दृश्यमान हुई है। यह आर्थिक रूप से आत्मनिर्भर,

अपनी उपलब्धियों पर गर्व करने वाली, आत्मविश्वास, अधिकार और समृद्धि से भरी 'पावर विमिन' हैं, जो पुरुषों की भी बॉस हो सकती हैं–

> "उसने अपने लिए भी सोचना और जीना सीखा है। पुरुष सहकर्मी के समान क्षमता साबित करने हेतु उसने कड़ी मेहनत की है और अपनी क्षमता को मात्र जैविक इकाई (स्त्री) से भिन्न 'व्यक्ति' के रूप में स्थापित करने हेतु जी तोड़ मेहनत की है। समाज में पुरुष से समानता की आकांक्षी इस स्त्री ने अपने लिए जगह बनानी चाही है।"[3]

स्त्री के कामकाजी होने और घर सँभालने की परम्परागत भूमिका से भिन्न भूमिका ने स्त्री की स्थिति एवं समाज में उसके दर्जे को प्रभावित किया। परिवार और समाज में उसके सम्बन्धों को भी प्रभावित किया। स्त्री ने अपनी नई भूमिका स्वीकार की, उसके लिए कड़ा संघर्ष भी किया, परिवार एवं समाज की स्त्री की इस बदली हुई भूमिका के प्रति क्या दृष्टि रही, उसकी मानसिकता में बदलाव आया या नहीं, उसका दृष्टिकोण प्रभावित हुआ या नहीं, यह भी उतना महत्वपूर्ण है, जित ना कि स्त्री का बदला हुआ दृष्टिकोण।

इस प्रकार हम देखते हैं कि स्त्री की अस्मिता को व्यापक स्तर पर सामाजिक स्वीकृति तो प्राप्त हुई, परन्तु हजारों वर्षों से एक परम्परा के रूप में चली आ रही पुरुष मानसिकता को बदलने में अभी और समय लगेगा। समकालीन हिन्दी कथा लेखिकाओं ने समाज में स्त्री की बदलती हुई छवि, उसके अस्मिता बोध, कामकाजी स्त्री के प्रति पुरुष मानसिकता, पुरुष वर्चस्ववादी समाज के बरक्स स्त्री के संघर्ष की पहचान अपनी रचनाओं के माध्यम से की है। उषा प्रियम्वदा, मन्नू भण्डारी, ममता कालिया, गीताजंलि श्री, सिम्मी हर्षिता, क्षमा शर्मा, प्रभा खेतान, मृदुला गर्ग, चित्रा मुद्‌गल, चन्द्रकान्ता, सुधा अरोरा, मधु कांकरिया, नासिरा शर्मा आदि से लेकर मृणाल पाण्डे, अर्चना वर्मा, अलका सरावगी, नमिता सिंह, रमणिका गुप्ता आदि महिला रचनाकारों की एक लम्बी फेहरिस्त है, जो अपने लेखन के माध्यम से स्त्री विमर्श के छुए-अनछुए पहलुओं को रेखांकित

कर रही हैं। प्रस्तुत शोध-पत्र के सन्दर्भ में समकालीन हिन्दी साहित्य में स्त्री की भूमिका का अवलोकन करने के लिए कुछ प्रतिनिधि रचनाओं का विश्लेषण प्रस्तुत है।

ममता कालिया का उपन्यास 'एक पत्नी के नोट्स' दाम्पत्य सम्बन्धों का पुनर्निरीक्षण करता हुए एक महत्वपूर्ण प्रश्न उठाता है कि क्या पति-पत्नी का सम्बन्ध मात्र सैक्स पर ही आधारित है? देह का आकर्षण समाप्त होते ही क्या विवाह से प्रेम गायब हो जाएगा? पुरुष की सौन्दर्यलिप्सा को सन्तुष्ट करने के लिए स्त्री शरीर की सजावट करने और पति को रिझाने-दुलारने में ही अपनी सम्पूर्ण शक्ति और मेधा[3] का हवन करती रहेगी? ताकि उसका पति एक सुन्दर स्त्री के पीछे भागना छोड़ दे। क्या आपसी समझ और आत्मीयता दाम्पत्य का आधार नहीं हो सकते?

क्षमा शर्मा ने अपने उपन्यास 'परछाईं अन्नपूर्णा' के माध्यम से कामकाजी स्त्रियों के परिप्रेक्ष्य को रेखांकित किया है। भूमिका में ही क्षमा शर्मा इस प्रश्न को बहस में लाती हैं कि स्त्री पैसा कमाने के लिए नौकरी करती है या आत्मविश्वास के लिए?[4] घर-बाहर के प्रश्नों में विवाह या कैरियर का चुनाव स्त्री के लिए शाश्वत प्रश्न रहा है। सामाजिक एवं पारिवारिक स्थितियों के परिणामस्वरूप विवाह करने और सन्तानोत्पत्ति के बाद घर परिवार के लिए कैरियर छोड़कर जाती स्त्रियों की संख्या कम नहीं हैं। बड़े पैमाने पर कामकाजी स्त्रियों में यह प्रवृत्ति देखी जा रही है।[5] ऐसे समय में जब आज भी समाज की मानसिकता स्त्री के लिए घर और बाहर में से एक के चुनने की है। "स्त्री को घर और नौकरी में से एक चुनना चाहिए।"[6] कैरियरिस्ट होना स्त्री के लिए गाली की तरह इस्तेमाल होता रहा है। "कैरियरिस्ट यानी एक छोटे लाभ के लिए सब कुछ दाँव पर लगाने वाली।"[7] 'परछाईं अन्नपूर्णा' की विभा घर से बाहर अपने लिए जगह तलाशना चाहती है, यह जानते हुए कि घर से सड़क पर आयी स्त्री चरित्रहीन घोषित कर दी जाती है।

'परछाईं अन्नपूर्णा' कामकाजी स्त्री से जुड़े महत्वपूर्ण प्रश्न, कार्यस्थल पर होने वाली यौन-यंत्रणा, यौन-शोषण को केन्द्र में लाता

है।[8] सहकर्मी पुरुष के मस्तिष्क की चीर-फाड़ विभा अपनी सखी विनीता के साथ विचार-विमर्श में करती है। "औरत की बात आते ही हमें उसके अन्दरूनी हिस्से याद आते हैं।"[9] स्त्री कार्यालय में उपस्थित हो अथवा नहीं, "उसका रूप एक सहकर्मी का न होकर एक ऐसी सामग्री के रूप में होता है, जो सिर्फ शारीरिक उपयोग का ही नहीं बल्कि वैचारिक उपयोग का भी शिकार बनती है।"[10] अन्तर्राष्ट्रीय श्रम संगठन (संयुक्त राष्ट्र संघ) की एक रिपोर्ट के अनुसाार 'पुरुषों के बराबर आर्थिक और राजनीतिक सत्ता पाने में औरतों को अभी हजार वर्ष लगेंगे, क्योंकि 'दुनिया की 98 प्रतिशत पूँजी पर पुरुषों का कब्जा है।'[11]

प्रभा खेतान के उपन्यास 'छिन्नमस्ता' का विश्लेषण करते हुए उपर्युक्त सन्दर्भ अपनी विशिष्ट भूमिका निभा सकते हैं। अपने होने का अर्थ खोजती प्रिया के जीवन के माध्यम से स्त्री विमर्श के इस महत्वपूर्ण प्रश्न से साक्षात् सम्भव है। प्रिया का परिवार जिस वित्त वर्ग का प्रतिनिधित्व करता है, वहाँ पैसों की कमी नहीं हैं, करोड़ों का व्यवसाय है, मौज मस्ती के लिए विदेश यात्राएँ हैं, परन्तु जब प्रिया ने अपने लिए पैसा कमाना चाहा तो सजा तो उसके हिस्से में आनी ही थी। उसे दो में से एक चुनने का अवसर मिला—परिवार अथवा व्यवसाय और उसने व्यवसाय को चुना। स्त्री को 'महत्वाकांक्षी होने के' अपराध की सजा मिलती है:-

> "मैं सीरियस हूँ। फिर कहता हूँ, यदि आज तुम लन्दन गयीं, तो मेरे घर में तुम्हारी जगह नहीं। यह भी साली कोई जिन्दगी है, जब देखो तब बिजनेस।"[12]

घर नरेन्द्र का है, उसमें प्रिया रहे या नहीं, यह निर्णय नरेन्द्र का अधिकार-क्षेत्र है। पति के धनाढ्य परिवार में, पति के नाम से जाना जाना प्रिया को स्वीकार्य नहीं, उच्च वर्ग के दिखावटी जीवन के मध्य वह सहज नहीं होती, बचपन व किशोरावस्था में माता-पिता के परिवार का उसके प्रति उपेक्षापूर्ण व्यवहार और रवैया भी कहीं, इसके लिए जिम्मेदार है।

चित्रा मुद्गल ने 'आवां' उपन्यास में मजदूर की बेटी नमिता पाण्डे के संकल्पों, संघर्षों, मोहभंग, पलायन और वापसी को सुरसामुखी

बाजार के हथकंडों और स्त्री को देह-मात्र मानने वाली पुरुष-प्रवृत्तियों को उघाड़कर समय और समाज के वृहत्त सन्दर्भों में परीक्षित किया है। उपभोक्तावाद-जो स्त्री को वस्तु मानकर उसकी कोख का भी व्यापार करता है और प्रेम जैसी अन्तरंग अनुभूति को सिक्कों से तौलता है। बाजार के इस शोषण के साथ चित्रा मुद्गल श्रमिक संगठनों में घुस आए स्वार्थी तत्वों और भ्रष्ट नीतियों का पर्दाफाश कर, मजदूरों के हित-चिन्तकों को भी मजदूरों का शोषक बनते दिखाती हैं। महत् उद्देश्यों और स्त्री पुरुष समता के हामी भी स्त्री की विचारधारा से पहले, उसकी देह से ही प्रभावित-लालायित होते हैं।

वैश्वीकरण से आए तमाम बदलावों के बाद, आज भी स्त्री अंधकार-युग की बर्बरता के बीच जीने को अभिशप्त है। आए दिन बलात्कार, स्त्री-दहन और पारिवारिक हिंसा की घटनाएँ घटती हैं। पुरुष जितना हिंसक होता जा रहा है, स्त्री उतनी ही उग्रता से प्रतिरोध करने लगी है। साहित्य इस प्रतिरोध को अभिव्यक्ति देता है। सुधा चोपड़ा की कहानी 'ताराबाई चाल, कमरा नं० 135' हो या मधु कांकरिया की 'एक रुकी हुई औरत', जहाँ स्त्रियाँ सवाल करती हैं कि जीने का आधार पुरुष ही क्यों, स्वयं जीवन क्यों न हो? नासिरा शर्मा मुस्लिम परिवेश में, धार्मिक सामाजिक रूढ़ियों की बन्दी स्त्री के लिए मुक्ति का आह्वान करती हैं, यद्यपि उस मुक्ति की आकांक्षा के लिए आज भी उसे 'संगसार' ही किया जाता है। लेकिन स्त्री भीतर से सचेत हो रही है, यह बड़ी बात है-वह चाहे 'ऐलान गली जिन्दा है' उपन्यास की 'रत्नी' हो, 'कथा सतीसर' की राज्ञा या काव्या हो, या अनेक-अनेक कथा, कहानियों की बदलती स्त्री।

कुल मिलाकर कहने का आशय यह है कि समकालीन समाज में आज स्त्री की छवि बदली है, वह अपनी अस्मिता और अधिकार-बोध के प्रति सचेत हुई है और सामाजिक संरचना में स्त्री की बदलती हुई इस छवि को समकालीन हिन्दी कथा लेखिकाओं ने अपनी रचनाओं में प्रतिबिम्बित किया है। समग्रतः मैं अपने इस शोध-आलेख का समापन सुप्रसिद्ध कथाकार नमिता सिंह की इन पंक्तियों के माध्यम से करना चाहूँगीः-

"स्त्री न केवल घर, परिवार बल्कि समग्र समाज की एक इकाई है। उसका अस्तित्व वैयक्तिक भी है और समूहगत भी है। उसकी चिन्ताएँ और सरोकार भी व्यापक होने चाहिए। वह हाशिए पर नहीं बल्कि मुख्यधारा के साथ संघर्षरत रचनाकार है। उसका वजूद एक छोटे समूह, एक खण्ड, एक टुकड़ा आकाश तक सीमित नहीं है। वह समग्र समाज की प्रतिनिधि है, उसे पूरी धरती और पूरा आकाश चाहिए। यही स्त्री विमर्श की अवधारणा है और यही स्त्रियों की रचनात्मकता का पटल है।"[13]

सन्दर्भ:-

1. साहित्य की वैचारिक भूमिका, डॉ. राजेन्द्र मिश्र, पृष्ठ 236।
2. रोज 1961 एवं कापड़िया 1959 के अध्ययन।
3. हंस, मार्च 2001, अभय दुबे का आलेख, पितृसत्ता के नये रूप।
4. परछाईं अन्नपूर्णा, क्षमा शर्मा, भूमिका।
5. हंस, मार्च 2001, पृष्ठ 37।
6. परछाईं अन्नपूर्णा, क्षमा शर्मा, पृष्ठ 31।
7. वही, पृष्ठ 31।
8. सुमन कृष्णकान्त, इक्कीसवीं सदी की ओर, राजकमल प्रकाशन, पृष्ठ 163।
9. परछाईं अन्नपूर्णा, क्षमा शर्मा, पृष्ठ 28।
10. उपन्यास बनाम स्त्री विशर्म, संजय सिंह, हंस, फरवरी 1998, पृष्ठ 84।
11. अरविन्द जैन, न्याय क्षेत्रे : अन्याय क्षेत्रे, पृष्ठ 258।
12. छिन्नमस्ता, प्रभा खेतान, पृष्ठ 14।
13. 'इरावती' के अक्टूबर-दिसम्बर 2006 के अंक में संकलित नमिता सिंह का आलेख, पृष्ठ 21।

37 भारतीय संगीत के शास्त्र पक्ष तथा कलापक्ष को समृद्धि प्रदान करने में समकालीन महिला संगीतकारों का योगदान

—ब्रजरानी शर्मा, बबिता सिंह

प्रत्येक भाषा का अपना शास्त्र होता है, व्याकरण होता है, बिना शास्त्र के किसी भी भाषा को हम भाषा की संज्ञा नहीं दे सकते। संगीत की भी अपनी भाषा है, उसका व्याकरण है और उसी आधार पर उसका शास्त्र है। जिस संगीत के कलापक्ष को शास्त्र के आधार पर अभिव्यक्त करते हैं, उसे हम शास्त्रीय संगीत की संज्ञा देते हैं। शास्त्रीय संगीत में अथाह गहराई, गम्भीर मंथन, सिद्धान्त, नियम एवं परम्परा समाहित है। शास्त्रीय संगीत का तात्पर्य शास्त्र पर आधारित मर्यादित एवं नियमों से बँधा हुआ संगीत है, जो निश्चित परम्परा में आबद्ध है। संगीत विषय का शास्त्रीय पक्ष इतना प्रभावशाली है कि जब इसने कला का रूप लिया तो सम्पूर्ण जगत को मोह लिया।

इतिहास के पृष्ठों से स्पष्ट है कि वैदिक एवं पौराणिक काल से हिन्दू काल तक नारी का इस कला में अद्वितीय स्थान रहा। यद्यपि हमारे प्राचीन संगीत ग्रन्थों में से किसी भी ग्रन्थ का प्रणयन महिला द्वारा नहीं किया गया है, किन्तु गायन, वादन और नृत्य जैसी व्यवहारिक कलाओं के साथ महिला वर्ग का सक्रिय सम्बन्ध रहा है। आधुनिक युग में, जबकि महिला हर क्षेत्र में पुरुषों की बराबरी कर रही है, तो संगीत तो उसका अपना क्षेत्र है। इसलिए महिला कलाकारों और शास्त्रकारों का एक स्वतन्त्र और महत्वपूर्ण स्थान है। चाहे वह संगीत की कठिनतम ध्रुपद, धमार जैसी मर्दानी गायकी हो या अवनद्ध वाद्य। सामान्यतः जिन विधाओं पर पुरुष अपना आधिपत्य मानता आया है, वे भी अब महिलाओं से अछूती नहीं हैं। आधुनिक संगीत जगत में कुछ विदुषी महिलायें जो बहुचर्चित हैं और जिन्होंने अपने कलापक्ष तथा शास्त्रपक्ष से संगीत को समृद्ध

किया है उनमें से कुछ के योगदान पर इस पत्र में प्रकाश डाला गया है।

संगीत के कलापक्ष के सन्दर्भ में यदि चर्चा की जाये तो सर्वप्रथम 'गंगूबाई हंगल' का नाम अग्रगण्य है। हंगल किराना घराने की स्थापित गायिका हैं, जिनकी आवाज में गूँज है। गमकदार तानों की आप लाजवाब गायिका रही हैं। गंगूबाई हंगल ने बहुत ही कठिन परिश्रम व उत्साह से संगीत सीखा। महिला होने के बावजूद प्रतिदिन ग्यारह मील को यात्रा कर 'कुंदगोल' जाकर आप संगीत सीखती थीं, तभी तो स्वर-शिरोमणि, 'पद्मभूषण' और 'संगीत नाटक अकादमी' पुरस्कार प्राप्त करने योग्य बनीं। इसी श्रेणी में काशी की 'गिरजा देवी' ने भी महिला कलाकारों की श्रेणी में उच्च स्थान प्राप्त किया है। गिरजा देवी ख्याल और ठुमरी की प्रसिद्ध गायिका तो हैं ही, इसके अलावा पूर्वी लोक गीत, होली, भजन, दादरा, कजरी और गजल को भी निपुणता के साथ प्रस्तुत करती हैं। आपको 'पद्मश्री' के अलंकरण से भी विभूषित किया गया है।

अपने समय की सुप्रसिद्ध गायिका श्रीमती मोधूबाई कुर्डीकर की सुपुत्री 'किशोरी अमोणकर' भी लोकप्रिय कलाकार हैं। आप घरानों के बन्धनों को पसन्द नहीं करतीं तथा प्रगतिशील धाराओं को अपनाती हैं। संगीत में नए-नए प्रयोग आपकी विशेषता हैं। नौगाँव (असम) की 'परवीन सुल्ताना' आज भारत की सुप्रसिद्ध गायिका हैं। श्रीमती सुल्ताना की आवाज बेहद सुरीली एवं ऊँचाइयों वाली है। अतितार सप्तकों में गाने वाली आप अकेली गायिका हैं। जिस निपुणता से आप ख्याल, तराना व ठुमरी गाती हैं, उसी खूबी से गजल और भजन भी गाती हैं। किराना शैली की गायिका 'प्रभा अत्रे' का नाम भी संगीत जगत में पर्याप्त लोकप्रिय है। इनके अतिरिक्त ठुमरी, दादरा, गजल तथा 'पूरब शैली' में बनारस के रंग को ठुमरी में पिरोने की महारथ हासिल श्रीमती शोभागुर्टू, रामपुर परम्परा की प्रतिनिधि गायिका श्रीमती सुलोचना ब्रहस्पति, बनारस निवासी श्रीमती निर्मला अनोखे, श्रीमती माणिक वर्मा, डॉ. सुनन्दा पटनायक आदि अनेक महान गायिकायें संगीत को समृद्ध बनाने में अपना योगदान दे रही हैं। इसके अतिरिक्त वाद्यवादन में भी महिलाओं का विशेष योगदान है। पं. रविशंकरजी की पूर्व

पत्नी सितारवादिका डॉ. अन्नपूर्णा देवी, वायलिन वादिका डॉ. एम. राजम्, सरोद वादिका शरणरानी तथा मुम्बई की जरीन दारूवाला एवं तबला वादिका के रूप में डॉ. आबान ए. मिस्त्री का नाम उल्लेखनीय है।

नृत्य जगत में तो महिलाओं का ही वर्चस्व रहा है। भारत की प्रतिष्ठित कत्थक-नृत्यांगना सितारा देवी, जो भारत सरकार द्वारा 'पद्मश्री' तथा संगीत नाटक अकादमी पुरस्कार से विभूषित हुईं, हेमामालिनी, सोनल मानसिंह, शोभना नारायण आदि अनेक महान नृत्यांगनाओं ने नृत्य को समृद्धि प्रदान की। इस प्रकार गायन, वादन तथा नृत्य जैसी समृद्ध विधाओं में महिलाओं का योगदान सराहनीय है। शास्त्र पक्ष की बात करें तो हमें यह नहीं भूलना चाहिए कि हमारे लगभग सभी पौराणिक ग्रन्थ 'संस्कृत वाङ्मय' में लिपिबद्ध हैं और आधुनिक युग में संस्कृत भाषा को अधिक प्रोत्साहन न मिलने के कारण उनके श्लोकों को समझना, पढ़ना तथा उचित व्याख्या करना एक ज्वलंत समस्या है। यद्यपि शास्त्र के आधार पर ही हम शास्त्रीय संगीत को प्रयोगात्मक रूप देते हैं और कदाचित उसके शास्त्र की बारीकियों के आधार पर ही उसमें निखार लाते हैं तथापि जितनी महारथ कलापक्ष में महिला संगीतज्ञों को है, उतनी संख्या में शास्त्र पक्ष में कुछ ही चुनिन्दा महिलाओं का नाम ख्याति प्राप्त शास्त्रकारों में लिया जा सकता है।

संगीत के शास्त्रीय पक्ष के प्रचार-प्रसार तथा उत्थान के लिए अपना सम्पूर्ण जीवन समर्पित करने में श्रीमती सुमति मुटाटकर जी का नाम अग्रगण्य है। आपने 'भारतीय संगीत का शास्त्रीय पक्ष' विषय पर शोधकार्य करके एक अनूठा शोधप्रबन्ध संगीत-शास्त्र जगत को दिया। देश-विदेश के सांगीतिक और सांस्कृतिक विद्यापीठों में संगीत विषय के प्रामाणिक वक्ता के रूप में आपने संगीत के शास्त्र पक्ष के सही रूप को उजागर किया। इसके अतिरिक्त संगीत शास्त्री डॉ. प्रेम लता शर्मा का नाम उल्लेखनीय है जिनके विभिन्न पत्र-पत्रिकाओं में लगभग चालीस शोध-पत्र प्रकाशित हो चुके हैं। हिन्दी, मराठी, पंजाबी, गुजराती, उर्दू, संस्कृत आदि सभी भाषाओं में अधिकार रखने वाली डॉ. शर्मा निरन्तर संगीत-शास्त्र

की समृद्धि में समर्पित हैं। 'तालमणि' की उपाधि से सम्मानित डॉ. योगमाया शुक्ल जी कलाकार और विदुषी दोनों रूपों में प्रसिद्ध हैं। आपके ग्रंथ 'तबले का उद्गम, विकास और वादन शैलियाँ' में दिये गये तथ्य अत्यन्त गवेषणापूर्ण, सुसंगत और प्रामाणिक हैं। तबला विषयक उभय पक्षों पर वैज्ञानिक आधार पर लिखित यह ग्रन्थ संगीत जगत के लिए अत्यन्त उपयोगी ग्रन्थ साबित हुआ है। इसके अतिरिक्त अनेक आधुनिक महिला शास्त्रकारों में मुम्बई की 'डॉ. आबान ए मिस्त्री' ने 'पखावज और तबला के घराने एवं परम्परायें' नामक ग्रन्थ लिख कर तालशास्त्र, उनके वाद्य, उनका इतिहास, वाद्यों के आविष्कार का समय, उनकी वादन शैलियाँ आदि पर प्रामाणिक जानकारी संगीत जगत को उपलब्ध कराई है।

निष्कर्ष रूप में हम कह सकते हैं कि वैदिक काल से आज तक संगीत कला में नारियों का योगदान सराहनीय है। चाहे वह शास्त्र पक्ष हो या कलापक्ष नारी-वर्ग धन्य है, जिसकी संगीत साधना विपरीत परिस्थितियों में भी पल्लवित होती रही।

38 बांग्ला कथाकार आशापूर्णा देवी की कहानियों में नारी मनोविज्ञान

—मंजु गुप्ता

बारहवें ज्ञानपीठ पुरस्कार से सम्मानित आशापूर्णा देवी आधुनिक बांग्ला साहित्य की श्रेष्ठ कथाकार हैं। उनकी छोटी-बड़ी कहानियों में जीवन के सामान्य एवं विशिष्ट क्षणों की ज्ञात एवं अज्ञात पीड़ाएँ मुखरित हुई हैं। आशापूर्णा देवी का लेखन-संसार उनका निजी संसार नहीं है। वह हम सबके घर-संसार का ही विस्तार है। इस संसार को वे जिज्ञासा के साथ देखती रही हैं-कभी नन्हीं सी बिटिया बनकर, तो कभी एक किशोरी बनकर, कभी नई नवेली वधू के रूप में, तो कभी ममतामयी माँ के रूप में, तो कभी प्रौढ़ गृहिणी बनी घर-संसार का दायित्व सँभाले हुए, तो कभी दादी, नानी और असहाय वृद्धा बनी किसी अभिशप्त काल कोठरी में पड़ी पूरे समाज के परिवर्तन को चुपचाप झेलती हुई।

आशापूर्णा देवी ने अपने सभी स्त्री पात्रों को अपने बीच से उठाकर सबके बीच रखा है। उसे रसोईघर की दुनिया से बाहर निकालकर वृहृत वातावरण देना चाहा है। इसमें जहाँ नारी का माँ-पत्नी और पुत्री वाला स्वरूप सुरक्षित रहा है वहीं उसका सामाजिक परिवर्तन की भूमिका में भी सक्रिय योगदान रहा है। 'जो नहीं है वही' कहानी की नायिका गायत्री को उसका पति घर की दीवारों में जकड़ कर रख देता है, जो उसकी मध्यकालीन कुण्ठा का परिचायक है जिसके लिये स्त्री मात्र भोग्या है। आज भी पुरुषों के एक वर्ग को स्त्री का स्वाध्याय, कलात्मक रुचि, सामाजिक कार्यों में योगदान फूटी आँख नहीं सुहाता है। इस तरह विवाह और बच्चों के जन्म के बाद स्त्री के जीवन का सामाजिक उद्देश्य कहीं खो जाता है, वह मात्र कुलीन नौकरानी का जीवन जीने लगती है।

'इज्जत' कहानी में एक उच्च वर्ग की महिला सुमित्रा द्वारा समाज के निम्न स्तर की एक बालिका को संरक्षण देने की मानसिकता

का वर्णन है जो पूरी तरह मनोवैज्ञानिक है। लेखिका ने उच्चवर्गीय परिवारों में भी स्त्रियों की विवशता एवं दयनीयता का मार्मिक चित्रण किया है, जहाँ अब भी वे कोई निर्णय लेने के लिए स्वतन्त्र नहीं है। 'नागिन की पूँछ' कहानी में अधिकार सम्पन्न महिला द्वारा अनावश्यक छूट लेने को सुधारने की सदाशयता के बावजूद अधिकारी के अधीनस्थ की पत्नी अपना सुखचैन गँवा बैठती है। 'किर्चिया' कहानी में हमारे परिवारों मे असहाय और अशक्त पड़ी वृद्धाओं की दयनीय अवस्था का अत्यन्त हृदयद्रावक चित्रण है। यह एक ऐसी विकट समस्या है जिसका सामना सभी को कभी न कभी करना है। अपनी आँखें खोकर केवल स्पर्श और आहट से आसपास की गतिविधियों को जान लेने वाली सरोजवासिनी यह नहीं समझ पातीं कि अपने ही नाते-रिश्तेदार और घर के लोगों ने उन्हें कितना अनावश्यक समझ लिया है, जब उन्हें इसका अहसास होता है तो उन्हें यह लगने लगता है कि इस कटुता को झेलने से अच्छा है कि उनकी समस्त संवेदना छिन जाये जिससे वह अपरिचित और अमानवीय होती जाने वाली दुनिया से अपने को अलग कर सकें। दृष्टिहीनता को भी वह ईश्वर का प्रसाद मान लेती हैं जिसने उन्हें विद्रूप हँसी और व्यंग्य करते विकृत चेहरों को देखने से बचा लिया। ऐसी मनोवैज्ञानिक परख की दृष्टि कम लेखिकाओं के पास है।

आशापूर्णा देवी ने पात्रों की चित्तवृत्तियों के ताने-बाने को बारीकी से अपने लेखन में समेटा है। इन पात्रों को उनके परिवेश ने ही नहीं, खुद उनके मानसिक विन्यास ने भी असहाय और अभिशप्त बनाये रखा है। उनकी सभी कहानियों में देखा जा सकता है कि अवचेतन की अदृष्ट सत्ता पात्र की चेतन सत्ता को किस सीमा तक प्रभावित करती है। इस दृष्टि से पात्रों के सारे ताम-झाम, ठाठ-बाट, अधिकार, पद, मान सब पीछे रह जाते हैं। तब अपने स्वभाव की दुर्बलता के नाते ये पात्र सामान्य से दयनीय और कातर जान पड़ते हैं। 'बेआसरा' कहानी में अपने आलसी और निकम्मे जवान बेटे की मृत्यु का समाचार पाकर भी बेसहारा माँ अन्ना मौसी अपने दूर के रिश्तेदार के यहाँ पड़ी रहती है-मृत्यु जैसे समाचार को अनसुना कर। बाद में वह यह स्वीकार करती

है कि यह पाप उससे हो गया है। यह कहानी एक निराश्रित नारी की मनःस्थिति व नियति को उसके पुत्रशोक जैसी मर्मान्तक पीड़ा की घड़ी में चित्रित करती है। जीवन में अपने किसी भी उद्देश्य में सफल न होने की निराशा से भी अधिक महत्वपूर्ण है दो मुट्ठी दाना और जब यह आसरा भी छिन जाए तो क्या रह जाता है? आशापूर्णादेवी ने सामान्य नारियों की विशिष्ट मानसिकता को सामान्य सन्दर्भों और प्रतिकूल परिस्थितियों में रखकर देखा है। 'ऐश्वर्य' कहानी में जहाँ पति पर स्नेह भरा अधिकार है वहीं उसके कदाचार की अनदेखी करते हुए पारिवारिक स्थितियों पर और उसकी मर्यादा पर पर्याप्त अंकुश रखना भी नारी की जिम्मेदारी है।

आशापूर्णा देवी की प्रारम्भिक कहानी 'अभिनेत्री' में पारिवारिक रूढ़ियों का अन्तर्द्वन्द्व देखा जा सकता है। स्त्री को एक ही पारिवारिक ढाँचे में अनेक भूमिकाएं निभानी पड़ती हैं- कभी प्रेमिका, कभी गृहिणी, कभी सास और कभी अभिभावक की। इस उत्तरदायित्वपूर्ण अभिनय में भावनात्मक व व्यवहारिक सन्तुलन बनाये रखना पड़ता है। यह अभिनय जीवन में जितनी कुशलता, तटस्थता, व स्वाभाविकता से निभाया जाए पारिवारिक जीवन उतना ही सफल व सार्थक होता है। एक योग्य स्त्री कटुता के क्षणों एवं व्यक्तित्व की टकराहट की स्थितियों को बड़ी सहजता से जीती व झेलती है। एक किशोरी नवेली बहू से लेकर युवा माँ और फिर प्रौढ़ा माता तक के तीन पड़ावों से गुजरती हुई 'अभिनेत्री' कहानी इन्हीं पात्रों की मानसी-यात्रा को रेखांकित करती है। 'हथियार' कहानी में नायिका असीमा के माध्यम से लेखिका ने उन कामकाजी महिलाओं के आत्मविश्वास को जगाया है जो केवल रूप या सौन्दर्य से नहीं वरन् अपनी दक्षता से समाज में एक वांछित व उपयोगी भूमिका निभा सकती हैं। उनकी परवर्ती कहानियों में भी आर्थिक और सामाजिक दबावों से उत्पन्न स्थितियों में नारी के संघर्ष और अस्पष्ट होती जाती नैतिकता और मूल्यहीनता के सन्दर्भ में नारी द्वारा खुद बनाये गये सन्दर्भों और आदर्शों के बीच झूलता उसका असमंजस है।

इस तरह आशापूर्णा देवी के रचना संसार की नारियाँ दरिद्रता के अभिशाप से लड़ती हैं किन्तु उच्च पदस्थ अधिकारियों की

त्वचा-लिप्सा के आगे घुटने नहीं टेकतीं, अहंकारी पति के कायरतापूर्ण रवैये के विरुद्ध जूझती हैं, जीवन के अन्तिम क्षण तक अपने अधिकार बोध को नहीं जतातीं लेकिन आत्मसम्मान के प्रश्न पर कभी समझौता नहीं करतीं। समाज के घृणित कारोबार से स्वयं को व अपने परिवार को अलग रखना चाहती हैं-उस आधुनिक सोच से बचाना चाहती हैं जहाँ कुछ भी वर्ज्य या त्याज्य नहीं है।

आशापूर्णा देवी की कहानियों में वक्तव्य, समस्या और मनोवैज्ञानिकता के गुण मिले-जुले हैं साथ ही जीवन के तिक्त, रिक्त और मधुसिक्त तीनों प्रसंग भी संयोजित हैं। वे अपने नारी पात्रों को गौरवान्वित नहीं करतीं-यही उनकी विशिष्टता है। उनकी कहानियों का समापन प्रश्न से होता है समाधान से नहीं और यह प्रश्न ही पाठकों को कोंचता व कुरेदता रहता है। उनके भारतीय व मानवीय दृष्टिकोण ने उन्हें अनुपम प्रतिष्ठा दी है और वे एक ऐसी लेखिका के रूप में प्रतिष्ठित हैं जो आदर्श और यथार्थ के समुचित तालमेल से भारतीय समाज को एक नया संस्कार देना चाहती हैं। वह नारी को समाज निर्माण के केन्द्र में रखना चाहती हैं और उसे उस प्रबल प्रवाह चक्र से उबारना भी चाहती हैं जिसमें सभी नारियाँ क्रमशः पिता, पति और पुत्र की आश्रिता बनकर ही जीने को अभिशप्त हैं।

39 समकालीन महिला कथा साहित्य में कामकाजी स्त्री ('शाल्मली' तथा 'एक पत्नी के नोट्स' के विशेष सन्दर्भ में)

—शिल्पा पाण्डेय

महिला जगत को आधी दुनिया कहा जाता है, फिर भी पहचान अभी बाकी है। युग ने करवट बदली है, नये प्रश्नों के साथ नयी समस्यायें और नयी दिशायें सूझने लगीं। पिछले दो दशकों में महिला उपन्यासकारों ने अपनी पहचान बनायी है। नारी ने घर की चहारदीवारी भारत में बहुत पहले पार कर ली किन्तु कर्मक्षेत्र में उसके अभिनव अस्तित्व को कुछ दशकों से ही पहचाना गया है। महिला 'सशक्तीकरण' शब्द अस्तित्व में आ चुका है। इससे अभिप्राय महिलाओं को सामाजिक, आर्थिक, शैक्षिक तथा राजनैतिक स्तर पर आत्मनिर्भर कर सशक्त करने से है। आजादी के बाद महिलाओं की जीवन शैली में काफी हद तक बदलाव आया है, घर-आँगन की परिधि से बाहर निकलने का साहस अब महिला ने जुटा लिया है और अब महिला को पुरुष के बराबर होने का गौरव प्राप्त हो रहा है। जहाँ किरन देसाई ने साहित्य के क्षेत्र में प्रतिष्ठित बुकर पुरस्कार जीतकर भारतीय मेधा का परचम लहराया है वहीं अन्य कामकाजी महिलाओं में डॉ. इन्दिरा हिन्दूजा, इन्दिरा नूई, अलका तोमर आदि ने नए कीर्तिमान स्थापित किए हैं।

कामकाजी महिला हिन्दी उपन्यास और कहानी दोनों में जीवन की चुनौतियों का सामना करते हुए स्वयं एक चुनौती के रूप में उभरी है। श्रम द्वारा धनोपार्जन करने की परम्परा निम्नवर्ग की नारियों में दीर्घकाल से पायी जाती है। मध्यवर्गीय समाज में कामकाजी महिला कुछ ही काल से सामने आयी है। कामकाजी महिला घर और बाहर जिन समस्याओं से रूबरू हुई है उन्हें समकालीन हिन्दी उपन्यासकारों ने यथासम्भव चित्रित किया है। आज की स्त्री अपने अधिकारों व कर्तव्यों के प्रति सजग है। वह समकालीन परिदृश्य

में प्रत्येक क्षेत्र में अपनी स्थिति की सुदृढ़ता के नये आयाम खड़े कर रही है और इन नारियों को अपनी साहित्यिक रचनाओं में स्थान देने वाली भी अधिकतर रचनाकार स्त्रियाँ ही हैं। बीते दो दशकों में महिला रचनाकारों में अलका सरावगी, ममता कालिया, क्षमा शर्मा, प्रभा खेतान, उषा प्रियंवदा, मन्नू भण्डारी, मंजुल भगत का नाम प्रमुख है।

स्त्री का कामकाजी होना आज के युग में फैशन अथवा महत्वाकांक्षा न होकर वर्तमान समय की माँग है, परन्तु इसी आवश्यकता को आवश्यकता न मानकर उच्छृंखलता मान लिया जाता है, क्योंकि परम्परागत मानसिकता से ग्रसित पुरुष समाज इसे स्वीकार ही नहीं कर पाता कि स्त्री उसे पीछे छोड़ते हुए सफलता के नये आयाम, नये कीर्तिमान स्थापित करे। स्वतन्त्रता के पश्चात् 1956 में हिन्दू कोड बिल के पास हो जाने के पश्चात् कानूनी दृष्टि से भारतीय नारी को पुरुष की भाँति जीवन के विविध क्षेत्रों में प्रगति के समान अवसर उपलब्ध हुए हैं।

गृहिणी के रूप में तथा पति के व्यवसाय के सहायक के रूप में नारी की भूमिका का अध्ययन करने के पश्चात् एक तथ्य स्पष्ट रूप से उभर कर सामने आता है कि घर तथा बाहर का कामकाज करने भर से नारी कामकाजी नहीं हो जाती। इसके लिए दो बातें विशेष रूप से अनिवार्य हैं:-

प्रथम उसका कार्य पति अथवा परिवार के सदस्यों से स्पष्ट रूप से या तो पृथक हो या मान्यता प्राप्त हो। दूसरा उसे श्रम का पूर्ण प्रतिफल प्राप्त हो।

प्रस्तुत शोधप्रत्र में नासिरा शर्मा के 'शाल्मली' उपन्यास में आर्थिक, सामाजिक दृष्टि से सक्षम नारी की मर्मव्यथा को मर्मभेदी रूप में एवं ममता कालिया द्वारा रचित 'एक पत्नी के नोट्स' में कामकाजी नारी पर पुरुष द्वारा किये जाने वाले सन्देह एवं सभी प्रकार की सामाजिक यंत्रणा के विषय में प्रकाश डाला गया है।

माँ-बाप के आँगन की कोमल कली शाल्मली शिक्षा दीक्षा से परिपूर्ण होकर जब नरेश के साथ विवाहिता के रूप में नया जीवन प्रारम्भ करती है तो पुरुष सत्ता का वर्चस्व उसके शिक्षित व्यक्तित्व

को नकारने का प्रयास करता है। नरेश जो कि एक मध्यवर्गीय रूढ़िग्रस्त मानसिकता से युक्त परिवार का लड़का है, विवाहोपरान्त शाल्मली की नौकरी पर रोक लगाने का प्रयास करता है पर जब वह उसे समझाती हुई नौकरी के ऊँचे पद पर पहुँच जाती है तो वह उसका भरपूर आर्थिक एवं सामाजिक दृष्टि से दोहन करने की चेष्टा करता है। वास्तव में नरेश समाज के उन पुरुषों का प्रतिनिधित्व करता है जो ये जानते हैं कि पत्नी यदि पति के साथ कंधे से कंधा मिलाकर जीवन संग्राम में उतरे तो इससे परिवार की भलाई होती है, परन्तु अपने कुंठित पुरुषार्थ और झूठे दंभ के कारण पत्नी का आर्थिक स्वावलम्बन, मानसिक परिपक्वता, सामाजिक प्रतिष्ठा उन्हें भीतर ही भीतर सालती है।

नासिरा जी ने अपने उपन्यास में एक और तथ्य उजागर किया है कि जहाँ शाल्मली नरेश के असभ्य परिवारीजन के हर अत्याचार को मूक बनकर सहती है, नरेश की माँ की अपनी माँ से बढ़कर सेवा करती है जिससे वे गद्‌गद् होकर अपनी बहू को बेटे से अधिक लायक मानती हैं वहीं नरेश शाल्मली के माता-पिता की सेवा करना तो दूर उनकी खोज खबर लेना भी अनावश्यक समझता है और शाल्मली द्वारा भी माता-पिता के लिये कुछ करने पर उसे आपत्ति होती है। लेखिका नासिरा शर्मा इस समाज के समक्ष यही प्रश्न रखती हैं कि क्या विवाह के बाद लड़की इतनी परायी हो जाती है कि अपना हाड़-माँस गलाकर पालन-पोषण करने वाले उसके माँ-बाप की सेवा करने का अधिकार भी उससे छीन लिया जाता है।

जहाँ तक शाल्मली के चारित्रिक विकास का प्रश्न है लेखिका ने उसके चरित्र को आधुनिकता के द्वन्द्व से बिल्कुल अछूता रखा है। वह एक भारतीय नारी के धर्म का पालन करती है परन्तु दुर्भाग्यवश सर्वगुणसम्पन्न होने के बावजूद उसे पति का प्यार न मिल सका। नारी विमर्श के पहलुओं पर विचार करने पर यही स्पष्ट होता है कि शाल्मली जैसी हजारों महिलायें आज भारतीय नगरों में नारकीय जीवन व्यतीत कर रही हैं। वे महिलायें बाह्य जीवन में सुखी और सम्पन्न दिखती हैं पर मानसिक तनाव और पारिवारिक उलझन उनके व्यक्तित्व को तार-तार कर देती है। एक

स्थान पर शाल्मली कहती है- "कभी-कभी मुझे लगता है कि मर्द एक ताकतवर घोड़े के समान है जो दौड़ना जानता है मगर उसकी आँखों में पड़ी पट्टी उसे केवल उतना ही छोटा रास्ता दिखाती है जिस पर उसे दौड़ना आता है।" शाल्मली के माध्यम से नासिरा शर्मा ने अपने उद्‌गार व्यक्त करते हुए कहा है कि औरतों के पास दो ही अभिव्यक्तियाँ हैं या तो सर झुका देना या समस्या को अधूरा छोड़कर सर कटा देना।

इसी श्रृंखला में ममता कालिया कृत 'एक पत्नी के नोट्स' भी दृष्टव्य है। ममता कालिया ने अपने उपन्यास में पति-पत्नी के आपसी मतभेद और तनाव के परिणामस्वरूप पत्नी के जीवन की टूटन तथा मन की घुटन को बड़े ही मर्मस्पर्शी रूप में चित्रित किया है। सन्दीप और कविता जो कि उपन्यास के प्रमुख चरित्र हैं, का वैवाहिक जीवन नाना वैषम्यों में झकोले खाता हुआ बिखराव के कगार पर आ जाता है। ममता जी ने बड़ी तन्मयता से आधुनिक नारी के वैवाहिक जीवन में गुँथी समस्याओं को चित्रित किया है।

सन्दीप एक सुन्दर, सुशिक्षित, स्मार्ट एवं होनहार आई.ए.एस. अधिकारी है। अपने कर्मक्षेत्र में वह जितना कामयाब है, व्यक्तिगत जीवन में उतना ही साहित्यिक, कला प्रेमी एवं कुशल वक्ता है। कविता और सन्दीप का प्रेम विवाह है और वह सन्दीप से प्रगाढ़ प्रेम करती है परन्तु वैवाहिक जीवन के टेढ़े-मेढ़े मार्ग पर चलते हुए उसने पाया कि उसका पति अन्य अफसरों की पत्नियों को अपनी ओर आकर्षित करने के लिए वाचाल हो जाता है और पत्नी को हेय सिद्ध कर परस्त्री की प्रशंसा करता है। यही बात कविता के अन्तर्मन को झकझोरती है।

वर्तमान समय में कामकाजी नारी समय-समय पर शोषण का शिकार भी हो रही है चाहे अपनों के द्वारा या अन्य से। इस पुरुषप्रधान समाज में कामकाजी महिलाओं पर शक किया जाना एक मामूली सी बात है। आमतौर पर अर्द्धशिक्षित या अशिक्षित पुरुष बात-बात पर अपनी पत्नी को दुश्चरित्र होने का ताना देता है पर कई संभ्रान्त परिवारों में सन्दीप जैसे पति यह जानते हुए कि उसकी पत्नी गंगा की तरह पाक-साफ है परन्तु मानसिक पीड़ा से उत्पीड़ित करने के लिए उसके चरित्र पर अँगुली उठाते हैं।

सन्दीप आधुनिक समाज में जीने वाला वह तथाकथित आधुनिक व्यक्ति है जो स्वयं दूसरों की पत्नियों से घुल-मिलकर बातें करता था परन्तु कविता पर हमेशा सन्देह करता था। परन्तु यह ताला-चाभी का प्यार उसका दम घोंट रहा था। यह उपन्यास भले ही सुखान्त हो परन्तु कविता जैसी पत्नियों का जीवन विडम्बनाओं और विद्रूपताओं से भरा होता है। एक ओर जहाँ नारी को सुशिक्षित पति की सहधर्मिणी एवं स्वयं एक सम्पन्न कामकाजी महिला होने का गौरव प्राप्त है वहीं दूसरी ओर घरेलू जीवन में उसे पग-पग पर पति द्वारा ताड़ना मिलती है। कविता जैसी नारियाँ अपने हृदय की वेदना किसी से नहीं कह पातीं, क्योंकि उन्हें अपने पति के सम्मान की भी चिन्ता रहती है। इस प्रकार संभ्रान्त परिवारों की चहारदीवारी के भीतर नारी की घुटन को लेखिका ने बड़ी तन्मयता से बयान किया है। मन में सन्देह की विषबेल पनपती हो तो यह परिवार का सर्वनाश कर देती है। सन्देह एक प्रकार की मानसिक विकृति है जिसका कोई निदान नहीं। ममता कालिया ने कविता के माध्यम से यही चित्रित किया है कि घर तथा बाहर दोनों क्षेत्र सँभालने के पश्चात् भी सुशिक्षित पत्नी को प्रायः पति के अत्याचारों से छुटकारा नहीं मिलता।

दहेज, बलात्कार, भ्रूण हत्या, घरेलू हिंसा आदि सामाजिक समस्याओं के अतिरिक्त भी कई समस्यायें हैं जो वर्तमान युग में कामकाजी महिलाओं से सम्बन्ध रखती हैं। चरित्र पर संदेह कर उस पर अकथनीय अत्याचार करना भी भारतीय समाज में नारी का शोषण करने का साधन है। निस्सन्देह आज से पचास वर्ष पूर्व की अपेक्षा नारी ने स्वतन्त्रता पायी है, अधिक सम्मान अर्जित किया है। पारम्परिक मान्यताओं को चुनौती देकर उसने अपनी स्थिति में सुधार लाने के लिए जो जेहाद छेड़ा है वह उसकी पहचान है, क्षमता भी और उपलब्धि भी और इसी दृष्टि से उसे यहाँ अध्ययन का विषय बनाया गया है। घर में पुरुषों की तुलना में कामकाजी महिला की स्थिति आज भी हीन है। इसका कारण पुरुष प्रधान समाज, पुरुष की अनुदारता तथा परम्परावादी नारी की संकीर्णता है। इसके लिए अकेली कामकाजी महिला का संघर्ष पर्याप्त नहीं पूरे समाज का सहयोग अपेक्षित है। यह तत्व धीरे-धीरे पनप

रहा है और इसे पनपना ही है। आलोच्य उपन्यासों का अध्ययन करने पर स्पष्ट है कि कामकाजी महिला ना पूरी तरह आधुनिकता को स्वीकार कर पाई है न ही परम्परा को नकार पाई है। परिणामस्वरूप वह दुविधाग्रस्त है जिसने प्रकारान्तर से उसे दुर्बल तथा तनावयुक्त बनाया है। उसे इन कमजोरियों पर विजय प्राप्त करनी ही होगी। समकालीन महिला साहित्यकारों की लेखनी आज भी इस दिशा में कार्यरत है।

सन्दर्भ ग्रन्थः-

1. डॉ. रोहिणी अग्रवाल, हिन्दी उपन्यास में कामकाजी महिला, पृष्ठ- 70, 194।
2. अभिनव प्रसंगवश (पत्रिका) पृष्ठ-62।
3. ममता कालिया 'एक पत्नी के नोट्स' 2003 पृष्ठ- 17, 39, 68, 38।
4. नासिरा शर्मा, शाल्मली, 1987 पृष्ठ- 85, 96, 102, 154।
5. हरेन्द्र कुमार, महिला सशक्तीकरण (लेख), समय आगम, पृष्ठ- 189।

40 समकालीन महिला कथा साहित्य में नारी विमर्श

—पूजा मित्तल

"नारी का तो जीवन ही प्रेम का इतिहास है, पहले माता-पिता, फिर पति, फिर पुत्र, कन्या-इन्हीं को लेकर उसका क्षुद्र संसार है। पुरुष जब अपना घोंसला छोड़कर ऊँचे उठकर गगन की सूर्योज्ज्वल नीलिमा में हर्ष से विचरण करता है उस समय नारी एकान्त में अकेली बैठी हुई उसी घोंसले की अपने पंखों से घेरे हुए रक्षा करती है। स्नेह, पुरुष के विश्राम का प्रमोद, आलस्य की चिन्ता और अवकाश का चित्त विनोद है, किन्तु वहीं स्नेह नारी का समस्त मुहूर्त, समस्त चिन्ता, समस्त कार्य, समस्त जीवन है। स्नेह ही में उसका जन्म, विनाश और मृत्यु है।"

-जयशंकर प्रसादः चन्द्रगुप्त

प्राचीन काल से ही स्त्री की शक्ति को अनदेखा कर उसे प्रताड़ित किया जाता रहा है। कभी अर्धांगिनी, कभी सहधर्मिणी, कभी सहयोगिनी, कभी सेविका, कभी दासी, कभी भोग्या आदि विभिन्न रूपों में उसके साथ भला-बुरा व्यवहार किया गया। इन्हीं आधारों पर उसकी सामाजिक स्थिति को आँका गया। भारत में आज भी समाज के एक बड़े हिस्से की स्त्रियों को अपमानित व प्रताड़ित होना पड़ता है। साहित्यकार अपने युग की उपज होता है। उसके युग की सामाजिक, धार्मिक तथा राजनैतिक परिस्थितियाँ उसके व्यक्तित्व का निर्माण करती हैं। कथा साहित्य समसामयिक समाज का सबसे बड़ा दर्पण है। कथा साहित्य अपने कलेवर में मानव जीवन की सम्पूर्णता तथा समग्रता को हर दृष्टि से अभिव्यक्ति प्रदान करता है। नारी लेखन आज सामाजिक चेतना का वाहक बन गया है। वह घर से बाहर आकर खुला संसार खुली आँखों

से देख चुकी है। उसमें इतनी सामर्थ्य है कि स्वयं शकुन्तला और उर्मिला की कहानी कह सकती है। अब और शोषण उसे पसन्द नहीं। स्वातन्त्र्योत्तर युवा नारी की छटपटाहट और संघर्षों को लेखिकाओं ने अपने उपन्यासों में अलग-अलग प्रकार से अभिव्यक्त किया है। आज लेखिका को सामाजिक चिन्ता से सरोकार दिखाई देता है और संस्कारों की रूढ़ियों के बीच दबती पिसती नारी के बदले नारी स्वातन्त्र्य के सन्दर्भ में स्वस्थ मानसिकता से भरपूर जीवन की सार्थकता दिखाई पड़ती है। इस सन्दर्भ में महादेवी वर्मा जी ने कहा है:-

> "हजार बुझे दीपक, एक दीपक नहीं जला सकेगा एक जला दीपक दीवाली मना सकता है। युग बदला, समस्याएँ बदलीं। आज अपना विवेक जाग्रत रखिए। आज हर एक नारी को सिंहवासिनी होना है।"

शिवानी ने अपने साहित्य में नारी उत्थान के लिए आवाज उठाई है:-

> "आज नारी पुरुष के समकक्ष खड़ी होने का दावा करती है तो फिर क्यों अपनी समस्याएँ स्वयं नहीं सुलझा पाती? क्यों कभी भी घर्षिता-शोषिता नारी समाचार-पत्रों का समर्थन चाहती है, क्यों प्रधानमंत्री का जहाँगीरी घण्टा बजाने भागती है? अपराधी को तत्काल स्वयं दण्डित क्यों नहीं कर पाती?"

मन्नू भण्डारी, कृष्णा सोबती, शिवानी, उषा प्रियंवदा, रजनी पन्निकर, मेहरून्निसा परवेज आदि लेखिकाओं का अपना अभूतपूर्व संसार है जो किसी सीमा तक पुरुष के संसार से अलग है। उनके नारी पात्र यदि एक ओर समाज की मर्यादाओं को बनाए रखना चाहते हैं तो दूसरी ओर अपने अस्तित्व की पहचान भी करना चाहते हैं। आज महिला उपन्यासकारों का लेखन व्यवस्था के प्रति रोष और यथास्थिति को लेकर शंका की नींव पर खड़ा है। उनकी दिलचस्पी का विषय आज यात्रा है, पड़ाव नहीं, तलाश है, मंजिल नहीं, जीवन है मृत्यु नहीं। पुष्पा भारती ने एक बड़ी तीखी और पैनी बात कही है:-

"नारी के पास जड़ से न उखड़ने के कारण अधिक प्रामाणिक अनुभव है। वह पुरुष की भाँति साहित्यिक आडम्बरों का जीवन जीने का दम्भ नहीं भरती।"

मृदुला गर्ग ने तो यहाँ तक कहा है कि हर सफल पुरुष लेखक के पीछे एक नारी होती है। हर लेखिका के पीछे कई नहीं तो एक पुरुष अवश्य रहता है जिसके कारण नहीं, जिसके बावजूद वह लेखन करती है। नारी लेखनी ने नारी के विविध रूप, संयुक्त परिवार में उनकी स्थिति, दाम्पत्य जीवन तथा टूटन, प्रेम विवाह, अन्तर्जातीय तथा बेमेल विवाह की विसंगतियाँ, तलाकशुदा नारी की सामाजिक स्थिति, नारी और नैतिकता, एकाकीपन आदि समस्याओं को उद्घाटित किया है। नारी के शारीरिक एवं मानसिक दोनों रूपों की चर्चा महिला उपन्यासकारों ने की है। उषा प्रियंवदा का उपन्यास 'रुकोगी नहीं राधिका' में आधुनिक परिवेश से उदिता नारी ही विषय है। उषा जी के शब्दों में:-

"एक ऐसी स्त्री का जो अपने में उलझ गई है और अपने को पाने की खोज में उसे अपने ही अन्दर बैठकर खोज करती है। राधिका का निपट अकेलापन और भारत में अपने को उखड़ा-उखड़ा पाना मेरी अपनी अनुभूतियाँ थीं जिन्हें कि मैं बेहद लाड़-प्यार के बावजूद भी नकार नहीं सकी। सो यह नारी के अकेले होने की स्थिति है।"

मन्नू भण्डारी वैयक्तिक चेतना से अनुप्राणित मूलरूप से नारी जीवन की ही उपन्यासकार हैं, जिन्होंने आधुनिक नारी को घर की चहारदीवारी से निकालकर कर्मक्षेत्र में ला खड़ा किया है और शिक्षित युवती के वैवाहिक जीवन की आन्तरिक त्रासदी की सूक्ष्म पहचान अंकित की है। मन्नू भण्डारी ने बड़ी ही ईमानदारी के साथ नारी के मन में उठने वाले भावों, स्थिति विशेष में पुरुष के मन में जगने वाली शंकाओं, ईर्ष्याओं आदि को अपनी कहानियों में चित्रित किया है। इनका चर्चित उपन्यास 'आपका बंटी' प्रेम का नया यथार्थ है जहाँ पति-पत्नी दूध-पानी की तरह नहीं बल्कि पानी-रेत की तरह मिलते हैं। प्रसिद्ध लेखक किशोर साहू ने दाम्पत्य जीवन की सार्थकता को स्पष्ट करते हुए कहा है:-

> "तुम्हारे आँचल में नरम-गरम, अच्छा-बुरा दोनों पड़ेंगे। घबराओ नहीं दोनों से निबाह करो। पति-पत्नी जब एकाकार होकर जीवन सागर मे गोता लगाते हैं तो उनकी मुट्ठी में सिर्फ मोती ही नहीं आते, कुछ मोती, कुछ सीप दोनों ही आते हैं। मोती- गोती रखकर सीप-सीप फेंक देना उचित नहीं। दोनों को' अपना लो, दोनों से प्यार करो। यह मत भूलो कि मोती सीप के अन्दर ही पैदा होता है।"

प्रसिद्ध उपन्यास लेखिका कृष्णा सोबती का 'मित्रो मरजानी', 'डार से बिछुरी' और 'सूरजमुखी अँधेरे के' क्रमशः स्त्री-पुरुष सम्बन्धों पर आधारित, बलात्कार की विभीषिका दर्शाती हुई रचनाएं हैं। इन उपन्यासों में बरसों से धूल, मिट्टी और अँधेरे की परतों के नीचे लुकी-ढकी नारी को चित्रित किया गया है। समाज पर लेखिका ने किसी प्रकार का मध्यवर्गीय लबादा नहीं ओढ़ाया। नारी की स्थिति समाज में क्या है? लगता है कृष्णा जी ने 'रति के घटित' को अपने अन्दर पहले सोख लिया हो और धीरे-धीरे औपन्यासिक शब्दों में पिघलाया हो-

> "वास्तव में स्त्रियाँ जल के समान हैं जो शान्त रहने पर अत्यन्त शीतल होती हैं और जब जल में तूफान आता है, तब वह ऐसा भयंकर हो जाता है कि बड़े-बड़े भयंकर जहाज भी टुकड़े-टुकड़े हो जाते हैं।"
>
> *-आचार्य चतुरसेन*

> "स्त्री का हृदय एक विचित्र वस्तु है, वह आज प्यार करती है, कल दुत्कार देती है। प्यार के लिए सब कुछ करने को तैयार हो जाती है, परन्तु प्रतिकार के लिए उससे भी अधिक भयानक कर्म कर बैठती है।"
>
> *-सुदर्शन*

शशिप्रभा शास्त्री ने नारी मन की जटिल गुत्थियों को सुलझाने की प्रक्रिया अपने उपन्यासों में प्रस्तुत की है। स्त्री की काम वासना को लेकर स्त्री-पुरुष सम्बन्धों को नई दृष्टि से देखा है। स्वयं इन्होंने अपनी रचना प्रक्रिया में कहा है कि "अब नारी को अपने अधिकारों

के लिए आवाज बुलन्द करते देखती हूँ तो सन्तोष होता है। अपने कर्तव्यों की इतिश्री करके नहीं, अपनी इच्छा-आकांक्षाओं के प्रति नारी को तड़पते और उसकी पूर्ति के लिए उलटे-सीधे यत्न और गलत-सलत कदम अब मेरी दृष्टि में स्वाभाविक और उचित प्रतीत होते हैं।" 'सीढ़ियाँ', 'अमलतास', 'वीरान रास्ते और झरना', 'क्योंकि' आदि में नायिकाओं के सुख-दुःख को उन्होंने गहराई से अनुभव किया। श्रीमती रजनी पन्निकर की कहानी 'मन की आँखें' की मालविका भारतीय नारी की प्रतीक है जो निःस्वार्थ सेवा आदि सद्गुणों से सास के विरोधी मन को भी अपने पक्ष में कर लेती है। 'पत्थर और संगीत' की निशा भी ऐसी ही शक्ति सम्पन्न नारी है जो अपने परिश्रम और सहनशीलता के बल पर राकेश जैसे शुष्क अध्यापक को भी द्रवित कर देती है।

नारी हृदय की वेदना और प्रेम की पीड़ा की गायिका अमृता प्रीतम पंजाबी की प्रमुख कथाकार हैं। ये साहित्य अकादमी और ज्ञानपीठ पुरस्कार से पुरस्कृत लेखिका हैं। उन्होंने अपनी रचनाओं 'पिंजर', 'डॉ. देव', 'अशू', 'आक के पत्ते', 'नागमणि', 'बन्द दरवाजा', 'बुलावा', 'एक थी अनीता', 'तेरहवाँ सूरज', 'यह सच है', 'उनचास दिन' आदि में नारी की वेदना के खुरदरे और उभरते चित्र प्रस्तुत किये हैं। अमृता प्रीतम ने अपनी कहानियों में नारी शरीर को समाज के हाथ का खिलौना पाया। उसे न प्यार का अधिकार है न विवाह का। यह लेखिका की विद्रोह भावना है कि उनकी प्रत्येक नायिका अपने 'मन की आवाज' सत्य को पाने के लिए संघर्षरत है-मगर क्या सत्य की प्राप्ति होगी? नहीं! नहीं! यही आवाज बार-बार जीवन की अन्तर्पीड़ा बन जाती है। समाज में नारी की विवश स्थिति पर अमृता की दृष्टि अधिक टिकी है। उसके बन्धन, उसकी छटपटाहट और उसकी पीड़ा का चित्रण ही इनकी रचनाओं का मूल स्वर है।

हिन्दी की सबसे अधिक लोकप्रिय लेखिका शिवानी की मर्मस्पर्शी कहानियाँ नारी मन की गहन पड़ताल करती हैं। उनके सुख-दुःख, उनके रिश्ते और उनके आपसी तनाव शिवानी के कथा-कौशल को रेखांकित करते हैं। 'मायापुरी', चौदह फेरे', 'कृष्णकली',

'कृष्णवेणी', 'चिरस्वयंवरा' आदि अनेक कहानियाँ तथा उपन्यास नारी के विविध रूपों का चित्रण करते हैं।

समकालीन कथा लेखिकाओं में चर्चित एवं लोकप्रिय नाम है--ममता कालिया, जिनका 'बेघर' और 'नरक दर नरक' प्रसिद्ध उपन्यास है, जिसमें दर्शाया गया है कि समाज का नारी के प्रति उपभोगवादी दृष्टिकोण है। मृदुला गर्ग ने विवाह नैतिकता यानी दाम्पत्य मान्यताओं पर प्रश्नचिह्न लगाया है। 'चित्तकोबरा' उपन्यास के माध्यम से विवाह सम्बन्धी विसंगति का चित्रण बड़ी गहराई से किया है। कमलेश बख्शी ने 'सुरंग के बाहर' लिखकर स्त्री-पुरुष सम्बन्धों से जुड़ी नई साहसपूर्ण दृष्टि का परिचय दिया है। 'अन्तहीन भटकन' तथा 'दिशा खोजती जिन्दगियाँ' एक ऐसी नारी की भटकन है जो जीवन भर चलती है पर कहीं नहीं पहुँचती, वह अन्तहीन है। मणिका मोहिनी ने 'प्रेम कहानी' उपन्यास के माध्यम से महानगरी की आधुनिकता, वर्जनामुक्त खुलापन व्यक्त करते हुए प्रगतिशील चेतना और नारी सम्बन्धी वैचारिक बोध को वाणी दी है।

इस प्रकार से कहा जा सकता है कि आज के आन्तरिक और बाह्य संकट बोध के अनेक सन्दर्भ तथा परम्परा बनाम आधुनिकता के सन्दर्भ के बीच सम्बन्धों का पुनर्निर्धारण इन कथा लेखिकाओं ने चित्रित किया है। इन उपन्यास लेखिकाओं ने नारी को संकल्प स्वातन्त्र्य के मूल्य से सम्भावित किया है तथा नारी को 'मानवी' रूप में प्रतिष्ठित किया है। नारी ने ही नारी जागरण और चेतना विकास का नितान्त उन्नत स्वरूप रूपायित किया है। आज शिक्षा ने नारी को घर की चहारदीवारी से बाहर निकाला है और पश्चिम के उदारवादिता के सिद्धान्त तथा प्रजातान्त्रिक परम्पराओं के सम्पर्क में ला बिठाया है। आज समाज में नारी का निजत्व उभरकर आया है। आशा है समाज में अपनी अहम भूमिका के साथ नारी का स्वरूप स्थापित होगा और अवश्य होगा, वह केवल मादा नहीं होगी, एक व्यक्ति भी होगी ताकि वह विश्व को भारतीय नारी की अस्मिता और गौरवमयी पहचान दे सके।

41 समकालीन सामाजिक संदर्भ एवं सूर्यबाला का कथा साहित्य

—अंजना गुप्ता

आचार्य रामचन्द्र शुक्ल ने साहित्य के अन्तर्गत उस सारे वाङ्मय को रखा है, जिसमें अर्थबोध के अतिरिक्त भावोन्मेष अथवा चमत्कारपूर्ण अनुरंजन हो अथवा उसकी विचारात्मक समीक्षा हो, कविता उनके विचार से जीवन की अभिव्यक्ति है। उन्होंने उसे हृदय की मुक्तावस्था का प्रकाशन माना है।[1] इसी तथ्य को मानते हुए अपने साक्षात्कारों और अपनी रचना प्रक्रिया पर टिप्पणियों के माध्यम से सूर्यबाला जी ने भी अपनी रचनाओं के प्रेरक तत्वों को रेखांकित किया है। उनकी रचनाओं का पहला प्रेरक तत्व समाज है इसलिए उन्होंने साफ कहा है- "क्योंकि साहित्य को कभी समाज से निरपेक्ष देखा ही नहीं जा सकता है।"[2]

सूर्यबाला ने भी अपने साहित्य के माध्यम से आज की परिस्थितियों को अभिव्यक्ति प्रदान की है। सूर्यबाला के साहित्य के विभिन्न रूपों और प्रतिरूपों को समकालीन परिवेश में देखने से पहले यह आवश्यक है कि पहले 'समकालीन' शब्द के अर्थ को समझ लिया जाए। 'समकालीन' का कोशीय अर्थ है-सामयिक, समवयस्क। हिन्दी शब्दकोश में 'समकालीन' का अर्थ है 'एक ही समय में रहने वाले' अंग्रेजी शब्दकोश में 'समकालीन' शब्द 'कन्टेम्परारी' का पर्याय है। इससे एक बात स्पष्ट होती है कि समकालीन का अर्थ उस समान काल से है जिसमें वे घटनाएं घट रहीं हैं या जिसमें एक व्यक्ति जी रहा है, रह रहा है, आन्दोलन चल रहा है। व्यक्ति के सन्दर्भ में समूचे जीवन प्रवाह को उसका समकालीन माना जा सकता है। काल विशेष के सन्दर्भ में सामाजिक, राजनीतिक एवं सांस्कृतिक निकष पर समकालीनता का अर्थ लगाया जा सकता है। अतः वास्तव में समकालीन से अभिप्राय उस काल या समय से है जिसमें

रचनाकार स्वयं जी रहा है। मूलतः यह तीन शब्दोंसे मिलकर बना है। प्रथम-सम, द्वितीय-कालीन, तृतीय-ईन। सम का अर्थ है समान, काल का अर्थ है समय, ईन का अर्थ है सम्बन्धित। इस प्रकार समकालीन का शाब्दिक अर्थ है काल विशेष से सम्बद्ध अर्थात् एक ही समयखण्ड से सम्बन्धित।

महिला कथाकारों में सूर्यबाला जी का प्रमुख स्थान है। उन्होंने कथित महिला कथालेखन की रूढ़ियों का अतिक्रमण करते हुए एक संवेदनशील लेखिका के रूप में अपनी पहचान बनाई है। सूर्यबाला ने निरन्तर नये विषयों पर कहानी और उपन्यास लिखे हैं, जिनसे पाठक जुड़ा रहते हुए भी अनभिज्ञ रहता है अथवा रहने की कोशिश करता है। उन्होंने न केवल अधिक मात्रा में लिखा अपितु गुणवत्ता और प्रभाव की दृष्टि से उनका लिखा हुआ महत्वपूर्ण है। वे मुख्यतः नारी की नियति का बखान करने वाली कथा लेखिका ही नहीं वरन् उसे आज के समाज की वास्तविकता को देखते हुए सशक्त रूप में प्रस्तुत करती हैं। उन्होंने समकालीन परिवेश की बहुआयामी चुनौती को न केवल स्वीकार किया है अपितु रचनाओं के माध्यम से उनसे मुठभेड़ भी की है।

यह तथ्य सम्भवतः समाज में द्रष्टव्य रहा है कि अनीति के प्रति विरोध समाज का मूलाधार है, जो समाज साहित्य की सहायता से समय-समय पर करता रहा है, परन्तु क्या घटित के प्रति विद्रोह की स्थिति ही सदैव काम्य अथवा उचित है तथा हितपूर्ण है? नहीं? विद्रोह से पूर्व विवेक तथा विनाश के पूर्व शांति मानव जीवन के संदेश हैं। वर्तमान समाज में ये प्रवृत्तियाँ लुप्त होती जा रही हैं। इस प्रवृत्ति का सूर्यबाला जी नें खण्डन किया है। जहाँ नैतिक मूल्यों का प्रश्न उठता है वे विद्रोह के स्थान पर स्वयं को गाँधीवादी विचारधारा का ही पोषक मानती हैं, वे कहतीं हैं:-

> "मानती हूँ कि जीवन की स्थितियों को देखने में मेरी दृष्टि ज्यादा गाँधीवादी रही है। मैं परिवर्तन और बेहतरी के लिए विद्रोह से पहले विवेक को रखती हूँ। विद्रोह की विध्वंसक भूमिका मुझे जीवनोपयोगी कभी नहीं लगी। अब भी मानती हूँ कि जीवन की बहुत कम स्थितियाँ ऐसी

हैं कि जिन्हें विद्रोह के माध्यम से सुलझाया जा सकता है वहाँ अभी पाने से पहले देना होगा। जीवन चरम काव्य सुख-शांति और सहायता के सन्दर्भ में विद्रोह की भूमिका नगण्य होती है।"[3]

लेखिका ने विविध कहानी संग्रहों तथा उपन्यासों में समकालीन प्रवृत्तियों व परिवेश को चित्रित करने के साथ-साथ नारी की वास्तविक स्थिति को अभिव्यक्त किया है तथा पुरुषों के निरंकुश एकाधिकार को कड़ी चुनौती दी है। 'यामिनी कथा' नामक उपन्यास के माध्यम से उन्होंने घरेलू नारी के जीवन के तनाव और विवशता का निरूपण किया है, जहाँ यामिनी अपने दूसरे और पहले पति की सन्तान के बीच सन्तुलन बनाये रखने का प्रयास करती है लेकिन वे दोनों ही उसे पीड़ित और अपमानित करते हैं। वह अपने अधिकारों की जमीन का एक टुकड़ा पाने तक के लिए तरस जाती है।

"जी में आया, दोनों तरफ मिले इस निर्वासन के हुक्मनामे पर पागलों की तरह बदहवास ठठाकर हँस पड़ूँ या फिर बारी-बारी से उन्हें झिंझोड़कर पूछूँ-यूँ हुक्मनामे या आदेश जारी करने का अधिकार क्या सिर्फ तुम्ही लोगों को मिला है, तुम लोग अनुमति दोगे तो तुम्हारी सीमा में आऊँगी और दुत्कार दोगे तो भिखारिन याचना की मुद्रा लिए खड़ी रहूँगी कि तुम पसीजो और मुझे मेरी जगह बहाल करो। मेरे पास अपनी जमीन का भी तो हाथ भर का ही सही एक टुकड़ा होना चाहिए जहाँ मेरी इच्छाएं अपनी चिंगलियों में ही सही दो घड़ी को सुस्ता सकें। मेरी सारी जमीन पर क्या सिर्फ तुम्हीं लोगों का हक, कब्जा रहेगा आजीवन?"[4]

गाँधी जी ने भी पुरुष प्रधान समाज में नारी को उचित स्थान दिलाने के लिए महिलाओं को परामर्श देते हुए 23 मार्च सन् 1947 के हरिजन में लिखा है:-

"स्त्रियों को मेरी सलाह है कि वे सभी अवांछनीय और निकम्मेपन के खिलाफ सविनय विद्रोह करें।"[5]

इस वास्तविकता से समाज अनभिज्ञ नहीं है कि दहेज के नाम पर आज भी कन्याओं को विवाह के पश्चात् प्रताड़ित किया जाता

है। रंग, रूप, सौन्दर्य आदि तथ्य जो प्रायः लड़कियों के सकारात्मक पहलू होते हैं तथा उनके व्यक्तित्व को उभारते हैं। अगर किसी किशोरी में ऐसी कोई विषमता होती है तो उसके विवाह के सम्बन्ध में बाधाएं उत्पन्न हो जाती हैं और क्षतिपूर्ति के रूप में दहेज की माँग की जाती है। कहानी 'पुल टूटते हुए' में उसकी सटीक अभिव्यंजना की गयी है:-

> "माँ पिताजी भी लड़की के टूटते मन का ख्याल कर घर में दिखाने के बदले पार्क, मन्दिर, रेस्टोरेन्ट में दिखाने ले जाने लगे। लेकिन जगह बदलने से जवाब नहीं बदले। जवाब तो कहीं चश्मे के बहाने, कहीं दबे रंग के बहाने वही रहे। इन क्षतियों की पूर्ति के लिए दान दहेज देकर मामला 'विचाराधीन' करने के लिए कहा जाता जिसे मान लेने के लिए पिता की औकात जवाब दे जाती।"[6]

सूर्यबाला के कथा साहित्य में वे किशोरियाँ भी हैं जो अपनी पारिवारिक कठिनाइयों और समाज के स्वार्थी नियमों के बीच अपनी प्रतिभा को नष्ट होते देख रही हैं। 'गीता चौधरी का आखिरी सवाल' आज की नारी का पहला सवाल है:-

> "अब इस नाप-जोख में मेरा यह वर्तमान तहस-नहस होता है तो किसी की बला से। वार्षिकोत्सव में पुरस्कार लेने जाने के बदले भाई के दोस्त के लिए पकौड़े तलना, और इन सबके बाद कभी भी किसी के ऊपर का गुस्सा भी अपने ऊपर उतार लेने देना।"[7]

समाज की मानसिकता को विभिन्न साहित्यकारों ने विभिन्न कृतियों के माध्यम से अभिव्यक्त करने की कोशिश की है। समकालीन जीवन के विविध सन्दर्भ कुण्ठा, निराशा, हताशा, आर्थिक विषमता आदि साहित्य में अभिव्यक्त हो रहे हैं। सामाजिक मूल्य, परम्पराएं, संस्कृति, धर्म, संस्कार, सभी आज बदलाव की ओर उन्मुख हैं। माता-पिता के प्रति प्रेम भाव मानो समाज में लुप्त होता जा रहा है, क्योंकि आज की पीढ़ी संभवतः पाश्चात्य संस्कृति की ओर अग्रसर है। लेखिका ने कहानी 'एक इन्द्रधनुष जुबेदा के नाम' के माध्यम से इसे अभिव्यक्त किया है।

"प्रायः मुझे लगता है, हमेशा पुरानी पीढ़ी नयी को जितना समझती है, उससे भी बहुत कम हम नये लोग पुरानों को समझ पाते हैं। नयों को दोष न दे पाने पर भी पुरानों के प्रति करुणा तो उभरती ही है। इसलिए इस कहानी के 'बापू जी' और 'माँ' को कहीं जाकर ढूंढना नहीं पड़ा।"[8]

सूर्यबाला ने 'गैस' कहानी की कामकाजी महिला का भी चित्रण किया है जो दिन-रात घर-बाहर खटने के बावजूद मानसिक तनाव और वाग्बाणों की व्यथा झेलने को विवश है। पति को उसकी इस पीड़ा से कोई मतलब ही नहीं होता वह सिर्फ अपने अहं को रखना चाहता है। पत्नी उसके अभिमान और कर्तव्य के बीच झूलती रहती है-

"महेश से पैसे भी नहीं माँगेगी। सिलिण्डर लाने को भी नहीं कहेगी वह खुद ही रिक्शा पर, सचमुच भयभीत हो उठी थी, पहले भी ऐसी धमकियों के बीच ही कई नौकरियाँ छोड़ चुका हैं-पैसे का अभाव, मानसिक क्लेश और अशांति रहती थी, वह तो रहती थी ऊपर से महेश की ईगो।"[9]

अतः कहने का तात्पर्य है कि समाज में आज जो भी घटित हो रहा है उसका यथार्थ चित्रण ही सूर्यबाला के साहित्य में मिलता है। समाज में चल रही वास्तविकता का लेखिका ने मात्र खुलासा ही नहीं किया वरन् मूल्यों की स्थापना भी की है, यथा-

"मम्मी देखो, ये मैले-कुचैले हाथों में मेरी सिन्ड्रेला वाली बुक गन्दी कर रही है। मैंने मोना को समझाया कि तुम्हें गरीबों के प्रति उदार होना चाहिए।"[10]

इस प्रकार के प्रसंगों से लेखिका ने जहाँ सकारात्मक सोच पैदा की है वहीं समाज में आस्था एवं मूल्यों की स्थापना भी की है:-

"त्याग, निष्ठा, संयम, धैर्य और विवेक एक युग विशेष के लिए उपयुक्त हों और दूसरे के लिए अनुपयुक्त ऐसा नहीं है-ये हर युग के सत्य हैं और अगर आज इन्हें नकारा या अस्वीकारा जा रहा है तो उस सबसे विद्रोह भी हमारी रचनात्मकता का एकमात्र अंग होना चाहिए।"[11]

मूल्यों में गिरावट से समाज में भ्रष्टाचार का उत्कर्ष हो रहा है सूर्यबाला की कहानी 'होगी जय, होगी जय, हे पुरुषोत्तम नवीन' के सरकारी भ्रष्ट अधिकारी अपने पद की गरिमा को भुलाकर अपनी आड़ में भ्रष्ट नेताओं से तस्करी ही नहीं करवाते हैं, बल्कि अपने कर्तव्यों की जान बूझकर अवहेलना करते हैं-

> "सस्पैण्ड करो साले को आखिर देर-सवेर उसे बर्खास्त तो होना ही है। ऐसे-ऐसे मूजी इस महकमे में कितने दिन चलेंगे इतना तो उनके ट्रक पकड़ने के साथ ही होना चाहिए था कि इस ट्रक को पकड़ने का क्या हश्र होता है? हमें भी तो ऊपर तक जबाब देना पड़ता है।"[12]

लेखिका ने समाज में व्याप्त भ्रष्टाचार के इस रूप को मुखर करते हुए आज के स्वार्थी, भ्रष्ट, दोहरे चरित्र वाले, फिर भी राजनीति की डोर को सँभाले रखने वाले नेताओं की विकृत मानसिकता को अभिव्यक्त किया है, यथाः-

> "लाल सूरज के छापे और त्रिशूल की निशानी वाले ट्रक दूर से ही अपनी पहचान बनाते हैं। निशानी बनाई किसलिए है? बेकार का अड़ंगा हटाने के लिए ही तो।"[13]

शैक्षणिक संस्थाओं में आज योग्यता और प्रतिभा की नहीं वरन् जो अर्थ की महत्ता है वह वास्तविक है- "मेरी भाभी का भाई तो कहता था कि पचास रुपये में जिस क्लास का चाहे, जिस डिवीजन का चाहे, ला देगा, वह जाली सर्टिफिकेट।"[14] वर्तमान समाज में 'विद्यार्थी शब्द के रूप में बदलाव आया है विद्यार्थियों के व्यवहार के साथ-साथ उनके आचरण तथा गुरू के प्रति उनकी भावनाओं के व्यवहार में भी परिवर्तन आया है जो कि विद्यार्थी जीवन के वास्तविक स्वरूप को छोड़ उसमें व्याप्त पथभ्रष्टता के सशक्त रूप का चित्रण करता है। उपन्यास 'दीक्षान्त' के अन्तर्गत लेखिका ने इसे अभिव्यक्त करने का प्रयत्न किया है-

> "मेरा मतलब था अगर आप ज्यादा कड़ाई न बरतें तो मैं पास हो सकता हूँ, लेकिन दसवीं में तुमने कितने साल लगाये यह मुझे मालूम है। उसकी बात छोड़िये सर, पर यह तो होम इग्जाम है, फिर आप जैसे शिक्षकों का फायदा ही क्या?"[15]

मीडिया, जनतन्त्र में मूल्यों का मुख्य समानार्थक तथा विरोधी तत्व है। विविध प्रकार की घटनाएं मीडिया के माध्यम से ही अभिव्यक्त होती हैं। केवल खबरों को छाप देने मात्र से ही देश में अमन व शांति की स्थापना नहीं हो सकती, समस्याओं का निराकरण भी आवश्यक है। कहानी 'सौदागर दुआओं के' के माध्यम से लेखिका ने इस स्थिति का निरुपण किया है यथाः-

"आप सब कलम, कैमरे वाले चाहें अपने मुल्क के हों या गैर मुल्क के, सिर्फ तबाहियों की बातें ही क्यों उछालते रहते हैं? इन तबाहियों से निजात दिलाने वाले मुद्दों की ताजबीज क्यों नहीं पेश करते? अमन की चाहत दिलाने वालों की एक पूरी जमात, पूरी दुनिया, पूरा जमाना आपके साथ होगा।"[16]

लेखिका ने अपने साहित्य के माध्यम से इस प्रकार की समस्याओं को चित्रित तो किया ही है साथ ही साथ समाज में व्याप्त कई अन्य कुप्रवृत्तियों को अभिव्यक्त करने का प्रयत्न भी किया है जिसमें जातिवाद की समस्या आज मुँह फैलाये खड़ी हैः-

"तुम झोपड़ी पट्टी में रहने वाले घुट्टी में ही जाँत-पाँत लेकर आते हो तभी तो तुम लोगों की बस्ती में इतना झगड़ा होता है, होता है ना!"[17]

स्वतन्त्र भारत में जनतांत्रिक मूल्यों की स्थापना एक युगान्तकारी घटना है। संविधान में हर तरह की असमानता को ध्वस्त करते हुए समानता, न्याय, स्वतन्त्रता आदि मूल्यों को व्यवहार में लाने का संकल्प लिया गया है। यह बात और है कि राजनेताओं, अफसरों और पूँजीपतियों की मिलीभगत से इन मूल्यों का पूरी तरह से प्रसार और व्यवहार नहीं हो पाया। कहानी 'दुआओं के सौदागर' में वे इसी बात को एक पात्र के माध्यम से अभिव्यक्त करती हैं कि-

"हमारी कौम यानी कि हिन्दुस्तानी कौम में अपना-पराया, हमारा-तुम्हारा जैसी बातें बेहद ओछी किस्म की समझी जाती हैं। हम हिन्दुस्तानी बँटने-बिखरने से बेहद घबराते हैं।"[18]

यह समस्त बिन्दु सूर्यबाला के कथा साहित्य में व्याप्त समकालीन परिवेश को अभिव्यक्त करते हैं। इससे स्पष्ट है कि परिवेश से उनका निरन्तर संवाद हुआ है। उनका साहित्य मात्र मानव हित के संकेत बिन्दुओं को लेकर नहीं चलता वरन् साहित्य में विभिन्न आधुनिक प्रवृत्तियों को दर्शाकर पाठक को वर्तमान स्थिति के प्रति सचेत करने में सहायक है। सूर्यबाला जी का साहित्य व्यापक है जो समाज के विभिन्न पक्षों को छूता है तथा यथार्थ की अभिव्यक्ति के साथ-साथ पाठक को सोचने के लिए विवश करता है कि वास्तविकता है क्या?

संदर्भः-

1. चिन्तामणि, भाग-1, आचार्य रामचन्द्र शुक्ल, पृ.सं. 193।
2. कात्यायनी संवाद, लिखना क्यों?, पृष्ठ सं. 10।
3. 'आजकल' जुलाई 1994, पृ.सं. 26।
4. 'यामनी कथा' पृष्ठ सं. 84।
5. समाज कल्याण अक्टूबर, 1995, पृष्ठ सं. 8।
6. 'दिशाहीन मैं', पुल टूटते हुए पृष्ठ सं. 43।
7. 'गृह प्रवेश', गीता चौधरी का आखिरी सवाल, पृष्ठ सं. 159।
8. 'एक इन्द्रधनुष जुबेदा के नाम' पृष्ठ सं. 78।
9. 'मुंडेर पर', 'गैस', पृष्ठ सं. 97।
10. 'दिशाहीन मैं', सिन्ड्रैला का स्वप्न, पृष्ठ सं. 119।
11. 'कात्यायनी संवाद', पृष्ठ सं. 12।
12. 'गृह प्रवेश', 'होगी जय, होगी जय, हे पुरुषोत्तम नवीन', पृष्ठ सं. 71।
13. 'गृह प्रवेश', 'होगी जय, होगी जय, हे पुरुषोत्तम नवीन', पृष्ठ सं. 67-68।
14. 'थाली भर चाँद', 'रहमदिल' पृष्ठ सं. 41।
15. 'दीक्षान्त' पृष्ठ सं. 64।
16. 'गृह प्रवेश', सौदागर दुआओं के , पृष्ठ सं. 63।
17. दिशाहीन मैं, सिन्ड्रैला का स्वप्न, पृष्ठ सं. 48।
18. 'गृह प्रवेश', सौदागर दुआओं के, पृष्ठ सं. 58।

42 परिवर्तनशील भारत में स्त्रियों की प्रस्थिति-एक समाजशास्त्रीय अध्ययन

—बीना मित्तल

भारतीय सामाजिक संरचना में भारतीय नारी के अतीत पर दृष्टि डालने पर यह चित्र उभरकर सामने आता है कि भारतीय नारी प्रकृति की सृजनशीलता एवं रचनात्मक शक्ति की प्रतीक है। मानव की आदिम अवस्था से लेकर आज तक पुरुष ने नारी के प्रति संरक्षण तथा नारी ने पुरुष के प्रति समर्पण भाव रखा है।

वैदिक साहित्य के अनुशीलन से यह ज्ञात होता है कि वैदिक काल में स्त्री का स्थान अतीव गौरव मण्डित था। वेदों में स्त्री को 'अबला' नहीं वरन् 'सबला' माना गया है। वह शिक्षा में बहुत आगे थी। यजुर्वेदों में उसे 'सोमपृष्ठा' कहा गया है। वेद मंत्रों का अर्थ बताने वाली विदुषी स्त्रियाँ ऋषिकाल में थीं जैसे- लोपामुद्रा, श्रृद्धा, सरमा, रोमशा, विश्ववारा, अपाला, यमी, घोषा आदि।

आध्यात्मिक ज्ञान के साथ-साथ धार्मिक क्षेत्र में भी स्त्री को पुरुष के समान ही अधिकार प्राप्त थे। इसका सबसे बड़ा उदाहरण 'रामचरितमानस' में उस समय मिलता है जब श्री रामचन्द्र जी द्वारा किए गये राजसूय यज्ञ में सीता जी की अनुपस्थिति में उनकी स्वर्णमूर्ति को उनके स्थान पर रखकर यज्ञ संपन्न किया गया।

वृहदारण्यक उपनिषद में ब्रह्मवेत्ता गार्गी की कथा का उल्लेख है जिसने राजा जनक की विद्वानों से भरी सभा में ऋषि याज्ञवलक्य के साथ शास्त्रार्थ किया था। भारत में मध्यकाल में स्त्रियों के अगाध पण्डिता होने के दृष्टान्त पाए जाते हैं। जिस समय शंकराचार्य ने अपने समय के प्रकाण्ड पण्डित मण्डनमिश्र को परास्त कर दिया उस समय उसकी पत्नी विद्याधरी ने शंकराचार्य को परास्त किया। स्त्री का यह युग भारत के इतिहास का स्वर्णिम युग कहा जा सकता है।

परन्तु यह समय देर तक न रहा। स्त्री के यही दिव्यगुण धीरे-धीरे उसके अवगुण समझे जाने लगे। जो स्त्रियाँ वैदिक युग में धर्म और समाज का प्राण थीं उन्हें श्रुति का पाठ करने के लिए अयोग्य घोषित किया जाने लगा। वैदिक युग का दृष्टिकोण जो स्त्री के प्रति दिव्य कल्पनाओं तथा पुनीत भावनाओं से परिवेष्टित था, अब पूर्णतया बदल चुका था। उनके मानसिक तथा आत्मिक विकास के द्वारों पर ताले लगा दिए गये थे। सनातन वैदिक काल के उच्च सुदृढ़ आदर्शों की इमारत ढह चुकी थी। पुरुष ने स्त्री को अपनी भोग्य वस्तु बना लिया था। धीरे-धीरे बाल-विवाह, पर्दे की बेड़ियाँ तथा अविद्या का अन्धकार नारी समाज के लिए अभिशाप बनने लगा। अठारहवीं शताब्दी में स्त्रियों की दशा जितनी दयनीय थी उसमें 19वीं सदी में कुछ सुधार आया। धार्मिक आडम्बर, रूढ़िगत विचार, परम्परागत सामाजिक संस्कार सभी ने मिलकर अन्धकार का ऐसा परिवेश भारतीय जीवन के चारों तरफ निर्मित कर दिया था कि उसे तोड़ सकना सम्भव नहीं था जिससे रही सही स्थिति भी घोर निराशा के कारण और भी शोचनीय हो गयी थी। इस बर्बर युग की प्रतिक्रियास्वरूप राजा राममोहन राय, श्रीमती एनी बेसेन्ट जैसे समाज सुधारकों ने नारी जाति पर होने वाले अनेक सामाजिक अत्याचारों पर रोक लगाने का प्रयास किया तथा स्त्री शिक्षा का प्रबन्ध किया। स्वामी विवेकानन्द ने भी स्पष्ट शब्दों में कहा था कि 'जब तक विश्व में महिलाओं की स्थिति में सुधार नहीं होगा तब तक विश्व का कल्याण नहीं होगा।'

आधुनिक युग में स्त्रियों की स्थिति में परिवर्तन आया इस परिवर्तन ने परम्परागत दृष्टिकोण को चुनौती दी। श्री पणिकर के शब्दों में, "वर्तमान समय में स्त्रियों द्वारा हिन्दू जीवन के सिद्धान्तों का पुनःपरीक्षण हिन्दू समाज के लिए एक सबसे बड़ी चुनौती है।" यह चुनौती वास्तविक भी है और इसके विभिन्न प्रतिबन्धों की प्रतिक्रिया भी है किन्तु इसका तात्पर्य यह नहीं है कि स्त्रियाँ भारतीय नारीत्व के सामाजिक आदर्शों को ठुकरा देने पर तुली हुई हैं। इसका तात्पर्य मात्र यह है कि जो रीति-रिवाज व परम्पराएँ प्रगति में बाधक हैं उन्हें बदलना ही अच्छा है। आज स्त्रियों की स्थिति में परिवर्तन अन्य कारणों से भी आ रहे हैं जैसे- पाश्चात्य संस्कृति

का प्रभाव, शिक्षा का विस्तार, यातायात व संचार के साधनों में उन्नति, औद्योगिकीकरण, संयुक्त परिवारों का विघटन, अन्तर्जातीय विवाह तथा राष्ट्रीय आन्दोलन आदि। अभी भी स्त्रियों के जीवन में अनेक समस्याएँ हैं। वर्तमान समय में ग्रामीण क्षेत्रों में बाल-विवाह अभी भी प्रचलित है। इसके साथ ही बेमेल विवाह, दहेज प्रथा, नातेदारी प्रथा, महिलाओं का पुरुषों द्वारा अनेक प्रकार से होने वाला उत्पीड़न आदि समस्याएँ घर किये हुए हैं।

भारत सरकार ने महिलाओं के कल्याण के लिए अनेक प्रयत्न किये हैं। उनके लिए अनेक कल्याण कार्यक्रम भी संचालित किए हैं। स्त्रियों की सामाजिक और आर्थिक स्थिति में सुधार करने की दृष्टि से समान वेतन अधिनियम पारित किया गया, मातृत्व हित-लाभ अधिनियम बनाये गये। ग्रामीण महिलाओं के कल्याण के लिए गाँवों में महिला मण्डल बनाये गये हैं। सन् 1990 को सार्क देशों द्वारा बालिका वर्ष के रूप में मनाया जाना महिला सशक्तीकरण के लिए सराहनीय कदम है। आज भारत सहित पूरे विश्व में महिला सशक्तीकरण आन्दोलन चरम पर है। नारी उत्थान के लिए यह आवश्यक है कि उसके समुचित विकास पर ध्यान दिया जाए। वह स्वावलम्बी बने और बढ़ती हुई आकांक्षाओं और आवश्यकताओं को पूरा करने में पुरुष के समान समर्थता प्राप्त करे। अब वह परिस्थितियाँ नहीं है जब उसे अबला नारी कहकर सम्बोधित किया जाता था। आज प्रत्येक क्षेत्र में स्त्रियाँ पुरुषों के साथ कन्धे से कन्धा मिलाकर चल रही हैं। राष्ट्र की उन्नति में वह अपना योगदान दे रही हैं तभी तो आज राष्ट्रपति पद को अलंकृत किए हुए प्रतिभा पाटिल, सर्वश्रेष्ठ सांसद के रूप में सुषमा स्वराज, मुख्यमंत्री मायावती, पुलिस अधिकारी किरन बेदी, अन्तरिक्ष में उड़ान भरने वाली सुनीता विलियम्स ने जन-जन के समक्ष एक आदर्श उपस्थित किया है।

निष्कर्ष यह निकलता है कि भारत में महिलाओं की स्थिति में परिवर्तन हो रहे हैं परन्तु इन्हें तब तक बड़े और महत्वपूर्ण परिवर्तन के रूप में नहीं माना जा सकता जब तक कि व्यवहारिक रूप से सब कुछ लागू नहीं होता। वैसे तो नारी को स्वयं प्रयत्न करना होगा। जो बैठा रहता है, उसका सौभाग्य भी बैठा रहता

है और जो चलता है उसका सौभाग्य भी प्रगति करता है। नारी को अपनी स्थिति सुधारने के लिए अपना उद्धार स्वयं करना होगा। जब तक शंकराचार्य के समान प्रखर वैराग्य सम्पन्न स्त्रियाँ पैदा नहीं होगीं तब तक उनका उद्धार कृष्ण, बुद्ध और गाँधी जी जैसे पुरुष भी नहीं कर सकते। आज नारी को दासी न बनकर सहचरी बनना है। समाज में स्त्री-पुरुष का सहजीवन होगा परन्तु इसकी एक शर्त अनिवार्य है कि परम्परागत भ्रान्त धारणाओं को छोड़कर स्त्री को स्वरक्षित होना होगा। आज समय की पुकार यही है कि स्त्री को स्वतन्त्रता दी जाए और उसका आत्मिक विकास किया जाये।

संदर्भ ग्रंथः-

1. Bloom, B. 1963: Stability and changes in human characteristics Wiley, New York
2. Kuppuswamy, B 1977: Social change in India. Vikas Publishing house, Delhi.
3. मैकाइवर एवं पेज : समाज, रतन प्रकाशन मंदिर, आगरा, 1992 हिन्दी संस्करण।
4. सिंह सरोज : समाज में परिवार का अध्ययन, स्टार प्रकाशन, आगरा 1989।
5. श्री निवास एम. एन., आधुनिक भारत में सामाजिक परिवर्तन, राजकमल प्रकाशन प्राइवेट लिमिटेड, फैज बाजार, दिल्ली-6, 1967।

Contributors

Patricia Prime is co-editor of the New Zealand haiku magazine *Kokako,* Reviews Editor of the online magazine *Stylus,* and a regular contributor to *Takahe.* She is also the assistant editor of the online journal *Haibun Today,* and one of the editors of *The Take Five Anthologies,* 2008 and 2009. Besides reviewing, writing poetry and articles, she also writes the traditional Japanese forms of haiku, tanka, renga, linked verse, cheritas and haibun. She was honoured with the Poet of the Millennium Award by the International Poets Academy in 2001. She has had several of her interviews published in *Takahe* and online in *Simply Haiku* and *Stylus.*

Dr. Eunice de Souza retired as Head, Department of English, St Xavier's College, Mumbai in 2000. She has authored *A Necklace of Skulls, Complete Poems* (Penguin, 2009) and has compiled and edited *Women's Voices* (Oxford, 2002), a pioneering work in women's studies in the 19th and early 20th centuries. She frequently writes for children.

Dr. Nibir K. Ghosh is Head, Department of English Studies & Research at Agra College, Agra & Senior Fulbright Fellow 2003-04, University of Washington, Seattle, U.S.A.

Kathleen Alcalá writes and teaches on Bainbridge and Whidbey Islands, U.S.A. She is the author of five books, the most recent being *The Desert Remembers My Name – on Family and Stories,* University of Arizona Press, 2007.

Dr. Shanker A. Dutt is Professor of English at Patna University, Patna & Chairman, Bihar Sangeet Natak Akademi.

Dr. T. S. Anand retired as Principal, GGN Khalsa College, Ludhiana. He is currently Professor of English at AlTahaadi University in Libya.

Dr. Rajesh Kumar Sharma is Reader, Department of English, Punjabi University, Patiala.

Dr. Muniba Sami is Professor in the Post-graduate Department of English, Patna University, Patna.

Dr. Sujata is Principal, Smt. B.D. Jain Girls Degree College, Agra.

Dr. Anju Bala Agrawal is Reader in the Department of English at R.C.A. Girls' P.G. College, Mathura.

Arpita Ghosh is Research Scholar in the Department of English at Banaras Hindu University (B.H.U.), Varanasi.

Dr. Neena Arora is Reader, Department of English, H.P. University Centre for Evening Studies, Shimla.

Dr. Smita Jha is Assistant Professor in the Department of Humanities & Social Sciences, Indian Institute of Technology (IIT), Roorkee.

Ashu Toor is Head, Department of English, Guru Nanak Girls College, Ludhiana.

Dr. Anuradha Gaur is Associate Professor, Department of English Studies & Research, Agra College, Agra.

Dr. Madhavi Nikam is Lecturer in the P.G. Department of English, R.K. Talreja College, Ulhasnagar, University of Mumbai.

Dr. Gunjan Chaturvedi is Reader, Department of English Studies & Research, B.D.K. Girls' P.G. College, Agra.

Deepti Vanjare is Research Scholar, Department of English, J.H. Govt. P.G. College, Betul (M.P.).

Dr. Ashish Gupta is Assistant Professor, Department of English, J.H. Govt. P.G. College, Betul (M.P.).

Dr. Pramila S. Chawla is Head, Department of English, B. D. Jain Girls' P.G. College, Agra.

Dr. Hemlata Srivastava is Associate Professor, Department of English Studies & Research, Agra College, Agra.

Dr. Ruchi Singh is Lecturer in English at Amity University, Noida.

Dr. C. Sharada is Assistant Professor in the Department of English at Nizam College (Osmania University) Hyderabad.

Dr. Atima Adhikari is on the Guest Faculty, Department of English, Rani Durgavati Vishwavidyalay, Jabalpur.

Dr. Sudhi Rajiv is Professor in the Department of English, Jai Naraian Vyas University, Jodhpur.

Ujjwala Tathe teaches English at Mahila Mahavidyalaya, Karad (Maharashtra).

Archna Sahni teaches in the Department of English at Punjabi University, Patiala, Punjab. She has recently published her first collection of poems titled First Fire (Calicut: Yeti Books, 2005).

Dr. Piyas Chakrabarti is Lecturer in the Department of English, Bagnan College, Bagnan, Howrah (West Bengal). He specializes in race and gender studies.

Ms. B.T. Seetha is Associate Professor in the Department of English at Nizam College, Osmania University, Hyderabad.

Dr. Hetu Bhardwaj retired as Principal, Parikh Mahavidyalaya, Jaipur. He is the Chief Editor of two reputed journals – *Aksar* and *Panchsheel Shodh Samiksha*.

Dr. Tribhuvan Nath Shukla is Professor & Head, Department of Hindi, Rani Durgavati Vishwavidyalay, Jabalpur.

Dr. Sunita Rani is Associate Professor in the Department of Hindi Studies & Research, Agra College, Agra & Visiting Scholar 2003-04, University of Washington, Seattle, U.S.A.

Dr. Santosh Gaba is Head, Department of Education, B.D. Jain Girls' P.G. College, Agra.

Dr. Bharti Parijaat is Head, Department of Hindi, B.D. Jain Girls' P.G. College, Agra.

Dr. Mukul Sharma is Reader, Department of Hindi, B.D. Jain Girls' P.G. College, Agra.

Dr. Beena Kumari Gupta is Head, Department of Sanskrit, B.D.K. Girls' P.G. College, Agra.

Dr. Ritambara Shukla is Reader, Department of Hindi, B.D. Jain Girls' P.G. College, Agra.

Dr. Shikha Sreedhar is Lecturer, Department of Hindi, B.D. Jain Girls' P.G. College, Agra.

Dr. Brij Rani Sharma is Reader, Department of Music, Tikaram Kanya Mahavidyalaya, Aligarh.

Babita Singh is Research Scholar, Department of Music, Tikaram Kanya Mahavidyalaya, Aligarh.

Dr. Manju Gupta is Lecturer in the Department of Psychology, B.D. Jain Girls' P.G. College, Agra.

Dr. Shilpa Pandeya is Lecturer in Hindi at ACME Institute, Agra.

Dr. Puja Mittal is Reader, Department of Hindi, B.D. Jain Girls' P.G. College, Agra.